A Radically Democratic Response to Global Governance

This book presents a critique of dominant governance theories grounded in an understanding of existence as a static, discrete, mechanistic process, while also identifying the failures of theories that assume dynamic alternatives of either a radically collectivist or individualist nature. Relationships between ontology and governance practices are established, drawing upon a wide range of social, political, and administrative theory. Employing the ideal-type method and dialectical analysis to establish meanings, the authors develop a typology of four dominant approaches to governance.

The authors then provide a systematic analysis of each governance approach, thoroughly unpacking and critiquing each one and exploring the relationships and movements among them that engender reform and revolution as well as retrenchment and obfuscation of power dynamics. After demonstrating that each governance approach has fatal flaws within a diverse global context, the authors propose an alternative they call Integrative Governance. As a synthesis of the ideal-types, Integrative Governance is neither individualist nor collectivist, while still maintaining the dynamic character required to accommodate responsiveness to cultural contexts.

Margaret Stout is an Associate Professor of Public Administration at West Virginia University in Morgantown, USA.

Jeannine M. Love is an Associate Professor of Public Administration at Roosevelt University in Chicago, USA.

Transnational Law and Governance
Series Editor: Paolo Davide Farah
West Virginia University, USA and gLAWcal – Global Law Initiatives for Sustainable Development, UK

In recent years the concepts of "transnational law" and "governance" have been explored by both scholars and practitioners with the terms taking on new meaning and significance, particularly in light of the ongoing economic crisis and a corresponding critical reappraisal of global institutional structures and governance. This multidisciplinary series aims to provide a home for research exploring these issues.

Transnational law covers a broad theoretical definition that includes studies emerging from disciplines such as international law, comparative law, international economic law and administrative law undertaken by legal scholars but also features extensive research undertaken by scholars from other disciplines, including but not limited to political sciences, international relations, public administration, sociology, history, philosophy and geography. Governance in particular is now seen as important when we refer to the general stability of the markets, to good faith and other key principles, which are fundamental to the notion of a fair market that is responsive to the needs of governments and citizens as well as businesses.

This series features cutting-edge works which critically analyse the relationship between governance, institutions and law from a variety of disciplinary perspectives.

Forthcoming titles:

Administrative Appeals in EU Law
Giacomo Gattinara and Alessandro Di Mario

A Radically Democratic Response to Global Governance
Dystopian utopias

Margaret Stout and Jeannine M. Love

LONDON AND NEW YORK

First published 2016
by Routledge
2 Park Square, Milton Park, Abingdon, Oxon OX14 4RN

and by Routledge
711 Third Avenue, New York, NY 10017

Routledge is an imprint of the Taylor & Francis Group, an informa business

© 2016 Margaret Stout and Jeannine M. Love

The right of Margaret Stout and Jeannine M. Love to be identified as authors of this work has been asserted by them in accordance with sections 77 and 78 of the Copyright, Designs and Patents Act 1988.

All rights reserved. No part of this book may be reprinted or reproduced or utilized in any form or by any electronic, mechanical, or other means, now known or hereafter invented, including photocopying and recording, or in any information storage or retrieval system, without permission in writing from the publishers.

Trademark notice: Product or corporate names may be trademarks or registered trademarks, and are used only for identification and explanation without intent to infringe.

British Library Cataloguing in Publication Data
A catalogue record for this book is available from the British Library

Library of Congress Cataloging in Publication Data
A catalog record for this book has been requested

ISBN: 978-1-138-65405-1 (hbk)
ISBN: 978-1-315-62345-0 (ebk)

Typeset in Galliard
by Wearset Ltd, Boldon, Tyne and Wear

Printed and bound by CPI Group (UK) Ltd, Croydon, CR0 4YY

We dedicate this book to our many mentors and colleagues, both past and present, in the Public Administration Theory Network, a group of scholars who share the belief that critical social theory has a place in understanding and changing administrative practice. Although it is little known to other disciplines, public administration theory has long been concerned about the impact of governance on peoples and places, with a tradition of promoting democratic practices and just outcomes. These administrative scholars grapple with the challenges of implementation—of moving theory into practice. For these reasons, we believe we have something of unique value to bring to governance theory and the pursuit of social, economic, and environmental justice.

Contents

List of figures	xi
List of tables	xii
Foreword	xiii
Preface	xvi
Acknowledgments	xviii

PART I
Barriers to global governance — 1

1 Introduction — 3

2 Why now? — 8
A crisis of sustainability 8
    The contemporary context of globalization 9
    Social crises 9
    Economic crises 11
    Environmental crises 14
A crisis of governance 17
    The question of sovereignty 17
    The question of governance 18
    The question of participation 20
The crisis in review 21

3 Grounding governance in ontology — 22
Ontological dualisms 23
From dualisms to typologies 25
The relationship between ontology and language 26
How ontology shapes governance 27
Ontological confrontation and colonization 33
The argument in review 36

viii   *Contents*

4   Crafting and using a Governance Typology   38

The value of typologies 38
  Significant focus 39
  Organizing capacity 39
  Coherency 39
  Summary 40
Constructing an ideal-type framework 40
  Identify a social phenomenon of interest 41
  Choose a culturally significant frame of reference 41
  Identify essential generic elements 41
  Interpret genetic meanings 42
  Employing dialectical analysis 42
The resulting Governance Typology 43
  Ontological assumptions and associated language 44
  Psychosocial theory 45
  Epistemological concepts 47
  Belief systems 47
  Ethical concepts 48
  Political theory 49
  Economic theory 50
  Administrative theory 50
Four governance approaches emerge 51

PART II
Primary governance theories   53

5   Hierarchical Governance   55

Ontological assumptions and associated language 56
Psychosocial theory 58
Epistemological concepts 60
Belief systems 61
Ethical concepts 62
Political theory 63
Economic theory 65
Administrative theory 66
Summary and illustration 68

6   Atomistic Governance   71

Ontological assumptions and associated language 72
Psychosocial theory 74
Epistemological concepts 76

Belief systems 77
Ethical concepts 77
Political theory 79
Economic theory 82
Administrative theory 83
Summary and illustration 85

7 Holographic Governance   88
Ontological assumptions and associated language 89
Psychosocial theory 92
Epistemological concepts 94
Belief systems 96
Ethical concepts 96
Political theory 97
Economic theory 100
Administrative theory 102
Summary and illustration 104

8 Fragmented Governance   107
Ontological concepts and associated language 108
Psychosocial theory 111
Epistemological concepts 114
Belief systems 115
Ethical concepts 115
Political theory 116
Economic theory 118
Administrative theory 119
Summary and illustration 121

PART III
Dystopian utopias   125

9 Analysis of the primary governance approaches   127
Dialectical analysis 127
Dialectic in the Governance Typology 128
Ontological differences and similarities 130
Establishing a dynamic model 133

10 The Arc of Reform   139
Liberalism's multiple personality disorder 140
The bondage of Hierarchical Governance 142

x   *Contents*

The isolation of Atomistic Governance 144
The dialectic between liberalisms 148
The calcification of the Reified Community 150
Schismogenic escalation 153
The absorption of Holographic Governance 154
The alienation of Fragmented Governance 156

11 The Arc of Reification

160

Existential crisis 160
*The dialectic between extremes: paradox of the **i**/Individual 161*
Untenable extremes: revolution or retreat? 164
The Reified State 168
The Reified Market 171
The Reified Community 174

PART IV
Affirmation of a radically democratic approach to governance

177

12 Why Integrative Governance?

179

Experiential rationales 179
Ontological rationales 182
Employing dialectical synthesis 186
Seeking synthesis 188
Ontological assumptions and associated language 189
Psychosocial theory 191
Epistemological concepts 191
Belief systems 192
Ethical concepts 192
Political theory 193
Economic theory 194
Administrative theory 194

13 Pursuing Integrative Governance

196

Next steps 200

References 202
Index 238

Figures

5.1	Transcendent source (One) of being (one)	57
5.2	Socially embedded individuality	58
6.1	Many immanent sources of being (O/one)	72
6.2	Socially independent Individuality	75
7.1	Transcendent source (One) of becoming (one)	89
7.2	*T'ai-chi T'u* symbol (*yin/yang*)	91
7.3	Socially embedded Particular Individuality	93
8.1	Many immanent sources of becoming (O/one)	110
8.2	Socially independent Singular Individuality	112
9.1	The Governance Arc	133
10.1	The Arc of Reform	140
10.2	Ontological dialectic in liberalism	141
10.3	Communitarian liberalism	151
11.1	The Arc of Reification	161
12.1	Dialectical progression	187
12.2	The ontological terrain of Integrative Governance	189
13.1	Pathways for discourse	199

Tables

3.1	Principal ontological dichotomies matrix	25
4.1	Ontological dialectics	42
4.2	Ontological assumptions	45
4.3	Language characteristics	45
4.4	Psychosocial theory	46
4.5	Epistemological concepts	47
4.6	Belief systems	48
4.7	Ethical concepts	49
4.8	Political theory	49
4.9	Economic theory	50
4.10	Administrative theory	50
4.11	Primary governance ideal-types	51
5.1	Governance ideal-types: Hierarchical	55
6.1	Governance ideal-types: Atomistic	71
7.1	Governance ideal-types: Holographic	88
8.1	Governance ideal-types: Fragmented	107
9.1	Static state governance ideal-types: Hierarchical and Atomistic	129
9.2	Dynamic state governance ideal-types: Holographic and Fragmented	129
9.3	Collectivist governance ideal-types: Hierarchical and Holographic	130
9.4	Individualist governance ideal-types: Atomistic and Fragmented	131
9.5	Streamlined ontological matrix	131
9.6	Dialectical differences and similarities in static state ontologies	135
9.7	Dialectical differences and similarities in dynamic state ontologies	136
9.8	Dialectical differences and similarities in collectivist ontologies	137
9.9	Dialectical differences and similarities in individualist ontologies	138
12.1	Dystopian pathologies	183

Foreword

Nowadays, it is impossible to ignore the voices blaming the existing systems of governance within the borderless globalization system for being incapable of adequately responding to the problems and needs of the current age. The rage and discontent of a growing portion of the population who feel they have been left aside or who feel more insecure within prosperous Western societies is demonstrated in the growing support for anti-system parties and candidates. Most recently—last but not least—the majority vote for "Brexit" in the referendum in the United Kingdom to leave the European Union, leaves us confronted with a burning question: What went wrong?

The necessity of finding an answer to this question has never been greater than today. The growing concerns regarding progressive climate change, rapid technological development, wars and conflicts affecting different parts of the world, terrorism, the migration crisis, an unstable and weak job market and the general insecurity of the populous cannot simply be criticized as collective paranoia against globalization. The rising inequality or insecurity of even the middle class related therewith puts pressure on the existing social order and elites who often fail to keep pace with these latest developments or to adequately respond to them in a time of crisis.

The authors of this book argue that in order to provide a sustainable and acceptable alternative to the current system, the existing concepts of governance need to be critically assessed. Similarly to medicine, the symptoms indicate that a purely technical solution remedying only the negative consequences will not be sufficient—a thorough diagnosis aiming to examine the roots and source of the problems is needed. With respect to governance it means that the philosophical underpinnings of the existing governance and administrative concepts, including the language and epistemological concepts or belief systems associated therewith, need to be critically assessed and evaluated. The philosophical analysis might then serve as a proper basis for an interdisciplinary analysis of governance systems from a perspective of ethics, political theory, economics, or theory of administration. This evaluation necessarily needs to include citizens, whose lives are shaped and influenced by the quality and system of governance and administration in their respective countries. This relationship is interdependent: citizens might be pillars of the public order and system, but history

xiv *Foreword*

teaches us that they might also be the first ones calling for its reform or over-throw. Existential crisis might be a first step toward revolution.

Even though many expressions of discontent with the system might be regarded as evidence of personal frustration, they might also be symptoms of the impact the social order and systems of governance have on individuals. Man is a social being, craving independence and freedom while seeking to belong somewhere. These contradictory aspects of Man's personality accommodate various philosophies, political theories, and religions, whereas they find their reflection in concepts of governance as well. The assumption that people can understand themselves and form their identity within social relationships led, for example, to the creation of a socialist utopia aiming to eliminate sources of oppression represented by the privilege and wealth preventing those relation-ships. On the other hand, the insecurity of the Hobbesian state justified the existence of a society based on hierarchical order, where the citizens agreed to sacrifice part of their freedom in order to preserve their liberty and existence, thus subjecting themselves to the authority of government. A softer alternative represents a social contract inspired by John Locke, which gives individuals more discretion to pursue their individuality and self-interest. Government in this meaning is understood as a necessary evil, which enables individuals to enjoy their freedom and pursue their happiness. Both of these last two altern-atives, the Hobbesian as well as the Lockean model, serve as a basis for different variations of liberalism.

The current crisis of most of the classical models of governance rests inter alia in the fact that—despite trying to do so—they are not fully capable of enabling satisfactory participation of citizens or responding adequately to the major issues of the current age. Even the democratic concepts of governance, based on the idea of representative democracy, cannot prevent erosion to what Francis Fuku-yama calls "vetocracy" and a feeling that the state has been in fact captured by the ruling class and elites elected paradoxically in free elections. The postmodern critique is to a large extent directed also against neoliberalism, blaming its ideo-logy of unregulated markets for turning social identities into market commod-ities driven by the forces of consumerism. What appeared to Friedrich Hayek as an alternative to the totalitarian state crushing the individual will seems now to unveil enough of its dark side to justify its reform. The business class and pro-ducers have the power to manipulate social narratives in order to shape the desires of individuals. The implications might go even beyond the realm of sheer consumerism; the latest news, for example the Panama Papers, or the 2008 fin-ancial crisis, demonstrate that the focus on individual gain might lead to an off-shoring of wealth and power. This form of individualism without borders is naturally insensitive to broader economic, social, cultural or environmental issues and the interests of the public in general. Since the logic of the market-place and consumerism applies also to the government, public affairs become in the end only an extension of the market. This approach is unsustainable in the long term and might lead inevitably to environmental or social crisis. Moreover, it may lead even to political crisis, since the focus on consumerism might effectively disempower the middle class and the poor, whose frustration might turn against the establishment and thus, contrary to Hayek's intention, might lead to totalitarianism. Examples from history demonstrate that totalitarian ideologies, such as fascism, draw their support mostly from those who feel that their voice is not being heard.

To overcome the existential crisis leading to anti-establishment tendencies, governance systems need to be adjusted so as to enable and guarantee economic, social, cultural and environmental sustainability. Despite trying to accommodate different interests and involve citizens in the process, current systems of governance are not able to adequately address the citizens' expectations, which results in a tendency to reject the system. But remedies seem to be at hand. Public participation is already an established instrument of environmental law, which effectively integrates citizens in the process of decision making in environmental matters. It represents a tool enabling public authorities to coordinate their steps with citizens, which results often in a compromise acceptable to all parties involved. Moreover, public participation is an essential step toward sustainable development. Different stakeholders involved in the process represent different interests—social, economic, or environmental—which need to be integrated to the widest extent possible. In fact, public participation as an integrative approach is, as the authors of the book suggest, radically democratic.

The rapid development of technologies and natural sciences often leaves the impression that social science is a few steps behind in its reactions to contemporary challenges. This book has the potential to prove the contrary. The crisis in governance systems is not yet at its peak, but the deficiencies are visible even to the average citizen. The interdisciplinary analysis undertaken by the authors of this book represents a valuable contribution to the discussion about the feasibility of governance systems, including identification of the roots of their deficiencies. It undertakes the bold step of envisaging the reform of governance systems, bringing them closer to citizens and adapting them to the reality of the current interdependent and interconnected world. The question of how to govern society in the twenty-first century then becomes not only a matter to be feared, but also a challenging task worth studying and thinking about.

Paolo Davide Farah
Editor-in-Chief for the Routledge Publishing Book Series
"Transnational Law and Governance"

West Virginia University, USA and gLAWcal – Global Law
Initiatives for Sustainable Development, UK

Preface

This book is the outgrowth of over seven years' research on this topic that resulted in a variety of conference papers (Love 2010b, 2011, Stout 2009a, 2010c, 2011, Stout and Love 2012), an encyclopedia entry (Stout and Love 2016), journal articles (Love 2008, 2012, 2013, Stout 2006, 2009b, 2010a, 2010d, 2010e, 2012a, 2012b, 2014, Stout and Love 2013, 2014a, 2014b, 2015a, 2015c, Stout and Salm 2011, Stout and Staton 2011), and books (Stout 2013, Stout and Love 2015b). As authors, we share a scholarly lineage that converges through Thomas Catlaw, who served on our respective dissertation committees (Love 2010a, Stout 2007) and suggested that we might be mutually interested in one another's work. We discovered our shared passion for exploring how fundamental philosophical assumptions shape governance practices and their outcomes. A collegial friendship was formed and blossomed with serial panel presentations at subsequent academic conferences.

After engaging in two such panels, we realized that each of our respective typologies was actually missing a type. In our individual attempts to explain and affirm what we now call Integrative Governance (Stout and Love 2015c) within a two-by-two conceptual matrix, we were missing its synthetic quality. By pulling it out of the matrix and inserting one another's missing types instead, the full dialectical character of each position was revealed. In short, this move resolved a number of conceptual shortcomings and illuminated the full argument presented herein.

In the interest of ontological disclosure, we would each like to say something about what brought us to these explorations in the first place. Margaret writes:

> My worldview and associated experiences have led me to be at odds with most practices in Western society. I find myself a stranger in a strange land where people behave toward one another based on self-interest and instrumental purpose rather than relating with one another as co-creators of a common good. I have little respect for authority based purely on patriarchal familial patterns or hierarchical organizational structures rather than on merit and leadership by example. I cannot comprehend the greed countenanced by capitalism nor abide by the social injustice it generates. I do not understand extreme prejudice and even hatred based on "us" versus

Preface xvii

"them". I cannot imagine a notion of selfhood based on a lack of connection to others and feel those who operate under such assumptions are irrational given our human condition of social being, if nothing else.

In short, I believe that the way I have been brought up, as strange as it may sound to many, provides a fairly good recipe for democracy as a way of life—one that I endeavor to express throughout my personal, political, and economic life. Frankly, I am quite tired of being colonized by the dominant model of Western society. I am weary of being derisively labeled "socialist", "anarchist", "Pollyanna", and even "delusional". I am worn down by being marginalized by majoritarian views. I am exhausted by the cognitive dissonance I constantly experience being democratic in an authoritarian world. But I am heartened by those who share this sensibility and are inspired to proclaim my truth.

(Stout 2010e)

Similarly, Jeannine writes:

I have always felt slightly out of place in the world around me. While I easily mastered the "game" of Western society—moving between situations of authority and places of competition—frankly, it always seemed a bit absurd. As a child I would often engage in mini-rebellions, ways of shrugging off authority, refusing to engage in the competition, and earning myself the label of "obstinate" from my parents. My childhood refusals expanded as I grew and I realized that what I was refusing were specific expectations of how to exist in the world. As I have moved through life I have become increasingly disillusioned by the assumptions that underlie our collective life, refusing assumptions that seem only to disintegrate the possibility of fostering community and understanding, which harm and oppress ourselves and others, breeding inequalities and destroying our world in the process.

However, simply refusing, always being at odds with the assumptions of the world around you, is tiring business. One seeks to not only refuse but also affirm. In place of these refusals I affirm a life in which I am formed through my relationships with others, recognizing the positive and negative impacts my relationships have on my own sense of self and those of others. I affirm a life in which I am not separate from other beings, human and nonhuman, but intricately connected with them. I affirm a life in which such recognition of interconnection supports not only community but also demands the hard work of mindfulness in my interactions with the world, for every action I take ripples out into the universe.

Acknowledgments

The authors would like to acknowledge institutional support for research that enabled completion of this manuscript. Margaret Stout received support from the West Virginia University Senate Grants for Research and Scholarship 2012 (R-12-026), 2013 (R-13-049), and 2016 (R-16-003). Jeannine Love received support from Roosevelt University in the form of a Faculty Research Leave in 2012.

All figures in the book were crafted by Eve Faulkes; we deeply appreciate her creative insight in illustrating complex concepts.

While permissions are in hand and all previously published sources are appropriate cited and included in the reference list, we would like to thank our publishers.

In Chapter 2, the section entitled 'A crisis of sustainability' draws from a literature review previously presented in:

> Stout, Margaret and Jeannine M. Love. 2015. *Integrative Process: Follettian Thinking from Ontology to Administration*. Claremont, CA: Process Century Press.

In Chapter 2, the section entitled 'A crisis of governance' draws from a literature review previously presented in:

> Stout, Margaret. 2013. *Logics of Legitimacy: Three Traditions of Public Administration Praxis*. Boca Raton, FL: Taylor & Francis Group, CRC Press.

Chapter 3 draws from arguments previously made in:

> Stout, Margaret. 2011. "Refusing Ontological Colonization." *Administrative Theory & Praxis*, 32(4), pp. 600–605.
> Stout, Margaret. 2012. "Competing Ontologies: A Primer for Public Administration." *Public Administration Review*, 72 (3), pp. 388–398.
> Stout, Margaret. 2012. "Symposium Introduction: Process Philosophy." *Administrative Theory & Praxis*, 34 (3), pp. 357–361.

Stout, Margaret. 2012. "Toward a Relational Language of Process." *Administrative Theory & Praxis*, 34 (3), pp. 407–432.

Stout, Margaret. 2014. "The Many Faces of Unity." *Public Administration Quarterly*, 38 (2), pp. 273–281.

Stout, Margaret and Love, Jeannine M. 2013. "Ethical Choice Making." *Public Administration Quarterly*, 37 (2), pp. 278–294.

Stout, Margaret and Love, Jeannine M. 2014. "Fraternity, Solidarity, and Unity: Concepts Grounded in Competing Ontologies." *Administrative Theory & Praxis*, 36 (3), pp. 421–429.

Stout, Margaret and Love, Jeannine M. 2015. "Relational Process Ontology: A Grounding for Global Governance." *Administration & Society*, 47 (4) 447–481 (early view, June 2013).

Chapter 4 draws from explanations made in:

Stout, Margaret. 2010. "Reclaiming the (Lost) Art of Ideal-Typing in Public Administration." *Administrative Theory & Praxis*, 32 (4), pp. 491–519.

Stout, Margaret. 2012. "Competing Ontologies: A Primer for Public Administration." *Public Administration Review*, 72 (3), pp. 388–398.

Chapters 5–8 draw from discussions of public encounters in:

Stout, Margaret and Love, Jeannine M. 2015. "Integrative Governance: A Method for Fruitful Public Encounters." *American Review of Public Administration* (early view, March 2015). DOI: 10.1177/0275074015576953

Chapters 10–11 draw concepts from:

Love, J. M. (2012). "From Atomistic to Interwoven: Utilizing a Typology of i/Individualisms to Envision a Process Approach to Governance." *Administrative Theory & Praxis*, 34 (3), 362–384.

Love, J. M. (2013). "A Society of Control: The People and the Individual." *Administrative Theory & Praxis*, 37 (4), 576–793.

Chapter 12 draws concepts from:

Stout, Margaret and Love, Jeannine M. 2015. "Relational Process Ontology: A Grounding for Global Governance." *Administration & Society*, 47(4) 447–481 (early view, June 2013).

Chapter 13 draws the explanation of integration from:

Stout, Margaret, and Jeannine M. Love. 2016. "Follett, Mary Parker." In *Encyclopedia of public administration and public policy*, edited by Melvin

xx *Acknowledgments*

J. Dubnick and Domonic A. Bearfield, 1503–1510. New York: Taylor & Francis Group.

Editorial notes: any type of emphasis (i.e., italic) in quotes is in the original, unless otherwise indicated by "emphasis added." Also we use the gender-neutral plural rather than gender-specific singular terms in our own narrative.

Part I
Barriers to global governance

Part I establishes the need for the project of examining existing approaches to governance and looking for a radically democratic approach to fit the global context. Chapter 1 provides an introduction to the book. Chapter 2 provides a sketch of our current crisis of sustainability. It ends with an overview of how contemporary governance theory is responding to this context, summarizing the conversation to which this book responds. Here, we find that attempts to establish a globally acceptable approach to governance elude us. Chapter 3 establishes the argument that a principle barrier in this search is the existence of multiple and competing worldviews. Specifically, governance practices are ultimately grounded in deep philosophical commitments. We first explain the concept of ontology and how it is related to language. We then explain how ontology serves as a basis for governance, including how worldviews shape political, economic, and administrative theory and practice—the core elements of governance. From this foundation, Chapter 4 explains the methodology of this inquiry and the conceptual elements of a Governance Typology that can be used to compare and contrast approaches and their likely outcomes. These primary governance ideal-types are labeled: Hierarchical, Atomistic, Holographic, and Fragmented.

1 Introduction

This book is part of a larger project to conceptualize and develop a radically democratic approach to governance in a global context. Herein, we explore both empirical evidence of and theoretical barriers to global governance and propose an approach that may be able to overcome those barriers through a more relational and dynamic praxis.

Part I provides the foundation from which to launch this theoretical exploration of the barriers to global governance. Here, we introduce basic definitions and the plan of the book. The term "radical" means going to the root or source (as opposed to going to extremes). In reference to democracy, this means grounding theory and practice in the individual subject or world-citizen.[1] *Radical* politics shifts the subject from a unified People or particular group identity to each and every person, and rights are no longer tied to community identity. Radical understandings of democracy move from liberalism's parties and elected representatives to direct, participatory democracy. Taken together, *radical democracy* is differentiated from conservative, liberal, and communitarian approaches to democracy. Following Deleuze, we might call this move *becoming-democratic* (Patton 2005, 64). This project builds a theoretical argument of both critique and affirmation, and offers empirical illustrations.

Chapter 2 provides a sketch of our current crisis of sustainability in the global context. It ends with an overview of how contemporary governance theory is responding to this context, summarizing the conversation to which this book responds. By *governance*, we mean all of the practices used to organize collective action in any societal context, from formal rules and institutions down to unstructured everyday interactions. Governance theory can range from the macro to the micro level of analysis and can be found in the context of both public and private organizations. It is both a political and administrative or management concept that is intra-organizational, inter-organizational, intergovernmental, intersectoral, and international in the contemporary context.

By *global*, we imply that many contemporary problems transcend the boundaries of jurisdictions and nations, thereby demanding global governance of some type. Yet in attempting such actions, we confront grave challenges to identifying globally acceptable approaches. These difficulties are evidenced in a global crisis of sustainability whether considering social, economic, or environmental

4 Barriers to global governance

indicators. These challenges are also evident in demands for deeper democracy within particular governments and conflicts among governments holding competing worldviews—whether they are declared or not.

Chapter 3 establishes the argument that political and administrative theory and practice—the core elements of governance—are framed by assumptions that can be traced back to a variety of philosophical commitments and core beliefs. In short, governance is always a matter of praxis. We argue that ontological concepts provide the foundational assumptions we use to frame our understanding of the world, ourselves, and others. Ontology is embedded in our very thoughts because it is represented in our languages; therefore, it is the grounding for all ideas that follow.

To inform our understanding of ontology, we look to diverse sources: philosophy, psychology, sociology, theology, and ethics. Furthermore, rather than limiting our literature review to a handful of leading scholars, we seek to bring at least some marginalized or nontraditional academic voices into the conversation. Our approach is similar to that of Progressive-era pragmatist Mary Follett (2013b), who drew from many disciplines to identify correspondences, correlations, and "cross-fertilizations" (xvii) for the philosophical underpinnings to her governance theories (Stout and Love 2015b). It may be that a different ontology "can be made plausible to more people and accepted by others as a worthy competitor for attention, if we draw upon multiple resources to express it" (Connolly 2011, 9). The goal of this book is to identify the need for a robust philosophical, metaphysical, and physical ontological grounding for a radically democratic approach to governance.

Using a broad literature, we construct and explain a typology that provides analogous comparisons across the key conceptual elements that inform and shape governance practices. As explained in Chapter 4, the ideal-type method can be used to compare and contrast approaches and their likely outcomes. In our Governance Typology, we explain in straightforward terms the principal positions that undergird the most common systems of governance, providing a conceptual map for clarifying the full meaning of competing prescriptions. We claim that the elements most important to governance practices are: ontological assumptions and associated language, psychosocial theory, epistemological concepts, belief systems, ethical concepts, political theory, economic theory, and administrative theory. These concepts fit together like the layers of an onion, with ontology at its core. In explaining each ideal-type, we follow a logical congruence from ontological commitment through administrative practice.

This conceptual layering approach is consistent with the notion of *stratalism* —that existence itself is layered in an interconnected fashion (Dziadkowiec 2011, 98). As mediated by language, ontological assumptions are embedded in each conceptual element, each working with the next as building blocks to shape forms of governance. Therefore, to change governance, we may need to work our way through conceptual strata to the anchoring ontological assumptions. In other words, we cannot simply implement change in theory or practice at any other conceptual level while keeping a mismatched ontology—eventually

Introduction   5

the ideas or behaviors will revert to congruence with our most fundamental assumptions.

By identifying pairs of logically fitting dialectical dualisms in each element, in Part II, Chapters 5–8, we develop four primary governance ideal-types grounded in an understanding of reality as a static, discrete, mechanical process, along with those that seek more dynamic approaches of either a radically collectivist or individualist nature. We begin with the static state ontologies most familiar in modern Western societies, then move into the less familiar dynamic state ontologies. Chapter 5 explains Hierarchical Governance; Chapter 6 explains Atomistic Governance; Chapter 7 explains Holographic Governance; and Chapter 8 explains Fragmented Governance. Each chapter ends with an illustration to demonstrate how the conceptual elements play out in lived experience.

In Part III, Chapters 9–11, we present a critique of these dominant approaches to governance, employing dialectical analysis to reveal the dystopian conditions created by each imagined utopia. Through a careful analysis explained in Chapter 9, we show that each possible position along the ontological continuum has fatal flaws that prevent us from achieving a sustainable future—one that ensures just and fruitful outcomes socially, economically, and environmentally. Differences among the approaches foster mutual critiques, while similarities enable hybrids between ideal-types. Hierarchical and Atomistic Governance are grounded in static ontologies that hold collectivist and individualist assumptions in dialectical tension. Holographic and Fragmented Governance are grounded in dynamic ontologies that carry collectivist and individualist assumptions to their logical extremes, breaking the static continuum into dynamic but opposing poles. These competing qualities create barriers to finding a globally acceptable approach to governance. Adopting any one of these options will fail to achieve universal acceptance and will maintain the polarizing tensions we find in the global governance context.

As explained in Chapter 10, resistance and reform efforts tend to push the mainstream static state approaches toward dynamic ontological terrain in what we call the Arc of Reform. This ontological dynamism can foment existential crisis in the individual or societal revolution, potentially causing a leap from one dynamic position to another. However, as explained in Chapter 11, in response to discomfort with instability in the dynamic positions, hegemonic systems typically generate counter-reforms that pull governance back from utopian extremes in what we call the Arc of Reification, forming hybrids that may obfuscate underlying philosophical commitments for manipulative purposes. Together, these chapters develop a deeper understanding of the implications of differing governance approaches, provide a new perspective on governance reform movements, and foster thoughtful choice making among philosophical assumptions.

Finding all four primary governance approaches as well as their hybrids to have fatal flaws within the global context, in Part IV we argue that an innovative approach to governance is needed. Chapter 12 explains why a relational process approach may be more fruitful in terms of both experiential and ontological

6 Barriers to global governance

rationales. As international relations scholar Sergei Prozorov (2014a, 2014b) notes, a universalism that will not produce particular substantive content that can become hegemonic or totalizing is difficult to find. In a globalizing context, the challenge is to provide an ontological grounding that is not dominating in its prescriptions, but rather flexible and culturally inclusive. Such a governance approach will need to meet the principal goals of the primary approaches while avoiding their pitfalls and generating more fruitful outcomes.

To craft such an approach, we must locate its core assumptions on ontological terrain. We demonstrate that rather than generating another reified hybrid, an ideal-type can be constructed through a *dialectical synthesis* of concepts found in the four primary approaches to governance. In Chapter 13, we argue this synthesis would provide a fundamentally different ontological ground while addressing the central concerns of each of the other four ideal-types. We believe this synthesis may provide a better approach to governing social, political, and economic institutions as they interact globally. We call this synthesis approach Integrative Governance following Follett's (1918, 1919, 1924) use of the term to describe dialectical synthesis in a non-Hegelian fashion (see Stout and Love 2015b). Its concepts can be found in a rapidly growing body of work from a vast array of disciplines and worldviews that share an understanding of reality as a dynamic and relational, organic process—what we call *relational process ontology* (Stout and Love 2015c).

Many scholars argue that a relational process understanding of existence has meaningful and positive implications for public policy and governance. However, these assertions and even prescriptions for alternative approaches typically lack a structure and framework that can anchor them into traditional understandings of governance of groups, organizations, and societies in a manner that can *effect change in practice*. As public administration scholars, we seek to close the gap between governance practices and emerging understandings of *political ontology*, which includes assumptions about the nature of human being, identity, and social life (Catlaw 2007a, Howe 2006). We look forward to continuing our project through theoretical development and empirical analysis using the Governance Typology presented herein and encourage others to do so as well.

Before embarking, we must note that while this phase of the project is an exercise in speculative philosophy and we draw upon particular philosophers in this project, this is decidedly *not* a book for scholars who wish to engage other scholars in robust and nuanced conversation about these philosophers' ideas. Our aim is to foster transdisciplinary cross-pollination by identifying shared concepts that can offer a foundation for broad-based discussion. In ideal-typing, the subtle differences in actual systems of thought or an individual's full set of propositions are lost in the necessarily broad brushstrokes and the demands for logical coherence across concepts. This is why *ideal-types are never real*. Presenting intact theories, schools of thought, and actual experience would lead to nuanced argumentation within each element of the typology that would serve to confuse. Actual situations pull the core logics in various directions, creating

Introduction 7

hybrids between ideal-types. Where such conflicts in logic are noticeable, we have called out contradictions in the narrative or end notes.

The typology is meant to identify *basic* characteristics, linking them to principal philosophers and theorists for the reader's further investigation. We make explanations as straightforward as possible to provide a framework for analytical comparison. Therefore, we anticipate that anyone deeply familiar with any of the philosophers and theorists mentioned may challenge our truncated presentation and logical arrangement of ideas. We invite this kind of critical dialogue, yet we have not let such possibilities deter us from our purpose of showing how ontological assumptions weave themselves into our theories and practices, compete for primacy, and generate barriers to global governance.

Note

1 We must note that the term "citizen" is problematic in radical political theory, given contested legal identities.

2 Why now?

As noted by Karl Marx, it is during unstable times that revisiting the relationship between the individual and society becomes crucial (Schaff 1970). We argue that dialectical escalation of mutual critiques of governance approaches push ideologies toward polarized ideals. Despite the difficulties encountered in instantiating radical democracy on any scale, we agree that "it is more important than ever to hold this utopian place of the global alternative open, even if it remains empty, living on borrowed time, awaiting the content to fill it in" (Žižek 2000, 325). While this book is primarily a theoretical inquiry into this endeavor, the motivation for changing governance practices comes from *lived experience*. This chapter provides a brief summary of the current social, economic, and environmental predicaments that drive a widely shared sense of global crisis and a growing desire for transformation of governance practices, thereby establishing the empirical rationale for this inquiry.

A crisis of sustainability

Together, collectivist and individualist approaches to political economy have managed to produce unprecedented levels of crisis in all areas of life. We live quite literally on the brink of destruction, to which many now argue the only reasonable response is total system change (Alperovitz *et al.* 2015). This section provides an account of the empirical conditions in which we find ourselves struggling for a sustainable—let alone flourishing—existence, carefully considering the implications as our world becomes increasingly globalized and a capitalist market-oriented worldview becomes more pronounced. We then highlight particular crises in the three pillars of sustainability—the social, economic, and environmental arenas of life. As similarly argued by others, we find the political effects of ontological competition have led us to the brink of disaster in all three pillars. This book joins the growing call to "reorient ourselves profoundly in relation to the world, to one another, and to ourselves" (Coole and Frost 2010, 6), and to uncover ontological foundations that "are prerequisites for any plausible account of coexistence and its conditions in the twenty-first century" (2).

Why now? 9

The contemporary context of globalization

There appears to be widespread agreement that the forces of globalization have impacted every natural and societal system. Drawing from a sample of theoretical physics, new materialism, process theology, post-humanism, relational sociology, and contemporary political theory, we can see the human condition is rife with crises. As theoretical physicist David Bohm (2004) puts it, "What are the troubles of the world? They seem so many that we can hardly begin even to list them" (55). However, we generally categorize them as social, economic, and environmental issues, with particular emphasis on "the major problems of climate change, global inequality, and warfare that face the world today" (Edwards 2010, 297). In each of the crises outlined below, the conditions are bleak.

Social crises

Relational sociologist Pierpaolo Donati (2014) argues that modern Western culture "has been governed by the principle of 'institutionalized individualism'" (9). Beck and Beck-Gernsheim (2001) describe the sociological impact of this ideal as *individualization,* an impossible dislocation from social life. Indeed, postmodern society is experienced as "'paradoxical community': a community made by people without any real community" (Donati 2014, 13), or a "a paradoxical collectivity of reciprocal individualization" that "assumes that individuals alone can master the whole of their lives" (Bauman 2001, xxi). Amidst such isolation, fruitful coexistence is difficult to achieve. Nor can a collective culture be fabricated through our standard attempts to balance freedom and control through social contract. While globalization is bringing more people into an ever-widening communications and economic community, the "ethic of individual self-fulfillment and achievement" is fracturing all other forms of community (Beck and Beck-Gernsheim 2001, 22). This leads to "a society where no one is any longer recognizable by anyone else" (Debord 1994, 152).

Yet despite this increasing drive toward individuation, globalization and technological advances mean that we are simultaneously becoming more interconnected. As Bauman (2001) explains, we are "increasingly tied to others, including at the level of world-wide networks and institutions" (xxi). However, by and large, this interconnection through technological and market systems does not represent a shift toward a sense of *ontological* or *psychosocial* interconnection. As Bohm (2004) argues, "in spite of this worldwide system of linkages, there is, at this very moment, a general feeling that communication is breaking down everywhere, on an unparalleled scale" (1). By this he means that our capacity for actual *dialogue*—the listening and sharing that enables mutual understanding—is decreasing. In many respects we are more diverse and less connected than ever before and have fewer skills to "make common" (i.e., communicate) shared meanings.

10   *Barriers to global governance*

Instead, individuals seek out other like-minded individuals to connect with, creating what Pariser (2011) describes as a "you loop" in which individuals use social media to foster groupthink while avoiding or attacking those who adhere to different political positions or worldviews. However, it must be noted that there is also tremendous potential inherent in such communication technologies to foster common ground and support for community action and social movements (Castells 2015). The increased ease of communication across geographic barriers is bringing together a wider range of individual voices and experiences, as seen in revolutionary actions such as the Arab Spring and resistance movements such as Occupy Wall Street and Black Lives Matter. As argued by Minkler, "Social media are effectively being used to engage thousands of people in a variety of issues to create social change" (as quoted in Satariano and Wong 2012, 269). Still, such movements are often more successful in linking individuals of common perspective to organize oppositional politics than engaging individuals in genuine dialogue across differences.

This may be tied to culture. For instance, in Western cultures we are typically engaged in discussion that aims to break up or analyze ideas rather than to find interconnections. Bohm (2004) argues that this occurs because Western languages and worldviews actually disable our abilities to be open, withhold judgment, and allow shared meanings to emerge. We use adversarial modes of deliberation and debate to proliferate our own understandings while resisting or refusing the understandings of others, thereby co-creating fragmentation and divisions (Bohm 2004, Keating 2013). In her analysis of such oppositional approaches, womanist AnaLouise Keating (2013) explains that "oppositional politics fragment from within" (3). As social agreements about everything from language meanings to identity and political ideology break down, the human condition is rapidly becoming that of the *fragmented individual* (Love 2012)— an isolated and decentered self that is at the effect of many shifting social constructions of identity that have less and less to do with an authentic self. While "society is based on shared meanings, which constitute the culture ... at present, the society at large has a very incoherent set of meanings" (Bohm 2004, 32). This condition corresponds with the social type of *atomism*, in which there is a very limited sense of group, thereby deteriorating social order (Douglas 1996). Proliferating identity politics thus serves to divide and separate individuals across various characteristics, while broadly inclusive communities disappear. As a result, society is rife with conflict—these conflicts become amplified rather than seeking out commonalities within our differences (Keating 2013).

To address the paradoxical situation in which the individual is rhetorically empowered while disempowered economically, socially, and politically—where communication technology is advancing means of self-expression while mutual understanding between individuals is atrophied—we must seek a "posthuman politics" (Braidotti 2006) that recognizes the primacy of relation, interdependence, and *life* writ large. Because we still waiver among eternal or lifeless ontologies, feminist theoretician Rosi Braidotti (2013) argues;

Why now? 11

Our public morality is simply not up to the challenge of the scale and complexity of damages engendered by our technological advances. This gives rise to a double ethical urgency: firstly, how to turn anxiety and the tendency to mourn the loss of the natural order into effective social and political action, and secondly, how to ground such an action in the responsibility for future generations, in the spirit of social sustainability.

(112–113)

Economic crises

Most contemporary critical social theory perspectives see advanced capitalism driving or exacerbating this human condition, and many characterize the globalizing process as an "Economization of the World" (Waldo 1988, 931), through which all forms of social relationship become transactions with an economic or market-like character (Ramos 1981). In this process "all living species are caught in the spinning machine of the global economy" and natural resources and living organisms alike are commodified in a "bio-technological industrial complex" (Braidotti 2013, 7). This machine has, in many ways, taken on a life of its own, such that it has created a "contemporary global condition that now exceeds the control of any market system, state, or network of states" (Connolly 2011, 127).

As such, many feel that globalization "is increasingly forcing us to live in an economy rather than a society" (Smadja 2000)—the result is an "economic polity" as opposed to a political economy (Wolin 1981, 31). Indeed, the citizen's role in government has almost disappeared—governance has been de-politicized (Stivers 2008) and we have replaced civic virtue with "civic commercialism" (Ventriss 1991, 121). We have become little more than "citizens of corporate-nations" (King and Zanetti 2005, 21). This "colonization of the life-world" (Habermas 1989, 54) has allowed the infiltration and hegemony of market values throughout all social institutions and the corresponding loss of other values is damaging political and civic life.

In this market-dominated context, attention to power dynamics illuminates the reality that producers are in control of market exchange—and therefore the primary means of social connection within capitalism—thereby demonstrating that the promise of consumer autonomy is merely rhetorical manipulation (Thorne 2010). The market-oriented policies and rhetoric of neoliberalism therefore increasingly obscure concentrated power within the globalizing market while creating a visible, though false, sense of individual empowerment (Thorne and Kouzmin 2006). Indeed, Debord (1994) likens the neoliberal marketplace of late capitalism to a flashy spectacle, because it is intended to distract and mislead the consumer in order to obfuscate power imbalances.

Ostensibly, individuals are free to consume as they choose. However, "the dynamics of consumption actually render the individual more rather than less vulnerable to control" (Barber 2007, 36). Even as the consumer strives to construct identity through consumption, they remain fragmented through the

12 Barriers to global governance

proliferation of niche markets. The "choices" offered are disempowering because desires are artificially fabricated and multiplied, often drowning out authentic needs (Marcuse 1964). Individual consumers become increasingly subject to manipulation by market forces (Barber 2007, McSwite 1997), vulnerable due to their yearning for a sense of identity (Kinnvall 2004).

More practically, despite indications of strengthening economic markets in some countries, the global economy is arguably in the worst condition since the Great Depression, as gaps in social and economic inequality are extreme and worsening. The global financial crisis (GFC) of 2008 and the following recession through 2012 or beyond are simply the most recent evidence of the fundamental flaws of the assumptions underlying capitalism: limitless natural resources, progress, and growth (Donati 2014). Yet despite the devastating global impact, capitalism's adherents have steadfastly refused to step back and question these assumptions, or capitalism itself. Indeed, Kakabadse *et al.* (2013) argue that economic responses to the crash doubled-down on late capitalist practices, merely exacerbating the originating problems. These responses bolster incentives for continued greed and corruption through policies such as "too big to fail" bailouts, regulatory capture, and ongoing failures in corporate governance that do not see past the hegemonic "group think" of the free-market mentality.

As a result, the GFC not only increased economic disparities in the short term but policies addressing it continue to fuel power and economic asymmetries and injustices. Resentment grows as the gap between expectations of consumption and self-reliance are no longer matched by earning capacity either within or among regions, exacerbating the "long-term and increasing gap between rich and poor [that] is sometimes called 'global apartheid'" (Griffin 2007, 104). Beck and Beck-Gernsheim (2001) describe this as a paradoxical situation in which self-sufficiency is rhetorically espoused but increasingly less feasible. These conditions amplify antagonisms and hostilities that impact both state and market processes, bleeding out into all social roles (Connolly 2011). It is a political economy that "leads to moral/ethical pervasions spawning rapacious greed and corruption" (Kakabadse *et al.* 2013, 81). Instead of diversifying economic and social perspectives, capitalist globalization tends to homogenize cultures in the model of atomistic self-interest: "It is an ideology that defines basic expectations about the roles and behaviors of individuals and institutions" (Kettl 2000b, 490).

Late market capitalism uses the fear of strong centralized control and the current wave of globalization to become a hegemonic force for deregulation and the hollowing out of governments (Love 2013). Political theorist William Connolly (2011) argues convincingly that capitalism now strengthens its "channeling apparatuses" with an "abstract" or "resonance machine" that brings together market, religion, civil society, and state to "tighten the decisional, disciplinary, and channeling modes of state sovereignty" (134). The resulting movement has been one that focuses on "deregulation as a form of freedom" in which "global corporatism and the 'utopia' of unlimited consumption prevail"

(Kakabadse *et al.* 2013, 81). Such market rhetoric "obscures how it itself requires a very large state to support and protect its preconditions of being" (Connolly 2013, 7). Kakabadse *et al.* (2013) similarly call out systemic collusion, noting that "the roots of the current GFC can be seen in the wave after wave of neoliberal ideological projections capturing government policy since the days of Thatcher and Reagan in the late 1970s" (81).

This hegemonic argument is difficult to deny, as the key actors in globalization and the push toward international governance include the World Bank, the International Money Fund, various United Nations economic development initiatives, the Organization for Economic Cooperation and Development, and the G20 summits (Fremond and Capaul 2002, Kettl 2000b). These organizations wield strong influence over public policy on international debt, aid, and trade, and generally attach governance requirements to grants of favorable trade status and development assistance. In their shared model, states must demonstrate democratic accountability, political stability, safety and security, effectiveness, lack of regulatory burden, rule of law, and lack of corruption (Fremond and Capaul 2002). *Good governance* in this model is defined as "transparency and accountability in government, economic liberalization and privatization, civil society participation, and respect for human rights, democracy and the rule of law" (Collingwood 2003, 55). But typically the expected role of government is to ensure "the rights of outside suppliers of equity finance to corporations are protected and receive a fair return" (Fremond and Capaul 2002, ii). Such policies use power imbalances and economic need to force capitalist market policies on populations regardless of whether such economic and governance structures are culturally appropriate or desired.

It must be noted that the economic crises of today are not recent phenomena. Writing in 1879, public intellectual Henry George was deeply concerned about the problem of poverty as a barrier to fulfilling democracy's promise. He pointed to the growing distrust of government as evidence that political equality paired with the unequal distribution of wealth in a capitalist system can lead only to "either the despotism of organized tyranny or the worse despotism of anarchy" (1929, 530)—an argument repeated by public administration theorist Frederick Thayer (1981) a century later as the excesses of hierarchy and competition. George (1929) felt that it was both unconscionable and mystifying that poverty could perpetuate and even worsen amidst the overall growth of wealth. Many would agree that late capitalism has led us even further down this regressive road. Scarcity, self-interest, competition, and the greed, corruption, and government austerity they engender threaten markets, governments, and civil society alike. George (1929) insists that the only source of such behavior is the fear of poverty; remove the threat of poverty and society will be free to advance.

According to George (1929), poverty persists because the means of production—land, labor, and capital—are privately owned. Land includes "all natural materials, forces, and opportunities" (38). Labor includes all human exertion. Capital is "wealth devoted to procuring more wealth" (37). It

14 *Barriers to global governance*

increases the power of labor by providing infrastructure of a physical or technical nature—tools, improved materials, organization to production, and information. In order to increase profits for the owners of land and capital, market exchange is increasingly competitive, demanding ever higher prices and volumes from consumers while providing ever lower wages to labor. These are the excesses of competition described by Thayer (1981) and the conditions that some believe will eventually inspire a middle-class revolution in the United States (Dolbeare and Hubbell 1996). These are also the mechanisms through which capitalists and landowners wield asymmetries of power. As noted by Thayer, capitalism is but another symptom of the more "generic" problem of hierarchy and its system of subordination (Catlaw 2008).

Donati (2014) similarly argues that capitalism frames the "institutional order of the whole society" (73). In the wake of failing communism and socialism, many resign themselves to a lack of any viable alternatives to this capitalist model and its attendant liberal democracy (Dryzek 1996). Challenges to its utilitarian assumptions are dismissed as "audacious" and "hopeless" simply because they represent "reforms which would interfere with the interests of any powerful class" (George 1929, 99). Indeed, advocates of capitalism argue that its political economy is the only or best type of self-organizing and self-regulating system (Alperovitz *et al.* 2015). Neoliberalism *"inflates the self-organizing power of markets by implicitly deflating the self-organizing powers and creative capacity of all other systems"* (Connolly 2013, 31).

Connolly (2013) suggests that because of these systemic beliefs, the GFC produced a sort of cultural disbelief—*How could government and the market allow this to happen?* But he argues that with more participants in various social movements making a critical account of neoliberal capitalism, we may be at a turning point in political economy quite similar to where religion stood before the Enlightenment and where the physical sciences stood as the Newtonian system began to collapse into quantum and complexity theory. The Next System Project initiative may be one such indicator (see Alperovitz *et al.* 2015).

Environmental crises

Capital's assumption of unending economic growth is also facing crisis in the form of limited natural resources. In particular, waning supplies of nonrenewable energy are of grave economic concern. Climate change also exacerbates stressors in the economy due to "higher fossil fuel and electricity prices" (Randolph 2012, 127). But on the environmental side of the coin, the use of these resources has led to ecological devastation and many argue that the natural environment is nearing disaster. The crisis is typically attributed to the technological and financial practices of advanced capitalism (Barry 2005, Klein 2014). In short, the development machine "encounters structural limitations in its external and internal environments" (Donati 2014, 19). While its internal limits are found in the economic crisis, its external limits are the natural environment's capacity to accommodate our technological practices. Today, these issues

Why now? 15

"acquire an urgency unimaginable just a generation ago" (Coole and Frost 2010, 16).

At this point in global history, the stakes are quite high—human beings are quickly becoming an endangered species. Bohm (2004) argues that attempts by science to explain the universe in its entirety has caused us to see it as something that can be controlled through knowledge and technology. We feel a sense of independence from and dominion over the world:

> Some people think we can survive by organizing nature, by finding species of trees and plants that can live despite pollution—producing new species through genetic engineering, or some other means. They think that we could industrialize our world so much that nature itself is industrialized.
>
> (105)

While there is growing concern over genetic and biotechnological engineering of food, animals, and people (see for example, Braidotti 2010, 2013, Coole and Frost 2010), the banner under which environmental concerns generally gather is the issue of climate change. At the time of this writing, while political arguments about its existence and causes continue, it is accepted by the scientific community that the impacts of climate change resonate around the globe, "from melting glaciers, sea ice and tundra, to extreme weather events and drought" (Randolph 2012, 127). Some coastal human settlements have already been inundated by rising seas. As Speth (2008) warns, "If you take an honest look at today's destructive environmental trends, it is impossible not to conclude that they profoundly threaten human prospects and life as we know it on the planet" (17).

In addition to climate change, agricultural and industrial practices also wreak havoc on biodiversity at local, regional, and global levels (Mies and Shiva 2014). Indeed, many biologists argue that a sixth mass extinction is already underway; one that is driven by human activity (Barnosky *et al.* 2011). For instance, the widely publicized 2010 oil spill from British Petroleum's *Deepwater Horizon* oil rig, occurred in part due to "a series of cost-cutting moves" on the part of BP and its contractors (Freudenburg and Gramling 2011, 15) and the catastrophe "initiated a previously unknown category of marine pollution" (Somasundaran *et al.* 2014, 19) the full impacts of which will not be known for some time. The use of hydraulic fracturing to reach ever more remote sources of natural gas have profound health impacts on local communities and wildlife populations through soil and water contamination (Kassotis *et al.* 2014, Osborn *et al.* 2011). The process is known to cause microearthquakes and not only has the number of events been increasing in areas with historically low risks, as the wells become deeper the severity of earthquakes induced are also increasing (Ellsworth 2013).

The demand for inexpensive products has also led to large-scale agricultural production which, while it has "been successful in increasing food production, it has also caused extensive environmental damage" (Foley *et al.* 2005, 570).

16 Barriers to global governance

Industrial farm animal production (IFAP) seeks to maximize profit by raising food animals in highly compact and often enclosed environments (concentrated animal feedlot operations, or CAFOs). This high concentration of animals results in the increased use of antibiotics and production of animal waste, polluting surrounding soil and water (Halden and Schwab 2008, Mallin and Cahoon 2003). These high-density operations also place unsustainable pressures on land and water resources to feed the livestock, resulting in nutrient depletion in topsoil, soil erosion and global deforestation (Halden and Schwab 2008) and have been calculated to have a larger cumulative impact on global warming than the transportation sector (Steinfeld *et al.* 2006). Intensive agricultural practices for food production utilize high levels of antibiotics, pesticides, and nitrogen-rich fertilizers, and are linked to pollution and degradation of soil, eutrophication of waterways that causes toxic algal blooms in critical water sources, loss of biodiversity, and smog (Kane *et al.* 2014, Mallin and Cahoon 2003, Tilman *et al.* 2002). These impacts compromise the health of the global ecosystem.

Despite the growing understanding of the widespread harmful impacts of energy and mass food production and distribution, such practices continue to be encouraged by an economic model based on the assumption of limitless growth (Kakabadse *et al.* 2013, Roy and Crooks 2011). These assumptions view natural resources as boundless means to profit. Demand for an ever-increasing quality of life—as determined by Western standards of material wealth—for ever-increasing numbers of people results in the mass harvesting of natural resources by large multinational corporations without attention to system limitations or impact on the overall ecosystem. This relegates the impacts on critical natural factors such as the ozone layer, underground aquifers, topsoil quality, and biodiversity to the status of externalities not quantified in cost–benefit calculations. But such "externalities" have profound *internal* implications for life on this planet. As zoologist and environmentalist David Suzuki argues, an economic model that dismisses environmental impacts as externalities "is not based in anything like the real world" (as quoted in Roy and Crooks 2011).

Due to the environmental crises of climate change and loss of biodiversity, the human *condition* has become a *predicament*—a devastating political and economic system has led us to the brink of ecological catastrophe that reveals the delicate balance of the ecosystem; what Connolly (2013) characterizes as "the fragility of things." The impacts cannot be isolated; these crises threaten everyone, regardless of nationality, but impact developing nations first and most severely (IPCC 2014, Kreft *et al.* 2015). Furthermore, these environmental crises create widespread "disruptive effects on our economic and social systems" (Randolph 2012, 127)—exacerbating the other crises of sustainability in a cycle of ongoing deterioration. This predicament demands a dialogue among philosophy, theology, and the sciences so that we can figure out how to both protect ourselves from life's dangers while investing in existential affirmation.

A crisis of governance

Clearly, the crisis of sustainability confronted in social, economic, and environmental arenas of life demands a response from governments and governance theory. Donati (2014) argues that the GFC of 2008 and the following recession demonstrates that political economies based on a tension between freedom (individualism) and control (collectivism) *"are not sustainable as long-term systems"* (45). Yet this "political–administrative sub-system of society" is "the institutional order of the whole society" (73) that permanently sets liberal competition and profit against socialist solidarity and redistribution. To resolve this dialectic, the entire political economy must change (Alperovitz *et al.* 2015). Here, we will consider the current conversation in governance theory regarding how to respond to the contemporary context of globalization.

We find ourselves in a situation in which there is less organizational hierarchy and control within the institutions of society, but there is more competition. We have not eliminated the original constitutional structures, but have changed many rules of engagement from what might be described as the authoritative dictates of classical conservative liberalism to the pluralist and market-like transactions of modern liberalism and neoliberalism. We may seem to be significantly more autonomous from hierarchical domination, but we are prevented from forming social bonds due to the overwhelming competitive spirit imbuing the political economy. People around the world increasingly challenge pluralistic representative democracy, demanding deeper, more participatory approaches. Therefore, contemporary governance theory is revisiting three fundamental questions: that of sovereignty, the role of government, and the methods of democratic participation.

The question of sovereignty

Sovereignty represents political power—the power to decide and to act not only for oneself, but in a manner that affects others. The sovereign is "above or superior to all others; chief; greatest; supreme … in power, rank, or authority … holding the position of ruler; royal; reigning … independent of all others" (Neufeldt 1996, 1283). Most representative democracies hold sovereign prerogative within the state or federated states that empower the political and administrative officials who comprise the state and control its laws (Ostrom 1989). When these officials are given authority to act on behalf of the government, citizens are denied political sovereignty.

Clearly, this is the meaning of sovereignty that governance theory cannot seem to escape. By establishing representative systems of democratic government, we retain *symbolic* sovereignty within the individual. However, through the supposedly voluntary will and consent of an abstraction called the People, we imbue institutions of the state with *operational* political authority (Catlaw 2007a). Through this system all those who are considered citizens are able to choose their representatives and temporarily lend their sovereignty to them until

18 *Barriers to global governance*

the next election. This political authority is then delegated at least in some part to public administrators who are made accountable and responsible through various mechanisms. Through increasing intergovernmental and intersectoral partnerships of various types, this delegation is stretched even further, with even less electoral influence and control.

In what may appear to be an expanding democracy globally, this process of representation increases tensions between the rhetorically sovereign individual and a functionally sovereign representative state. The individual finds themselves under the purview of authority given to another entity (White 1990). But the proliferating social identities outlined above ensure the impossibility of adequate representation (Sarup 1989). The supposedly sovereign individual only has political voice through *group representation* that continually contests definitions of the People without questioning the principle of representation itself. Follett (1998) describes this type of representation as imitation in crowds, herds, masses, and mobs. Public administration theorist Thomas Catlaw (2007a) argues that these attempts to fit ourselves into group identities cause problems of inclusion and exclusion. But more problematically, *no individual* is actually represented by the People, because it is an abstraction empty of substantive content. It is a simply a placeholder for sovereignty used in representative democracy.

In this system, political authority concentrates in the hands of a few "sovereign Individuals," elevated by their relative power within the market and, therefore, within the political sphere (Thorne 2010). In the US context, economic elites have been found to have "a quite substantial, highly significant, independent impact on policy" while average citizens "have little or no independent influence on policy at all" (Gilens and Page 2014, 572). Through the proliferation of democracy around the world, this system of representation acts as a "midwife [to] a new world order" (Witt 2010, 924)—one that produces the globalized social, economic, and environmental crises of sustainability described above.

The question of governance

Through neoliberal reforms, govern*ments* themselves are increasingly decentered among other actors across sectors. "Government—the State—is no longer the defining ingredient" (Stivers 2008, 104). A key element of this phenomenon is the push toward government load-shedding of functions and privatization of service delivery exemplified in reform movements like Reinventing Government (Gore and Clinton 1993, Osborne and Gaebler 1992) and the New Public Management (Hood 1996). In short, the public good is increasingly coproduced by governments, corporations, and a variety of nonprofit Non-Governmental Organizations (NGOs) through the contracting out or elimination of government functions altogether. Govern*ance* is increasingly conducted by a "marble cake" not just of governmental agencies in various geopolitical regions, but of intersectoral actors including public, private for-profit, private nonprofit, voluntary associations, and individual citizens engaged in the actions of governance (Bingham *et al.* 2005, Grodzins 1966).

In fact, by 2005 in the US, the direct provision of goods and services by the federal government accounted for only 5 percent of its overall activity (Salamon 2005). In local governments, for which direct services account for a higher level of government activity, over a quarter of all services have been privatized—with government contracting seeing sector growth even through the 2008 recession (Epstein 2013). It is clear to many that privatization "is not merely another management tool but a basic strategy of societal governance. It is based on a fundamental philosophy of government and of government's role in relation to the other essential institutions of a free and healthy society" (Savas 2000, 328). This philosophy largely rejects the notion of publicness and embraces the expansion of market values. Because of this shifting perspective, the entire notion of *publicness* has come into question (Bozeman and Bretschneider 1994, Emmert and Crow 1988, Wettenhall 2001).

To this inter*sectoral* complexity, we must also add inter*national* blurring (Keohane and Nye 2000) because "events have fueled a global connectedness or interdependence that transcends national boundaries and is manifested in financial, political, environmental, technological, and cultural ways" (Yoder and Cooper 2005, 298). In our contemporary context, governance is spread throughout a global system in which "processes and structures continually interact and a new order emerges in response to disruptions" (Crosby 2010, S71). This is an era characterized by the "absence of any clear definition of what constitutes 'a people' or 'a nation'" (Carlsson and Ramphal 1995, 74). The nation-state is rapidly losing its status as the "locus of governance for collective life" (Yoder and Cooper 2005, 298). This has significant implications for both governance theory and practice that have only begun to be explored—issues that "spill over onto the most basic questions of ... governance" (Kettl 1993, 211). Globalization is becoming "thick" through the increasing density of intersectoral organizational networks engaging in governance activities that reach beyond national borders (Keohane and Nye 2000, 108).

Unfortunately, the slipping away of borders among social sectors and nations does not necessarily mean a blending of worldviews. In fact, competing worldviews perpetuate conflicts because they prevent us from communicating understandably—we talk past one another (Stout 2012a), while global economic elites gain greater influence not only in national policy (Gilens and Page 2014) but also in international policy, including using their influence in representative systems to manipulate conditions of international trade and structural readjustment programs (Perkins 2004, Stiglitz 2007). Furthermore, the competition among worldviews tends toward hegemony and domination (Brigg 2007). In this globalizing context, while operational practices may be readily adopted by non-Western governments, the underlying cultural values in Western governance may not be as welcome. Schultz (2004) frames the problem nicely: *What happens when the practices, norms, values, and principles that guide behavior differently in particular settings are no longer situated and therefore in competition?*

20 Barriers to global governance

Which set of ethical rules dominates? Unfortunately, neoliberal governance has "a dominating and homogenizing character that is of concern in global governance" (Kettl 2000b, 490). The "massive prescience and truth of these analyses" (Critchley 2005, 220) can be found in the original communist critique of cosmopolitanism as the pseudo-internationalization of atomistic individualism (Marx and Engels 1998).

The question of participation

Some argue that *who* makes governance decisions is not the only problem in questions of sovereignty; it is also *how* those decisions are made. "An important distinction is to be made between the *locus of decision* and the *mode of calculation*" (Wildavsky 1979, 123). As the sector where governance happens becomes less important, how decisions are made becomes more important—the degree to which the process is *democratic* is of core concern. For example, citizens of European nations worry that European Union decisions are made by appointed experts rather than through representative political deliberation (Kettl 2000b). In response, scholars urge politicians to "play a key role in efforts to improve the democratic anchorage of governance networks" (Sørensen and Torfing 2005, 215). In short, international and intersectoral governance demands a reframing of democracy, civic agency, and politics (Boyte 2005)—a project that Follett understands as employing the integrative process of democracy throughout all sectors of social life (Stout and Love 2015b).

Publicness must therefore be reaffirmed and may be measured by "commitment to the common good and civic involvement" (Carino 2001, 60). However, *who* in the public is included is also in question. Indeed, Follett (1998) recognizes that the further we get from engaging citizens—the individual sovereigns—in participatory practices, the less democratic governance becomes. Direct involvement of the governed enables governance as a function of both moral and instrumental choice. It is this participatory mode of association that "provides the link between theories of communicative action, deliberative democracy, and new forms of global governance" (Risse 2004, 293). These approaches can help us determine "how to design and manage the immensely complex collaborative systems" (Salamon 2005, 10–11), and in doing so create "the possibility that improved participation and dialogue can fill the gaps that have appeared in the ideals and practices of representative and responsible government" (Bevir 2012, 110). Participatory governance practices must accommodate cultural diversity, non-rational human behavior, and demands for inclusive citizenship beyond mere consumer choice (Kelly 1998). They must also reach into theories of political economy as the new paradigm in order to address "big issues" like democratization, societal equity, and ethics (Klingner 2004).

This notion of the degree to which governance includes active engagement in democratic deliberation was conceptualized by Arnstein (1969) in her Ladder of Citizen Participation model. Using evaluations of participation practices in urban revitalization, she identified a typology that includes nonparticipation

Why now? 21

(manipulation and therapy), tokenism (informing, consultation, and placation), and citizen power (partnership, delegation, and control). In pointing to the issue of decision-making power, she revealed "the central issue of the participation debate" (Fagence 1977, 122). Contemporary empirical studies of participatory democracy support this claim (see for example, Kathlene and Martin 1991, Stout 2010b). To be democratically authentic, participation efforts must represent a "genuine devolution of authority" (Carley and Smith 2001, 198). Therefore, participation cannot be repressive or it will devolve into the inauthentic practice of cooptation (Selznick 1949). Follett (1998) recognizes authentic participatory practices as the only "true democracy" (156)—something she argues has not yet been tried on a large scale. Following Follett's lead, we join in the search for a radically democratic approach to global governance.

The crisis in review

Taken together, these many crises are implicated in one another in an inextricable fashion. Representative democracy has been infiltrated by market interests, hollowing out government itself as functions and authority have been outsourced to the private sector. This shift of power has produced social, economic, and environmental crises. The recognition that democratic governments, let alone more authoritarian regimes, are at the helm causes the global governed to demand political voice. Social movements indicate the level of dissatisfaction with representation; people increasingly insist upon practices of direct and participatory democracy.

3 Grounding governance in ontology

As noted in Chapter 2, competing worldviews present a significant barrier to resolving global crises of sustainability, including that of governance. Such worldviews are "the composite of all the values, beliefs, and attitudes you hold toward the world, which assists you both in describing what you see and in prescribing what you should do" (Abigail and Cahn 2011, 270). This chapter explores the basic differences among the ontological assumptions of those worldviews, the relationship between ontology and language, and the manner in which ontology shapes governance. It then lays out the primary experiential reason that we should care about these issues: ontological colonization. In essence, when ontologies differ and confront one another they typically compete for primacy, thereby establishing the conditions for hegemonic and counter-hegemonic dynamics in governance practices. Maintaining these differences in antagonistic tension generates stalemate at best, war at worst, while differentials in political and economic power prevent a more productive agonism (Mouffe 2005).

Ontology is the most general branch of metaphysics concerned with the nature of being and generally stems from philosophy, religion, or physics. Ontologies are theories of existence, origin myths, or "onto-stories" as some have called them (Bennett 2001, Howe 2006). Ontology is how we frame an understanding of ourselves and the human condition within what we presume reality to be. Reality is the ontic—the phenomena we actually experience. These assumptions prefigure the beliefs, theories, and practices that follow (Tønder and Thomassen 2005b, White 2000). Therefore, ontological assumptions are implicated in action. As Connolly (2011) argues, "belief, spirituality, desire, and role performance are involved with each other, with a change in one helping to consolidate or weaken a change in another" (91). However, we argue that without changing ontological assumptions, changes in the other elements will eventually revert to logical congruence with beliefs.

Therefore, ontological assumptions drive our behavior, but are nearly invisible to those holding them unless specifically questioned or confronted by differing perspectives. As cultural developments, these ontological ideas have evolved over time in different places. As described by administrative theorist Louis Howe (2006), the ontology of Western society changed radically in response to modernity, draining the world of intrinsic meaning or transcendent

Grounding governance in ontology 23

purpose through modern science and formal governmental rationalities; the world became what sociologist Max Weber (1993) described as *disenchanted*.

However, this trend did not fully eliminate metaphysical ontologies from society, nor from all political philosophies and social science; even this "disenchanted" perspective retains an underlying, if altered, ontology. Furthermore, the ontology of science has not fully displaced other ontological assumptions and beliefs grounded in different explanations of existence. These differing views drive increasing insurgences in political debate and governance practices. Therefore, it is important to develop an understanding of multiple ontologies to clarify the deeper meanings and consequences of such debate.

Ontological dualisms

In Western philosophy, most discussions trace back to the pre-Socratic Greek philosophers, Parmenides and Heraclitus (Graham 2002, Heidegger 1992), whose dialectical positions can help make sense of ontological alternatives. The two philosophers' respective positions on the nature of being and knowing can be described as: (1) singular (unity, One) versus plural (fragmentation, Many), (2) continuity (being) versus change (becoming), (3) transcendence versus immanence, and (4) Truth versus truths. These positions may be an accurate depiction of dialectic, or it may be an interpretation that serves to simplify the nuances of their positions to a point whereby a dialectical relationship can be devised. In other words, the two perspectives can be understood as ideal-types or caricatures.

Parmenides is considered the grandfather of most Western philosophy (Palmer 2008) and the positivist science that followed. Based on an allegorical revelation from the goddess Truth, Parmenides claims that reality *is* (static) a unity (whole). The Way of Truth shows that reality is one unchangeable, timeless, indestructible whole. Existence is assumed to be eternal because nothing can come from nothing. "Nothing" is referred to as the void, which cannot exist. There is only one Truth, which can be perceived through reason, but which is clouded by sensory perceptions. Our perception of change (dynamic) and difference (plural) is merely the Way of Appearance—illusions of plurality and change that hide the truths of unity and continuity from humanity. Because that from which all things are made never disappears, the appearance of many different things materializing and transforming is merely an illusion of difference. In this way, human beings are caught in a conflict between the appearance of a phenomenal world of plurality and the truth of underlying wholeness.

In short, this is an essentialist view of the nature of being and "Plato and Aristotle both came to understand Parmenides as a type of generous monist" (Palmer 2008, section 3.5, paragraph 9). By generous monism, it is meant that the essence of all things is necessarily unified, while its phenomenal manifestations are plural but not necessarily differentiated. "What Is imperceptibly interpenetrates or runs through all things while yet maintaining its own identity distinct from theirs" (Palmer 2008, section 3.5, paragraph 11). The source of

24 Barriers to global governance

being is also transcendent or metaphysical—separate from the physical (immanent) universe. Putting a theistic spin on this concept, Thayer (1981) describes this experience as the ancient understanding that knowledge of oneself is knowledge of God—we are *all* God. However, Parmenides at no time refers to the Way of Truth as being divine or godlike in any manner. His "distinction among the principal modes of being ... qualify him to be seen as the founder of metaphysics or ontology as a domain of inquiry distinct from theology" (Palmer 2008, section 3.5, paragraph 12).

On the other side of the dualism, Heraclitus has been called the father of process philosophy (Christ 2003). Heraclitus argues that reality *becomes* (dynamic) and is therefore a multitude (plural) across time, if nothing else. Thus, there are many truths. Heraclitus asserted that the only universal principle is change and all that exists is in a constant state of becoming and dissolving, which produces a particular harmony at any given point in time. Yet he notes that the substance of each state (formation and dissolution) is the same—there is an essence of becoming that expresses itself in many potentialities, as noted in the common phrase "from all things one and from one all things." Therefore, the source of existence is immanent.

The opposing processes of becoming and dissolution are the source of a creative conflict through which all things exist, and all things can be identified as a part of a binary such as life and death. As one comes into being the other disappears, and vice versa. "Contraries are the same by virtue of constituting a system of connections: alive–dead, waking–sleeping, young–old. Subjects do not possess incompatible properties at the same time, but at different times" (Graham 2008, section 3.2, paragraph 4). However, neither half of the binary can be said to exist separately from the other; they comprise a whole. This brings to mind the symbol for *T'ai-Chi T'u*; the Eastern philosophical understanding of the *Tao* (life) as a non-dualistic whole comprised of two opposing forces of *yin* and *yang* in an ever-changing pursuit of balance (Capra 1999). This view can be described as a form of dynamic monism—a unifying process, but one that is ever changing over the course of time. As Heraclitus claimed, you can never step into the same river twice.

Based on these fundamental differences, Parmenides and Heraclitus are set into an irresolvable dialectic that undergirds many philosophical and theoretical debates to this day. For example, Parmenides' monism is used to defend the notion that the Way of Truth can be perceived by some and can therefore be represented and enforced by them onto the Way of Appearances. In other words, a unity can be legitimately coerced by some as representatives of the One dominating the Many. A liberal rejection of this notion puts the ability to perceive the Way of Truth into everyone's hands, enabling competition as opposed to domination. Such pluralists may also draw upon Heraclitus and his notion of difference as a defense of the Many as opposed to the One.

The most recent formulation of ontological dualism is characterized by competing assumptions of abundance versus lack at the core of existence (Tønder and Thomassen 2005b). Brought into play through post-structuralist critique,

Grounding governance in ontology 25

philosophers argue whether the nature of human beings starts from embodied matter (ontological) as opposed to signification or social construction (epistemological). While both positions tend agree to the concept of a void at the heart of existence, one perspective understands it to be full of nonmaterial potentiality while the other sees it as empty of worldly signification. The former focuses on the freedom to co-create while the latter focuses on freedom from domination.

In the exploration that follows herein, we will consider how two sets of ontological dualism exist in dialectical tension with one another, thereby producing a typology of four governance ideal-types. We will then consider how we might develop a synthesis of those ontological positions in a fifth governance ideal-type.

From dualisms to typologies

To explore divergent ontologies, it is helpful to employ an ideal-type method (Weber 1949b, 1994a) to draw out principal characteristics and their differences (Stout 2010d). Considering the concepts provided by Parmenides and Heraclitus, we can see that differing ontological assumptions include whether reality has: a static or dynamic state, a transcendent or immanent source, and a singular or plural expression (Stout 2012a). *Static* state means that reality simply *is*—we can know its truth through various means. *Dynamic* state means that reality is continually becoming, and so understanding it is difficult beyond temporary "snapshots" of its expression. *Transcendent* source means that the ground of being is beyond that which exists. *Immanent* source means the ground of being is within that which exists—they are one and the same. *Singular* expression means that the source of existence is complete—it cannot be broken apart in some way. Therefore, individual parts are not necessarily differentiated. *Plural* expression means that there are many sources of existence; therefore individual parts are clearly differentiated. These characteristics will be used throughout the book to understand fundamental differences among governance approaches.

If we put these characteristics into a two-by-two matrix, we can start to shape a description of four ideal-type positions (see Table 3.1) that describe *existence*. Indeed, these differing ontological positions represent incompatible stories about reality and therefore refer to very different ways of being in the world. As such they yield strikingly different theories and practices regarding how we can

Table 3.1 Principal ontological dichotomies matrix

Static state	*Static state*
Transcendent source	*Immanent source*
Singular expression (One)	*Plural expression (Many)*
Dynamic state	*Dynamic state*
Transcendent source	*Immanent source*
Singular expression (One)	*Plural expression (Many)*

26 Barriers to global governance

and should live together. Such an ideal-type model can be used to examine such theories and practices to identify their underlying ontological assumptions.

The relationship between ontology and language

We accept certain arguments of cognitive linguistics and philosophy suggesting that language shapes consciousness and identity and therefore prefigures all intellectual thought and forms of social relationship. The notion that language creates a predisposition for particular types of social action is based on the understanding of language as a tool of social construction that impacts our way of perceiving and understanding the world around us and our place in it. In each instance, these ontological assumptions shape the very language we use to formulate our theories and describe our world. In turn, the structure of this language reinforces our ontological assumptions.

This section will summarize briefly this highly complex argument and concur with it only to a point. While Western philosophers make a convincing case for the manner in which language shapes us and the very real dangers of its dominating effects, this characteristic is culturally situated, not inherent in language per se, as frequently argued. This is eloquently described by Henry George (1929):

> What is more ingrained in habit than language, which becomes not merely an automatic trick of the muscles, but the medium of thought? What persists longer, or will quicker show nationality? Yet we are not born with a predisposition to any language. Our mother tongue is our mother tongue only because we learned it in infancy.
>
> (489)

We take this one step further, suggesting that our ontological assumptions are reflected in our languages and that languages differ based on those assumptions.

Some cognitive linguists suggest that the human brain is the only type with a language acquisition device (Chomsky 1965), suggesting that the term refers only to linguistic utterances. However, language in this discussion will include all forms of discourse—words, symbols, and practices that represent something else. Since other species are able to utilize sign language, for example, this discussion diverges from some linguistic theories. Language thusly defined is comprised of representations. The concepts we use to describe nature are not features of reality, but creations of the mind—they are "parts of the map, not of the territory" (Capra 1999, 161). Many "things" are represented in language—what is perceived through the physical senses, intellectual knowledge, emotional feelings, and intuitions—some of which are conscious and many of which are unconscious. Once experience is translated into language, it is altered. Therefore, some suggest that language cannot be disaggregated from consciousness. From this perspective, the rational knowledge of consciousness discriminates, divides, compares, measures, and categorizes. It enables us to create an abstract intellectual map of reality that is linear and sequential in nature, helping us to navigate in the material world. Associated concepts, symbols and language frame

Grounding governance in ontology 27

our thinking to match. Because of its capacity to structure consciousness, language deeply shapes our sense of self, others, and the world around us, thereby channeling our behavior and action.

These linguistic suppositions and their impact on governance practice have been carried forward in public administration theory through a variety of views on the social and political implications of discourse (see for example, Farmer 1995, 1997, 2002a, 2005b, Fox and Miller 1995, Miller 2000) as well as dialectic (see for example, Carr 2000a, 2000b, Carr and Zanetti 1999, Rutgers 2001). Perhaps most notably, several theorists utilize social theorist Jacques Lacan's reformulation of Freudian psychoanalytical theory to explain the impact of discursive processes on identity (see for example, Catlaw 2005, 2006, 2007a, 2007b, Catlaw and Jordan 2009, Harmon and McSwite 2011, McSwite 2000, 2001a, 2001b, 2002, 2003, 2004, 2005, 2006, White and McSwain 1993).

Lacan argues that because language constructs the subject, it inherently creates dominating relationships that rob individuals of any capacity for agency (Fink 1998, Žižek 2006). We challenge this assertion along with others: "Is it possible to struggle against, and change, the language and ideology of patriarchy, or are we forever formed in this way?" (Barker 2000, 87). We argue that given what is evident in many non-Western languages, it is reasonable to assert that it is possible to change the dominating language of Western culture to reflect alternative ontological assumptions. In other words, language itself is not *inherently* dominating and hierarchical in nature. Instead, Western language in particular has been constructed in a dominating and hierarchical manner; this manner is not universal (Mitchell 1974).

Given the evolutionary nature of language, it is logically possible that a language that constrains, alienates, and controls consciousness and identity can be replaced with one that expands, connects, and enables individuality. Indeed, many have argued that the task of philosophy "should primarily be the clarification of language" (Mesle 2008, 11). This proposition is supported by Saussure's (1960) original notion that "different language structures or systems create different 'worlds' of meaning and hence different lived worlds" (White and McSwain 1993, 23). Therefore, we will consider the implications of language in explaining the ontology of each approach to governance.

How ontology shapes governance

It has been claimed that "public administration exists to realize the governance of society" (Raadschelders 1999, 288). Yet remembering that governance is comprised of all of the practices used to organize collective action in any societal context, what society believes governance to be changes over time and across place. We ground our Governance Typology in ontology, arguing that ontological concepts provide the foundational assumptions we use to frame every other concept or action. In this sense, ontology is no longer "the arcane philosophical study of being" (Howe 2006, 423)—it is important to all social and environmental concerns because it frames our understanding of self

28   Barriers to global governance

and others, including other beings and things. As Allan (1993) notes, metaphysical, ideological, and political positions can be assessed by considering "the concrete actions of our daily lives" (284). In other words, "Ontology is not a separate, allegedly more fundamental dimension that is extraneous to praxis ... its object is nothing but this praxis itself and the beings involved in it" (Prozorov 2014a, xxix).

Because of this relationship between ontology and action, "the *quality* of existential orientations to the human predicament plays a significant role in ethical, political, and economic life" (Connolly 2013, 179, emphasis added). As Ayn Rand (1982) notes, politics and economics presuppose ethics, and "before you come to ethics, you must answer the questions posed by metaphysics and epistemology" (4). A similar understanding of philosophical commitments has been described as an "ethical–political constellation" of norms and perceived possibilities that shape practical philosophy and praxis (Bernstein 1991). Ontological assumptions drive everything from the question of sovereignty to a public ethic and the proper institutions of government. It shapes how we go about living together, thereby directly impacting public policy (Christ 2003).

Ontology is therefore important to governance theory and practice because it *frames presuppositions about all aspects of life and what is good and right.* In short, the relationship between politics and ontology is reflexive; political philosophies adopt specific ontological assumptions about the nature of reality and offer prescriptions for political forms that fit these ideas. These political forms structure social action, reproducing that which is assumed (Giddens 1984). New institutionalism refers to this phenomenon as "path dependency" (North 1990) through which the original assumptions are reinforced by the institutions they shaped—what *is* frames what *should* be; what *should* be perpetuates what *is*. Identifying such fundamental assumptions makes clear how particular political forms are thought to be appropriate or even logically necessary based on the nature of existence. This is also why they typically remain unchallenged. To open up the questions of governance, the notion of ontology and the political must be linked (Catlaw 2007a, Tønder and Thomassen 2005a).

Indeed, ontological commitments are not easily brushed aside and demand logical congruence all the way from beliefs to practices so that incongruence does not generate "ontological angst" (Evans and Wamsley 1999, 119). Ideas or practices will eventually revert to congruence with our most fundamental assumptions to avoid such contradiction. Furthermore, if the nature of reality is in conflict with how we perceive it, then our socially constructed reality and institutions will be existentially problematic. To change governance practices, the ontological assumptions to which they are anchored must be altered. Therefore, our goal is to think through how ontology, political form, and resulting practices can be aligned in a logical manner that leads to desirable results in the current context.

We concur that "divergent understandings ... reflect different ontological commitments towards identity, its relationship to difference and its importance in theorizing politics and subjectivity" (Widder 2005, 32–33). To challenge an

Grounding governance in ontology 29

ontology that has negative implications for the political subject, we must first identify and describe that ontology and then locate an alternative. In this endeavor, we recognize that some theorists are vehemently opposed to grounding the political subject in any ontology, arguing "politics is a disruption of the ontological domain and separate categories are required for its analysis and practice" (Critchley 2005, 225). However, we follow the contrary line of thought, which assumes that ontology shapes language and language shapes thought; therefore, it stands to reason that ontology prefigures virtually everything that follows. A different ontological grounding, rather than no ontological grounding, is necessary for a new political praxis.

Many recognize the need to unpack the underlying philosophical assumptions in governance. For example, public administration scholars invest a good deal of attention in the problem of how epistemology shapes administrative *study* (see for example, Adams 1992, Box 1992, Farmer 2010, Houston and Delevan 1990, Raadschelders 1999, 2000, White 1986) as well as *practice* (see for example, Farmer 2010, Hummel 1991, 1998, Schmidt 1993). These scholars explore how thought and knowledge shape action. In some ways, this epistemological focus has deflected attention from deeper philosophical commitments that have a direct bearing on our political practices. In short, *why do we think and know the way we do?*

Other public administration scholars seek to ground theories about legitimate claims to political authority in notions of human nature (Caldwell 1988) or "what we think of as being human" (Spicer 2004, 354). This underlying nature of the human being and social relationships has been referred to as the problem of the social bond (McSwite 2006). Therefore, we must explore psychological and social theories—psychosocial theories—and their notions of *self* and *other*, and the dynamics of bonding or otherness that this relationship generates. The concept of *alterity* concerns the decentered "moral other" as opposed to an objectified, cognitive other (Johnson 1990). Ascertaining how we can and should live together is necessarily influenced by who we think we are and in what ways we are, or are not, connected to one another (Love 2010a, 2012).

As an example, modern liberalism assumes self-interested, atomistic human beings, which engenders pluralist political forms as a matter of course. If you believe this description of the human condition, political institutions must be based on the individual. In this way political theory depicts both what *is* and what *should be*—it describes what is believed to be the constitutive Good: the source of good, as well as good ends (Taylor 1989). This notion is reflected in the writings of political theorist Carl Schmitt (1985), who asserts that theories of the state are secularized theological concepts. In other words, the state is a stand-in for God; citizen is to society as person is to God. Thayer (1981) makes the same point in suggesting that the principal problem for political theory is ultimately, "Who is authorized to speak for God?" (A-14). From a secular perspective, this is similar to the problem of who is authorized to speak for the People (Catlaw 2007a).

30 *Barriers to global governance*

In the context of governance, the associated roles of citizen, elected representative, and appointed administrator create role-associated alterity—"How should an administrator [or representative or citizen] behave in relationship to others?" (Farmer 1995, 227). The possibilities include relationships of dominance and submission, as in the master–servant metaphor, as well as difference without domination among governance actors (Carr and Zanetti 1999). These very different ideas about how we relate to one another are reflected in our political ontology and enacted in administrative praxis.

Accordingly, contemporary political theory has turned away from unthinking adoption of the philosophical commitments that characterize modern Western culture, both critiquing its underlying assumptions about human nature and offering affirmative modifications or alternatives. For example, Love's (2010a) ideal-type model unpacks the psychosocial assumptions underlying traditional public administration scholarship. Similarly, Hendriks' (2010) ideal-type model of democracy links political practices to the societal cultures underlying them. In a sort of reverse engineering process, social practices are deconstructed and analyzed in order to understand the types of human nature that is presupposed.

However, many argue that we must go further even than the complex assumptions about the nature of human being, identity, and social life. We cannot limit discussion to epistemology or psychosocial assumptions—we must examine ontology. Such inquiry would serve to link "a fundamental conception of reality (ontology) with a specific epistemological position … with a distinctive form of the political" (Catlaw 2007a 11). This logic assumes that ontology is the most deep-seated philosophical commitment and is therefore the most fundamental basis for claims about all aspects of governance. As Robert Cox (1995) asserts, "the first task of a contemporary political theory is to declare its ontology" (36).

In his groundbreaking study of political philosophy, Stephen White (2000) argues that ontology prefigures political philosophy and is therefore an appropriate topic of study for social and political theorists, as does political theorist William Connolly (2011). This "ontological turn" (Prozorov 2014a) is increasingly prevalent in philosophy, political theory, and public administration theory. Many of these scholars call for political action rather than stopping at theoretical speculation—fully linking new ways of thinking to action (Braidotti 2013). However, many fail to extend political action into the realm of policy implementation. To address this gap, there is a small but important lineage of public administration scholars suggesting that to understand the deepest problems of governance, we must consider philosophical issues and their implications for practice (see for example, Appleby 1952, Catlaw 2007a, Cooper 1984, Denhardt 2000, McSwite 1997, 2006, Morstein Marx 1946, Waldo 1984).

Daring to delve this deep, public administration theorist Gary Wamsley (1996) insists that ontological disclosure is the only appropriate platform from which one can make normative claims about the way things should be. Traces of this argument can be found in early texts of the field. Morstein Marx (1946) argues, "Perhaps our sorest lack is doctrine in the theological sense to govern

Grounding governance in ontology 31

the flow of cooperative energies in a free commonwealth" (503). Rectifying this lack is a project that political scientist Dwight Waldo (1984) began in his 1948 critique of the administrative state: "Any political theory rests upon a metaphysic, a concept of the ultimate nature of reality" (21). In his analysis, Waldo argues that in moving from governance based on the assumed legitimacy of elected representatives—the political state—to a form of governance based on the assumed legitimacy of expert administrators—the administrative state—modern governance is shifting its metaphysic, or in our terms, its ontological position.

Following suit, a growing number of public administration theorists are taking up the question of ontology in particular as the most fundamental basis for claims about all aspects of governance (see for example, Catlaw 2007a, Catlaw and Jordan 2009, Evans 2000a, Evans and Wamsley 1999, Farmer 2002b, Howe 2006, Hummel 2002, King and Kensen 2002, King and Zanetti 2005, McSwite 2006, Mingus 2000, Murray 2000, Stivers 2002a, 2002b, Stout 2007, 2010a, 2010e, Stout and Salm 2011, Wamsley 1996). Some of these scholars are in search of ontological grounding to justify the field of public administration as it stands, suggesting that competing claims among theories (e.g., public management versus public administration) are ontological struggles to prove administration's "legitimate role in the governance process" (Evans and Wamsley 1999, 123). Other scholars are simply seeking to understand the ontological grounding of competing claims so that better governance choices might be made (Catlaw 2005).

An example of such exploration is Stout's (2013) ideal-type model of public administration traditions, linking a variety of administrative practices with ontological and psychosocial assumptions. Similarly, Kooiman (2001, 2003) develops a philosophical framework for three ideal-typical governance modes: hierarchy, market, and interactive (network). Each governance type is comprised of different ontological, epistemological, and behavioral assumptions. Once governance theories are "unpacked" (Crowley 1997) in this way, the philosophical commitments and associated values can be assessed considering their implications for social outcomes. In short, what we believe about reality guides what we do, and sometimes we don't like the results. So, we critique those assumptions using a variety of theoretical lenses (e.g., critical social theory, postmodern philosophy, feminist theory, cultural studies, etc.) in order to recommend change. This overarching purpose follows the logic that what we believe is what we do; if we want to change what we do, we need to change what we believe— even if it means deeply held beliefs about the very nature of reality and the self. Fortunately, these beliefs are not immutable. As noted in the *Manifesto of the Communist Party*, changes in our condition can prompt a new consciousness that will enable change: "Does it require deep intuition to comprehend that man's ideas, views, and conception, in one word, man's consciousness, changes with every change in the conditions of his material existence, in his social relations and in his social life?" (Marx and Engels 1998, chapter 2).

In sum, a growing number of governance scholars agree that specific administrative structures are embedded within particular political socioeconomic

32 *Barriers to global governance*

systems and must be changed at that level of analysis (Kirlin 1996, Ostrom 1997). "If the result desired is an inclusive, democratic polity, then these organizations ought to be grounded in theories, assumptions, and understandings of reality that advance knowledge of, and give direction toward, attaining such a polity" (Kelly 1998, 201). Therefore, identifying the underlying assumptions of political ontology is critical not only to understand and evaluate legitimacy claims in governance, but to establish normative goals for practice. The question is, *which type of ontology would best help us flourish together?*

A conference panel at the 1999 American Political Science Association and a follow up journal symposium in *Administration & Society* launched an important dialogue on this question, focusing primarily on Heidegger (Farmer 2002b). Without explicating an alternative ontology in detail, these essays made problematic the prevailing individualist ontology that imagines being-in-the-world as fundamentally separate from everything and everyone else (Hummel 2002), as well as problematizing representation of either a political or expert nature (Stivers 2002b). *If we are worlds unto ourselves, then how can anyone represent another? If we are independent or isolated individuals who must create social space before any type of political relation is possible,* how *do we do so?* In other words, "Which view of reality helps us to find meaning in public life?" (Stivers 2008, 93).

While the preliminary dialogue on ontology in public administration is encouraging, it by no means fully elucidates answers to the implications of its prefigurative role in governance. Nor have subsequent articles and books by these and other public administration scholars exhausted the topic. For example, in the pursuit of a more participatory approach, there is some discussion about the assumed ontological condition of the subject in Lacanian psychoanalysis (Catlaw 2007a, Catlaw and Jordan 2009, McSwite 2006), a call for a *politics of the subject* (Catlaw 2007a), a proposal for *enchanted materialism* in public ethics (Howe 2006), adoption of "Heidegger's ontology [of] Being-with" (Stivers 2008, 92), and a description of what has been broadly labeled "relational ontology" as opposed to the predominant "individualist ontology" (Stout and Salm 2011, 216) based on the work of Mary Follett and Alberto Guerreiro Ramos.

We agree that "the challenge that commands attention for public administration is to begin conceiving the social relations and subsequently governing structures and practices that are rooted in a different political ontology" (Catlaw 2005, 471). We must identify the ontology that would help us "*practice* critical theory" (King and Zanetti 2005, xviii). However, the question remains; *what* exactly *is the ontology that fits the emancipatory, participatory, approach to governance that is being pursued?*

Building on preceding work by our colleagues, this book seeks to provide a more robust answer. We respectfully suggest that the alternatives proposed to date are lacking in two fundamental ways. First, not all describe an ontological position that fully fits the radically democratic approach to practice being sought. Neither the ontological condition of lack in the post-analytic Lacanian subject nor the aesthetic mutual appreciation of enchanted materialism and its

Grounding governance in ontology 33

ontological abundance addresses the concept of innate relatedness in an open-ended process. While Heidegger's understanding of *being-with* addresses relatedness, it does not provide an ontological understanding of the dynamic process of *becoming* (Shaviro 2009) assumed in participatory practice. Nor does Heidegger reach beyond the non-Cartesian phenomenology of *social* reality to explain a non-Newtonian physical universe.

It is this last issue that points to the second deficiency: positivist ontology provides an explanation for *all* aspects of reality, not just the human elements. Limiting discussion to largely psychosocial or epistemological explanations of the human experience of reality as opposed to an explication of its ontological necessity leaves the rationale open to considerable challenge. To simply say "we have to start at bedrock and *assume* that we are all already connected, just as we have assumed in the past that we were not" (Stivers 2008, 93–94) is insufficient explanation. The received supposition of disconnection is undergirded by a fully explicated system of positive science in both its physical and social branches; it is defended by "the verdict of science" (Waldo 1984, 21). To blithely replace that assumption with another without a similarly complete explanation lacks the rigor required to do so convincingly. We must explain not just our understanding of human or social reality but also how we understand its physical and non-physical attributes. In other words, to withstand positivist critique, ontological explanation and grounding is required.

We agree with Catlaw (2007a) that Waldo's (1984) project of establishing the metaphysic of public administration remains unfinished and that the field's recent focus on postpositivist and skeptical postmodern epistemologies have deflected attention from this inquiry. While Catlaw (2007a) does a terrific job of linking representation and liberal democracy with positivism, this same task remains for linking participatory democracy to an alternative more fitting than epistemological post-positivism. To explicate fully and defend a radical form of participatory—as opposed to representative—democracy, we must go beyond epistemology to the underlying ontology. We must show why such a political form is logically sensible based on the nature of *all* aspects of reality.

Ontological confrontation and colonization

Assuming the relationship between ontology and governance, in the global context there remains the problem of *choice*. The notion that multiple ontologies exist and compete with one another has been suggested elsewhere, as well as the usefulness of clearly identifying their fundamental differences (see for example, Brigg 2007, Tønder and Thomassen 2005b). A call has been made in both political theory and public administration theory to more fully understand alternatives to the principal Western ontology—one that has been called "a political ontology of representation" (Catlaw 2007b). This is a quite difficult task, as most Western ontologies are variations on one of two themes—the One and the Many—both of which support the notion of representation, which tends toward domination, as described above. Many contemporary understandings of political

34 *Barriers to global governance*

ontology agree that both ontological and psychosocial difference defies legitimate representation (Widder 2005). Therefore, this book offers a critical analysis that will provide a basis from which to identify an ontology that resists becoming hegemonic.

On the point of hegemony, with multiple ontologies at play in the global context, *what happens when those with incommensurable characteristics confront one another?* Following Follett (2003a, 2013b), we argue that either domination or unsatisfying compromise result. In either case, those who lose experience *ontological colonization* (Stout 2010e). Indeed, Griffin (2007) argues that, historically, the winning worldviews are those that perpetuate the social–political–economic status quo, while the losers are the worldviews that threaten those interests.

Ontological colonization is reflected in the lived experience of deep "cognitive dissonance ... from competing metaphysical systems" (Verney 2004, 139). Attempts to conciliate competing notions of being and relating can cause psychological distress and even existential crisis. Many people struggle with pursuing "democracy in the polis, alternating meritocracy and autocracy in the workplace, and some odd combination or complementarity of the three in our neighborhoods and homes" (Stout 2010e, 601). On the surface, this may seem to be the practical necessity of balancing public and private action; however, the struggle is much deeper. Attempts to split the world into spheres of the *public* (i.e., government) and *private* (i.e., market) and *civic* (i.e., community) are generated by competing ontological assumptions that drive calls for reform and revolution to emphasize one sphere over the others. These further create conflicting understandings of the social relationship that fracture the self through the "paradox of the i/Individual" (Love 2008, 2010a, 2012)—we can neither be independent individuals nor simply express our functional roles in groups.

This is by no means a unique experience. Alternative ontologies subsist within what is assumed to be Western culture based on geography (e.g., the global North) as well as (post)colonial contexts elsewhere. This includes a broad spectrum of peoples found globally—indigenous peoples, Eastern mystics, pagans, feminists, LGBTQIA folk, deep ecologists, process philosophers, quantum physicists, and the list goes on to include all those who refuse to accept Newtonian/Cartesian reality as a natural given. These views may be marginalized by the dominant culture, but refusal and resistance of both philosophical assumptions and governance practices are an increasing trend, as evidenced in a broad range of philosophical and cultural studies (see for example, Amoah 2010, Beeman and Blenkinsop 2008, Brigg 2007, Christ 2003, Deleuze and Guattari 1987, Howe 2006, Keating 2013, Marcuse 1964, 1969, Pesch 2008, Smith 1999, Stewart-Harawira 2005, Waters 2004a).

For example, in its project to deconstruct supposedly gender-neutral concepts feminist theory seeks "a comprehensive overhaul" (Zanetti 2004, 141) of mainstream Western philosophy and its "Eurocentric masculine conventions" (Pulitano 2003, 30). Similarly, indigenous peoples around the world reject the "Eurocentric metaphysics, epistemology, and worldview" (Waters 2004b, 105).

Grounding governance in ontology 35

Indigenous scholars describe an ongoing state of cognitive dissonance in which they must live in two worlds at once, managing a dualism that is founded on competing understandings of reality itself (Amoah 2012, Brigg 2007, Smith 1999, Stewart-Harawira 2005, Waters 2004a). In short, they find individualist ontological arguments foreign to their inner sense of what *is*.

From such perspectives Western/global North worldviews have become *ontologically hegemonic* (see for example, Amoah 2010, Beeman and Blenkinsop 2008, Brigg 2007, Christ 2003, Stewart-Harawira 2005, Howe 2010, Waters 2004a). This means two things—first, there are multiple ways to understand existence and the dominant worldview is only one of many. At core, this is a problem of otherness or alterity; if we conceive of fellow human beings as "others" or "them" rather than "us," the potential for domination is perpetuated (Farmer 1995). When alternative worldviews cannot be ignored, the reaction by the dominant worldview is one of assumed superiority. "When confronted by alternative conceptions of other societies, Western reality becomes reified as representing something 'better,' reflecting 'higher orders' of thinking, and being less prone to the dogma, witchcraft and immediacy of people and societies which were so 'primitive'" (Smith 1999, 48).

Second, this assumed superiority leads to the dominant worldview marginalizing others:

> We think that in conjunction with its political and military branches, Modwestcult [modern Western culture] is engaging in a much less obvious form of colonization—that is over the territory of what kind of being is permitted to be recognized as human.
>
> (Beeman and Blenkinsop 2008, 97)

While science and modern liberalism may have freed us from the domination of more theistic ontologies, they have created a different oppression based on psychosocial assumptions about atomistic individualism. This has led to ever-increasing homogenization in spite of superficial attention to diversity based on things like race or aesthetic cultural preferences (Keating 2013). But there is more to difference than mere cultural adaptation or nuance on this pluralist theme: there are differences in our very understanding of human *being*.

Therefore, postcolonial critique cannot simply consider the manner in which "new forms of economic, political, and military colonialism are reshaping both colonizing and colonized societies" (Kinchloe 2006, 181). We must delve deeper, assessing the manner in which ontological assumptions impact the ways we operate in a globalizing society. In so doing, we can move beyond unwitting ontological domination and perhaps even discover the potential of other ontologies as better foundations for governance.

Together, critical theories of gender and race as well as indigenous systems of thought are some of the richest sources of current discussion on the relationship between ontology and power in its social, economic, and political aspects. Feminists of color and indigenous peoples "have a much more radical understanding

36   *Barriers to global governance*

of the limitations of elite white male traditions of thought" (Christ 2003, 159). However, these theorists are joined by a host of process philosophers (see for example, Cobb Jr. 2002, Faber *et al.* 2010, Griffin 2007, Keller 2003), post-anarchists (see for example, Rousselle and Evren 2011), post-humanists (see for example, Braidotti 2013), new materialists (see for example, Coole and Frost 2010), quantum physicists (Bohm 1980, 1985, Capra 1983, 1999), contemporary biologists (see for example, Margulis *et al.* 2011, Maturana and Varela 1987), and deep ecologists (see for example, Bell 2006).

Considering such critiques most broadly, White (2000) makes an argument that "weak" ontologies are better suited to pluralist contexts than "strong" ontologies because they are either open to contestation and plurality or they embrace change and the fluidity of existence, which enables adaptation. Such malleable assumptions have also been called "*unstable ontologies*" (Marchart 2005, 26). Contrarily, strong ontologies are fixed and rigid in character, claiming to represent permanent Truth or natural law. As such, they are hegemonic and colonizing in nature when confronting alternatives.

Therefore, we must continue ontological exploration in terms of critique and refusal, but also in affirmation of alternatives that will not be colonizing. In short, a synthesis that accommodates the One and the Many while maintaining a dynamic, mutable understanding of existence is what is required to meet the tests of a weak ontology. Such an ontology may reintroduce "wonder and modesty" (Howe 2006, 423) to governance practices, thereby eliminating ontological hegemony. However, weak does not connote thin. Weak ontologies can provide a robust and detailed explication, and yet remain fluid in character as amendable normative affirmations.

The argument in review

Ontology shapes our understandings of the world and the language we use to frame our very thoughts. Therefore, language serves as a constant reaffirmation of our worldview. Because there are multiple and substantially differing ontological perspectives, we cannot assume that any one is inherently right and must assume that the assertion of one will be met with contestation from others (Brigg 2007). Because of this competition and the fact that ontology prefigures our understanding of ourselves and others, the study of ontology has recently been extended by social and political theory (White 2000).

A growing number of scholars in a variety of disciplines argue that ontology prefigures which particular social and political forms are deemed appropriate or even possible. Political philosophy is based on beliefs about how to achieve the Good, assuming the ontological nature of human being. Governance practices are grounded in political philosophy. For these reasons, governance theory cannot overlook or merely assume the ontological underpinnings of the political philosophy from which it cannot be severed. Taken together political ontology guides our answers to questions such as: *How should we relate to others? How should we relate to nature? What is right and good and how do we pursue these ends?* Because the answers are in large part instantiated in the practices of governance, Howe (2006) urges the field of public administration to grapple with these ontological presuppositions to public discourse and action—attending to the myriad theoretical and practical implications.

If we do not do this philosophical work and merely try to change practices to achieve different results, the attempts are likely to fail. We cannot put a bandage of technique on a symptom of poor philosophical grounding and achieve better results—we must adapt our assumptions to fit the needs of the context, allowing practice to follow logical suit. It is to this project that we turn. Herein we will identify the reasons why principal approaches to governance and their hybrids do not fit the contemporary global condition and perpetuate hegemonic colonization. We will then propose an alternative ontology that could meet the unstable and weak characteristics thought to be most promising for a non-hegemonic approach to governance.

4 Crafting and using a Governance Typology

In this inquiry we employ dialectical analysis of concepts from various literatures to construct a typology of four ideal-type approaches to governance, illustrate key concepts of each approach using concrete examples, and complete mental experiments of critique on each approach and hybrids among them. We then propose the basis for a fifth ideal-type that is constructed through a dialectical synthesis of the original four approaches to governance.

The value of typologies

Typologies are particularly useful because they enable a combination of description, critique, and affirmation (Stout 2010d). Once developed, typologies are used in empirical analysis that compares evidence against the ideal-types in order to draw critical or affirmational conclusions. It is important to note that ideal-types are intentionally caricatured simplifications of the complexity of actual experience or particular perspectives. They are designed to accentuate the characteristics of a concept in order to focus attention on a specific aspect of the phenomenon in question. In this way conceptual logic can be used as a measure of actual phenomena to determine what they are most like and what logical implications can be inferred from that similarity.

This particular typology is meant to describe varying approaches to governance. Assuming that ontology shapes language, language shapes thought, and thought prefigures virtually everything that follows—including how we choose to govern action in the human and nonhuman world—we need a way to break down the social phenomenon of governance into conceptual elements. To reiterate, by *governance* we mean all of the practices—from formal rules and institutions down to unstructured everyday interactions—used to organize collective action in any societal context. Because the political and administrative reflect different aspects of governance, both must be included in a typology and examined separately.

Ideally, theoretical frameworks should: direct attention to critical features that have general consistency with lived experience, provide a foundation for inquiry, specify classes of variables and how they fit together in a coherent structure, and specify who or what motivates action (Schlager 1999). Many scholars

Crafting and using a Governance Typology 39

offer similar criteria for frameworks, theories, and models (see for example, Dye 2002, Easton 1966, Lazarsfeld and Barton 1951). Using these ideas as evaluative criteria, theoretical frameworks should have: a significant focus, organizing capacity, and coherency. Such a framework will help us understand why particular governance choices are made at different times and in different places.

Significant focus

In constructing frameworks, scholars must decide which attributes of a topic are relevant and important. In fact, the criterion of relevance is often deemed more important than rigorous data collection and analysis—what has been referred to as "hyperfactualism" (Easton 1966, 3). It can easily be argued that governance is a topic of significant focus, as it impacts virtually all aspects of social, economic, and environmental life. It enjoys discussion in numerous disciplines and fields of practice, including political science, public administration, public policy, law, sociology, economics, business, and others.

Organizing capacity

Theoretical frameworks can be useful in trying to grasp the big picture in the transdisciplinary study of governance. Theories differ in what they seek to explain as well as in what they consider and can be classified according to characteristics such as their scope, their function, or their level of analysis. Regardless of the organizing strategy chosen, the classification "needs to be assessed according to the purposes for which it is used" (Easton 1966, 12). Ideally, the framework will establish a comparative basis from which various theories can be clearly differentiated, but that also identifies a common denominator from which to evaluate.

Devising an organizing dimension can be tricky:

> If the classification is kept very simple, with only a few broad groupings, it will combine many elements which are not very similar. Important distinctions of a more detailed sort will be lost completely. On the other hand, if the classification preserves all distinctions which may be of any significance, it will contain too many groups to be surveyed and handled conveniently.
>
> (Lazarsfeld and Barton 1951, 157)

This causes the typologies to be rich in description, but thin in analytic usefulness. The organizing logic should create exhaustive and mutually exclusive categories if possible.

Coherency

Coherency refers to the degree to which the variables or meanings attributed to them tie together in a logical manner. For example, a framework that coherently

40   *Barriers to global governance*

links normative principles, values, policies, and action would not have logical contradictions among ideas (Fischer 1995). Instead, coherent sets describe the issue at hand in the most comprehensive manner (Dryzek 1990). This approach enables the identification of disconnects between values and actions that may hinder the success of a given approach. It also accommodates the problem of incommensurable principles (Paris and Reynolds 1983).

Summary

Given the value of theoretical frameworks to sense making and knowledge building, we construct a framework that endeavors to meet the criteria of significant focus, organizing capacity, and coherency. Governance is a social phenomenon that includes both actors and institutions. Given this combination of individual and societal levels of analysis, it makes sense to use sociologist Max Weber's (1949b, 1994a) ideal-type method in its construction. With a Governance Typology in hand, we can use the characteristics of the ideal-types to uncover the ontological assumptions at play in governance theories and case studies.

Constructing an ideal-type framework

Well-crafted ideal-types consist of two components: generic elements and genetic meanings (Stout 2010d). *Generic elements* compose the ideal-type framework. They are of value to theoretical inquiry as the concepts necessary to understand a given phenomenon and why it happens the way it does. They are also culturally significant characteristics with importance to social actors. *Genetic meanings* refer to the particular definitions of the generic elements that create logical coherence within an ideal-type. The *genetic* meanings of the *generic* elements compose each ideal-type within the framework. The Governance Typology presented herein can be used to examine both theories and practices to identify their underlying ontological assumptions and then either critique or affirm those assumptions based on empirical or theoretical bases.

Following the ideal-type method, first, a specific social phenomenon of interest must be identified. Second, a culturally significant organizing characteristic must be chosen and specified as the frame of reference. Third, the generic elements essential for identifying causal relationships must be identified. The set should be culturally significant, as comprehensive as possible, and the manner in which these elements are thought to be related must be explicated in a logical manner. Fourth, mutually exclusive meanings of each element must be interpreted so that the genetic character of the ideal-type is clear. These meanings must also be logical and coherent in their relationships with one another and plausible in comparison to experience. The following sections will explain how these steps were executed.

Crafting and using a Governance Typology 41

Identify a social phenomenon of interest

In this inquiry, the social phenomenon of interest is *governance*, which includes both actors and institutions in its definition. It is also the subject of considerable scholarship and is therefore deemed of sufficient import to warrant study. However, the phenomenon is not studied empirically, but rather through cultural evidence found in texts. *Texts* can come in the form of written texts, social practices, social institutions, or "other arrangements or activities" (Farmer 1995, 21). In this case, philosophical and theoretical written texts are the object of interpretation. Texts were used as formative data for the ideal-types because language generates "ideas, approaches, intuitions, assumptions, and urges that make up our world view; it shapes us" (Farmer 1995, 1).

Choose a culturally significant frame of reference

Once a social phenomenon of interest is formed, the ideal-type method calls for choosing a culturally significant frame of reference—in other words, a lens with which to look at the phenomenon that matters to the members of the culture. The frame of reference herein is *ontology*, which means that as texts were read, statements or meanings that imply ontological characteristics were noted and categorized. Given the discussion in Chapter 3, scholarly arguments that political theory and administrative theory are grounded in ontology make it a culturally significant frame of reference to governance.

Identify essential generic elements

The next step in building an ideal-type framework is to identify all the essential concepts that are important to the phenomenon under study. To inform causal hypotheses, the set of generic elements should be culturally significant, and as comprehensive as possible, and the manner in which these elements are thought to be related must be explicated in a logical manner. Process philosopher Alfred North Whitehead (1966) describes this quality as "importance" and notes that generic concepts are those that will reveal the features that are important for each situation. Because governance is grounded in ontology, this is the logical place to start. However, governance includes a vast array of concepts that require consideration of all manner of philosophical and theoretical ideas. Acknowledging that this is a system of our own making (see McCutcheon 2005), the conceptual elements we feel are necessary for a robust understanding of governance are: ontological assumptions and associated language, psychosocial theory, epistemological concepts, belief systems, ethical concepts, political theory, economic theory, and administrative theory. The first four elements provide a philosophical foundation while the latter four elements explore the implications of those philosophies in practice. It is our supposition that ontology encodes each of these conceptual elements with a particular character—a sort of governance DNA.

42   Barriers to global governance

Together, these elements are comprehensive enough to formulate a well-rounded framework of governance theory to be used in empirical research. Each element was deemed necessary to achieve a sufficient understanding of the social actions of governance actors and the social structures of governance, as well as various causal relationships. The assumptions of each element rest on one another in a building-block fashion that formulates a coherent set.

Interpret genetic meanings

Mutually exclusive meanings of each essential element must be interpreted so that the genetic character of the ideal-type is clear. These meanings must also be logical and coherent in their relationships with one another and plausible in comparison to experience. To identify key differences among statements made about the various elements, categorization uses *logico-meaningful* interpretation, whereby the central meaning or mental biases of a given cultural perspective are identified and used to craft a consistent and integrated set from logically related concepts (Sorokin 1957). This process utilizes both interpretive and critical reasoning in order to make category assignments (White 1999) to genetic types (Weber 1949b).

To make this critical assessment, we employ a dialectical analysis of various literatures, seeking concepts that are logically in oppositional tension with one another. Furthermore, we compare each concept to the foundational ontological positions to determine which one it most resembles. Based on the ontological frame of reference explained in Chapter 3, the characteristics of existence are: state (static versus dynamic), source (transcendent versus immanent), and expression (singular versus plural). To construct a two-by-two matrix for four differing ontological positions, state is on one axis, while source and expression are on the other, as shown in Table 4.1. Texts are interpreted and categorized as to which of these assumptions appear to be most logically coherent with propositions and claims. Those that do not fit into any category are considered either as possible hybrids or a true synthesis of the four ideal-types.

Employing dialectical analysis

While dialectical analysis will be further explained in Chapters 9 and 12, the notion of dialectic has been present in Western thought since the time of Socrates, and is noted in Plato's *Republic* and explained in Aristotle's *Topics*. Dialectic

Table 4.1 Ontological dialectics

	Transcendent source, singular expression	Immanent source, plural expression
Static state	Ideal-type 1	Ideal-type 2
Dynamic state	Ideal-type 3	Ideal-type 4

Crafting and using a Governance Typology 43

has been a method used by leading philosophers, scholars, and scientists, including Hegel, Engels, Marx, Horkheimer, Adorno, Marcuse, Gadamer, Lacan, Popper, and Gouldner. Stemming from Hegel's interpretation of both Aristotle and the Chinese Taoist *yin/yang* symbol (which will be discussed herein), dialectical logic has three moments: thesis, antithesis, and synthesis (Adorno 1973, Popper 1940). As explained by process philosopher Zhihe Wang (2012), Hegel understood dialectic to be the fundamental principal of life that generates a unity or synthesis of opposites; one position cannot exist without the other. Furthermore, one cannot be understood without the other, so meaning can only be understood in the context of the whole and the relationship with the other is what makes it concrete, as opposed to pure abstraction. As typically interpreted in the West, dialectical concepts (thesis and antithesis) exist in essential conflict, rather than complementarity.

As a form of critical logic, dialectic is a manner of thinking or thought process in which contrasting perspectives are used to reveal important insights that would not be apprehended otherwise (Padgett 2002). Understanding the relationship between the two opposing positions can lead to an awareness of the whole that the two positions are actually creating. Aristotle developed the concept of dialectic in the *Topics*, taking it beyond Socratic dialogue for the purpose of instruction to a form of intellectual inquiry or philosophical science (Shields 2013). Dialectic is used to cross-examine competing *endoxa*, or widely believed principles, in order to test their staying power. Furthermore, this process can lead to the discovery of first principles, which for Aristotle are the ultimate truth.

Today, dialectic is used as a method of interpreting social phenomena, particularly those associated with change: (1) an explanation of the problem of unintended consequences as stemming from paradox or ironic reversals in the course of events; (2) a way to understand goal shifts and displacements; (3) a method of revealing how an existing structure prevents transformation to a more effective one, or how its success paradoxically brings about its downfall; and (4) a lens that reveals development or progress through conflict, oppositeness, paradox, contradiction, and dilemma (Schneider 1971). These approaches to interpretation are equally valuable to this inquiry and are considered in an analysis of the four primary ideal-types as well as attempts to hybridize or conciliate them (Part III) and how we might synthesize them (Part IV).

The resulting Governance Typology

The ideal-type framework presented herein builds on previous four-type frameworks explicated in dissertations, conference papers, and publications as noted in the Preface. However, by revising and combining the preceding frameworks we have filled critical gaps in both. In examining the two original typologies in light of one another, it became clear that each typology was missing one type in an effort to identify an alternative. Through this realization and subsequent analysis, the dialectical pairings in each element became clear. The preferred ideal-type actually represents a synthesis of all potential pairs, both vertically and

44   Barriers to global governance

horizontally. It is a *fifth* ideal-type: a synthesizing alternative to the two-by-two matrix rather than a position within it. With these revisions, the typology is more robust and logically coherent.

The generic elements we consider necessary to formulate a comprehensive typology of governance are: ontological assumptions and associated language, psychosocial theory, epistemological concepts, belief systems, ethical concepts, political theory, economic theory, and administrative theory. *Ontological assumptions* reflect our understanding of the source of existence that informs our worldview or cosmology. Language reflects our understanding of ontology and is discussed within this element of the framework. *Psychosocial theory* refers to our understanding of self and other human beings and the manner in which we relate. *Epistemological concepts* describe how we know about existence. *Belief systems* are traditions of faith and scientific "truths" that explain ontology, psychosocial condition, and epistemology. *Ethical concepts* describe values that guide action, drawing from the preceding philosophical commitments. *Political theory* describes how we structure social institutions. *Economic theory* describes how we structure distribution of material and human resources. *Administrative theory* describes how we administer and manage political and economic systems.

The first four elements of the ideal-type framework (ontological assumptions and associated language, psychosocial theory, epistemological concepts, and belief systems) form the driving philosophical commitments behind governance. The latter four elements (ethical concepts, political theory, economic theory, and administrative theory) frame governance forms and practices that are often referred to as *political economy*. By considering these generic elements as coherent sets, the typology serves exploration of the relationships between various approaches to governance and the philosophical commitments that inform or even prefigure them (Hendriks 2010, White 2000). In exploring the genetic meanings of the generic elements, we identify a series of conceptual binaries that generate two-by-two matrices of four coherent ideal-type positions, as explained in the following subsections. The genetic characteristics of each ideal-type is discussed in Part II.

Ontological assumptions and associated language

To reiterate from Chapter 3, political ontology has been used to describe complex assumptions about the nature of human being, identity, and social life and the reflexive relationship between ontology and the political (Catlaw 2007a). Because political ontology is taken as a given in most of the public administration literature, one must look to a variety of other sources to identify and describe the assumptions in use, including philosophy, psychology, sociology, and theology. This brings us back to ontology proper: the most general branch of metaphysics concerned with the nature of being, which generally stems from philosophy, religion, or physics.

On the ontological level of analysis shown in Table 4.2, the vertical axis shows the dialectic of *states of existence*, either static or dynamic, while the horizontal axis consists of two dialectical pairs: transcendent or immanent *source*

Crafting and using a Governance Typology 45

Table 4.2 Ontological assumptions

	Transcendent source, singular expression	*Immanent source, plural expression*
Static state	Hierarchical	Atomistic
Dynamic state	Holographic	Fragmented

of existence and singular or plural *expression of existence*. The labels used in the ontological assumptions and associated language name the political ontologies of the ideal-types. Based on their characteristics, we derive metaphors we believe express the underlying logic of each type, all of which is explained in Part II.

In regard to state of existence, *static state* means that existence simply *is* (*being*), while *dynamic state* means that existence is continually *becoming. Transcendent* means that the source of existence is beyond that which exists, while *immanent* means the source of existence is within that which is actual. In regard to expression of existence, *singular* means that the source of existence is complete (One)—it cannot be broken apart in some way, while *plural* means that there are many sources of existence (Many). Discussion of these opposing characteristics traces back to Parmenides and Heraclitus, as discussed in Chapter 3.

These ontological assumptions engender differences in language, which in turn reinforces them through the shaping of consciousness, identity, knowledge, and beliefs (Derrida 1976, Gadamer 2004, Heidegger 1996, Lakoff 2003, Saussure 1960). As shown in Table 4.3, the primary difference found in language families lies on the vertical static–dynamic axis that produces a noun-based, subject–object orientation versus a verb-based, subject–subject orientation. On the horizontal singular–plural axis language differences are more nuanced within static versus dynamic families. Holistic language tends to emphasize the group and is accentuated in the Holographic position in a firm We, as opposed to I-within-the-group. Binary language tends to emphasize the individual and is accentuated in the Fragmented position as a subject resisting social construction.

Psychosocial theory

These varying understandings of the nature of existence and being have similarly different implications for human being and social life. Here, we discuss psychosocial theories associated with ontological suppositions by indicating the type of

Table 4.3 Language characteristics

	Holistic	*Binary*
Noun orientation	Discrete, hierarchical	Discrete, nonhierarchical
Verb orientation	Gerundial, holistic	Gerundial, discrete

46   *Barriers to global governance*

subjectivity assumed. As shown in Table 4.4, the psychosocial character of individuality is made up of two dialectical pairs: *identity* is either unitary or decentered within a *social condition* that is either embedded or independent. These characteristics prefigure the type of relationship anticipated among individuals.

A *unitary* identity is contained within itself in a cohesive fashion (Descartes 1980), whether the subject is considered as part of a plurality of subjects or an abstract single whole. From an ontological perspective of being (Whitehead 1979) the individual simply *is*. Unitary identity also endures through time and experience (Hales and Johnson 2003). Although the physical body may change over time (Mesle 2008), identity is a static, coherent narrative on a linear teleological path. A *decentered* identity is fluid and responsive to changes either internal or external to the subject (Harper 1994); the individual is always *becoming* and is a qualitatively different being at different times and in different contexts (Whitehead 1979).

An *embedded* social condition means that pre-existing social institutions define identity and human relations through designated roles, with the difference being the stability of the social institutions framing identity. An *independent* condition means that individuals are understood either as pre-social beings with no *a priori* social bond (independent from others) or as post-social beings where identity resists the effects of the social context, but may not be able to access an authentic self.

Following Love (2010a, 2012), lowercase individuality indicates a socially situated identity, while capitalized Individuality indicates an identity ostensibly free of such external influence. The use of capitalization as a distinction has been used in a variety of contexts. This application is largely influenced by the "big–little" distinction as applied to t/Truth in pragmatism (James 1907), the o/Other in psychoanalysis (Lacan 1977), and p/Politics and the p/People in representational democracy (Catlaw 2007a). In each case, the capitalization (big-T, big-O, big-P, big-I) represents a myth or fabrication—something that "never existed in the first place" (Žižek 1997, section 2, paragraph 1). When the subject is recognized as embedded within a social framework (Hierarchical and Holographic), this is indicated through the use of the lowercase "i" in *individuality*. When the subject is seen as isolated from societal influences (Atomistic) or stripped of social identity altogether (Fragmented), this is indicated through the upper-case "I" in *Individuality*. Following ontological discussions of particularity and singularity, we augment these labels for the dynamic ideal-types (Holographic and Fragmented).

We should point out that these psychosocial characteristics are very similar to the cultural and ideological grid/group system developed by anthropologist

Table 4.4 Psychosocial theory

	Embedded condition	*Independent condition*
Unitary identity	individuality	Individuality
Decentered identity	Particular individuality	Singular Individuality

Crafting and using a Governance Typology   47

Mary Douglas (1996). In her model, "grid" refers to the manner in which agency is fostered or controlled while "group" refers to the relationship between the group and the individual that forms identity. "High grid" means there are rigid rules that structure behavior. "High group" means there are strong allegiances and sense of shared identity. Low levels of each refer to the lack thereof. These characteristics combine forming differing cultural biases or ideologies, which she labels Individualism, Fatalistic, Hierarchy, and Egalitarian Enclave. In Part II, we make note of the differences and similarities between our typologies.

Epistemological concepts

The combined meanings of the first two elements, the assumptions about existence and human existence in particular, prefigure how we come to know the world. *Epistemological concepts* describe how knowledge is structured and how truths are justified. Epistemologies have been a principal focus in public administration and governance scholarship because as leading social theorists such as Michel Foucault and Bent Flyvbjerg argue, "power defines what constitutes knowledge and rationality; indeed, power ultimately defines 'what counts as reality'" (Brooks 2002, 91). Distinctive patterns of decision making may be based on "embedded assumptions and social constructions of reality" (Schneider and Ingram 1997, x). As shown in Table 4.5 epistemological concepts fall along a *structuration* axis, where knowledge is based on either foundations or coherence, and a *justification* axis of how truth is validated through either internal or external means.

Knowledge grounded in *foundations* assumes that there are static truths upon which all knowledge is built. Alternatively, if existence is in a dynamic state foundational truths are not possible. We can only know through what we accept as truth or through temporary "snapshots" that are artificially fixed. Therefore, we seek *coherence* among ideas. Internal justification means that truth is validated through intellectual logic or *a priori* assumptions. External justification requires validation *a posteriori* through reliable experiential evidence or social agreement.

Belief systems

For the purpose of this model, belief systems codify our ontological, psycho-social, and epistemological assumptions. As Dilthey (1988) explains, a belief system is "a state of affairs bound up not only with mythical thought, but with

Table 4.5 Epistemological concepts

	Internal justification	External justification
Foundations structure	Rationalism	Empiricism
Coherence structure	Idealism	Epistemological anarchism

48 Barriers to global governance

metaphysics, and with self-reflection" (158). Belief systems gather together the sets of assumptions that frame a particular perspective or worldview. Like onto-logical prefiguring, "attending to one leads to a very different sense of reality and of one's place in it than attending to the other" (Cobb Jr. 2002, 53). Griffin argues that "different religions produce people with significantly different structures of experience" (Wang 2012, 149).

As shown in Table 4.6, beliefs reflect our ontological and psychosocial assumptions. Therefore, along the axes we find both static and dynamic *state* descriptions of metaphysical (transcendent) and natural (immanent) *sources of existence* commonly expressed as the One and the Many. This is the basis of the dichotomy of the divine and the earthly, the metaphysical and the physical, the sublime and the mundane. However, the assumption of static versus dynamic state generates further differentiation that will be discussed in each ideal-type.

Ethical concepts

Before embarking upon explication of the last four elements of the typology, it must be noted that because much of the social theory most influential in Western governance has been written by scholars in the United States and European nations, the meanings described are primarily from these sources. It would be fruitful to expand the typology with non-Western and pre-modern explanations of ethics, political theory, economic theory and administrative theory—particularly in the Holographic position. However, there are some fundamental differences in assumptions even within contemporary Western theory that can be reasonably aligned with the four basic ideal-types in this framework.

As previously noted, the set of concepts explained thus far form the rationales for varying ethical concepts. Ethics are systems of criteria used to measure the moral worth of a decision or action. This typology draws on Christian theologian H. Richard Niebuhr's (1963) typology of ethical stances, which seeks to understand the relative authority of both humankind and God.[1] In his framework, human nature is realized in three distinct ethical stances: man-the-citizen, who is answerable to the social order, man-the-maker, who determines the social order, and man-the-answerer, who is mutually obligated with others. Each type has a unique way of being in the world that can be related to other conceptual elements.

As shown in Table 4.7, the ethical dialectic on the vertical axis is between internal or external *sources of ethical guidance* (Darwall 1998). External sources are described as criteria while internal sources are described as motivation. One way to

Table 4.6 Belief systems

	Metaphysical One	*Natural Many*
Static state ontology	Monotheism	Naturalism
Dynamic state ontology	Pantheism	Anti-essentialism

Crafting and using a Governance Typology 49

Table 4.7 Ethical concepts

	Normative Right	*Normative Good*
External criteria	Deontological obligation	Consequentialism
Internal motivation	Moral imperative	Moral skepticism/relativism

think about this difference is the relationship between self and other. Lyons (1983) finds evidence that there are two distinct ways of describing the self in relation to others: connected or separate/objective. The former is related to relationships that generate internal motivations, while the latter is linked to judgments based on ethical concepts. On the horizontal axis, the dialectic of *normative structure* either prioritizes Right as a proper action or Good as an end value (Kagan 1998).

Political theory

Political, economic, and administrative theory are closely linked; however, each component will be explained separately for the purpose of conceptual clarity. Complex political forms have been predicated on the notion of representation because if nothing else, as Dahl (1998) points out, most social groups are too large to function without some kind of representation. Yet what is deemed proper or legitimate representation is a widely debated question, particularly in democratic societies.

Thayer (1981) posits that any form of governance creates the problem of who speaks for God, which we interpret here as the ontological source of existence to accommodate nontheistic beliefs. He argues that Western culture has tried two ways of answering that question: through hierarchy and through competition. In other words, representation can be decided either through dictate or through pluralism. The political theories shown in Table 4.8 are formulated on the horizontal axis primarily on the basis of whether they employ hierarchy or competition to establish the *structure of authority*. Added to this on the vertical axis is the *relative strength* of that structuration, moderate or strong. However, it must be noted that labeling the political philosophy associated with the ontological positions is difficult because differences that are important to some get lost. For example, those who hold to a classical republican philosophy may reject being grouped with classical conservative liberalism; we group them thus based on Clark (1998) and MacIntyre (1988).

Table 4.8 Political theory

	Hierarchical authority	*Competitive authority*
Moderate	Classical conservative liberalism	Modern liberalism
Strong	Socialism	Individualist anarchism

50 *Barriers to global governance*

Economic theory

As with political philosophy, the preceding assumptions have profound implications for economic institutions and systems orchestrating the use, exchange, and distribution of resources. As shown in Table 4.9, economic theories closely follow the political theories with which they are typically associated. The dialectical axes for the economic positions are type of *regulation*, either external or internal, and the *intensity* of that regulation, relatively weak or strong. External regulation refers to government intervention in economic activities while internal regulation refers to an economy free of government intervention.

Table 4.9 Economic theory

	External regulation	*Internal regulation*
Weak	Welfare state	Market exchange
Strong	Collectively planned economy	Self-sufficiency and barter

Administrative theory

Administrative theory includes a number of concepts in the public milieu, including: political authority and scope of administrative action, criterion of proper administrative behavior, administrative decision-making rationality, and organizing style (Stout 2013). Together, these concepts shape the administrative role and administrators' actions, along with the relationship with both politicians and citizens. As with the other elements of the typology, the specific meanings associated with these concepts build identifiable schools of thought that can be linked coherently with the philosophical ideas that prefigure them. Here, we attempt to identify central ideas around which schools of thought cluster, acknowledging that they are often by no means ideal-typical in nature, but rather hybrids that lend themselves more or less to the ideal-type positions.

As shown in Table 4.10, following political theory, administrative theory is classified predominantly along the horizontal axis of *organizing* via hierarchy versus competition (Thayer 1981) with differences on the vertical axis being the *relative strength of administrative authority* in relation to society, including both politicians and citizens.

Table 4.10 Administrative theory

	Hierarchical organization	*Competitive organization*
Weak authority	Orthodox Administration	New Public Service
Strong authority	New Public Administration	New Public Management

Four governance approaches emerge

The assumptions of each generic element inform one another to form a coherent, interlocking set. Ontological assumptions about the state, source, and expression of existence prefigure our language. These conceptualizations shape our understanding of self, others, and the world around us. These ideas, in turn, shape how we think and build knowledge of existence and our beliefs about the world, whether based on physical or metaphysical ideas. Together, these philosophical commitments shape ethics and systems of value, along with political, economic, and administrative theories. In sum, the first four elements of the framework (ontological assumptions and associated language, psychosocial theory, epistemological concepts, and belief systems) compose the driving philosophical commitments behind governance. The latter four elements (ethical concepts, political theory, economic theory, and administrative theory) frame governance forms and practices.

The diverse meanings of these elements are drawn from a variety of dialectical concepts whose pairs are linked coherently. A sketch of these meanings is provided in Table 4.11. Collectively, we describe the four primary ideal-typical positions as: (1) Hierarchical Governance, (2) Atomistic Governance, (3) Holographic Governance, and (4) Fragmented Governance. Each type is explained in

Table 4.11 Primary governance ideal-types

	Hierarchical Governance	*Atomistic Governance*
Ontological assumptions	Static state, transcendent source, singular expression	Static state, immanent source, plural expression
Language characteristics	Discrete, hierarchical	Discrete, nonhierarchical
Psychosocial theory	individuality	Individuality
Epistemological concepts	Rationalism	Empiricism
Belief systems	Monotheism	Naturalism
Ethical concepts	Deontological obligation	Consequentialism
Political theory	Classical conservative liberalism	Modern liberalism
Economic theory	Welfare state	Market exchange
Administrative theory	Orthodox Administration	New Public Service
	Holographic Governance	*Fragmented Governance*
Ontological assumptions	Dynamic state, transcendent source, singular expression	Dynamic state, immanent source, plural expression
Language characteristics	Gerundial, holistic	Gerundial, discrete
Psychosocial theory	Particular individuality	Singular Individuality
Epistemological concepts	Idealism	Epistemological anarchism
Belief systems	Pantheism	Anti-essentialism
Ethical concepts	Moral imperative	Moral skepticism/relativism
Political theory	Socialism	Individualist anarchism
Economic theory	Collectively planned economy	Self-sufficiency and barter
Administrative theory	New Public Administration	New Public Management

52 *Barriers to global governance*

its own chapter in Part II. The continuing methodology of dialectical synthesis and the possible ideal-type of Integrative Governance is explained in Part IV.

Note

1 His thinking has been applied to public administration theory in the past (see Harmon 1995).

Part II

Primary governance theories

Part II provides an explanation and discussion of the four primary governance ideal-types beginning with those associated with static state ontologies most familiar in modern Western societies, and then moving to those associated with the dynamic state ontologies that are less familiar. As each one is considered, it is important to remember that ideal-types are pure utopias, while lived phenomena are a heterogeneous expression of multiple ideal-types and their hybrids. But to even begin to sort out these possibilities, the competing ideations require full explication across associated theoretical dimensions. Only then can they be rigorously compared normatively or tested empirically. Each chapter presents an ideal-type using the same conceptual framework with mutually exclusive meanings to enable such analysis. Chapter 5 explains Hierarchical Governance; Chapter 6 explains Atomistic Governance; Chapter 7 explains Holographic Governance; and Chapter 8 explains Fragmented Governance.

We argue that such theoretical depth is necessary. As Dr. Martin Luther King, Jr. reportedly commented, "They aren't interested in the *why* of what we're doing, only in the *what* of what we're doing, and because they don't understand the why they cannot understand the what" (Fischer 1992, 325). Understanding *why* helps us determine *what* to do, even when the contextual situation differs. However, we acknowledge that for many, theory quickly becomes arduous when considered purely at an abstract level. Indeed, public administration as a whole has long believed that it is critical to link theory to practice (Bowman 1978). In short, these types of reflections "make sometimes difficult critical theoretical views communicable to students and practitioners" (Kensen 2008).

Philosophy needs illustration to bring abstract concepts into practical perspective. Ideas become more compelling when they are connected to experiences and phenomena to which we can relate or which we care about. We need to imagine ourselves in the situation and think about how we feel about it. Case studies are the mainstay of public administration research and pedagogy (see for example, Bailey 1992, Barzelay 1993, Eisenhardt 1995, Jensen and Rodgers 2001). Collections for use in graduate programs abound (see for example, Denhardt and Hammond 1992, Golembiewski *et al.* 1997, Lerner and Wanat 1998, Meyer and Brown 1989, Miller and Alkadry 1998) and some actually frame

54 Primary governance theories

introduction courses in their entirety (see for example, Garvey 1997, Lutrin and Settle 1992, Stillman 2005). A more recent approach seeks to use practice stories to inform theory (Elias 2010, Hummel 1991, King and Zanetti 2005, Stout 2010b).

Accordingly, each chapter uses illustration to help make sense of the conceptual elements and how they can play out in lived experience. First, we use the concept of "public encounters" developed by administrative scholar Koen Bartels (2013) to describe hypothetical dynamics the governance ideal-types are likely to generate (also see Stout and Love 2015a). This mental experiment reveals the dynamics likely in terms of how each approach: (1) handles conflict, (2) gathers input (facts and values), (3) comes to agreement on goals and methods, and (4) engenders expected behavior. As Bartels (2014) notes, this type of evaluation is needed in the practice of public administration, policy, and planning. We also use actual case studies of a common policy issue to illustrate. Given our attention to global crises and the immediacy of the environmental implications of global warming, we will use agricultural production to consider each primary approach to governance in action.

However, before turning to our explication of each governance approach, we must note that our interpretations of texts considered are made from our own particular worldviews, which are themselves grounded in ontological, psychosocial, and epistemological assumptions. Because our assumptions (as disclosed in the Preface) differ from each of the perspectives under study in Part II, as "outsiders" we can only do our best to "reproduce as faithfully as possible" those perspectives (McCutcheon 2005, 17). However, living in a cultural time and place that is largely shaped and influenced by three of the four primary approaches to governance, we feel some level of confidence in our familiarity and interpretations. However, we must acknowledge a particular deficiency in our interpretation of what we identify as Holographic; we hope that readers holding these basic perspectives will be forgiving of the rudimentary sketch we offer.

5   Hierarchical Governance

A summary of Hierarchical Governance is provided in the upper left quadrant of Table 5.1. In sketch, all of creation is assumed to be an imperfect copy of a transcendent source that is whole and complete. Human beings have an individuality characterized by stable identities that are socially embedded within the group. People seek to become more perfect copies of the source of existence through logic and attention to moral rules; thus, this perspective fits with monotheistic religions that believe in an external divine source of existence and lends

Table 5.1 Governance ideal-types: Hierarchical

	Hierarchical Governance	*Atomistic Governance*
Ontological assumptions	Static state, transcendent source, singular expression	Static state, immanent source, plural expression
Language characteristics	Discrete, hierarchical	Discrete, nonhierarchical
Psychosocial theory	individuality	Individuality
Epistemological concepts	Rationalism	Empiricism
Belief systems	Monotheism	Naturalism
Ethical concepts	Deontological obligation	Consequentialism
Political theory	Classical conservative liberalism	Modern liberalism
Economic theory	Welfare state	Market exchange
Administrative theory	Orthodox administration	New Public Service
	Holographic Governance	*Fragmented Governance*
Ontological assumptions	Dynamic state, transcendent source, singular expression	Dynamic state, immanent source, plural expression
Language characteristics	Gerundial, holistic	Gerundial, discrete
Psychosocial theory	Particular individuality	Singular Individuality
Epistemological concepts	Idealism	Epistemological anarchism
Belief systems	Pantheism	Anti-essentialism
Ethical concepts	Moral imperative	Moral skepticism/relativism
Political theory	Socialism	Individualist anarchism
Economic theory	Collectively planned economy	Self-sufficiency and barter
Administrative theory	New Public Administration	New Public Management

56 *Primary governance theories*

itself to rationalist epistemology and an ethic of deontological obligation. These assumptions require political representation—someone or something with superior reason must speak for the source of being. The assumptions thus fit logically with traditional forms of political monism (royalty or the church), as well as classical conservative liberalism (republicanism). In the economic sphere these assumptions lead to a paternalistic welfare state hierarchically administered by the government functionaries of Orthodox Administration.

Ontological assumptions and associated language

Hierarchical Governance assumes existence to be in a static state determined by a transcendent source that is singular in expression—the One that *is* throughout time, whether it is understood as everlasting or created by a transcendent being *ex nihilo* (Griffin 2007). In other words, the source of being (i.e., God) is beyond the natural world, eternal, and creates all that could be and is. There is a hierarchy between the divine and the mundane that creates a primary relation of domination (i.e., God over people). This monist perspective is aligned with Parmenides who asserts, based on a revelation from the goddess Truth, that reality is one unchangeable, timeless, indestructible whole (Palmer 2008). Existence is assumed to be eternal because nothing can come from nothing.

However, whereas Parmenides' form of monism is generally understood as arguing that the appearance of differentiation of individuality is an illusion (see Holographic Governance), in Hierarchical Governance the singular, transcendental source of existence creates differentiated and related parts that exist in mechanistic complement as a separate whole, as shown in Figure 5.1. Indeed, the machine-like precision that pervades the natural world from this perspective is given as proof that such a transcendental and purposeful source of existence must exist—a teleological argument sometimes referred to as the watchmaker theory of God, in which universal order is by purposeful design (Hume 1988). This is also seen in theories of cosmological order such as Plato's (2004) interpretation of the universal Form. Form is a nonmaterial, singular thing that causes plural representations of itself in particular objects in the physical world, which are imperfect copies. Thus, the transcendent source of existence is ideal (One) and man's (one) proper role is to mimic the One as closely as possible. Like Plato's Forms, the One also represents Truth, Good, and Right.

In later cosmologies, God is understood as the creator of existence from nothing—*creatio ex nihilo*—from which a great chain of being extends in hierarchical order (Lovejoy 1964). A being or object's place in that hierarchy depends on the relative proportion of "spirit" and "matter" it contains. Specifically, the more spirit and the less matter, the higher its position. Various types of inanimate objects and elements are at the bottom of the hierarchy. Above them are various classes of plants, followed by animals, humans, and angels, with God at the top. Within each class more nuanced hierarchies exist, again based on characteristics corresponding to spirit and matter.

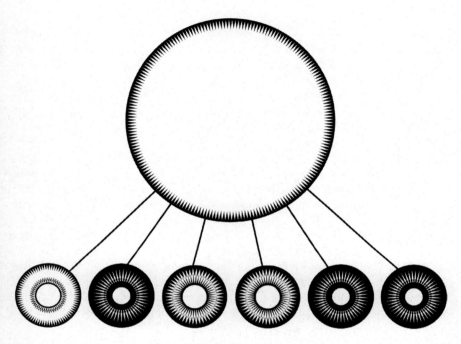

Figure 5.1 Transcendent source (One) of being (one).

In Hierarchical Governance, the language is static in form, but includes holistic ideals and hierarchical ordering. The One is represented through metaphors that emphasize the group or the whole. For example, in the United States individual citizens are referred to collectively as the People, thereby reifying the group identity (Catlaw 2007a). However, within that whole, noun-based, analytical languages describe the arrangement of objects, giving them a permanent position in relation to one another. More specifically, binaries infer value judgments through which differences are evaluated. In essence, binaries establish the opportunity for one of the two sides to be dominant (Derrida 1981). In this way, hierarchy is embedded in language. Philosophers of language show the inherently hierarchical nature of such binaries in Western culture (Derrida 1976).

Thus, language in this ideal-type includes hierarchical imagery, even when using organic metaphors such as "the body politic" with "heads of state" (Goodnow 2003, Hobbes 2000) or when the top of the hierarchy (One) is likened to the brain of the organism and each individual worker—distinct and static (one)—exists within "the system as functioning parts" (Katz and Kahn 1978, 53), fulfilling specific roles set forth by nature. However, metaphors are sometimes more mechanistic than organic, using machine language to show how different parts (one) unite in service to the One.

Psychosocial theory

Hierarchical Governance assumes that the individual has a centered (self-contained), unitary *identity* within an embedded *social condition*; individuality reflects a coherent identity, which fulfills a specific role within the group hierarchy (see Figure 5.2). It is the group identification and the designated role within the group that gives definition and differentiation to that identity. To understand this socially embedded expression of individuality, we will explain each psychosocial dimension—unitary identity and embedded social condition—and then consider their implications for the social bond.

Within Hierarchical Governance, individuality only emerges from interaction within the social sphere and, in particular, it is one's function within the whole that defines this identity. Thus, this "social whole" is depicted as "an 'organism' or living whole made up of differentiated members, each of which has a special function" (Cooley 1922, 36). In other words, identity is a matter of individuated function—a specific purpose only that particular individual fulfills. However, because each person is also attempting to be like the source of being, individuals (one) are understood as rather homogeneous in reference to the One, even though they have role differentiation in reference to one another. In this way, individuality is defined in accordance with the relationship to the whole, and that whole may be all of creation or mundane representations of the One in sociopolitical and religious institutions.

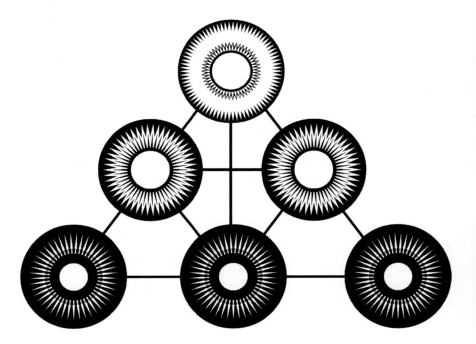

Figure 5.2 Socially embedded individuality.

Hierarchical Governance 59

Roles within the group are reflective of the hierarchical ordering of humans. As argued by Plato, people have varying degrees of ability to know and mimic the Forms. In fact, he makes this argument in his ideas about philosopher kings and his ranking of people into castes according to the metal of their souls (gold, silver, and bronze) (Plato 2004). Because the cosmos is hierarchically ordered and reality is static, there are certain individuals who are best suited to speak for the One and therefore embody a position of authority *over* everyone else. In short, as some are more perfect copies than others they are placed in a social relationship that looks something like a modern organizational chart (see Figure 5.2). The hierarchical arrangement *en masse* becomes the body politic directed by those at the top. Indeed, Douglas (1996) calls her corresponding social form *hierarchy*. In this high grid (rules and laws), high group (social identity) ideal-type, one's identity is based on one's predetermined place in the social (or cosmological) order and rules from above guide rational action. Such a structure engenders a feeling of group solidarity, giving meaning to the most mundane tasks and providing a sense of purpose and honor for even those who find themselves at the bottom of a deep hierarchy.

Thus, following from the ontological assumptions of Hierarchical Governance, the individual (one) is always an imperfect copy of a transcendent source that is whole and complete (One). Regardless of the group, system, or society within which individuals find themselves, "that individuality must always be defined and qualified by means of relation to some form of institution" (Kaufmann 1998, 3). The relationship between human beings and society can therefore be explained in a manner analogous to the relationship between human beings and a transcendent God (Schmitt 1985). Indeed, because the social hierarchy is a replication of the relationship between person and God, attempting to forge an independent identity (i.e., Atomistic) is neither possible nor would it be laudable.

This type of individuality assumes that a world without enforced social order is chaotic and unsafe (Hobbes 2000). Governor John Winthrop, the author of the sermon "A Modell of Christian Charity," held this ideal of indivisibility so strongly that he argued "true liberty requires subjection to authority" (Kaufmann 1998, 22). The reliance on institutional affiliations for personal identity places institutions themselves in a place of central importance for society. Thus, "to strengthen these institutions was also to strengthen, not diminish, one's sense of self" (Kaufmann 1998, 3). These interrelated roles are understood as specialized units (Gulick 1937a) that come together as a single organism, each performing a specific function according to predetermined rules to achieve the goals of the whole (Barnard 1968, Katz and Kahn 1978, Urwick 1937). Interactions between individuals are guided by respective roles within this social order, with each fulfilling the demands of the particular set of duties and expectations that correspond with their place within the social order.

As a result of this psychosocial theory, an inherent social bond is assumed in Hierarchical Governance. This presumed relationship exists within a predetermined framework. Following the great chain of being and its innate hierarchy,

60 *Primary governance theories*

individuality is defined by specific roles within the hierarchical order of society. As Box suggests, "virtually all human endeavor involves the formation of hierarchies of leaders and followers, a tendency that can be shaped or resisted, but rarely eliminated" (King *et al.* 1998, 166). Hierarchical Governance is presented as a means to impose rational order in a potentially chaotic Hobbesian world. The emphasis on role fulfillment within the whole leads to a corresponding notion of duty in which the individual submits to the collective (Box 2004), aligning self-interest with group interest.

The social bond in Hierarchical Governance demands a particular set of civic virtues: a devotion to fellow citizens, a sense of duty to participate in governance, a concern for the common good, and an ideal of equality (Cooper 1991). As Box (2004) explains, in classical republicanism, if these shared ideas and values are neglected, then the social glue that holds us together fails. Without shared values, individuals are independent, civil society erodes, and social institutions disintegrate. To prevent this from occurring Will (1983) describes the moral obligation of all citizens to preserve regime values as *soulcraft*. The social bond is manifest as the predetermined duty of citizenship as "a public office" (Cooper 1991, 137).

Epistemological concepts

Grounded in a static ontology, knowledge in Hierarchical Governance is foundational because there is an absolute Truth that exists beyond the material world. We ascertain Truth through internal reason or a form of divine revelation or epiphany (Graham 2002). From these foundational truths we must derive all that we can know through the process of logical reasoning.

Following Aristotle (1908), this system of knowledge is deduced in a rational and orderly fashion through internally justified logic from a set of foundational assumptions. However, whereas Aristotle asserts that deductive reasoning must be grounded with empirical observation, in Hierarchical Governance, deductive reasoning is applied to *a priori* truths drawn from revelation. We must not be fooled by empirical observation because the material world is an imperfect copy of the Forms (Plato 2004). Therefore, justification of truth is internal; it is based on reason rather than empirical observation. Indeed, "rationalism standardly affirms a doctrine of innate mental content" (Newman 2013, chapter 10, section 3). Thus, Hierarchical Governance is most aligned with rationalist epistemology, in which the "criterion of the truth is not sensory but intellectual and deductive" (Runes 1962, 263). Rationalism has also been described as "Cartesian Dualism," which emphasizes the mind as the ordering aspect of human being that is closer to the Truth than simple bodily experience can reveal (Mesle 2008, 93).

Rationalism is often aligned with Descartes' emphasis on innate ideas as the primary foundation of knowledge (Newman 2013). In his *Third Meditation*, Descartes (1980) splits ideas, and therefore sources of knowledge, into three potential categories—innate, adventitious (empirical observations), and fabricated. Of these, it is the innate ideas that form the basis of rational knowledge.

Hierarchical Governance 61

Due to the mind–body dualism, adventitious, or experiential ideas must always include an element of doubt because physical phenomena cannot cause ephemeral phenomena. Fabrications should be ignored as they are imaginary or fictitious. Thus, for Descartes all true knowledge must come from ideas that are innate (Adams 1975).

These innate ideas can be logically deduced because God "provides a guarantee for the reliability of reason" (Lennon and Shannon 2012). In other words, it is through the application of reason that innate—or true—knowledge is accessed. Malebranche (1980) insists that "only God enlightens us, and that He enlightens us only through the manifestation of an immutable and necessary wisdom or reason" (613). All knowledge comes from God as the ultimate source in the natural hierarchy and Reason; His Word provides the rules through which knowledge is obtained. Man's ability to reason has thereby historically discounted those who are determined to be less reasoned (e.g., women, peasants, indigenous peoples, animals, and so on).

In more secular terms, this epistemology is aligned with sociologist Max Weber's description of *formal rationality* (1994d). According to Weber, formal rationality (*Wertrational*) is deontological, being based on established predetermined absolute value, often in the form of law or belief.[1] Weber (1994b) later describes formal rationality as a combination of legal (absolute) and technical (utilitarian) rationality, which is the basis of legitimacy in his ideal-type description of bureaucracy.

Belief systems

Static state metaphysical belief systems support various interpretations of a personalized deity—the One that can be described as an actual entity which exists beyond the earthly plane and guides all of creation in a timeless, unchanging manner (Wang 2012). These characteristics broadly describe *monotheism*. Theism holds to the notion of a divine being. Monotheism in particular believes in a single, personal divine being with whom creation has an active relationship (Wang 2012). Monotheistic traditions "believe that their god is active in history and can be experienced in actual events in this world" (Armstrong 2005, 105). However, this activity is creative and directive in manner, in that the deity is separate from and hierarchically above the physical universe rather than manifest within it.

The importance of deference to the One is critical in most monotheistic traditions. Dictate comes down from the deity, who is responsible for all creation. Most ordinary individuals cannot use reason to discover divine laws. Therefore, divine laws must be revealed to elite individuals (e.g., prophets, clergy, royalty, etc.) who then promulgate Truth in a hierarchical fashion. For those who have not received these edicts, "using reason to discuss the sacred [is] about as pointless as trying to eat soup with a fork. Theology [is] only valid if pursued together with prayer and liturgy" (Armstrong 2005, 116) as determined by the head of the religion.

62 *Primary governance theories*

Ethical concepts

Hierarchical Governance assumes that the One determines the Form of the Good (Plato 2004). Because only the most advanced in society have reliable knowledge of the Good, universal laws must be devised in order to guide right action. Such guidance is beneficial to all roles within society because all social functions must work in coordination toward the greater good. Thus, the rational interest of the individual is understood to be synonymous with the interests of society. The guiding "social ethic" (Whyte 1956) is one in which functionaries within any organization focus on maintaining stability and homeostasis by fulfilling their roles. The social ethic therefore prioritizes deference to the needs of the group (Bercovitch 1978, Kaufmann 1998, Whyte 1956). In contrast, evil stems from selfish, irrational (and therefore unpredictable) individuals who attempt to define themselves outside of the whole.

Ethics in Hierarchical Governance accepts a form of deontological determinism in which Right is prioritized over Good; indeed, the only way to achieve Good is through Right action. Because Right is determined externally, "ethical judgments, and their truth conditions, are independent of motivation" (Darwall 1998, 235). Furthermore, because Right is universal and unchanging the ethical status of a given action can be externally validated by comparing action to these universal truths.[2] As such, moral theory for this type closely adheres to rule-based deontological obligation, in which actions are intrinsically right or wrong, aside from considerations of consequences.

Deontological obligation is perhaps most clearly articulated in *rule utilitarianism*, in which established universal moral laws determine which rules will yield the greatest amount of utility (Darwall 1998). Rule utilitarianism can be seen in Berkely's *Passive Obedience*, in which he insists that universal laws, derived from natural law, can be expected to advance utility "since God's aim in designing the laws of nature is the well-being of humankind" (Häyry 2012, 5). Once these rules of Right are established, promoting Good requires universal application: "It must indeed be allowed, that the rational Deduction of those Laws is founded in the intrinsick Tendency they have to promote the Well-being of Mankind, on Condition they are universally and constantly observed" (Berkely 1712, Sec. XXXI).

In the role that Niebuhr (1963) calls "man-the-citizen," the individual exists within a social order bound by law. Man-the-citizen is a deontological being who exists "under the rules of the family, neighborhood, and nation, subject to the regulation of our action by others" (53). "This man lives as moral self in the presence of the law first of all, not of other selves. What is over or against him as that which limits and attracts him is a commandment, a demand, a requirement" (70–71). Connecting this ethical position with the hierarchical social contract, Niebuhr (1963) explains that each person's "relation to other selves is a relation under the law" (71). This understanding of man-the-citizen echoes Montesquieu's (1989) depiction of the "good citizen" (26) in monarchy where "each person works for the common good, believing he works for his individual interests" (27). The principle of "honor" guides such actions, holding the body politic together and giving substantive ethical and political guidance to all stations of society.

From the Hierarchical Governance perspective, rules are necessary to control human nature, which tends toward self-interest and conflict due to imperfection in comparison to the source of existence. Hobbes (2000) asserts that the natural state of humankind "is always war of every one against every one" (64). Therefore, external authority is required to mandate and enforce appropriate behavior. This state of nature justifies the establishment of strong governments and laws to ensure just conduct. Thus, rather than imagining the individual citizen as sovereign, moral rules create requirements for conduct that are imbued with sovereign authority, which demands acquiescence; as parents often say, *because I said so*. The result is "a general ontological stance that rests on constitutional values and draws on philosophical pragmatism and democratic theory" (Evans and Wamsley 1999, 124), which can be described as a deontological ethic (Brady 2003), an ethic of duty (Hart 1989), an ethic of justice that protects rights (Starratt 1996, 2003), or a statist ethics in which the institutions of government embody and express the values of the whole as opposed to constituent factions (Huddleston 1981).

To prevent such factions, fairness is the primary democratic value, particularly the notion of fair treatment under the law (procedures, rules, etc.), which is prioritized to ensure procedural equity rather than equality of outcomes. Ronald Dworkin's (1986) theory of law is exemplary of such procedural fairness in that law has integrity with communal moral principles, particularly justice and fairness. Similarly, John Rawls' (2000) theory of justice fits within this perspective in that justice as fairness allows for differences in social station, thus rejecting equality of outcomes if the social order is arranged so as to benefit the least well-off. From this perspective, any person would ostensibly choose mutually acceptable, fair principles of justice. While this reasoning itself is procedural, the outcomes would also be fair because rational people will choose to benefit the least fortunate in society, in case they should find themselves in that situation.

Political theory

In Hierarchical Governance, designing social institutions with unchallenged authority is the primary concern of political theory. Based on Hobbesian ethical assumptions, men will abstain from a state of war only through fear of a power that is above them and with the assurance that all other men live under that same authority. To maintain stability, a society must agree to cast out those who break these rules. This justifies the need for civil states and laws; a paternalistic state is needed for a good and orderly quality of life. This rationale is the basis of an enforced social contract, or in Hobbesian terms, the generalized covenant. Therefore, the state's coercive power to exclude reinforces the social contract through fear. These assumptions lend themselves to any form of government claiming sovereignty over individuals, whether led by an individual monarch, an

64   Primary governance theories

executive, or a parliament or legislature that represents the collective will of the People.

This perspective is found in classical conservative liberalism[3] or what some refer to as republicanism.[4] Its architects include philosophers such as Thomas Hobbes (1588–1679), Francis Bacon (1561–1626), and René Descartes (1596–1650) (Clark 1998). These thinkers share the Enlightenment belief that the world order is an objective *given*, with humankind's place in it guided by laws of both God and Man. Only those who have a special position in the social hierarchy can demand compliance with God's image of Good (Thayer 1981 A-14).[5] As argued by Schmitt (1985) an analogous relationship is transposed onto the sovereign state's authority over its citizens.

Conservatism was initially hardly distinguishable from classical liberalism (Clark 1998). However, Edmund Burke (1729–1797), Thomas Carlyle (1795–1881), Joseph Schumpeter (1883–1950), and Leo Strauss (1899–1973) offered a clear conservative alternative to what would become modern liberalism. This classical conservative liberalism draws philosophically from Protestantism, English common law, natural rights, and social contract theory (MacIntyre 1988). Citizens are gathered together by an authorized sovereign. Such unified societies have existed "under the aspect of religion, or politics, or economy, or family, but all these interpenetrated one another and constituted a single reality" (Walzer 1984, 315). Once these Enlightenment thinkers banished organizing the state under religion, a new narrative was necessary. MacIntyre (1988) traces the roots of conservatism to Aristotelian thought, which emerged from a Homeric crisis of the gods' desertion of society. Without divine law, members of society were left to determine how to organize themselves.

As articulated by Berlin (2013), classical liberal conservatives believe that giving this type of positive liberty to all citizens is a dangerous proposition. Left to their own devices under traditional negative understandings of liberty as the right to master oneself places society at risk of devolving into the Hobbesian chaos feared. Therefore, society requires strong authority and obedience to that authority. In the nineteenth century, this argument was used to defend paternalism and rational control over human destiny. Governance should be guided by moral traditions and maintain authority to ensure order. For example, Leo Strauss (1899–1973) argues that government should act as a moral force in society to sustain values such as civility, loyalty, patriotism, chivalry, duty, obedience, courage, faithfulness, deference to authority, graciousness, and honor (Clark 1998). Citizens are expected to work in unison toward perfecting the institutions of authority that ensure these values (Hodgson 2009, Kaufmann 1998, Vowell 2008). While democracy is preferred over totalitarianism, it must be led by society's wisest and most virtuous leaders, with limited popular participation (Rossiter 1999). Impartial and wise governors will maintain order to achieve a just society.

Thus, in classical conservative liberalism the state is a stand-in for God and only the wisest and most moral leaders can demand compliance with the state's image of the Good (Spicer 2004); indeed, these leaders determine the state's "moral compass" (Friedrich 1940). Such ideas are evident in views espoused by the founding fathers of the United States, both in the *Federalist Papers* and in the Constitution itself (Rossiter 1999). People are described as self-interested and often irrational. To protect society from a tyranny of the masses and pluralist factions, elite leaders who are more reasoned than others should have decision-making authority. This perspective is carried forward in classical conservative liberalism by political philosophers like Walter Lippmann (2004) who maintain suspicions of the general populace and insist on a special role for the governing class. Authority is legitimized by traditional characteristics of leadership: those who possess more truth and virtue. Common citizens are equal only in the sense that they are similarly beholden to the authority of the social structure.

The political theory that follows has been characterized as *democratic elitism* (Bachrach 1967). Because the social order mimics the cosmological order, well-reasoning political elites are better able to formulate moral rules in accordance with natural law (Häyry 2012). This is the fundamental basis of the political ontology of representation (Catlaw 2007a)—the notion that an external authority can represent what is True, Right, and Good. This is manifest in a citizenry that comes together as a People to create a state that will determine for all what is Right and Good and is thereby legitimately authorized to ensure that all behave accordingly. Representatives are chosen based on their "better" virtue and character,[6] and are guided toward the public interest through a sense of *noblesse oblige.*

The public interest is determined by these representatives through their interpretation of universal laws. Replacing both kings and priests, modern democratic laws are made by elite leaders and codified as rulings from legislative, judicial, and executive political sources. Guided by morality, laws create rules of conduct that are imbued with political authority and demand acquiescence through the coercive power of the state. As noted by Berlin, such civil association is a form of rule-based governance reflective of the Constitutional order (Spicer 2004). Obedience to this order reflects good citizenship.

In sum, classical conservative liberals envision a fixed, highly rational, mechanistic world where individuals are driven by self-interest and thus need hierarchical oversight. This results in a predict-and-control approach to governance (Kooiman 2001, 2003). Through a predetermined voluntary agreement, individuals give their political authority to society via the state in exchange for the protection of rights and the promise of better obtaining the good things of life.[7] From this perspective, government is meant to ensure stability, order, security, and loyalty within both the organizations of government and society itself.

Economic theory

Hierarchical Governance assumes that humans are social beings that are part of a whole in which each fills a particular role to create an orderly and coordinated system. In economics, this occurs through the market interactions of households and firms as well as labor and capital. However, from the perspective of

66 *Primary governance theories*

classical conservative liberalism, self-interested actors left to their own devices will create chaos. Therefore, the economic system must be managed in a way that reinforces role definition while using constraints to order transactions. This is achieved through state regulation of the capitalist market moderated by the value of equality of rights. In this way, government represents what is Right in its oversight of economic activity in pursuit of Good.

The term *welfare state* has specific meaning that is in keeping with ethical assumptions about self-interest and the need for beneficent political rulers. Although Adam Smith later promoted free-market exchange, he asserted in his *Theory of Moral Sentiments* that market inequalities must be mitigated by civil society in some manner to ensure appropriate moral sentiments: "Society may subsist, though not in the most comfortable state without beneficence" (Smith 2000a, 147). Following this line of thought, the welfare state recognizes that market actors must work in an ethical fashion to ensure benefits for all, which are generally defined in materialist terms.

In combination, the welfare state and capitalism work together to ensure material progress through government control of the market. Due to self-interested human nature, on the one hand only coercive controls can ensure the order and security necessary for capital accumulation. On the other hand, only government regulation of capitalists can prevent grossly inequitable distributions to protect the general welfare. Thus, sociologist T. H. Marshall (1950) described the welfare state as a unique combination of democracy, welfare, and capitalism. As described by sociologist Lester Frank Ward in his theory of American social liberalism, the welfare state should be a paternalistic endeavor designed to countervail the power of the market (Commanger 1950). In fact, he suggested that private enterprise enjoyed the largest share of government protection and that its regulation should be equally turned toward the aid of laborers.

To achieve this objective, Rawlsian justice is applied to economics, producing the maximum–minimum criterion for determining economic policy. According to this understanding of utility function, welfare is maximized when the utility of those in society who have the least is improved the most. Therefore, government regulation should ensure that economic activity increases social welfare by improving the position in society of its members who are the worst off. Following this line of thinking, the welfare state produces labor laws, social insurance programs, social welfare programs, regulatory policies, and progressive taxation. Together, these policies redistribute wealth among economic classes, thereby ensuring the general welfare while maintaining social hierarchy.

Administrative theory

In the United States context, Hierarchical Governance aligns most closely with what has been called the Constitutional Tradition of public administration (Stout 2013), the characteristics of which are frequently described as "traditional" or "orthodox" (Denhardt 2000, White and McSwain 1990). They are also typically associated with earlier historical time periods within public administration (Ostrom 1976, Peters 1992, Stivers 2000). It is the weakness of authority delegated to administrators that aligns this school of thought with Hierarchical Governance.

Orthodox administration is characterized by a constitutional separation of powers and strict limitations on delegated administrative authority. Implementing the hierarchical role definition of this perspective, it advocates a politics/administration dichotomy in which administrators are mere functionaries directed by the elite leaders of the state and its laws. This dichotomy assures administrative legitimacy by demanding accountability through a hierarchical chain of command to the separated powers of government with elected leaders at the helm, and through them, the People. Waldo (1984) suggested that the political theory of public administration defined the Good Life as something efficient and productive, with a good measure of equality and peace. Society is planned and nature is mastered with the help of competent administrators.

While all members of the society live under the auspices of the law, political actors *make* those laws while administrators merely *execute* them. In this hierarchical arrangement the elected representatives deliberate and define what is right for "the public good" and set forth policies and laws to guide action accordingly. As noted in the ethical concepts section, rule utilitarianism is designed to control self-interest (Schultz 2004) and ensure regime values (Rohr 1989). Accountability in achieving what is right becomes the standard of measurement for administrators. This purpose leads to Finer's (1941) prescription for political oversight and hierarchical rules and procedures guiding neutrally competent administrative action. In deferring to political authority, administrators are unburdened by discretionary decision making, acting within clearly demarcated roles and rules that remain subject to the authority of the sovereign (Thompson 1975).

The origins of the orthodox approach in the United States can be found in the civil service reform movement of the 1870s to 1890s, which sought to professionalize administration in order to reduce government corruption (Rosenbloom 2009). This approach prioritizes the values of expertise, neutrality, effectiveness, efficiency, and economy. The organizational structure tends toward centralized bureaucratic hierarchy, based on its understanding of depersonalized individuals. The structural functionalist elements of this approach were cemented in Taylor's dogged pursuit of efficiency through scientific management principles, which coincided with the emergence of public administration as a discipline (Waldo 1984). These management principles were touted by government reformers of the Progressive era through the "Bureau Men" of the Municipal Research Bureaus (Stivers 2000). For them, progress is achieved through efficiency, scientific rationality, and procedural principles.

These principles are embodied in the efforts of scientific management to identify the "'one best way [for each job or function],'" and, further, to identify the "'one best man'" for each task as well (Taylor 1911, 59). Here the authority of managers over workers in the determination of efficiency and fit yields

68 Primary governance theories

optimal outcomes for all as "the true interests of the two are one and the same" (10). Such order and precise role definition ensures that administrators can mechanistically follow "the most economical, productive, and effective ways" of achieving predetermined goals (Caiden 1984, 51). In this way, public servants can be trusted to carry out their duties in the most utilitarian and non-discretionary fashion.

Hierarchical Governance thereby anticipates an administrative role that Stout (2013) calls the *bureaucrat*. Administrators are merely *tools* of the elected representatives used to accomplish public goals (Box 2004). They are value-free implementers who follow procedures as dictated by elected officials (Box 1998). Another role conceptualization is that of *servant*, which implies both responsibility to the Constitution and neutral competence (Wolf and Bacher 1990). Other metaphors include: (1) a functionary who is fully subordinate and instrumental to politically defined ends, and (2) a professional or expert who is a competent analyst and implementer (Catron and Hammond 1990). In other words, bureaucrats are passive public servants (Reich 1990). In a government *of* the People (i.e., elected representatives), passive, competent service is the proper administrative role.

Citizens are viewed by such administrators as political constituents to be guided according to legal and procedural standards that ensure the just treatment of individuals as well as the pursuit of the public interest as a whole. A depersonalized view (Rosenbloom 2009) of the citizen is meant to ensure equitable treatment of all through a focus on procedural rules and due process. But because citizens are at risk of becoming overly self-interested or an "irrational mass," lawmakers must make right decisions on their behalf. Vigoda (2002) suggests that the view of citizens as subjects of an authoritative sovereign government emphasizes coercive tendencies. In her summary of possible administrator–citizen role pairs, Roberts (2004) identifies two that are applicable to Hierarchical Governance: (1) citizen as subject in an authority system in which all are accountable to the ruler, and (2) citizen as client who defers to an administrative state. Similarly, this perspective would pair Box's (1998) neutral administrative implementers of rules and laws with free-rider citizens who rarely engage with government.

Summary and illustration

Hierarchical Governance assumes a static ontology with a transcendent source: the One and individuals (one) exist within a natural hierarchical order. This leads to a foundational approach to knowledge in which truth is established by the One and can be ascertained through rational inquiry. This fits a monotheistic belief system. The One determines Right, which in the democratic context means Law, as opposed to God or King. Good can only come from law-abiding action; thus, Good is determined by Right through deontological obligation. As such, ethical theory closely adheres to what Niebuhr (1963) calls "man-the-citizen," who exists within a social order bound by law. In this classical conservative

Hierarchical Governance 69

liberalism, elected representatives are chosen based on their superior qualities to determine Right through the making of law, including rules that constrain capitalism through the welfare state. Administrators are expected to follow the rule of law as consistently and when rules are not written, they must follow the mandates of political leaders. They view citizens as subjects classified into different legal categories (e.g., eligible voter, welfare recipient, etc.) who are also beholden to those rules and laws as they pertain to the specific characteristics and roles that citizens play within society. These considerations determine the proper application of policies and rules for each individual circumstance.

This governance approach fosters public encounters (Bartels 2013) that are hierarchically ordered and canalized by role expectations. In an effort to control administrative discretion and ensure equal treatment, such encounters require truncation of individuality as defined by specified roles, with potential actions and interactions circumscribed by place in the hierarchy, as noted in Weber's (1968) ideal-type of bureaucratic rationalization (see for example, Denhardt 1981, Farmer 2005b, Fox and Miller 1995, Hummel 2008, Ramos 1981).

Using agricultural policy as an illustration, we would expect to see an understanding of the natural world as hierarchically ordered, in which human actors fulfill specific roles. Policy would be orchestrated through centralized, top-down governing where political elites and experts rationally determine and regulate the processes of production by farmers. Guided by a moral obligation to do what is right, production goals would be aimed at providing sustenance for all, although distribution could be expected to match one's place in the social order. Agricultural goods would be sold through heavily regulated market mechanisms, with substantial welfare programs for redistribution. Administration would occur through the establishment and authorization of accountable bureaucracies.

Considering the United States, in 1862 President Lincoln transferred authority over agricultural lands from the Department of the Interior to the Department of Agriculture (USDA). At that time, the US economy was largely agrarian. The initial mission of the USDA was to centralize research, planning, and oversight to prevent loss of production, whether due to weather, farming practices, or both (Helms 1992). Because individual landowners could not be trusted to voluntarily adopt appropriate farming or soil and water conservation practices, the federal government set forth to determine and promulgate best practices. The role of the state was one of a "paternalistic state delivering markets and societal infrastructure" (Lang and Heasman 2015, 282). These early policies and administrative agencies continued to proliferate and specialize through administrative divisions and programs overseeing all areas of agricultural production, as well as forestry and watershed management (Helms 1992).

In this Hierarchical Governance approach, agricultural policy follows a Productionist paradigm that aims to produce more food in order to "deliver progress, health and well-being" (Lang and Heasman 2015, 100). Practices employ advances in industrial technology and animal husbandry to assert "ecological dominance" (100) over nature, producing ever-increasing amounts of food. For

70 *Primary governance theories*

example the USDA's Green Revolution developed strains of F1 hybrid seeds that would result in larger and more consistent yields, but which were also "dependent on agrichemicals, irrigation, monocropping, machinery and other labour-shedding managerial approaches" (142).

To support farmers in adopting these technological advances, a complex bureaucratic system was built that ensured compliance with regulation and cooperation with government in both practices and production goals. For example, in response to the extensive Dust Bowl drought in the 1930s, the Soil Conservation Act of 1935 (Public Law 46–74) authorized the USDA to create the Soil Conservation Service (now the Natural Resources Conservation Service or NRCS) to work with farmers and ranchers, local and state governments, and other federal agencies and programs like the Civilian Conservation Corps (CCC) and Works Progress Administration (WPA) "to maintain healthy and productive working landscapes" (NRCS 2016, paragraph 1). In order to receive technical assistance from Agricultural Extension, production resources from the USDA, and in some cases labor through the CCC or WPA, farmers were required to sign short-term cooperative agreements to install conservation measures (Helms 1992).

As illustrated here, in a Hierarchical Governance approach, a centralized governmental agency may use incentives to get citizens to voluntarily cooperate with administrative experts to plan and manage their production, including planting and irrigation as well as grazing and watering techniques. However, this approach can just as easily use regulatory enforcement to demand specific management procedures and environmental protection as well as disincentives. For example, a failure to comply with particular standards limits access to other government assistance programs.

Notes

1 For Weber (1968), this made formal rationality "less" rational than instrumental rationality.
2 In a secular context this means human law and in the religious context it means divine law.
3 Today, Conservatism is hardly distinguishable as a separate perspective, but is rather a subset of classical liberalism as juxtaposed to modern liberalism (Clark 1998). Therefore, Orion White (1990) uses the label "classical conservative[ism]" to combine the ideas.
4 Labeling the political philosophy associated with the ontological positions is difficult because differences that are important to some get lost. For example, those who hold to a classical republican philosophy may reject being grouped with classical conservative liberalism. We do so based on Clark (1998) and MacIntyre (1988).
5 Traditionally, the church and royalty represented this transcendent monotheistic source of existence.
6 This is the onto-story that enables both hierarchy and competition (Thayer 1981). The hierarchy is established by those who are authorized to speak for God (in the case of religion) or the Good (in the case of governance), and competition emerges among those who aspire to that station.
7 The Good Life is assumed to be something to which government aspires. However, political theories define this end differently (Waldo 1984).

6 Atomistic Governance

A summary of Atomistic Governance is provided in the upper right quadrant of Table 6.1. In sketch, existence is understood in physical terms that can be perceived through the senses. In this understanding, temporal beings and objects evolve from nontemporal finite sources (i.e., the Big Bang, Nature) (Griffin 2007). Individuality is characterized by stable identities that are pre-social and independent of the group. Each person is a psychophysical "universe of one." Enlightenment thinking employs empiricist epistemology and consequential

Table 6.1 Governance ideal-types: Atomistic

	Hierarchical Governance	**Atomistic Governance**
Ontological assumptions	Static state, transcendent source, singular expression	Static state, immanent source, plural expression
Language characteristics	Discrete, hierarchical	Discrete, nonhierarchical
Psychosocial theory	individuality	Individuality
Epistemological concepts	Rationalism	Empiricism
Belief systems	Monotheism	Naturalism
Ethical concepts	Deontological obligation	Consequentialism
Political theory	Classical conservative liberalism	Modern liberalism
Economic theory	Welfare state	Market exchange
Administrative theory	Orthodox administration	New Public Service
	Holographic Governance	*Fragmented Governance*
Ontological assumptions	Dynamic state, transcendent source, singular expression	Dynamic state, immanent source, plural expression
Language characteristics	Gerundial, holistic	Gerundial, discrete
Psychosocial theory	Particular individuality	Singular Individuality
Epistemological concepts	Idealism	Epistemological anarchism
Belief systems	Pantheism	Anti-essentialism
Ethical concepts	Moral imperative	Moral skepticism/relativism
Political theory	Socialism	Individualist anarchism
Economic theory	Collectively planned economy	Self-sufficiency and barter
Administrative theory	New Public Administration	New Public Management

72 Primary governance theories

ethics—knowing and judging through observation. This worldview fits naturalist belief systems that endow all beings with natural rights. In this perspective political representation is possible because identity is fixed—one can know one's own and others' interests and speak for them and against them in pluralist competition. Thus, it fits the political theory of modern liberalism. Stressing competition and individual preferences, this perspective leads to the ideal of free-market exchange within the social contract. The administrative theory that best fits this pluralist approach to both governance and economics is New Public Service.

Ontological assumptions and associated language

Atomistic Governance assumes existence to be static in state, immanent in source, and plural in expression. This means that the Many are material beings and static in terms of a consistent and substantive animating core. As shown in Figure 6.1, the ontological position assumes that there is no source of being beyond oneself, as denoted by "O/one." Instead, each O/one is a unique and self-generated entity within a universe of Many—all beings are immanent and independent.

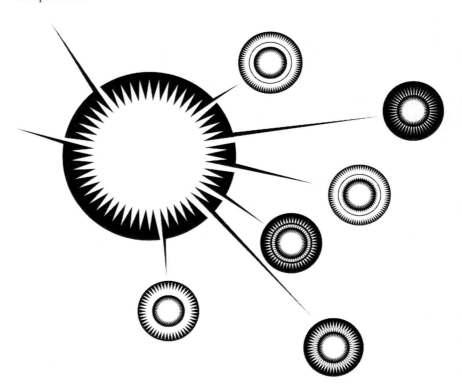

Figure 6.1 Many immanent sources of being (O/one).

Atomistic Governance 73

This materialist ontology assumes an external reality to which we have direct access through observation. Parmenides is considered the father of this Western philosophy (Palmer 2008) and the positivist science of cause and effect that followed. However, while the Atomistic type aligns with Parmenides' argument that reality is static, it departs from his ideas by insisting that being is plural rather than unitary in expression. Materialism rejects unified metaphysical explanations of existence, deferring instead to nature and its physical laws.

Ancient understandings of this materialist, determinist ontology come from the Greek atomists Leuccipus and Democritus (Adams 1975). Both held that everything is composed of atoms (similar to the modern understanding of molecules), which are physically divisible but indestructible. Between atoms lies empty space. Therefore, all phenomena can be understood as interactions among atoms—bodies acting on other bodies. Aristotle continued this tradition in his natural philosophy, adding explanations of motion through causation, place, and time. However, his assumption of a metaphysical source moves him out of this ontological position.

While making amendments through mathematics and geometry, materialist ontology is carried forward in mechanical philosophy in which physical laws determine the motion of matter (Descartes 1980). This understanding of materialism imagines matter (or its state as energy) as the only thing that exists. Therefore, all phenomena are simply the result of material interactions. Leibniz (1991) carried forward similar atomistic ideas in his conception of monads as the elementary particles of being. Leibniz's monads are eternal, indecomposable, individual, subject to their own laws, and not interacting. It must be noted, however, that he assumed these monads existed within universal unity (One). Although his conception of a predetermined harmony is in seeming opposition to laws of cause and effect, the notion that this order is embedded in internal instructions somewhat mirrors the laws governing subatomic particles and other laws of nature and fits with the notion of ontological stasis.

Similar to the static terminology found in Hierarchical Governance, but adding these atomistic assumptions, the language associated with positivist ontological concepts uses the subject–object orientation in a binary manner. As Bohm (1980) explains, Western languages follow a subject–verb–object structure that inherently divides—nouns are privileged and constructed as discrete elements only connected through verbs. "This is a pervasive structure, leading in the whole of life to a function of thought tending to divide things into separate entities, such entities being conceived of as essentially fixed and static in their nature" (29). This is the language of what James (1997) calls "our normal waking consciousness, rational consciousness" (305).

Rational consciousness discriminates, divides, compares, measures, and categorizes. It enables us to create an abstract intellectual map of reality that is linear and sequential in nature, helping us to navigate in the material world. Associated concepts, symbols, and language frame our thinking to match. As Hummel (1990) points out, "modernity is an analytic world" (214); therefore, language concepts are discrete and analytical, binary, and object-based. Specifically,

74 *Primary governance theories*

Western science and language share a "habitual way of seeing the world that is ingrained within our language and culture. It has the tendency to label everything—to stop the world through nouns" (Parry 2004, 7). When we understand reality as atomistic in nature, we conceptualize objects with clear and distinct boundaries that separate and divide in order to understand them. In short, differentiation creates static and stable meaning.

Difference cannot be denied in our experience of physical being (Christ 2003). From the Atomistic Governance perspective, one of the principal ways differentiation is explained is through binaries. Semiotics is an analytical technique for understanding how binaries create meaning (Leach 1974). When objects are understood as separate and discrete, concepts tend toward binaries because we describe what something is by analyzing what it is not. As Foucault (1972) notes, it is being in relation with other objects that "enables [an object] to appear, to juxtapose itself with other objects, to situate itself in relation to them, to define difference, and even perhaps its heterogeneity" (45). For example, *white* can only be understood in relation to *black*.

The separation of discrete objects also engenders a linear understanding of cause and effect that "concentrates on … goals" (Adler 1986, 38). For example, traditional concepts of space and time in physics hold that "elementary particles act on one another" (Bohm 1980, 47). Because objects do not change ontologically, but rather based on their properties in cause and effect relationships, the universe can be described in laws abstracted to the level of pure mathematical formalism.

Psychosocial theory

Atomistic Governance places the source of being in the natural world, of which individual human beings are a part. Therefore, the human being is the Hobbesian (or Lockean) individual in the state of nature (Stivers 2008), or the classical Cartesian subject within whom the "I" resides and does not change (Farmer 2005b). As shown in Figure 6.2, Individuality is unitary because it has a single linear, teleological life narrative—a unified, cohesive *identity* that continues through time (Farmer 2005b, Hummel 2008). However, as a pre-social being, such Individuality experiences a *social condition* of independence. Love (2010a, 2012) calls this psychosocial condition *atomistic individualism*. To understand this socially independent expression of Individuality, we will explain each psychosocial dimension—unitary identity and independent social condition— and then consider its implications for the social bond.

Individuality is understood as autonomous and self-reliant, where individuals are personally responsible for their own fates, interacting only voluntarily. This description corresponds with the social form of *individualism* in which competition establishes social order (Douglas 1996). In this low grid (rules and laws), low-group (social identity) ideal-type individuals have "few constraints and wide scope for forging and severing network connections freely" (Caulkins 1999, 111). Because each person is a "universe of one," social bonds must be created through mechanisms like contracts or compacts.

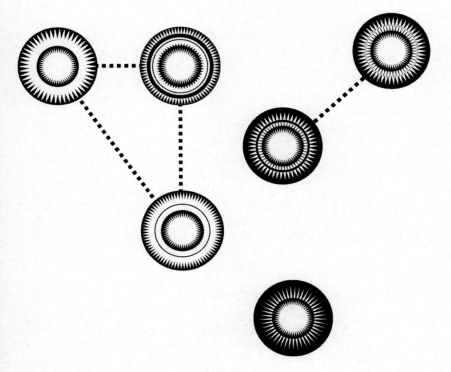

Figure 6.2 Socially independent Individuality.

Specifically, Atomistic Governance draws from a Lockean interpretation of the social contract in which groupings are neither natural nor permanent, but are voluntarily entered into and dissolved in accordance with the needs and desires of the individuals involved.

> Men being, as has been said, by nature, all free, equal, and independent, no one can be put out of this estate, and subjected to the political power of another, without his own consent. The only way whereby any one divests himself of his natural liberty, and puts on the *bonds of civil society*, is by agreeing with other men to join and unite into a community, for their comfortable, safe and peaceable living one amongst another[.]
>
> (Locke 1980, 52)

According to Follett (1998) the social contract became necessary to reunite atomized individuals in any form of social action (162). Because Atomistic Governance is inherently low-group (Douglas 1996), social groupings must be fabricated through voluntary action, but once agreement is reached Individuality is bound by the agreed upon terms of the group (Fischer 2008).

76 *Primary governance theories*

The extraction of Individuality from the hierarchical social order may be traced to Descartes (1980), whose separation of mind and body elevates the mind over all physicality. This separation allows humans to manipulate the physical world toward their own ends, no longer as part of a predetermined cosmological chain of being. However it was not until John Locke's *Human Understanding* appeared in 1690 that our current understanding of individuality emerged. Even then, the word was only used adjectivally ("individual Man") and not as a noun (Williams 1983, 163). While the term *individual* was originally used as a noun in biology and logic, it was in Adam Smith's *The Wealth of Nations* (1776) that "a crucial shift in attitudes [could] be clearly seen in uses of the word" (Williams 1983, 163). Dewey (1993) further explains that it was during this American Revolutionary era that " 'individualism' was born, a theory which endowed singular persons in isolation from any associations, except those which they deliberately formed for their own ends, with native or natural rights" (175). Indeed, Farmer (2005b) describes this subject as a "self-contained, self-mastering individual" for whom "stability and reliability exude" (43).

Epistemological concepts

In Atomistic Governance, scientific objectivity and supposedly neutral facts reign over all other ideas. This materialistic view "holds that there is only non-experiencing matter" (Mesle 2008, 94). Its epistemology assumes that basic foundational truths can only be known *a posteriori*, or after the fact. External justification is necessary through systematic observation of the natural world, i.e., *evidence*. Empirical proof is the only reliable source of information for understanding the nature of reality (Comte 2009). Thus, the epistemological perspective is logical positivism (Ayer 1959) or empiricism (Hempel 1959). Carnap (1959) describes this approach as "the *logical analysis of the statements and concepts of empirical science*" (133). Logical and empirical positivism reject any form of transcendent metaphysics, appealing instead only to that which can be verified or falsified through empirical means (Ayer 1952) using the "verification principle" or "criterion of verifiability" (Ferré 1998, 180).

While nature is static and thus knowable, there is a critical distinction from the reasoned rationalism of Hierarchical Governance. In addition to superior reason, careful empirical observation is required to fully understand it. This position can be described as the disengaged reason of Enlightenment thinking that undergirds positivist science (White 1990). This privileging of scientific knowledge derives from Aristotle's epistemological discussions (Shields 2013). Specifically, while logic in the form of syllogistic deduction is correct, the originating assumptions need to be based on empirical observation, or *episteme*. Only this approach can produce mind-independent, objective knowledge. Further, because individuals will have access to different empirical observations but can never have access to all empirical data, they should collectively pool information for verification and triangulation of observations (Hayek 1973). In this way, society can build knowledge from which to make sound judgments and decisions for action.

Atomistic Governance 77

This positivist empiricist epistemology undergirds instrumental rationality—what Kooiman (2001, 2003) refers to as an "agential ontology." Similarly, Ayn Rand's objectivism links rationality to autonomy (Peikoff 1991, Rand 1964). Critical theorist Jürgen Habermas divides such purposive rationality into *instrumental* and *strategic* forms (Erikson and Weigard 2003). Like Weber's *Zweckrational*, instrumental rationality pursues utilitarian ends in the most technically efficient manner, seeking to maximize benefit while minimizing cost.

Belief systems

Atomistic Governance supports belief systems grounded in natural laws that guide all beings (the Many). *Naturalism* denies any form of noumena and asserts a material world made up of many individual phenomena, as assumed by science. However, adding the psychosocial ideals of the Enlightenment, a secular humanist perspective on the natural order may be a more fitting system of belief than simply science. Humanism emphasizes the value and agency of human beings but prefers individual thought and evidence over faith-based rationales for beliefs. This anthropocentric perspective aligns with the emphasis on individual agency and competition in the survival-of-the-fittest context assumed by science. Thus, a belief in human superiority arises because human beings are seen as more perfect manifestations of Nature due to their ability to use reason.

Secular humanism emerged in the early 20th century as a rejection of theistic morality and revealed knowledge (Davies 1997). The movement affirms the dignity and worth of all human beings and posits that they are capable of being ethical and moral based on personal reasoning and ethical choice. Auguste Comte (1883) figured prominently in the establishment of humanism through his efforts to establish a religion of humanity that would support progress from the theological phase of human history to a metaphysical period that would eventually give way to a fully rational, positivist science.

Ethical concepts

Atomistic Governance moves the constitutive good from a metaphysical, predetermined end to one that is discovered through actual experience (Taylor 1989). Human beings naturally pursue Good by virtue of what is rationally deemed desirable. Good is immanent in the material world and can be ascertained only through objective analysis. Right action is therefore determined retrospectively based on the goodness of externally validated consequences. Authority is delegated to the individual to determine Good as well as how to pursue it. For example, Ayn Rand's ethical objectivism employs empirical rationality, autonomy, and individual rights in the pursuit of desired ends (Peikoff 1991, Rand 1964). Niebuhr (1963) refers to the individual in this ethical position as "man-the-maker" for whom "right is to be defined by reference to the good; rules are utilitarian in character; they are a means to ends" (55).

78 Primary governance theories

The metaphor of *maker* has been used since Aristotle's *Physics* and *Nichomachean Ethics* to depict such agency; Man makes himself and causes things to happen toward a desired end (Shields 2013). The image of maker is one that has been "refined and criticized in the course of its long use, by idealists and utilitarians, hedonists and self-realizationists. But it remains the dominant image" (Niebuhr 1963, 49). Man-the-maker is a self that "understands itself as existing primarily in relation to ideas and ideals. It defines itself as rational, living in the symbiosis of reason with its objects, be they ... scientific theories, or common-sense facts" (55).[1] This self is an agent in the sense of "a being in charge of his conduct" (48), an empowered, *teleological* being "who, acting for an end, gives shape to things" (49).

Thomas Aquinas follows this line of agential thinking to assist in the movement from a worldview based on deontological principles to one that accommodates the teleology of Enlightenment thinking. In short, Man is a master of his own acts by the use of reason and will and is unique in this capacity (MacIntyre 1988).[2] Teleology focuses purely on consequentialism, such as act utilitarianism (economic or preference maximization) (Bentham 1988, Mill 1999, Weimer and Vining 1999), ethical egoism (Sidgewick 1884), or objectivist ethics based on self-interest (Rand 1964). Simply put, human beings pursue that which is in their self-interest (Buchanan 1966). It is founded on the utilitarian pursuit of efficiency, assuming rational actors in the model of *economic man* (Jenkins-Smith 1990, MacRae and Wilde 1979).

These perspectives assume that because Good is naturally desirable, individuals in pursuit of their own self-interest will produce Good for all. In *Nichomachean Ethics* Aristotle (2000) defines Good by explaining that: (1) the *highest* good is desirable for itself, (2) it is not desirable for the sake of some other good, and (3) all other goods are desirable insofar as they help to achieve the highest good. For example, if human flourishing is the ultimate good, health, wealth, and happiness are pursued as contributors to that highest good. Thus, individual interest and the public interest are one and the same. The utilitarian principle "requires that social welfare be maximized" (Paris and Reynolds 1983, 157), thereby accommodating the highest Good.

In this ethical context, Right action is determined based on the ability to achieve the common good, the public good, or the public interest, often defined as well-being (Kagan 1998). So, the first problem is to determine "what are the criteria?" (Appleby 1945, 48). Differing political philosophies influence the values one pursues (Simon *et al.* 1974). Deliberation is a rational act in which individuals reach agreement without forfeiting their autonomy—what Habermas refers to as communicative ethics (Erikson and Weigard 2003). In his ideal speech situation consensual value decisions are made based on the best argument (Habermas and Cooke 1998).

Drawing from these principles, humanism is described as a democratic and ethical life stance (Institute for Humanist Studies 2013). As indicated by Comte's (1883) definition of "altruism," humanists embrace the notion of an ethical purpose to pursue fulfillment, well-being, and justice for all individuals

Atomistic Governance 79

and humankind, supported by knowledge produced through reason, evidence, critical thinking, and an open exchange of ideas.

The theory of utilitarianism is perfected in modern liberalism, arguing that utility applies equally to non-economic "pleasures" such as liberty and justice, and ensuring that normative concerns can be addressed alongside more materialistic benefits (Mill 2000, 167). Utilitarianism suggests that the lack of predetermined substantive values forces us to rely on the lowest common denominator of rights-based procedure (Zanetti 2004). This procedure is known as *competitive pluralism* (Kooiman 2001, 2003)—each citizen has a right to participate in the competition of interests either directly or through representatives. Good is determined by competitively chosen values that are interpreted through technically rational processes. According to Weber (1994d), the most rational approach (*Zweckrational*) is based on a technical utilitarian calculus of discrete individual ends. The end, the means, and the secondary results are all taken into account and weighed as costs and benefits in a teleological fashion.

In sum, Atomistic Governance idealizes the ethic that Adam Smith (2000b) advocates in *The Wealth of Nations* (1776); self-interest promotes the common good "more effectually than when [man] really intends to promote it" (151). These assumptions undergird a teleological ethic (Brady 2003) designed to facilitate the pursuit of self-interest (Schultz 2004). Writ large, the public interest is Good as decided among aggregations of individuals who determine the social order. In this polity-based ethic, values are drawn from pluralist competition to determine Good (Huddleston 1981). Once established, individuals are responsible for producing desirable outcomes. To assess responsibility both technical and ethical values must be translated into operational criteria (Gulick 1937b).

Political theory

Modern liberalism is by far the dominant ideology in most Western nations (Clark 1998). Indeed, Simon *et al.* (1974) argue that its atomistic individualism is a founding characteristic of the American psyche and resulting forms of government. This form of liberalism has been prevalent since the seventeenth century and is based on the Enlightenment's science and technology and the rationalized, centralized administrative nation-state (Wolin 1981). These ideas were developed by John Locke (1632–1704), David Hume (1711–1776), and Adam Smith (1723–1790) (Solomon 2000) and extended by Jeremy Bentham (1748–1832), John Stuart Mill (1806–1873), John Maynard Keynes (1883–1946), and John Rawls (1921–2002) (Clark 1998). In rebelling against practices associated with Hierarchical Governance, "The easiest way out was to go back to the naked individual, to sweep away all associations as foreign to his nature and rights save as they proceeded from his own voluntary choice, and guaranteed his own private ends" (Dewey 1993, 175).

While the Hobbesian (2000) potential for chaotic and fierce self-interest is not entirely rejected, the modern liberal view follows John Locke (1980) in a

80 *Primary governance theories*

belief that self-interest is generally rational (White 1990). Individuals are willing to moderate their self-interest and autonomy in order to garner the protection of their own rights and to participate in the benefits of collective life and progress. Therefore, individuals will voluntarily enter into a social contract that ensures order and security so long as it remains minimally restrictive. "From these tenets, it was a short step to the conclusion that the sole end of government was the protection of individuals in the rights which were theirs by nature" (Dewey 1993, 175). Thus, the modern liberal ideas of social contract theory, utilitarianism, and pluralist choice are rewoven in a manner consistent with democracy's demands for liberty and equality, leaving the coercive authority of conservativism behind.

Political authority is considered a necessary evil to ensure progress, but coercive action on the part of the collective must be minimized. As argued by James Madison,

> If men were angels, no government would be necessary. If angels were to govern men, neither external nor internal controls on government would be necessary. In framing a government which is to be administered by men over men, the great difficulty lies in this: you must first enable the government to control the governed; and in the next place oblige it to control itself.
>
> (Rossiter 1999, 322)

The goal of politics is to minimize constraints on one's individual freedom to pursue happiness while maximizing one's right to do so. Here, the emphasis is on negative liberty, wherein an individual's actions must not to be coerced by interference or restraint imposed by others (Berlin 2013, Hayek 1978). The social contract is forged around several core liberal notions: individualism, freedom from government coercion, equality of political rights, the protection of property rights, and self-interested rationality.

The pluralist approach to the social contract requires only a "minimal set of individualistic values, procedures, or legal frameworks" (Howe 2006, 435). Pluralist competition is the method through which the public interest—Good—is determined. Within this institutional structure, individuals compete to determine and produce the collective good. From this perspective, to ensure liberty and sufficient levels of equality, the government can use interventions like taxation, subsidization, and regulation minimally to: (1) protect rights and enable the pursuit of the public interest, (2) address market failures to maximize material progress, and (3) provide public goods that are not produced by the market.

Thus, the structure of authority in the political realm is determined through pluralist competition as opposed to hierarchy. However, the strength of this competition is assumed to be relatively moderate or agonistic because of a stable social contract and the value placed on political equality. Furthermore, because Individuality is static in nature, people can know their own interests and express them through preferences that can then be represented by either elected officials or by interest groups. Representatives can be legitimately chosen based on similarity of beliefs and the right to represent is won through competition and majority rule. Once the competition results in a ruling vote, the majority choice becomes the public will, which remains static until challenged or opened for reconsideration.

Pluralist competition of ideas is also beneficial because it allows for incremental change due to evidence derived from ongoing empirical analysis. Box (1998) describes pluralism working well when citizens are sufficiently active in the policy making process. This requires that they have: time to participate, access to the information needed, and a consensus based on multiple views, agenda setting, framing, alternatives, decisions from discussions, just outcomes, and fair procedures. Mouffe (2000) also argues that pluralism works best when conceived as *agonism*, in which individuals with differing interests interact in the public sphere as adversaries, rather than as enemies. Agonism accepts the ineradicable nature of differences in values as not only inevitable but beneficial, even necessary for the existence of democracy, provided all engaged accept a "shared adhesion to ethico-political principles of liberal democracy" (102).

This perspective elevates the individual, the importance of equal opportunity and property rights, and rational choice. Within classical liberalism (White 1990), such individualism asserts that each person is sovereign by natural right and autonomous in their thoughts, preferences, opinions, and choices. Naturally self-interested individuals compete in an effort to maximize their own benefits while minimizing their own costs. No predetermined resolution is offered for the resulting conflicts between interests such as human rights and property rights, freedom and equality, or individual and community. Instead, these tensions are acknowledged as inherent features of the human condition that get balanced out through an ongoing pluralist exchange. These assumptions lead to a "'political economy' [that] conceives of order in human associated life as a result of the free interplay of its members' interests" (Ramos 1981, 31). Thus, the public sphere is a place "where bargaining between individuals, each with their own preferences, is conducted" (MacIntyre 1988, 338). Rational decision making, cost–benefit analysis, and public choice frame "virtually every sphere of public activity" (Wolin 1981, 28). Kooiman (2001, 2003) refers to this approach as *market governance*, which is based on an agential ontology and positivist epistemology that leads to competitive pluralism.

In sum, because individuals have stable identities, representatives can be legitimately chosen based on similarity of beliefs or policy preferences. When individuals come together to form groups, organizations, or societies through pluralist, competitive processes, the ties that bind them are dissolvable. In this political form, representation is won and the public interest (Good) is determined through competition among sovereign individuals and majority rule. Modern liberalism seeks to allow individuals the greatest independence from societal infringement (negative liberty). However, liberty is moderated by the social contract because of the countervailing value of equality.

82 *Primary governance theories*

Economic theory

In Atomistic Governance economic transactions are largely internally regulated within capitalist markets (Wolin 1981). Rather than having an external authority determine economic outcomes, the market is allowed to determine the most efficient outcomes through economic transactions and competition in a manner similar to political pluralism. This is described as *market exchange* (Davis 2003), where mechanisms of supply and demand are ideally in equilibrium, but are moderated by minimal government intervention. Internal regulation is best illustrated by Smith's (2000b) metaphor of the invisible hand of competition: producers and consumers engage in ongoing free-market exchange that results in incremental adjustments that consistently lead to a static equilibrium that provides maximum utility for all. Through these natural forces, social progress and the wealth of nations are made.

Therefore, coercive interventions from government are unnecessary and the market needs no support from government to succeed in its agenda—all property is privately owned and the government exists only to protect individuals from coercion by others (Commanger 1950, Rand 1966, Ricardo 1911, von Mises 1998). Yet because of market failures, modern liberalism admits that some government intervention is warranted to provide public goods that the market will not generate and to regulate some market processes (Mill 1909, Weimer and Vining 1999), effectively balancing individual and social goals. In other words, when autonomous transactions fail to produce the common good, the state must step in to moderate, guide, or control outcomes, mitigating greed and quelling conflict. Therefore, as with political authority, the strength of this internal market regulation is moderate.

Market exchange is grounded in the assumption of pre-social individuals that populate the world of "all-against-all" (Hobbes 2000) in competition for scarce resources, albeit moderated by Locke's (1980) rational utilitarian human nature (i.e., *homo economicus* or the rational actor). From this perspective, an individual is both "exogenous to the process" and left fundamentally unaltered by exchanges within the marketplace (Davis 2003, 11). Atomistic individuals are guided by a sense of self-interest "connoting economic advantage" (Follett 2013b, 35). They compete within the economy in an effort to maximize their own benefits while minimizing their own costs, with little or no regard for the implications for others—the definition of individual self-interest. Indeed, self-interest is typically monetized in some fashion to equate desires with some type of material advantage. Thus, George (1929) notes that in the prevailing political economy, progress is measured primarily in terms of material advancement and accumulation.

This interpretation of interest allows the notion of limited material resources to enter into the equation, imagining now a static, albeit plentiful supply of resources available to fulfill individual interests of all types. This idea of the self-interested individual in competition with others for scarce resources and benefits is the basic assumption in the economics of market exchange. The assumption of scarcity necessitates, perpetuates, and increases the competitive spirit because competition among individual interests must be a zero-sum game—what one party wins another party loses. Yet it is this ethic of competition that spurs progress and builds wealth.

Administrative theory

Within the modern liberal approach to pluralist politics, administrators are given discretion only sufficient to ensure citizens' maximum negative liberty. Administrators are actors within the political milieu, engaged in the pluralist competition of policy formation in the public sphere (Rosenbloom 2009, Spicer 2010). However, as participants in the social contract, administrators are obliged to enact the policies that emerge from that pluralist process. Thus, the strength of authority for administrators in the Atomistic Governance ideal-type is relatively moderate. This perspective calls for administrators to provide both expertise to and facilitation of the pluralist competition among public values and ideas, while maintaining a commitment to uphold the public interest that results from that pluralist process.

As in political theory, it is widely accepted that economic theory and its assumptions about human nature are prevalent underpinnings of contemporary administrative theory. In Atomistic Governance, pluralist competition characterizes both politics and economics. Lockean assumptions of rational human nature and utilitarian logic undergird the pluralist political thought and market theories that weave themselves throughout all types of organizational theory (Ramos 1981) that we associate with this approach. This utilitarian philosophy has been described as a bureaucratic, as opposed to a democratic ethos (Denhardt 1989, Pugh 1991). However, pluralistic competition is not firmly one or the other. We argue that the ideals of Atomistic Governance align most closely with New Public Service, which amends other schools of administrative theory with postmodern, pragmatist, and critical theory (Denhardt and Denhardt 2007). While Stout (2013) associates the New Public Service with more collaborative approaches to public administration, she notes that it is a stretch because of the continued empowerment of experts in facilitating pluralist deliberation.

Scholars aligning with New Public Service carry forward an expert role for administrators in pursuit of the public good, but they augment this expertise with direct citizen engagement in deliberation, thereby lessening the authority granted to both elected representatives (Orthodox Administration) and discretionary administrators (New Public Administration and New Public Management). While the role of facilitator becomes critical, other forms of expertise remain an "on tap" as opposed to "on top" position. Through this more egalitarian, participatory, pragmatic approach, a synthesis of technical and value-oriented concerns is sought within the pluralist process among elected representatives, administrators, and citizens. In short, administrators are legitimately engaged in all aspects of policy making short of actual partisan politics (Overeem 2005).

84 Primary governance theories

This *political* approach to public administration (Rosenbloom 2009) is rooted in the New Deal and World War II era. It seeks to empower administrators in political processes by valuing representativeness, responsiveness, and accountability to elected officials and citizens through transparency and direct participation. Therefore, the organizational structure accommodates decentralized pluralism whereby group identities are formed by aggregating interests. Similarly, Stillman (1996) links this approach to James Madison, who viewed public administration as part of the political system (legislative, executive, and judicial branches). Madison believed in maximizing and balancing interest group demands and using government to control the evils of faction. Therefore, administrators should be responsive to the changing balance among competing interests while acting as a vertical check and balance on the three branches of government.

From any of these perspectives, the social roles of politicians and administrators are not eliminated, nor are the functions of policy making. Therefore, it might be more accurate to view administrative theory in Atomistic Governance as a *shifting of the line of demarcation between politics and administration*, which places slightly increased political authority in the hands of administrators and broadens their scope of action in pluralist competition. One argument for such administrative discretion—administrative representation—mirrors the political notion of demographic representation (Kelly 1998, Kingsley 1944, Krislov 1974, Long 1954, Redford 1969, Rosenbloom 1983). In this theory, administrators are more likely to be demographically like the citizens they serve than elected officials and are thereby more representative. Alternatively, administrators who are more in touch with citizens on a daily basis can better advocate on behalf of specific interests (Mosher 1968). This is possible through a principal-agent relationship between administrators and the citizens they serve (Kass 1990).

Atomistic Governance thereby fits an administrative role Stout (2013) calls the Steward. In the political process, administrative Stewards are responsive to the affected citizenry by acting as facilitators of deliberation and stewards of the public trust (Roberts 2004). An ethic of stewardship takes the form of a principal-agent relationship between administrators and the citizens they serve (Kass 1990). Yet, with appropriate humility, the Steward does *not* hold ultimate authority. In fact, "stewards who forget their place and begin to assume that they are autonomous, or are at liberty to do as they please with 'the servants,' will be severely punished" (Hall 1990, 35). Putting these ideas together, "tomorrow's public administrators will be facilitators, educators, and co-participants, rather than deference-demanding experts or independently responsible decision makers" (Adams *et al.* 1990, 235–236). This role requires what has been called a "technology of administrative politics" (White 1971, 80). This know-how includes specific techniques and skills in interpersonal relations, political assessment, and problem-solving appropriate to the pluralist political process. Such administrative Stewards view citizens either as voters in a representative system or as interest group advocates (Roberts 2004). Similarly,

Stewards function as "helpers" who facilitate "active citizens" who seek to influence public sector decision making, or "watchdog citizens" who seek to advocate for their own interests (Box 1998, 73).

Summary and illustration

In sum, Atomistic Governance brings the source of being into the natural world, in which discrete human beings exist prior to, and potentially outside of, society. A combination of natural law and atomistic individualism prefigures empiricist epistemology and humanist belief systems. Within the social contract, both the responsibility for Good and the teleological agency of "man-the-maker" guide the pluralist competition of modern liberalism. These principles lead to moderate regulation of the market, in which individual preferences guide free-market exchange. The administrative theory that best fits this pluralist approach to both governance and economics is New Public Service because it ideally engages all actors equally in pluralistic policy making and implementation.

This governance approach fosters public encounters (Bartels 2013) that are ordered through pluralist competition at any level of analysis and in all social groupings. Public officials "play an important role in governance by balancing community values, legal and organizational constraints, and a variety of other factors in a manner that can be legitimized relative to a particular situation" (Denhardt and Crothers 1998, 151). In so doing, public officials transact business "with *customers* and *clients* in service delivery" (Bartels 2013, 472). Both public officials and citizens take a strategic stance toward getting what they want, with encounters being characterized by bargaining, debate, and compromise. Therefore, these encounters privilege "the ability to articulate logical, rational, and reasonable arguments" (477). Individuals set themselves against one another in order to win through persuasion. Through these negotiations, more innovative and cost-effective actions lead to the highest degree of satisfaction possible for all.

Using agricultural policy as an illustration, we would expect to see an understanding of the natural world, in which human actors choose and enact roles based on self-interest, as competitively ordered. Policy would be made through pluralist competition in which political leaders respond to advocacy and lobbying from special interest groups. Guided by utilitarian ideas of how best to produce the good, production goals would be aimed at maximizing yields and minimizing waste. Agricultural goods would be sold through moderately regulated market mechanisms, with minimal government welfare programs for redistribution. Administration would be facilitated by empowered and expert government agents.

Returning to the story of the USDA's drought response efforts, to increase the adoption of soil and water conservation practices, legislation was passed in 1937 to enable states to form Conservation Districts, which would be governed by locally elected or appointed board members (Helms 1992). Following the standard law, district formation would be put to the voters through referendum.

86   Primary governance theories

If passed, the district board members would be elected and they would sign an agreement with USDA to implement federal policy by tailoring it to local conditions. The districts would then, in turn, enter into conservation agreements with landowners. These changes were meant to increase local political control over administrative rulemaking and implementation.

While earlier laws were enacted to prevent "anticompetitive" behavior, such as the Packers and Stockyards Act of 1921, which prevented the manipulation of meat and dairy markets, subsequent efforts to deregulate markets have eroded these controls and have led to a consolidation of agricultural production (Wilde 2013). Today, elected officials continue to set policy but "corporations ... may be more important in shaping food systems than governments" (Lang and Heasman 2015, 2). This approach is reflected in the concept of "agribusiness" in which "food production would be market-driven rather than government supported or directed" (Gottlieb and Joshi 2010, 82). Such shifts can be seen in the Federal Agriculture Improvement and Reform Act of 1996 (PL 104–127), or Freedom to Farm Act, which began reducing or phasing out many traditional price supports and subsidies.

Government regulation of production, pricing, and subsidies are now largely guided by pluralist politics. Competing agricultural interests such as farmers, distributors, and social service providers lobby to influence governmental policies such as price supports, tariffs, regulatory requirements, and international free trade agreements (Wilde 2013). Within this approach there is a move toward market mechanisms such as crop insurance programs and marketing assistance loans to farmers where loan repayment plans are based on expected equilibrium prices for specified crops. The terms of these policies are left to pluralist politics, resulting in expanding agricultural interest group lobbying efforts. For instance, in 2015 US agribusiness spent a combined $132.3 million on lobbying (Center for Responsive Politics 2016).

These efforts have resulted in an emphasis on global market structures in which large corporations dominate food policy and production mechanisms while the role of the state is to "balance of public and private sector" (Lang and Heasman 2015, 282). Decentralizing authority and leaving food policy to competitive market mechanisms has transformed agricultural production. In the US in 2010, 70 percent of the net agricultural value added to the US economy was produced by farms classified as very large family farms or corporate farms, with only 18 percent produced by small family farms (Wilde 2013). Likewise, the heavy reliance on contract exchange means that most family-owned farms produce under contract with corporations in which production decisions are heavily dictated.

As illustrated here, in an Atomistic Governance approach, market mechanisms are the preferred means for determining production type, quantity, and processes, as well as distribution to consumers. The means of production are privately held and controlled, and to the extent that government is involved in regulating the agricultural sector and providing incentives for production, these decisions are influenced by pluralist politics driven by special interest groups.

Notes

1 Here Niebuhr also includes Platonic ideas and Aristotelian entelechies which do not fit Atomistic Governance.
2 Here Aquinas differs on the point of his comparison of human beings to angels and God.

7 Holographic Governance

A summary of Holographic Governance is provided in the lower left quadrant of Table 7.1. In sketch, all of creation is encompassed within and perfectly reflects the transcendent source of existence. As a part of the whole, Particular individuality is characterized by a decentered identity that is socially embedded. The assumption that the divine is both internal and external to self leads to epistemological idealism. These assumptions can be seen in pantheistic religions in which all beings are considered parts of the divine being. Action is guided by an

Table 7.1 Governance ideal-types: Holographic

	Hierarchical Governance	*Atomistic Governance*
Ontological assumptions	Static state, transcendent source, singular expression	Static state, immanent source, plural expression
Language characteristics	Discrete, hierarchical	Discrete, nonhierarchical
Psychosocial theory	individuality	Individuality
Epistemological concepts	Rationalism	Empiricism
Belief systems	Monotheism	Naturalism
Ethical concepts	Deontological obligation	Consequentialism
Political theory	Classical conservative liberalism	Modern liberalism
Economic theory	Welfare state	Market exchange
Administrative theory	Orthodox administration	New Public Service
	Holographic Governance	*Fragmented Governance*
Ontological assumptions	Dynamic state, transcendent source, singular expression	Dynamic state, immanent source, plural expression
Language characteristics	Gerundial, holistic	Gerundial, discrete
Psychosocial theory	Particular individuality	Singular Individuality
Epistemological concepts	Idealism	Epistemological anarchism
Belief systems	Pantheism	Anti-essentialism
Ethical concepts	Moral imperative	Moral skepticism/relativism
Political theory	Socialism	Individualist anarchism
Economic theory	Collectively planned economy	Self-sufficiency and barter
Administrative theory	New Public Administration	New Public Management

ethical moral imperative; both Truth and Right can be found through careful introspection. Representation is possible because individuals are interchangeable expressions of the whole. This worldview lends itself to the ideal of socialism and its collectively planned economy. Because these empowered citizen planners seek to ensure both social and economic outcomes, it is best aligned with New Public Administration.

Ontological assumptions and associated language

In Holographic Governance, the source of being is transcendent and expresses itself through what are perceived as many immanent beings and things but are in reality only components of the singular whole. As shown in Figure 7.1, the transcendent source of existence (One) contains all that could become, contains all that is becoming (one), and is within all that exists (One). This Absolute encompasses all that is, permeates all that is, and yet transcends all that is. With an ontological unity of both divine and mundane elements in the universe, there is no actual differentiation among apparently individual parts, similar to the Hindu understanding of *Brahman* or the Buddhist understanding of *Tao Te Ching* (Brodd 2003). Furthermore, existence is dynamic in nature, with all of

Figure 7.1 Transcendent source (One) of becoming (one).

90 *Primary governance theories*

creation changing along with the transcendent source. This flux stems from "an infinite, indivisible reality in which the transient data of the world cohere ... the Godhead" (Easwaran 2007, 24).

It is this complete absorption of both all potentiality and all that exists that gives rise to the label "ontology of abundance" in contemporary philosophy and political theory (Tønder and Thomassen 2005a). While theories included under this banner are by no means homogeneous and many pertain to aspects of Integrative Governance, some describe a totalizing substantive universalism in which the individual loses all distinction, identity, and autonomy. For example, some theorists draw from Hegel's (1977) unity of Identity, which is inclusive of all, eliminating all difference (Widder 2005). In this view, the core of each being is completely filled with the Absolute.

The seventeenth-century philosopher, Leibniz (1991), described the universal One, or the Pythagorean monad, as an absolute, all-knowing God that created the best universe out of infinite possibilities. This entire universe, including past, present, and future, can be seen in the essence of any individual substance within that universe, if only by God. As the American Transcendentalist poet, William Blake (2008) puts it, if we could see the world as God does, we would see the world in a grain of sand. Taking away Liebniz's assumption that all beings and things are also monads, each substance is an image of God. If people were able to apprehend the nature of existence,

> We would understand that our own being, like all other discrete beings, is simply an aspect of a single reality (the ultimately formless Godhead). We would see that we are all facets of one diamond, *different reflections of one Source.*
>
> (Bourne 2008, 136, emphasis added)

It is from this type of explanation that we draw the label Holographic Governance. In a hologram, the whole image can be constructed from any part of the recording medium. This metaphor is used in quantum physics to describe the principle of holism (Bohm 1980). More specifically, string theory suggests that the entire universe can be explained by the information inscribed on the surface of its boundary (Susskind 1995). Because the whole is reflected in each part, the parts are interchangeable and not particularly important as discrete entities.

This holism is particularly evident in Hinduism's advaitavāda (non-dualist interpretation). Deutsch (1969) notes that "the central concern of the Advaita Vedānta is to establish the oneness of Reality" (47). This oneness is manifest as Brahman,[1] the transcendent and immanent reality of the one godhead or supreme cosmic spirit. Brahman is "the ultimate reality. It is ubiquitous, formless, and essentially indescribable" (Watanabe 2009, 100)—the infinite, absolute, ultimate essence of material phenomenon. The non-dualism uniting all of creation within the godhead further asserts that all seeming binaries (e.g., being and non-being, life and death, good and evil) "are viewed as manifestations of the Absolute which is immanent in the universe and yet transcends it" (Sharma

1996, 1–2). In short, God is the universe and everything within it, but is not bound by its physical laws or linear time (Griffin 2007).

This form of mysticism denies the experience of separation in physical reality and views time as an illusion. This is not a claim that there is no physical world, but that when we see the world as somehow outside ourselves, we are falling prey to an optical illusion—we see only the diversity of the superficial physical world and miss the underlying unity of reality below the surface (Easwaran 2007). If we see with our minds rather than our senses, we see that "Brahman is real, the world is a dream" (Siddheswarananda 1998, 49). In Hindu mysticism this "cosmic illusion" (Yogananda 1993, 47), or *maya*, is a "veil" that hides reality (137). It is *maya* that "creates a sense of differentiation in us" and creates in us an attachment to the physical world rather than a recognition of our oneness with Brahman (Pandit 2005, 158).

The holistic nature of spirit and matter is found in other forms of Eastern mysticism as well. While there are several characteristics within its symbolism that better fit Integrative Governance, the symbol *T'ai-chi T'u* or the *Diagram of the Supreme Ultimate* places generic opposites within a whole (see Figure 7.2). The combined concepts of *yin* and *yang* represent all expressions of becoming, such as receptive/active, dark/light, matter/energy, body/spirit, yielding/firm, female/male, intuition/reason, and so forth. Rather than being understood as separate and hierarchical, unity "reconciles all opposites, and fulfills all man's highest intuitions of reality" (Underhill 1920, 21).

This symbol also illustrates the ontological dynamism perceived in the Holographic perspective. *Yin* and *yang* are in a dynamic state of rotational symmetry, representing the ceaseless motion of cyclic patterns of coming and going, expanding and contracting; this movement is represented by the curved line separating *yin* and *yang*. The paired concepts are engaged in a constant process

Figure 7.2 *T'ai-chi T'u* symbol (*yin/yang*).

92 *Primary governance theories*

of transformation, in which balance and harmony within the whole are sought (Capra 1999).

Noting the expanding influence of Eastern mysticism in the West, psychologist Edmund Bourne (2008) provides a summary of dominant themes in what he describes as a "new worldview" (2) that shares some ideals with Integrative Governance. The primary differentiating feature pertinent to Holographic Governance, however, is the assumption of transcendence, which retains the notion of a source of existence beyond materiality that is somehow distinct while also being the ultimate manifestation of all that exists. Thus, while existence is multi-dimensional, its dimensions are wholly connected via consciousness; "Though we appear to exist in separate bodies, our minds, at the deepest level, are joined in a collective consciousness. At the level of our deepest soul, we are all one" (Bourne 2008, 2).

The metaphors used to describe this ontological status are organic as opposed to mechanistic, holistic and systemic as opposed to distinctly functionalist. The part may play a changing role within the whole rather than being dedicated to one specific position. This is expressed well by the contemporary understanding of the pluripotentiality of cells within living organisms, in which individual cells contain the potential to become any type of cell or tissue within the body (Sidhu *et al.* 2012). Beneath their apparent roles within the system, the differentiated parts are all the same.

Psychosocial theory

Carrying these ontological assumptions into considerations of human beings, Holographic Governance assumes a Particular individuality that is universal within the whole. Within this perspective each individual is fundamentally the same and apparent difference is merely an illusion (Yogananda 1993). This concept can be found in Hegel's (1977) unity of identity that is inclusive of all, eliminating all difference (Widder 2005). In this view, the core of each being is completely filled with the Absolute: "*first*, as belonging to the unity whose *existence is still only implicit*, they are not let go by it but are rather borne by it as their substrate and are filled by it alone" (Hegel 2010, 334, section 21.382). This "allows the principle of subjectivity to attain fulfillment in the *self-sufficient extreme* of personal particularity, while at the same time *bringing it back to substantial unity* and so preserving this unity in the principle of subjectivity itself" (Hegel 1991, 282). Critiques of ontologies of abundance target this understanding of particularity because there is no room for differentiated identities (Tønder and Thomassen 2005b).

As shown in Figure 7.3, this Particular individuality is strongly embedded in an all-encompassing *social condition* and has a decentered *identity* because ontologically each part is a mirror reflection of the whole; there is no individual self, only a group-self. To understand this expression of individuality, we will explain each psychosocial dimension, including both decentered identity and embedded social condition, and then consider their implications for the social bond.

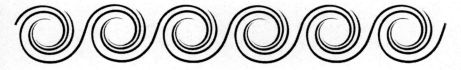

Figure 7.3 Socially embedded Particular individuality.

Particular individuality does not lend itself to any familiar Western notion of individualism, except for what we find in science fiction and fantasy. A good example would be the Borg Collective of *Star Trek* (Frakes 1996) in its original conception, in which there was no queen. Perhaps the closest idea would be the collective *un*conscious devised by psychologist Carl Jung (1969); a sort of genetic repository that organizes personal experiences in a similar way within every human being. In other words, it is an ordering structure of human consciousness common to all. "It consists of pre-existent forms, the archetypes, which can only become conscious secondarily and which give definite form to certain psychic contents" (43). As an inherited trait similar to instinct in all animals, there must be an originating source that precedes the individual, however it is conceived—whether natural (e.g., DNA) or supernatural (e.g., God).

Some Eastern traditions provide a metaphysical explanation for such shared consciousness. For example, "the individual self (atman) is ultimately the same as the single, formless Brahman. But it appears to be different, due to primeval misconstrual" (Paranjpe 1989 quoted in Watanabe 2009, 99). While individuals experience themselves as layers of experience in flux—"senses, emotions, will, intellect, ego" (Easwaran 2007, 25)—these parts do not make a separate whole but are just manifestations of energy within the whole of the universe. Indeed, "the ego-principle, *ahamkara* (I do), is the root cause of dualism or the seeming separation between Man and his Creator. *Ahamkara* brings humans under the way of *maya* (cosmic delusion)" (Yogananda 1993, 47). All beings underneath their seeming differences are one and the same "Self" (Easwaran 2007, 26).

A lack of individual identity lends itself well to the organism metaphor that asserts "each of us is a 'cell' in the collective 'body' of humanity" (Bourne 2008, 255). In communal traditions such as the Akan in Ghana, humans are understood as both embodiments of the divine and inherently social: "When a man descends from heaven, he descends into a human society" (Gyekye 1995, 155). Similarly, the Bantu-speaking peoples of Africa often interpret the concept of *Ubuntu* to mean that the individual is simply part of the whole; "*The community must therefore make, create, or produce the individual* ... whatever happens to the individual happens to the whole group, and whatever happens to the whole group happens to the individual" (Mbiti quoted in Eze 2008, 387).[2] In Western perspectives, this unity is reflected in the ideals of collectivist anarchists who view the collective as part of "a natural order—an organic wholeness that forms the basis of society" (Newman 2005, 37).

94 *Primary governance theories*

These assumptions of unity infer an *innate* social bond that leads to what Douglas (1996) calls the Egalitarian Enclave. This low grid (rules and laws), high group (social identity) ideal-type includes "egalitarians or sectarians who emphasize group solidarity and deplore extensive social differentiation" (Caulkins 1999, 111). These characteristics are what suggest the label of Particular individuality, in which identity is shared with the particular social group inhabited by the individual. Assuming this innate sense of connection, classical radicalism holds that society is a living organism that precedes the individual, and that human beings can only realize their full potential through community (Clark 1998). Yet to be considered moral, society must be constructed in a manner that enables each individual to fully realize their potential as a unique subject.

Epistemological concepts

Due to its dynamic nature, Holographic Governance rejects the possibility of an unchanging Truth, either *a priori* or *a posteriori*. The assumption is that the divine is coterminous with the self and the cosmos; therefore Truth changes along with it. Further, as the material world is merely a manifestation of the divine, the mind–spirit connection is the most direct way to understand "reality." Therefore, intuition, rather than reason or empirical observation, is necessary for knowledge production. Truth is accessed through ongoing introspection: "radical knowledge is given in the radical intuition of the *ātman*" (Siddheswarananda 1998, 49). As Murdoch (1992) explains "we must believe in our duty and ability to discover and make our own the truths which we first intuit or make out as shadows" (434–435). Some attribute the source of this intuition to be the collective unconscious (Jung 1969).

This approach is best reflected in Eastern traditions that are sometimes loosely identified as epistemological idealism, such as Yogācāra, which examines the way consciousness shapes our understanding of the physical world (Lusthaus 2002). Such perspectives hold that the external world "can only be apprehended via its interface with our present mental state" (Shun'ei 2009, 4) and thus reality is always "*transformed by our own consciousness*" (5). In other words, we must recognize that what is experienced is one's own reinterpretation of the physical world. Indeed, some call into question the very notion of physical reality as something separate from ourselves (Lusthaus 2002). By questioning the physical world as an illusion of materialism and the mind as an illusion of rationalism, this approach seeks instead a universal spiritual source of knowledge. However, this does not *necessarily* lead to the conclusion that there is a collective unconscious that unifies all minds.

A similar perspective is found in Western traditions. For instance, although assuming a static source of existence, Plato (1961, 1993) hypothesizes that based on reincarnation, one need only "remember" knowledge from past lives through a process he called *anamnesis*. Socrates argues that the soul is immortal and eternal, and therefore all knowledge is in the soul. While this knowledge is

Holographic Governance 95

forgotten due to the trauma of birth, it can be recalled and understood in the present lifetime (Plato 1961). The manner in which this can be approached is through *katharsis*, an experience through which the illusion of physical existence bound by time and space is stripped away to reveal the Truth of the soul. Once the soul is recognized as the true Form of existence, knowledge is obtained through contemplation, or *noesis* (Plato 1993). *Noesis*, in turn, enables the recollection of *anamnesis*.

Similarly, transcendental idealism holds that space and time are not qualities of things in themselves but are projected from subjective human consciousness (Rohlf 2010). Knowledge of reality is obtained *through* the mind, as opposed to being derived directly from empirical observation.[3] Kant (1998) similarly asserts that the physical world can never be experienced directly, but is always mediated through the mind. His epistemology asserts that objects conform "to the constitution of our faculty of intention" (110). What is perceived by our senses adapts to preconceived categories, requiring the individual to integrate that which is apprehended with that which is known *a priori*. This leads Kant to claim that *a posteriori* knowledge must be suspect due to the impossibility of ever knowing the physical world directly (Rohlf 2010). Saint Augustine similarly distrusts what we learn through the senses and warns that "the mind is also subject to a certain propensity to use the sense of the body ... for the satisfaction of its own inquisitiveness. This futile curiosity masquerades under the name of science and learning" (Augustine 1961, 241).

From these perspectives, the veil of illusion imposed by physical reality must be pierced in order to access the Truth. James describes the process of moving beyond these physical limitations and illusions as making contact with God through introspection; when "the threshold lowers or the valve opens, information ordinarily shut out leaks into the mind of exceptional individuals" (James 1996, 299). In Eastern traditions this is a process commonly referred to as enlightenment. Through *moksha* (enlightenment), we disentangle our consciousness from the illusion of everyday life (Yogananda 1993); "the solid outlines of individuality melt away and the feeling of finiteness no longer oppresses us" (Suzuki 1968, 183–184). In Buddhism enlightenment is referred to as *satori*, or a full comprehension of the situation (Kapleau 2000). The fullness of Truth accessed by an individual will be dependent upon variations in their ability to make the mind–spirit connection, or to access the Absolute. In many Buddhist traditions this variation in intuitiveness, or mindfulness, is reflected in the practice of gurus or masters. When a person is able to simultaneously see the two aspects of reality at all times, a level of enlightenment is attained that enables the choice of staying on the earthly plane and becoming a teacher, or *bodhisattva* (Dalai Lama and Chodron 2014). Such gurus dedicate their lives to helping others develop their own intuitive faculties, thus fostering direct connections to knowledge in all. The ultimate enlightened being is one who becomes the fullness of Absolute consciousness.

Such intuitive introspection may be described as an application of *idiomodific logic*, meaning "to modify one's individuality" (Watanabe 2009, 93). This is

96 *Primary governance theories*

best illustrated in Zen or Yoga meditation techniques, where one not only sees the Truth but also "becomes that truth" (93). It is similar to the spiritual belief "that knowledge of God was the same as knowledge of one's inner self" (Thayer 1981, A-9). Because each knower is connecting to the Absolute source of existence, ongoing introspection allows for the creation of a collective consciousness (Bourne 2008) and therefore a coherent Truth. Once observation of the physical world has been re-witnessed through introspection, one finds that "each experience of empirical truth is an experience of the Real (Brahman) in its totality" (Siddheswarananda 1998, 89).

Belief systems

Holographic Governance is aligned with transcendental belief systems that support various interpretations of an impersonal divine force (Wang 2012), the changing nature of which is revealed through the diversity of creation. There is no personal subject–object relationship with this being because one is simply part of that being. Belief in an impersonal, all-encompassing divinity is described as *pantheism*—all is God—a complete unity of both divine and mundane elements in the universe, the ultimate whole, identical with the cosmos (Mander 2013). Therefore everything within creation is simply an expression of God.

Pantheism is generally found in Eastern religions but one form, *expressivism*, was espoused by the American Transcendentalists (Taylor 1989). Since all beings are parts of the divine whole, every individual has the capacity for revelation through purely individual practices. For example, Quakers hold that each individual has a direct relationship to God and therefore religious institutions are not necessary to facilitate this relationship (Kaufmann 1998). Traditional meetings consist of silent worship or contemplation, during which the individual seeks guidance and revelation from God and shares if moved to do so.

In some Eastern traditions of meditation, devotees seek to transcend the illusions of the physical world through various forms of introspective practice. This is a daily ritual in which practitioners seek a state in which "consciousness is so acutely focused that it is utterly withdrawn from the body and the mind, it enters a kind of singularity in which the sense of a separate ego disappears" (Easwaran 2007, 26). When this occurs, meditation is a means to achieve the state of *turiya*, passing into a higher state of being or unity. As Krishna asserts in the *Bagavad Gita* (2007), when devotees free "themselves from the taint of self-will, with their consciousness unified, they become one with Brahman" (6:27).

Ethical concepts

Because Holographic Governance views the individual (one) as coterminous with the source of existence (One), there is no meaningful distinction between what is right for the individual and what is right for the whole. As believed by American Transcendentalists, all expressions of God should have an aesthetic

appreciation and understanding of one another as the same in some fundamental way (Taylor 1989). A fitting universal ethic would be along the lines of
the maxim of the Golden Rule: *Do unto others as you would have done to yourself.*
In some African traditions, this is articulated "by words like *simunye* ('we are
one,' i.e., 'unity is strength') and slogans like 'an injury to one is an injury to
all'" (Louw quoted in Eze 2008, 390). This translates into a moral imperative
of reciprocity whereby one feels obligated to do what is right for both self and
others. In Eastern traditions this is expressed in the concept of *dharma*, in
which one acts in accordance with the balance and harmony of the universe.
"Thus it means rightness, justice, goodness, purpose rather than chance" (Easwaran 2007, 32). The nature of oneness means that "any disturbance in one
place has to send ripples everywhere … until balance is restored" (32). As such,
introspective reflection on one's dharma, or duty, is of utmost importance to
shape action. This is a *transcendent ethic* in that moral guidance is drawn directly
from shared spiritual or non-rational sources (Huddleston 1981).

Appropriate to idealist epistemology, what is right in any given situation is
identified through introspection. Determining Right considers which action, if
followed by all, will promote the greatest good. In Western philosophy this is
seen in Kant's categorical imperative; "maxims (rules), as dictates of Reason, are
universal, applying to all rational beings in similar situations … such rules are
also of great *generality*" (Murdoch 1992, 34). As situations change, the categorical imperative changes. From this perspective, moral determinations "can
only be consulted in each individual bosom, not blindly accepted on external
authority … an understanding and practice of goodness clarifies the intuitions
of it which arise in the soul" (435). All are capable of accessing the "absolute at
the centre of human existence" (439) to obtain an understanding of what is
right.

Political theory

Following from the holistic philosophical elements of Holographic Governance
and its expression in an ethic of moral imperative, a political theory of socialism
logically follows. While it is difficult to sever political economy in this perspective,
we will endeavor to do so for comparative purposes. Political theories of socialism can be found in the writings of Jean Jacques Rousseau (1712–1778), Georg
Wilhelm Friedrich Hegel (1770–1831), Friedrich Engels (1820–1895), and Karl
Marx (1818–1883) (Clark 1998). At first, these sources may seem like strange
bedfellows for the philosophical sources drawn upon thus far. However, considering his studies of Eastern philosophy, Hegel draws holistic beliefs into Western
philosophy, albeit with a more humanistic interpretation.

Rousseau's challenges to self-interest and individualism were extended by
Hegel and, subsequently, by Engels and Marx. Hegel (1977) believed that
people can only understand themselves within social relationships; therefore,
identity can only be formed within the context of community. Rationality and
action are not based on individual choice, but are rather embedded within

98 *Primary governance theories*

family, civil society, and governance (Hegel 2000). He believed this social process occurs on a historically deterministic path, leading inexorably toward a predetermined utopian endpoint of communism.

Engels and Marx extended Hegelian ideas of the socialist utopia. For Engels and Marx, the socialist utopia offers a state in which self-actualization, family and social relationships, politics, religion, and ideas would flourish (Engels 2000, 175). These classical socialists believed in "the vital concrete possibility for every human being to bring to full development all the powers, capacities, and talents with which nature has endowed him, and turn them to social account" (Rocker 2004, 16). A truly communist political economy would restore the joy of labor and its benefits to families, reinstating social relations based on the whole person. Thus, socialism seeks to eliminate all sources of human oppression that prevent these relations, such as privilege and inordinate wealth. These thinkers see capitalism as the modern source of authority and domination that had traditionally been held by the church and the state in various forms of aristocratic rule. They argue such domination is unacceptable from any source, be it government, religion, or market.

Socialist ideas are echoed in the *collectivist* school of classical anarchist thought exemplified in the work of Proudhon (1809–1865), Bakunin (1814–1876), Kropotkin (1842–1921), and Malatesta (1853–1932) (Clark 1998). This form of anarchism both rejects authority rooted in tradition (e.g., church, state, caste, class) and promulgates a view of social connection that is disentangled from the state (Goodwin 2007) but reflects a "notion of indivisible unity" (Proudhon 1979, chapter X). There is an emphasis on absolute equality and eradication of difference through efforts to "abolish class distinctions, and to equalize the powerful and the powerless, the rich and poor, master and slave" (Newman 2005, 33). As Proudhon (1979b) notes, this project to promote homogeneity required rejection of anything "that may divide their will, break up their mass, create diversity, plurality, divergence within themselves" (chapter X). This leads to an understanding of liberty as a value that can only be found through the group: "The unlimited liberty of each through the liberty of all, liberty through solidarity, liberty in equality" (Bakunin 1972a, 45). Similarly, "I am free only when all men are my equals (first and foremost economically)" (Bakunin 1972b 20).

These principles are reflected in the socialist ideal, as manifest in both large-scale communist nation-states and small-scale intentional communities, or "'communes'" (Bookchin 2002, 10). On the national scale, the state is depicted as a uniform body politic. "They call themselves the People, the Nation, the Multitude, the Mass; they are the true Sovereign, the Legislator, the Power, the Ruler, the Country, the State" (Proudhon 1979, chapter X). The nation-state is then further broken into localized assemblies, *soviets*, or councils that are coordinated within the whole. For instance, Lenin (2002b) describes governing assemblies of the workers, insisting that "the Soviets of Workers' Deputies are the *only possible* form of revolutionary government" (58). Similarly, in his "Report on an investigation of the peasant movement in Hunan" Mao

Tse-Tung (1965b) describes the centrality and power of the local peasant association that "actually dictates all rural affairs, and, quite literally, 'whatever it says, goes'" (25).

Shifting this local focus to communes, critical-utopian socialists "dream of experimental realisation of their social Utopias, of founding isolated 'phalansteres,' of establishing 'Home Colonies,' or setting up a 'Little Icaria'—duodecimo editions of the New Jerusalem" (Marx and Engels 1998, chapter 3). There has been a tradition of communal living in the United States tracing back to at least 1735; these communities "aspired to establish an ideal society" (Oved 1988, 4). Such attempts at utopia through the equalization of all members was evidenced in communities such as Ephrata, established in the 1730s, in which "every newcomer had to hand over his property and to accept the collective way of life in production as well as consumption" (20).

While the focus is on unity and equality through homogenization, following from the philosophical principles above, this political theory has a place for leaders who serve as beneficent liberators and teachers. Such leaders may be depicted as "masters" in a secular sense—those who are more practiced in the art of introspection and therefore more in tune with the Absolute, even where it is stripped of religious undertones. Thus, the polis is *led*, but the basis for leadership is wholly different from Hierarchical Governance because leaders are ostensibly interchangeable within an egalitarian whole. Ideally, anyone could emerge as a leader by awakening from a false consciousness. Yet due to the unity of the whole, the structure of this authority is strong; it is unquestionable as it is rooted firmly in an absolute Truth.

When considered on a societal scale, the role of political leaders becomes one of awakening the masses from false consciousness and urging them toward political revolution. Those who have perfected their intuition are best able to articulate what is in the interest of the collective. These enlightened individuals become the leaders within Holographic Governance, asserting a form of positive liberty (Berlin 2013). These determinations override any conflicting individual interests because such conflicts are understood as a deviation from the metaphysical Truth and are therefore symptomatic of false consciousness.

An example of this sort of leadership can be found in Lenin's call to the Soviets of Workers' and Soldiers' Deputies to act as the "vanguard of the revolution, the vanguard of the people, which is capable of carrying the masses with it" (Lenin 2002a, 120). Similarly, Mao Tse-Tung (1965b) argues that there is a need "to lead the peasants to put their greatest efforts into the political struggle" (46). However, once individuals are freed from false consciousness and the revolution is successful, the state must be transformed into "the actuality of the ethical Idea ... the actuality of the substantial *will*, an actuality which it possesses in the particular *self-consciousness* when this has been raised to its universality" wherein "the *highest duty*" of citizens is as "members of the state" (Hegel 1991, 275). Thus, in Holographic Governance, citizens have a duty to recognize their unity within the whole and align with it through introspection and action.

100 *Primary governance theories*

Regardless of the actual events of the Russian Revolution, this ideal does not necessarily lead to centralized control of the citizens. For example, the South Korean program of Saemaul Undong, which began in the late 1960s, used central government experts to train rural villagers in community development, but then funded and empowered them to develop their own leadership, work teams, and projects (Korea Saumaul Undong Center 2014).[4] Furthermore, this does not mean a static unity. Grounded in a dynamic state ontology, the Party may change its policies and positions over time in response to an evolving context. For example, the 18th Central Committee of the Communist Party of China (the National Congress) recently adopted an official stance that the nation would pursue an ecological civilization, a concept that has been emerging in China since its first appearance in a report to the 17th National People's Congress. This concept demands that all citizens align themselves with this new shared purpose through "ecological reforms ... to reconcile contradictions between economic development and the environment." In April, 2015 the plan was restated, with the release of a document outlining "the acceleration of moves to establish an ecological civilization" (Zhang 2015).

Economic theory

While supportive of socialist political theory, Bakunin (1972b) argues that "political Freedom without economic equality is a pretense, a fraud, a lie" (21). According to Marx and Engels (1998), the central aim of socialist thought is to transform material or economic life. In a nutshell, the production process in a society exerts a profound influence on all other aspects of life, including self-actualization, family and social relationships, politics, religion, and ideas. Socialism abhors capitalism as an economic system and argues private ownership of property in the form of land and the means of production reinforces attachment to the material world and self-interest; socialist arrangements reflect a "suspicious attitude toward individual wealth" and practice "elements of communal sharing" (Blasi 2009, 23). Thus, capitalism prevents the socialist utopia from emerging (Engels 2000) and an alternative economic system must be forged.

Specifically, capitalism and private ownership produce a division of society into classes of owners and laborers. Socialists recognize that political equality is not possible "so long as people are separated into classes on the basis of their owning or not owning property, classes whose mere existence excludes in advance any thought of a genuine community" (Rocker 2004, 9). To eliminate class differences, the idealized economy would be comprised solely of laborers who individually own nothing more than the fruits of their own labor. Everything else would be held in common for the benefit of all, "to assure abundance to everyone" (10).

It is this socialist goal of transforming property and production into "a means to insure to man his material subsistence and to make accessible to him the blessings of a higher intellectual culture" (Rocker 2004, 2) that leads to the claim that private property constitutes theft from the group (Kropotkin 1992,

Holographic Governance 101

Proudhon 2007). Land and the means of production must belong to the public collectively. By putting land and the other means of production into common trust, government would be transformed into an egalitarian and participatory administrative organization charged with providing for the public good, using the rents from land and the means of production as its sole source of revenue (George 1929). Abilities should be applied and contributions should be made; however, everyone should have what they need regardless of production contribution. The role of government is to create these conditions and to facilitate collective action. Such equality will create greater efficiency through less waste of talent, social order without repression, and enhanced human rights and quality of life.

Egalitarian economic systems are therefore rooted in a form of mutualism in which individuals work together in a collective effort to provide for all (McKay 2011); the political economy must be equal in terms of opportunity, process, and results. As Bakunin (1972a) argues, economic equality

> must realize itself through the free organization of labor and the voluntary cooperative ownership of the means of production, through the combination of the productive workers into freely organized communes, and the free federation of the communes. There must be no controlling intervention of the state.
>
> (45–46)

Syndicalism is one method of achieving mutualism organized by workers in relationship with one another in production or trade (McKay 2008). It removes both hierarchy and competition, replacing it with an economic system of cooperation in which all individuals are on equal social and economic footing, participating in collective coordination of economic production. This mutualism can be seen in Bakunin's (1972b) call for The Council of Action, an "economic, political, and social organization" (24) that "federates from below and wills from a thousand quarters" (23) through the equal participation of all workers in a coordinated process of decision making.

In Holographic Governance the economy would be collectively planned in the sense of public decisions being made by the community. Regulation is therefore external to the producer (although the producer participates in both politics and administration) and strong because the means of production (including land) are owned by the community. However, asserting collective ownership over property and collectively planning the economy does not mean that Holographic Governance supports centrally planned economies such as those found in totalitarian regimes. Such central planning would require a hierarchical social structure that is explicitly rejected as a hindrance to the fulfillment of individual potential (Proudhon 2007). As Mao Tse-Tung (1965b) argues, "The peasants really need co-operatives, and especially consumers', marketing and credit co-operatives" (54).

Despite restrictions against hierarchy and central planning, there is still a place for leadership by the enlightened within socialism. Due to pervasive

102   *Primary governance theories*

poverty and economic inequality Marx predicted that capitalism would eventually collapse through proletariat revolution and be replaced by communism (Marx 2008). Yet given the strong psychological hold of capitalist ideology, leaders must free individuals from false consciousness (Baradat 2012). Leaders illuminate the intentional construction of class difference and the myth of upward class mobility (Marcuse 1964), both of which prevent social unity. Here the parallels to Platonic *noesis* or the Hindu awakening from *maya* are notable. In each tradition, material dependence is laced with the idea of being enslaved by the mundane aspects of life and thwarted from self-actualization.

Leadership also plays an educative role until all are capable of collective governance. For instance, Mao Tse-Tung (1965b) emphasizes the need for "proper guidance" (55) to allow the movement to spread: "We must actively lead peasants in solving such difficult and essential problems in production as labour power, draught oxen, fertilizer, seed and irrigation" (Mao 1965a, 142).

Administrative theory

Given the idealistic commitment to equitable distribution—"From each according to his ability, to each according to his need" (Marx 2008, 27)—Holographic Governance aligns most closely with New Public Administration (NPA) (Frederickson 1971, 1997). It is important to note, however, that it is difficult to identify a school of Anglo-American administrative theory that aligns with the Holographic ideal-type. Because administrative theory is practice-oriented it necessarily responds to existing conditions within contemporary society. While NPA shares philosophical ideals with Holographic Governance, it is more appropriately identified as Neoconservative—a hybrid position that is explained in Chapter 11.

NPA is a reformulation of the more normative, as opposed to instrumental, aspects of Orthodox Administration because of its emphasis of substantive values. Many of its principles are rejections of the technical approach to legitimacy and its prioritization of efficiency and effectiveness at the expense of other values such as ethics and equity (Denhardt 2000). A similar approach to substantive values is offered by the public administration scholars involved in the "refounding" movement (Wamsley *et al.* 1990, Wamsley and Wolf 1996). For these scholars "the purpose of government is to extend the protection of regime values to all citizens" (Frederickson 1997, 47). The art of governance is therefore the virtuous pursuit of the public interest (Caldwell 1988). In short, skilled bureaucrats should form an "aristocracy of talent" (Waldo 1984, 96) to ensure the Good Life is attained by all.

Of particular interest to this group of scholars is the notion of *equity* (Frederickson 1997, Hart 1974). Equity embodies constitutional values of equality and fairness, but also gives form to the ambiguous notion of the public good. Much argument is made in political theory about what constitutes equity, particularly whether it is an issue of fair opportunity (Nozick 2000) or fair outcomes (Rawls 2000). The NPA focus on equitable social and economic outcomes and the

Holographic Governance 103

administrator's responsibility to help produce this social good is aligned with the latter perspective. Toward this end, Frederickson (1971) offers a quite detailed argument;

> Embracing equity as the third normative pillar of public administration requires public servants to seek out and work toward more just allocations of public goods and services, to represent those who do not otherwise have access to public policy processes, to seek the public interest or greater good, and to respect the dignity of individuals (public employees as well as other citizens) and tirelessly safeguard their rights.
>
> (113)

As hinted by this quotation, "ethics" captures the notion of substantive values that are not easily translated into quantifiable factors but which may be reflected upon through careful introspection. This claim is fitting to epistemological and ethical concepts in Holographic Governance.

Because of obvious contradictions with a free-market economy, a commitment to achieving social equity requires a strong administrative government that is not unduly influenced by interest group demands. It is the strength of collective authority that aligns this school of thought with Holographic Governance. However, it must be noted that NPA empowers administrators with positional authority that does not fit this approach. Nonetheless, imagining this role as a function that coordinates how the revenues from land and other means of production are utilized for the common good of the community is not a giant leap. These theories make normative arguments for a wise and beneficent administration to countervail potentially corrupt political and economic forces (Adams *et al.* 1990, Box 2008, Dolbeare and Hubbell 1996, King *et al.* 1998). Indeed, this "discretionist" role has been likened to the Platonic Guardian Class (Fox and Cochran 1990).

Continuing with analogous comparison, NPA trusts in the ability of administrators—or Men of Reason—to use wisdom based on experience and intuition to make discretionary decisions (McSwite 1997). There is a sense in which problems are understood as part of the greater whole, without separation of problems and solutions, past and present (Flyvbjerg 2001)—these are all part of the ongoing process of experience and reflection. Because "experience cannot necessarily be verbalized, intellectualized, and made into rules" (19), experts are those who are best able to understand the situation through introspection.

Because intuitive and experiential wisdom is such a key element of NPA, it advocates for high levels of discretion decentralized throughout the administrative state. However, as with other elements of Holographic Governance, not all members of society are equally capable of determining the public good for administrative purposes. In fact, writing with Ralph Chandler, Frederickson suggests that we must "stop denigrating the role of authority; doing so only debilitates the process of governance. All mature societies have secular 'priesthoods' in which institutional wisdom is preserved" (Frederickson 1997, 222). Therefore,

104 *Primary governance theories*

administrators are expected to represent the People, interpret law, and act as virtuous citizens on their behalf, taking on responsibility for upholding "regime values" (Rohr 1986, 1989, 1990). These expectations can be found in studies of street-level bureaucrats (Lipsky 1983, Maynard-Moody and Musheno 2003).

A quick tour through the literature provides eloquent claims to such legitimacy. Public administrators are "protectors of our Republic and democratic way of life. They are *administrative conservators*, a distinction and vocation worthy of honor and respect" (Terry 1995, 183). The terms *virtucrat* and *discretionist* are also used to indicate responsibility for upholding ethical standards and values. As *trustees*, they are "competent to define the public interest on their own authority" (Frederickson 1997, 210) and can safely act as "an effective and ethical agent in carrying out the republic's business" (Kass 1990, 113). And, if the term *entrepreneur* is widened and liberated from financial meanings (Bellone and Goerl 1993), it can include all types of skillful and "vigorous responsible leadership" (Kobrak 1996, 213), becoming linked with modifiers like *public*, *policy*, *social*, and *civic* (Drayton 2002, Hart 1984, Henton *et al.* 1997, Kingdon 2003, Lewis 1980, Waddock and Post 1991).

From this perspective, public administrators have "a greater responsibility to understand the nature of our society, democracy, and government than do most citizens" (Box 2004, 4). The special role and strong authority given to enlightened public servants is reflected in NPA as "an alignment with good, or possibly God" (Frederickson 1971, 329). Public administration "plans, it contrives, it philosophizes, it educates, it builds for the community as a whole" (Dimock 1936, 133). In sum, public administration is central to Holographic Governance in maintaining the idealist moral imperatives of socialism as well as administering the collectively planned economy.

Summary and illustration

Holographic Governance assumes a transcendent, dynamic Absolute source of existence that encompasses and permeates all of creation. There is no meaningful distinction among individuals and knowledge of the changing Truth can be accessed by all through introspection. These assumptions lead to pantheistic belief systems or ideologies that focus on increasing understanding of Truth. Spiritual practices such as contemplation and meditation are devised to increase one's ability to do so. Due to the complete connection among all, there is no difference between what is Right and Good for the individual versus the whole. A moral imperative is felt by each person to do what is right in each situation. Representation is possible because individuals are equal. These qualities lead to a socialist political economy. Members of the community or society are expected to participate in political decision making and administrating economic activity for the public good.

This Holographic Governance approach fosters public encounters (Bartels 2013) in which government officials use their better judgment through discretion (Friedrich 1940), acting as "helpers" (Kanter 1972, 191) to other citizens.

Although public officials are committed to values of equality and fostering individual growth, maintenance of the social bond requires careful training or indoctrination (Leviatan 2013) and one must maintain a "mechanical solidarity" that emphasizes similarities and discourages differentiation (Durkheim 1984). Thus, Holographic Governance encounters "remove the repressive control of distant, impersonal institutions" found in Hierarchical Governance encounters and "replace it with the control of the intimate, face-to-face group of peers, which is perhaps a more benign kind of coercion" (Kanter 1972, 231).

Using agricultural policy as an illustration, we would expect to see an understanding of the natural world as holistically ordered, in which human actors accept socially determined roles. Policy would be made by group leaders charged with ensuring the good of the whole. Guided by ideals of right action, production goals would be aimed at maximizing production for fair redistribution to all according to need. Agricultural goods would be collectively owned and produced and distributed through cooperative group mechanisms to ensure these outcomes. Administration would be coordinated by group trustees charged with ensuring fair production expectations and equitable distribution of produce.

The Holographic Governance approach is well illustrated by group farming practices similar to those found in China. Building on traditional mutual aid practices (Wong 1979a), the people's communes program began in earnest in the 1950s after the communist revolution of 1949 and progressed in "four distinct phases: land reform, cooperativization, collectivization, and communization" (Wong 1979b, 90), culminating in the Great Leap Forward in 1958.

The process began with reforms that broke up feudal land and redistributed allotments to the peasants, who were then encouraged to begin the process of cooperativization through the creation of Mutual Aid Teams (MATs). In the next phase, MATs were organized into larger collectives known as Agricultural Producers' Cooperatives (APCs); all members contributed their land and then received earnings from the collective (Wong 1979b). With the initiation of the Great Leap Forward, there was a push to bring all collectives into a nationwide system of communes (Zhong 2003). In this final phase all land became collectively owned and no longer earned dividends for private owners.

Within these people's communes local government functions and economic agricultural policy making were combined into one localized entity (Zhong 2003). An economic system of collectivization of resources was created in which "land, livestock, farming implements, and all other means of production and commonly held assets were transferred to the commune" (Jisheng 2008, 167). Communes were organized into production brigades and production teams to make decisions about production and to collectively cultivate shared land (Wong 1979b), with all leaders selected from local peasant communities rather than appointed state agents (Zhong 2003).[5] These people's communes were thus "the basic planning unit in the agricultural sector" (Wong 1979b, 92).

Local township government was replaced by collective management through various committees within the commune (Zhong 2003) and each commune

106 *Primary governance theories*

existed as a "unified, self-reliant entity" (Wong 1979b, 92). The highly orchestrated process of moving from cooperative to collectives to communes was understood as necessary for providing peasants with political education that built on existing ideals of mutual aid and fostered "a high degree of self-awareness and self-direction on the part of the farmers" (Wong 1979a, xiv). The people's communes were abolished in 1982 and political (but not economic) power was restored to townships (Zhong 2003).

As illustrated here, Holographic Governance decentralizes decision making to local leadership through committee systems entrusted with providing for the good of the whole. Property ownership is communal with all working together toward collectively determined production goals, and distribution of goods determined by need. Through careful political education, all members of society learn to value communal organization and to fulfill their role within the whole.

Notes

1 It is important to separate the central idea of Brahman from the traditional caste system of Hinduism. The bhakti tradition in Hinduism, wherein the traditional caste system is rejected, fits more closely with Holographic Governance at the psychosocial level than the older caste-centric Vedic tradition. However, the belief in Brahman is present in both traditions.
2 Although this is a common interpretation of Ubuntu, Eze (2008) argues for an understanding that better aligns with Integrative Governance.
3 Because transcendental idealism assumes a static universe it is not perfectly aligned with Holographic Governance.
4 Many elements of this program reflect a more Integrative Governance approach.
5 It should be noted, however, that in practice the communes were tightly controlled by the Chinese Communist Party (CCP) (Jisheng 2008, Zhong 2003); thus the ideals of the Holographic approach were never fully achieved.

8   Fragmented Governance

A summary of Fragmented Governance is provided in the lower right quadrant of Table 8.1. In sketch, there is no essential foundation from which any aspect of reality can be understood or described. Singular Individuality is characterized by a disconnection from both a substantive core self and human groups. Identity is continually formed through individual choice in response to experience. This decentered atomism leads to both empirical and ethical relativism—no one's truth or idea of the good can supersede anyone else's. Political representation is

Table 8.1 Governance ideal-types: Fragmented

	Hierarchical Governance	*Atomistic Governance*
Ontological assumptions	Static state, transcendent source, singular expression	Static state, immanent source, plural expression
Language characteristics	Discrete, hierarchical	Discrete, nonhierarchical
Psychosocial theory	individuality	Individuality
Epistemological concepts	Rationalism	Empiricism
Belief systems	Monotheism	Naturalism
Ethical concepts	Deontological obligation	Consequentialism
Political theory	Classical conservative liberalism	Modern liberalism
Economic theory	Welfare state	Market exchange
Administrative theory	Orthodox administration	New Public Service
	Holographic Governance	***Fragmented Governance***
Ontological assumptions	Dynamic state, transcendent source, singular expression	Dynamic state, immanent source, plural expression
Language characteristics	Gerundial, holistic	Gerundial, discrete
Psychosocial theory	Particular individuality	Singular Individuality
Epistemological concepts	Idealism	Epistemological anarchism
Belief systems	Pantheism	Anti-essentialism
Ethical concepts	Moral imperative	Moral skepticism/relativism
Political theory	Socialism	Individualist anarchism
Economic theory	Collectively planned economy	Self-sufficiency and barter
Administrative theory	New Public Administration	New Public Management

108 *Primary governance theories*

not possible because identity is ever-changing and there is no legitimate basis for authority over any individual. Therefore, individualist or libertarian anarchism emerges as the only viable political form—governance by none. Individuals must be free to pursue their own self-sufficiency or engage in trade with others without government interference. The administrative theory most aligned with this type is New Public Management, given its promotion of privatization of previously public functions and deregulation of all types of private action.

Ontological concepts and associated language

The Fragmented Governance worldview can be described as *postmodern* in nature. Postmodernity refers to "two interconnected dimensions: (1) as a new historical period or different social formation and (2) as a specific body of philosophical critique and theory that calls into question basic assumptions regarding modernity, reason, and the Enlightenment" (Catlaw and Stout 2007, 1524). As a social formation, the availability of global communications paired with the cultural diversity encountered leads Bohm to note that "the pervasiveness of fragmentation" is a key characteristic of contemporary life (Nichol 2004, xx). As a philosophical perspective, anti-essentialism makes it difficult to find *affirmations* of the Fragmented Governance perspective, as much of the literature stands in critique of the postmodern condition—which we reserve for discussion in Part III. Yet a refusal of all external attempts to represent or control the individual form the affirmational core of the Fragmented Governance perspective.

The postmodern perspective challenges virtually all social, political, economic, and cultural institutions, particularly those based on domination through power obtained through both hierarchy and competition. These multiple resistances allow many previously excluded groups, discourses, and ideas to force their way into mainstream society. This refusal to accept imposed subject positions is championed by some skeptical postmodern philosophers (Rosenau 1992) and "cultural pessimists" (Simons 2005, 155) who deny any type of ontological stability. For these theorists, the Many is described as a multitude of singularities in a dynamic state of cause and effect with neither a fixed external reality nor stable internal reality to which we can have direct access. In other words, they are skeptical of the assertion of reality as objective, static fact. They are also skeptical of our ability to access an authentic self that is not mediated by social influences. Observations that might seem true are nothing more than subjective experiences of socially constructed facts (Berger and Luckmann 1966).

This post-structuralist perspective is grounded in an affirmation of the negative. The ontological terrain is described by philosophers such as Jean-Paul Sartre, Jacques Lacan, Slavoj Žižek, Alain Badiou, Ernesto Laclau, and Chantal Mouffe as a void, or nothing, at the core of existence around which a symbolic order is built. This "ontology of lack" (Tønder and Thomassen 2005a) assumes that there is something in the individual that escapes social construction, but that it is largely unknowable: "The crack in the symbolic network itself" is always just out of reach (Žižek 2007, 215). Thus, this ontology is implied by

Fragmented Governance 109

psychosocial theory, as opposed to preceding and thereby generating psychosocial assumptions. An ontology of lack is focused not on being-*qua*-being but rather on being-*qua*-understanding (Marchart 2005).

This is a decidedly Lacanian interpretation of being. Lacan (1977) categorizes different ontological domains, blending ontology with psychoanalytical theory. His psychoanalytic theory is composed of three "registers": the *real*, the *symbolic*, and the *imaginary*. How these registers exist in relation to one another determines the dominant societal discourse (Master, University, Hysteric, or Analyst). The *real* is what exists prior to or outside language; it is an undelimited source of potentiality, "a sort of unrent, undifferentiated fabric woven in such a way as to be full everywhere" (Fink 1995, 24). However, Lacan argues the futility of ontological speculation based on his understanding of the real as something that "cannot be comprehended in a way that would make an All out of it" (Lacan as quoted in Žižek 2007, 210). The real lies beyond the reach of first-person access and is therefore incomprehensible. Instead, because we can never exist outside of language, the *symbolic* "creates 'reality'" and it is through the symbolic that meaning and categorization, or the *imaginary*, is fabricated (Fink 1995, 25). Stavrakakis (2005) argues that when the real encounters the symbolic/imaginary, the ontological domain destabilizes the ontic in infinite multiplicity, opening up a political moment in which singularities can assert their differences.

Based on these descriptions, we *can* derive some basic characteristics of the real. First, the existence of a metaphysical source cannot be known, so immanence may be assumed. Second, entities must be plural in expression (Many) because difference is experienced, even if mediated through the symbolic/imaginary. There is no defensible reason to assume some form of social connection or foundational One. Finally, existence must be dynamic, because identities are in a constant state of flux.

As an example, although Deleuze and Guattari's (1987) full body of thought is more aligned with Integrative Governance, their concept of singularity helps explain the understanding of plural expression found in Fragmented Governance. While entities are immanent (Many), there is no substantive source of becoming (O/one). Instead, as shown in Figure 8.1, a constitutive lack remains elusive while the boundaries of each entity are porous and constantly changing through the process of assemblage (verb). In this process of becoming, each entity is vulnerable to externally imposed incursions, through which the singularity changes in both character and nature as a singular assemblage (noun).

Due to this ontological permeability, resistance to social construction through language becomes a central issue of focus from this perspective. It is from the postmodern critique itself that we have come to understand the power of language to construct what we accept as real. Language structuration is explored in depth, particularly by the European (continental) philosophers. As noted in Chapter 3, because of its capacity to structure consciousness, language deeply shapes our sense of self, others, and the world around us, thereby channeling our behavior and action. For example, Heidegger (1998) asserts, "Language is the

110 *Primary governance theories*

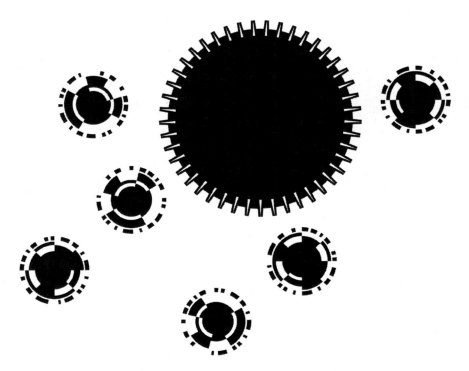

Figure 8.1 Many immanent sources of becoming (O/one).

house of being, which is propriated by being and pervaded by being" (254). This structuralist perspective suggests that language organizes (structures) our thoughts and actions at a deep and fundamental level (Saussure 1960).

In contrast, for Lacan, "there is no such thing as a metalanguage or metadiscourse that would somehow escape the limitations of the discourses ... for one is always operating within a particular discourse" (Fink 1998, 44). The real is always mediated through the symbolic into categorizations within the imaginary. As noted in the discussion of Atomistic Governance, we can understand these processes through semiotics, which is a technique for analyzing language through binaries that create meaning (Leach 1974). Again, the concept *white* can only be understood in relation to *black*. Carrying these ideas forward, Gadamer (2004) suggests ontology itself is hermeneutic in nature, whereby the world is linguistically constituted through ongoing discourse, substantive understanding, and agreements among people.

Post-structuralism extends these concepts in several directions. For our purpose, Derrida (1976) suggests that not only are meanings binary and mutually referential, they are merely representations or signifiers of the actual whose meanings can never be fixed; as our conceptualization of *white* shifts, so does our understanding of *black*. Further, language is always an abstraction formed

Fragmented Governance 111

between the signifier (symbol) and the signified (referent). In other words, language cannot provide a one-to-one representation of reality—it cannot reflect what *is*. As Harvey (1990) explains this linguistic disorder:

> When the signifying chain [within language] snaps, then "we have schizophrenia in the form of a rubble of distinct and unrelated signifiers" ... the effect of such a breakdown in the signifying chain is to reduce experience to "a series of pure and unrelated presents in time."
>
> (53)

Thus, language itself is a fundamental barrier to an experience of reality ontologically, psychologically, and epistemologically; the real always resists signification (Lacan 1977). As Lakoff (1987) notes, the more rigorous rational abstraction becomes, the more inflexible and detached it is from the actual.

Psychosocial theory

The emphasis on the social construction of reality via language has profound implications for psychosocial theory. The subject of Fragmented Governance is an entity without any externally imposed positive identity, one that constructs identity through processes of identification within the structure of society (Norval 2005). Thus, freedom is interpreted as the ability to negate or disengage from the realm of causal and determinate being, where this lack-of-being is the source of desire and is therefore generative (Marchart 2005) or constitutive (Thomassen 2005). "By inscribing a *lack* in our dislocated positivities, it fuels the *desire* for new social and political constructions and identifications" (Stavrakakis 2005, 186). As the point of autonomy, then, this "lack is precisely the *locus* of the subject" (Laclau 1990, 210); it is the gap between the ontological self and the ontic self. To understand this expression of the individual, we will explain each psychosocial dimension—decentered identity and independent social condition—and then consider their implications for the social bond.

From a post-structural psychoanalytical perspective, the ontological self is described as radical difference (Tønder and Thomassen 2005a) or an ineradicable excess that escapes societal signification (Norval 2005). *Identity* is a subject position formed within the symbolic order that prevents a subject's radical difference from being freely expressed. Without access to an internal, authentic self and without direct access to the empirical world unmediated by language, individual identity is permeable and decentered through the multiple narratives that each individual experiences (Deleuze and Guattari 1983). In other words, "self is only a 'position in language,' a mere 'effect of discourse'" (Rosenau 1992, 43), but because of the fluidity of language there is no one-to-one correlation between the sign (language) and the signified (self). Psychosocially, what is deconstructed in the contestations of identity politics is the ideograph (Miller 2004), which can be understood as a fabricated static, cohesive identity. Should one succeed in stripping away the metanarratives and language games that craft these identities, the Fragmented Governance perspective holds that no authentic self can be discovered (McSwite 2006).

Following post-Marxism, dynamic identity is formed through an ongoing refusal of societally imposed subject positions (Foucault 1980) and the counter-hegemony of the subject against society (Laclau and Mouffe 1985). The "social subject itself seems to dissolve in this dissemination of language games" (Lyotard 1984, 40). Ramos (1981) describes this postmodern identity as a "fluid" self (50). Stirner (1995) describes it as the "un-man" (125)—that which escapes signification and serves as a "non-essentialist position of resistance to ideology" (Newman 2005, 81).

As shown in Figure 8.2, the broken and misaligned fabric signifies a multifaceted identity that is constantly being made and remade in response to the social context. The differentiated subject exists in an ongoing struggle of resistance against the world's order; Singular Individuality attempts to close off the external impositions in order to gain autonomous control over identity.

Yet for many philosophers of ontological lack, this "resistance is fertile." Playing on the *Star Trek* Borg Collective motto, these theorists transform the pessimistic view of social construction into an affirmation of autonomy (see *New Internationalist* 2004). As individualist anarchist Max Stirner (1995) argues, "I am not nothing in the case of emptiness, but I am the creative nothing [*schöpferische Nichts*], the nothing out of which I myself as creator create everything" (7). While the postmodern context strips subjects of stable

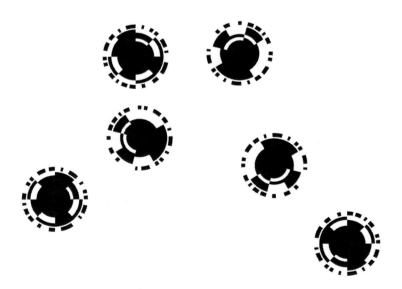

Figure 8.2 Socially independent Singular Individuality.

symbolic identities, it instead "offers them imaginary identities—ways to imagine themselves enjoying. These identities shift and change, taking on different meanings and attributes in different contexts" (Dean 2006, 99). Similarly, Deleuze and Guattari (1983) argue that decentered subjects act as "desiring machines" as opposed to rational beings. For such individuals, desire is a motivating force, the fuel for all potential action. Inverting traditional psychological theory, it is not *need* that creates *desire* but desire itself that then identifies a corresponding lack in need of fulfillment. Singular Individuality is thus a pastiche of shifting identities that are adopted and discarded in an ongoing process of choice.

Lacan describes this internal, independent psychosocial process as "the unknotting of the subject's Borromean knot (at the point where the Symbolic and the Real intersect for the subject...) and its re-knotting anew through the production of the *sinthome*" (Derbyshire 2007, 96). The *sinthome*, or symptom of one's unique neurosis, is a desire that in some way escapes social construction and lacks signification by any external discourse. This singularity cannot be copied or modeled in any way; therefore, representation through language is impossible. Singular Individuality is "an 'anonymous' existence" with "no positive identity of any substantive character" (Rosenau 1992, 55) that can be permanently attributed. Ideally, the Lacanian post-analytic subject "actively creates itself with its *sinthome*" (Derbyshire 2007, 97).

From this understanding of Singular Individuality, it is difficult to imagine a social bond of any type. There is no ontological social bond and without stability between the sign and the signified, individuals cannot craft a common set of signifiers through which to create community (Anderson 2006). In resistance to external impositions of social construction, social relation is limited to identification with others in a shared struggle. Therefore, Žižek focuses on desire as a basis for relation. In short, when one recognizes that one's own experience of lack is also experienced by the Other, rather than looking to the Other to fulfill the lack through imaginary identification, we enter into symbolic identification with one another. This recognition of mutual lack fabricates a social connection that can provide common ground for political action (Marchart 2005), which some argue provides a basis for relation (McSwite 2006, Catlaw 2005, 2006, 2007a, 2007b).

However, a social bond based merely on symbolic identification grounded in refusal makes productive social action difficult because it eliminates any basis for normative affirmations (Fraser and Nicholson 1988). Again reflecting the general critique of this perspective, the result is what Douglas (1996) calls Fatalism—a high grid (rules and laws), low-group (social identity) condition in which exterior social forces seek to control one's behavior without the assumed benefit of a secure identity. In other words, Singular Individuality stands in constant refusal of societal norms while accepting a shifting sense of self and identification with others. Morse (2006) describes this condition as *atomism* in which there is no group and thus no social order. However these interpretations disable the positive meaning of Singular Individuality as generative.

114 *Primary governance theories*

Epistemological concepts

The failure of modernity to produce satisfactory universal Truths has led to an epistemological crisis. Laclau and Mouffe argue that all attempts to fix meaning are a project of hegemony that must be met with deconstruction due to the undecidability of any concept (Norval 2005). Rather than trying to resolve the crisis, Fragmented Governance rejects the possibility of both foundational and coherentist universal Truth, discovered either *a priori* or *a posteriori*. Due to the impossibility of accessing reality without the mediation of language, this perspective holds that knowledge can only be fabricated in socially constructed narratives. However, the circular logic of self-referential signifiers creates a "fragmented, disjointed, and discontinuous mode of experience" (Best and Kellner 1991, 284). There can be many truths, none of which can claim to be truer than another. At best, truth can be understood as a temporarily coherent agreement among those within a particular time and place that must be justified based on the situation—although even this fleeting agreement faces severe challenges.

This perspective is explained well in Feyerabend's (1993) theory of *epistemological anarchism*, which holds that there are no rules for assessing or ordering the value of forms of knowledge. Rather, individual knowledge production must remain fully free in its pursuits and must remain so in order to fulfill its emancipatory function. Similarly, epistemological pluralism argues that there are different ways of knowing things and different methodologies for attaining understanding. Berger and Luckmann (1966) call this the social construction of knowledge and reality. Drawing on the phenomenology of Alfred Schutz (1967), they explain how meaning emerges through social interaction, creating intersubjective agreement about "truth" at specific times and in specific places. Intersubjectivity is a term developed by Husserl (1982) to describe how relational, subjective experience plays a fundamental role in the constitution of self, other experiencing subjects, and the objective world itself.

Even if there could be sufficient conceptual stability to seek social agreement on what will be considered true at a given time and place, the postmodern critique emphasizes that such social processes are rife with power dynamics. Rather than accepting the modern assumption that logic is the basis of rationality—of either a deductive or inductive nature—knowledge production itself is a strategic endeavor. Strategic rationality pursues substantive ends under uncertain social conditions. Therefore, it seeks the most effective argument oriented to success (Erikson and Weigard 2003). A particular idea is held firmly throughout a pluralist competition of ideas that allows for strategic trading and negotiation among parties until decisions are reached through either victory or other forms of agreement (Rein and Schön 1993).

Through such competition, the grand narratives of the past have been replaced by local narratives associated with smaller groups or even individuals within society. Meaningfulness is thus limited to place and time. As a result, "in contemporary society 'reality' has dissolved into fragments" (Best and Kellner

Fragmented Governance 115

1991, 257). At this extreme, there can only be epistemological relativism, which in turn increases the possibility for the clashing of narratives among groups (White 1999, 157).

Belief systems

It is difficult to attach any system of belief to Fragmented Governance because the notion of such a system is antithetical to its nature. A dynamic, natural, radically pluralist belief system would refute the possibility of a universal Truth from any origin—theistic or nontheistic, personal or impersonal. Instead, there are simply emergent, multitudinous possibilities that cannot be legitimately evaluated. As an example, Marcuse (1964) promotes the "great refusal" as the systematic opposition to all methods of social control. We must reject dominating narratives of any type.

From this anti-essentialist perspective, all religious or scientific systems of belief are depicted as competing metanarratives. A metanarrative, master narrative, or grand narrative, is a totalizing statement about knowledge and experience that is purported to be universally true. Lyotard (1984) was the first philosopher to introduce postmodernism as a general "incredulity toward metanarratives" (xxiv). However, as MacIntyre (1988) notes, such narratives are not only in conflict, but are incommensurable in their grounding. Therefore, none have a legitimate claim to being right, nor can we have a fruitful discussion about their differences. Thus, we use the term anti-essentialism to describe a belief system congruent with Fragmented Governance, noting that anti-essentialism itself is a metanarrative—just one that lacks substantive content (Wang 2012).

Ethical concepts

Fragmented Governance provides no firm ontological foundations or psycho-social stability on which to build normative structures. Furthermore, its relativist epistemology does not allow for a stable external source of ethical guidance in Truth. Instead, our internal motivations are informed by what we personally deem to be good. Thus, value terms such as Right and Good cannot appeal to universals of any type. In short, "there are no objective values" (Mackie 1990, 15). Instead, as with truth, value claims are understood to be mere social constructs. Norms are reflective of social context and such contexts are multiple and fluid. This postmodern fragmentation of social values (Box 1999) leads to ethical skepticism—both metaethical and normative (Mackie 1990).

Ethical skepticism is the belief that nothing is objectively right or wrong, therefore ethical concepts have no purpose (Archie 2010). Moral facts, the basic conceptions of ethics, cannot exist and notions of good or right can never be true or false. Instead all moral statements are devoid of substantive meaning and normative claims of goodness or rightness are purely subjective, with definitions changing based on the prevailing view of a particular individual, culture, or

116 *Primary governance theories*

historical period (Mackie 1990). As a result, everyone determines for themselves what is good: "The only obligation which I have a right to assume is to do at any time what I think is right" (Thoreau 2004, 90). Indeed, to the extent that any "common ground" of morality can be found it will only be "what emerges (temporarily) when one party wins the right (through war, elections, dynastic succession) to determine the decorums of appropriate behavior" (Fish 1999, 170). In other words, any supposedly common good is achieved through coercion or hegemony.

Political theory

Due to the problems of language signification—at the ontological, psychosocial, and epistemological levels—stability of any kind is unattainable, thereby ensuring a corollary impossibility of representation (Sarup 1989). Fragmented Governance calls for approaches that are not founded on fabricated universal ideals, or group or individual identities. According to political philosopher Antonio Negri, "the multitude is a set of singularities that persevere as singularities during their political and productive exercise" (Fernández de Rota 2011, 147). In short, representation of Singular Individuality is *not* possible because of ever-changing identifications. If some sort of political identity is claimed, it is a mere fabrication (see Catlaw 2006, 2007a, 2007b). Therefore, modernist notions of political rationality, individualism, property rights, and representation are all challenged.

This oppositional position is not conducive to political organizing because no person or idea can be represented, no social agreement can be stable without being suspected of domination. From an inability to form social bonds and the breakdown of political representation, the ideal of *individualist* anarchism emerges. These ideas stem from classical radicalism, which attempts to resolve the conflict between the democratic aspirations of the Enlightenment and the dominating power of society. The principal architects include philosophers Thomas Paine (1737–1809) and the Marquis de Condorcet (1743–1794) (Clark 1998). This form of radicalism is further developed by individualist and libertarian schools of anarchist thought found in writers such as Josiah Warren (1798–1874), Max Stirner (1806–1856), and Henry David Thoreau (1817–1862), all of whom reject authority and insist upon autonomy.

Individualist anarchism opposes domination of the individual by any authority external to themselves (Godwin 1842). There is a prioritization of the individual over any kind of social group, society, tradition, or ideology (Proudhon 2007). Any obligation to others must rest purely on the desire of the individual and there can be no assumed human nature that would impel an individual to make such a commitment. There are no legitimate limits on the pursuit of one's own desires (Stirner 1995). The individual is the absolute authority over themselves and all that they acquire through original appropriation, trade, or gift (Butler 1980).

While individualist anarchism originated in the 19th century, the postmodern critique of representation supports its ideal because the state is viewed as a

Fragmented Governance 117

progenitor of grand narratives and the misguided attempt to control the disjointed bits of society under illegitimate domination. From this perspective, the only viable political alternative is for individuals to extricate themselves from these grand narratives and the imposition of power they represent: "A lot of what passes for anarchism today is a crusade for an escape from a society of total alienation, and for the salvation of the individual psyche" (Goodwin 2007, 128). This linkage between anarchism and postmodernism has been made in the emerging theory of "post-anarchism" found in new social movements (Evren 2011). While many of these perspectives are associated with Integrative Governance, some share individualist anarchism's tenets: particularly the critique of representation and the resulting impossibility of social agreements among collectives of any sort.

From this perspective, politics is an ongoing process of contestation against hegemonic attempts to close ideas and identity through state-enforced signification and subject positions. This essentially replicates the psychosocial process of the constitutive lack subverting the process of identity formation; we are *becoming-minoritarian* (Deleuze and Guattari 1987). In fact, most "majorities" are not more numerous. They are merely more powerful because they hold multiple characteristics of power, i.e., white, heterosexual, male, English-speaking, and so forth. Such identity politics have expanded our understanding of the social world through analysis of and resistance to social construction. Becoming minoritarian is a refusal of naming and representation per se (Patton 2005). Such refusal gives political voice to all possible modes of existence, thereby challenging representative politics and deterritorializing systems of power and control. To be clear, this refusal is differentiated from identity politics, which are more generally characterized as counter-hegemonic *particular* identities that resist the hegemonic universal identity by claiming an alternative identity with equal rights.

In the same way privileged minorities generate a hegemonic majority, Žižek carries forward Rancière's concept of the *singulier universel* in his call for *all* excluded groups to band together in resistance to those who stand only for their particular interest (Coles 2005). In other words, there is no attempt to claim the seat of power and no demand for specific policy changes or rights from that privileged group as this would legitimate their position of power. Instead, there is only a demand that the powerful release their privilege. From a Lacanian perspective, the demand is to relinquish the horizon established by the dominant order (Žižek 2009). Today's Occupy social movement comes to mind. These social movements refuse to demand particular rights and instead demand that the system of privilege itself be abolished.

In this individualist post-anarchism, the only universal "identity" is the void in the social order that is defined as the point of exclusion in which all may participate. We understand one another's un-representable lack, prefiguring an emancipatory politics that seeks to maintain this freedom from social construction (Marchart 2005). The political solidarity built on this recognition of the common struggle against both naming and exclusion from power is void of

118 *Primary governance theories*

substantive content and must remain so. Indeed, Josiah Warren argues that all forms of society are artificial constructions (Butler 1980), and Max Stirner (1995) repeatedly refers to all forms of collectivity, including society itself, as a "spook" (221).

Therefore, as pointed out by Deleuze and Guattari (1983), "there is no general recipe" (108) for achieving the political ideal of multiplicities. The best that can be done is to "locate the most egalitarian and natural forms of social organization" (Bertalan 2011, 217). The common denominator is revolutionary and counter-hegemonic action (Adams 2011). While "this nihilism is active" (Fernández de Rota 2011, 147)—active in resistance and opposition to existing forms of governance—individualist anarchism rejects the project of organizing society beyond simply leaving it up to the individuals engaged in any given situation. These perspectives ultimately argue for elimination of the state in order to promote individual sovereignty and prevent all forms of manipulation at the hands of the state (Stringham 2007, 2005). Individuals would then become self-sufficient and all previously public functions would be provided by private means.

Economic theory

Following individualist anarchy, the ideal economy in Fragmented Governance would be completely unregulated exchange in order to prevent manipulation at the hands of the state (Stringham 2005, 2007). All liberal ideas about coordinated economic action are rejected (Godwin 1842). Individuals would be freed from any state-backed economic system (Morris 1993). Furthermore, consumers would be freed from "dominant meanings disseminated by the culture industry" (Simons 2005, 159) to prevent manipulation at the hands of the market. In this perfectly free economy, individuals would produce for themselves, consume what they want, trade if they want, or maintain self-sufficiency if they want, without consideration of other consumers or producers beyond their own trade interests (Stirner 1995). The ideal would be for producers and consumers themselves to self-organize all economic activities, where populist "consumers" would "make their own meanings and find their own pleasures" (Simons 2005, 159). These characteristics fit well with the ideals of individualist anarchism.

This approach to economics offers two potential solutions: to transform capitalism through resistance and direct action, or to exit capitalism. Some individualist anarchists tend toward the latter because they distrust the type of collective endeavor that would be necessary to transform capitalism. However, coordinated direct action against capitalism is the topic of much interest in anarchistic studies, particularly during and since the self-organizing action against the World Trade Organization (WTO) Ministerial Conference in Seattle in 1999 (Adams 2011, Day 2011, Evren 2011). Demonstrations against global trade and economic policy conventions and summits, like the WTO, the World Bank, the International Monetary Fund (IMF), the Free Trade Area of the

Fragmented Governance 119

Americas, and the Group of Eight+ (G8), have increased in strength in the past two decades. Coalescing somewhat around the crises of globalization, these direct actions involve national and international NGOs, labor unions, environmental groups, student groups, faith-based groups, and anarchists. Tactics include peaceful civil disobedience as well as vandalism against corporate property. Despite increases in their frequency, a high level of disagreement remains as to the purpose of these actions, beyond opposition; some argue in favor of reforming or transforming capitalism while others seek to replace it.

While the capitalist system persists, others use the approach of economic secession, which entails abstention from the prevailing monetary system and government-regulated capitalist markets. Rejection of the system requires the replacement of corporately produced goods and services with those produced by oneself, another individual producer, or cooperatives of producers (Morris 1993). It also requires replacement of money with other forms of exchange, such as barter and swapping, work hour trade, or commodities like gold (Lietaer 2013). For instance, Warren argues that economic exchanges must be limited to those in which individuals "give an equivalent in labor, and nothing but labor, for labor received" (Butler 1980, 433), therefore preventing the creation of money, interest, and banking systems and providing protection to individuals from manipulation, coercion, and exploitation.

Another approach to economic secession is found in the self-sufficiency movement recently popularized by author Barbara Kingsolver (2007), with tactics like homesteading and off-grid sustainability. Producing one's own food, potable water, and energy, along with other do-it-yourself skills have become increasingly popular in the twenty-first century (see for example, Emery 2012, Gehring 2011, Kaplan and Blume 2011, Seymour 2009). In the United States, this movement has its roots in Henry David Thoreau's *Walden* (1854)—"the original sacred text of homesteading" (Gould 2005, 3)—and in the work of Ralph Borsodi (1927, 1929, 1933) whose influence was such that it sparked a national homestead movement (Carlson 2004). While Thoreau's work was a reflection on a personal, and perhaps spiritual, journey, Borsodi rejects the market's manipulation of desire and advocates a radical decentralization of production in which individuals return to an agrarian model of self-sufficiency.[1]

Scholars working from these perspectives promote a completely unregulated system of barter that protects individual sovereignty and prevents all forms of domination (Stringham 2005, 2007). With government and capitalism thus eliminated, individuals would become fully self-sufficient, with needed goods and services provided through self-directed mechanisms of free barter and exchange.

Administrative theory

In Fragmented Governance, if the political economy were to follow the tenets of individualist anarchism, there would be no administrative theory or practice, because neither government nor markets would be administered. In the historical movement *toward* the individualist anarchist ideal, however, there are

120   *Primary governance theories*

administrative theories and practices that mimic market transactions. Albeit a weak connection, Fragmented Governance aligns most closely with the entrepreneurial nature of New Public Management (NPM) and the discretion given to administrators to establish and fulfill the public good (desire) through market mechanisms (Lynn 1996, Ostrom 1989). It is important to reiterate that it is difficult to identify a school of Anglo-American administrative theory that closely aligns with Fragmented Governance. Because administrative theory is practice-oriented it necessarily responds to existing conditions within contemporary society. While NPM shares philosophical ideals with Fragmented Governance it is more appropriately identified as *neoliberal*—a hybrid position that is explained in Chapter 11.

NPM began in countries like New Zealand, Britain, and Germany, and then later influenced reforms in the United States (Kettl 2000a). The original idea was that government could be transformed into small, decentralized boards overseeing private performance-based organizations that deliver public goods and services most efficiently and effectively. Actual provision of goods and services by the government would be minimized in the interest of keeping decision making as close to the individual as practicable. This theoretical movement extends the position that government should play a minimal role to advance economic growth, which culminated in the United States in the late 1980s and 1990s with the Reinventing Government movement (Hood 1991, Lynn 1996, 2006, Osborne and Gaebler 1992, Simon 1946, 1947, 1976).[2]

Accordingly, the principles of government reinvention are in line with free-market, consumerist, ideals: (1) eliminate unnecessary regulation and control, (2) put customers first, (3) empower employees to get results, and (4) reorganize and reengineer for increased efficiency and effectiveness (Gore and Clinton 1993). These reform efforts lead to increasing privatization and deregulation, including a relinquishment of governmental functions or oversight and control to private entities (Savas 1982). While these theories greatly empower managerial experts, they are more likely to be located outside government agencies. This movement toward privatization and the emphasis of individual choice clearly resonates with Fragmented Governance.

Although this school of thought leaves one foot in Atomistic Governance, by pushing further toward market mechanisms these administrative theories call for increasing reliance on laissez-faire economic principles that presume that the free market—based on aggregated individual decision making—administers society better. Therefore, public service is handed over to competing market forces that are thought to be more responsive to individual consumers. This pattern reinforces the market ascendency associated with postmodern consumerism. As Fox (1996) aptly points out, Osborne and Gaebler's *Reinventing Government* is itself a postmodern exercise, combining elements of market economics, public choice, empirical rationality, community and citizen empowerment, anti-hierarchical structuring, increased accountability, and increased discretion. This mish-mash of recommendations defies any sense of internal consistency, instead providing a little something for everyone, yielding a

Fragmented Governance   121

fragmented postmodern "paradigm" that is wholly defined by its slogans (Kamensky 1996).

In regard to the relationship between the state and the individual, Singular Individuality provides the perfect citizen-consumer in a market-oriented approach such as NPM. The practical impact of fragmenting identity in governance has been explored by several public administration scholars (Farmer 2005b, Hummel 2008, White 1999). By breaking citizens into identity fragments, the administrator focuses only on the particular aspect that is deemed relevant to their function while ignoring all other characteristics. In this way, persons are reduced to a select number of prespecified features (Hummel 2008). The dynamic nature of Singular Individuality means the person can also be further broken down into time slices (Farmer 2005b). From the skeptical postmodern worldview, such disjointed bits are the most to which administrators can respond. Fragmented Governance is therefore ushered in by an autonomous, discretionary, expert administrative role that Stout (2013) calls the Entrepreneur. In sketch, Entrepreneurs view citizens as customers or consumers (Roberts 2004) or watchdog citizens advocating for their own interests (Box 1998) to be served according to performance objectives established through pluralist competition.

Summary and illustration

In sum, within Fragmented Governance there are no ontological or epistemological foundations, thus all such metanarratives with substantive content are suspect. Assuming such anti-essentialism, there is no stable or common ground for developing a coherent identity or social context; therefore, all notions of the Good or Right are meaningless, and representation of any type is impossible. This leaves Fragmented Governance with no choice but to reject all forms of organized government and economy as they represent domination by select groups with no grounds for legitimacy. We see this occurring in challenges to government action in the social and economic spheres, where extreme fragmentation causes people to simply exit the system. What administration is left mimics market transactions to the greatest degree possible.

This approach to governance fosters public encounters (Bartels 2013) in which negative liberty reduces the capacity to agree upon even minimalist procedural approaches to determining collective action (i.e., pluralism). Denying any basis for communal good or right choice, the emphasis is instead placed on individual actions, wherein "the values of individual satisfaction are judged to be more important than the values of achieving collective democratic consensus" (Frederickson 1996, 267). The result is individualist anarchism throughout the political economy, only allowing transitory affiliations with others based on present interests.

Considering agricultural policy as an example, we would expect to see a suspicion of government intervention of any type in food production and distribution. A strong preference for individual autonomy in both production and

122 *Primary governance theories*

exchange would be evident. Individuals would seek to become self-sufficient to the largest extent possible, submitting to trade and barter only based on need or personal preferences. If administrators were to be involved in these activities at all, they would need to be working in service to each individual.

The Fragmented approach is well illustrated in the homesteading movement. Writing in response to both the devastation of the Great Depression and the resulting New Deal social assistance policies in the United States, Borsodi (1933) calls for a return to family farming in which individuals provide for their own sustenance through growing, harvesting, and preserving produce; raising livestock; and building one's own shelter. He insisted "the threat to human freedom ... cannot be escaped in the present program of adjusting man to the regimentation of technological, industrial, and urban civilization" (xx). He believed the only answer is to remove oneself from society and return to the land. Indeed, it is the "evil effects of this interdependence" (147) in society that is the central ill to be overcome.

To accomplish this independence, homesteading draws upon the tenets of self-reliance, urging self-sufficiency through individual production as the best answer both for the individual and for society in general. As Borsodi (1933) argues,

> Domestic production, if enough people turned to it ... would release men and women from their present thralldom to the factory and make them masters of machines instead of servants to them; it would end the power of exploiting them which ruthless, acquisitive, and predatory men now possess; it would free them for the conquest of comfort, beauty and understanding.
>
> (9)

These ideals are also found in the contemporary survivalist movement in which individuals learn mechanisms for obtaining, purifying, and storing their own water sources in addition to foraging and growing their own food (Cobb 2014). Like homesteading, survivalism reflects a "dramatic doubt, in a rhetoric of radical skepticism toward the prospects of contemporary institutional orders" and sees "modernity not as the irresistible advance of bureaucratization but as a failing project near its end" (Mitchell Jr. 2002, 11). From this perspective the anticipated systemic failure is certain to lead to catastrophic events—from economic collapse, to war, wildfires, famines, or pandemics—for which individuals must prepare.

As illustrated here, a Fragmented Governance approach turns decision making over to each individual or household so that they can determine their own needs and provide for them to the greatest degree possible through self-sufficiency. Property ownership is private and any needs that cannot be met by individuals are satisfied through processes of exchange or barter. To the extent that production is social, it is limited to sharing the information needed to foster self-sufficiency through learning to grow, harvest, and store the means to survive.

Notes

1 While Borsodi's early work advocated homesteading and extreme decentralization in production, his later work shifted to other terrains that align with the collectivist ontologies, including arguing for a hierarchical social order, and later planned communities (Carlson 2004).
2 Osborne and Gaebler's *Reinventing Government* (1992) argues for a market-centered polis peopled by consumers as opposed to citizens. It was influential in spurring the National Performance Review (2004) of Vice President Al Gore.

Part III

Dystopian utopias

The chapters in Part III provide a dialectical analysis and critique of the primary approaches to governance, as well as hybridizations commonly produced by reform efforts. In the spirit of ontological disclosure (Cox 1995, Wamsley 1996), we have both stated our individual perspectives in the Preface, revealing that we come to this inquiry from a decidedly relational process perspective, one that aligns well with certain theories of radical democracy. Therefore, we examine and critique each of the governance approaches herein from what could be considered an "outsider" perspective.

Chapter 9 explains the use of dialectical analysis within the ideal-type method, considering the differences that engender mutual critiques among the primary approaches to governance and the similarities that enable hybridization in practice. Chapters 10 and 11 explore the dialectical dynamics through which hybrids are generated. Because ideal-types rarely exist in pure form, it can be expected that actual manifestation will yield hybrids. However, these hybridizations do not reflect ontological fickleness or poor logic. In essence, each primary governance approach presents a utopia that is rarely realized because it would generate dystopian experiences if it were fully actualized. We argue that in pure form, ontological positions generate particular forms of psychosocial pathology or existential angst that drive ideological change.

Specifically, resistance and reform efforts tend to push the mainstream static ontologies toward dynamic ontological terrain. In response to ontological instability in those positions, existential angst engages a reverse critique. Counter-hegemonic reforms pull governance back from utopian/dystopian extremes, forming static hybrids that may obfuscate underlying philosophical commitments for manipulative purposes. As Proudhon (1979b) wrote, "authority retreats and liberty advances" (chapter X) in regress and progress. While progressive impulses advance ideology into dynamic positions, conservative impulses cause retrenchment toward static positions.

Based on the ontological similarities between individualist and collectivist ideal-types examined in Chapter 9, vertical movement is enabled between static state and dynamic state approaches to governance. Similarly, horizontal movement between the collectivist and individualist static state ontologies is also quite evident in governance theory. However, the differences between the

126 *Dystopian utopias*

individualist and collectivist positions are accentuated as ideas move from static to dynamic state ontologies and become more difficult to bridge. Therefore, we reconfigure the ideal-type matrix as an arc.

Dialectics among approaches generate countervailing processes that are reflected in the direction of movement—toward or away from a particular position. When movement is in response to the pathologies of the static approaches, it is along what we call the Arc of Reform; reforms push away from positions at the top of the Arc down toward the bottom on either side. When movement seeks to quell the existential angst generated by the pathologies of the dynamic approaches, we see a reverse pulling back toward the apex of the Arc in what we call the Arc of Reification. These movements of ideological critique and retrenchment are explored in Chapters 10 and 11.

Together, these analyses are meant to develop a deeper understanding of the implications of each approach to governance, clarify the reasons behind political and philosophical governance reform movements, foster thoughtful choice making among philosophical assumptions, and establish the foundational argument for dialectical synthesis. Thus, the analyses in this section set the stage for explicating and affirming Integrative Governance in Part IV, an alternative approach that seeks to resolve the pathological dynamics of the primary governance approaches without producing dystopian, reified hybrids.

9 Analysis of the primary governance approaches

Recalling Chapter 4, once constructed, ideal-types are used "not as an end but as a *means*" (Weber 1949c, 92). A robust typology is ultimately designed to explore anticipated implications (Doty and Glick 1994). This can be accomplished through mental experiments in logic as well as empirical research. Mental experiments explore what might happen if the ideal-type were fully manifested in order to make recommendations based on logical implications. Weber (1949c) asserts, "This procedure can be indispensable for heuristic as well as expository purposes ... it is no 'hypothesis' but it offers guidance to the construction of hypotheses" (90). Following this understanding, the Governance Typology presented herein is meant to provide strong "conceptual instruments for *comparison* with and the *measurement* of reality" (97). Here, we compare competing theories to see what is importantly different in order to ask questions: *Why is it different? What are the implications?*

Therefore, our inquiry continues with mental experiments that make comparisons between governance approaches. These explorations offer a platform for critical analysis in Chapters 10 and 11. Following Weber, we think through "what a behavior pattern or thought pattern (e.g., a philosophical system) would be like if it possessed completely rational, empirical and logical 'correctness' and 'consistency'" (Weber 1949a, 42). Specifically, we use dialectical analysis to explore the implications of the governance approaches using the lens of each ideal-type's ontological grounding and how those assumptions logically carry through the other elements of the typology.

Dialectical analysis

As noted in Chapter 4, we use dialectical analysis to compare and contrast the concepts within the approaches to governance with a view toward dialectical synthesis, as discussed in Part IV. In some interpretations of dialectics, an antithesis emerges due to unintended consequences of the thesis (Schneider 1971). Critical awareness of these contradictions promotes the recognition of their unity within an ongoing dialectical tension. As such, it is very useful in understanding the development of theory (Popper 1940). As our focus is on governance, public administration theory provides illustrative examples. Conciliatory

128 *Dystopian utopias*

public administration theories accept the contradictions that emerge between competing approaches (King and Zanetti 2005). Some critical theorists feel that maintaining the dialectic in this way is better than attempting resolution because any synthesis is suspected of actually being a dominating or obfuscating compromise (Adorno 1973).

Public administration theory also presents many concepts in a dichotomous or dialectical manner. For example, it has been argued that there is not one language of public administration (Farmer 1995) but two, which can be characterized as simply modern versus postmodern, traditional versus post-ist, or traditional versus post-traditional (Farmer 1999, 2005a, 2005b, 2006). Alternatively, there are two approaches to the field that can be characterized as technical versus normative, positivist scientific versus democratic and humanistic, traditional Orthodox Administration versus New Public Administration, New Public Management versus New Public Service, rationalist versus nonrationalist, hard-core rationalist versus soft-core rationalist, and so forth (see for example, Denhardt 2000, Denhardt and Denhardt 2007, Harmon 1995, King *et al.* 2000, McSwite 1997). Finally, dialectic is seen in Harmon's (1990, 1995) explication of what he calls the Answerer/Maker dialectic in public administration: "Responsibility and freedom need to be understood as reciprocally related to one another rather than diametrically opposed" (1995, 122).[1,2] Administrators must maintain both accountability and responsibility in the performance of their duties. We maintain that these dichotomies are directly linked to the logical differences between the One and the Many: the collectivist and individualist ontologies. However, the arguments found in the public administration literature do not differentiate between static and dynamic assumptions, thus leaving the impression of one rather than two dialectics as developed herein.

Dialectic in the Governance Typology

As a precursor to theoretical analysis and discussion, it is useful to reiterate that the first four philosophical elements of the typology—ontological assumptions and associated language, psychosocial condition, epistemological concepts, and belief systems—prefigure the latter four action elements of the typology—ethical concepts, political theory, economic theory, and administrative theory. In this way political ontology depicts both what *is* (ontologically) and what *should be* (theoretically and ethically). It describes what is believed to be the constitutive Good: both the source of good as well as good ends (Taylor 1989). Therefore, we can consider the underlying ontological assumptions of each approach to governance as the driver of problematic outcomes.

Placed in a two-by-two matrix, the four primary approaches to governance can be considered as related pairs based on fundamental qualities on either the vertical or horizontal axes of the matrix. For example, when considering the four approaches in pairs across the horizontal axis, we find that they can be paired as *static* versus *dynamic* types. Of these pairings, the static ideal-types shown in Table 9.1 are most familiar. Considering the dialectical oppositions

Analysis of primary governance approaches 129

Table 9.1 Static state governance ideal-types: Hierarchical and Atomistic

	Hierarchical Governance	*Atomistic Governance*
Ontological assumptions	Static state, transcendent source, singular expression	Static state, immanent source, plural expression
Language characteristics	Discrete, hierarchical	Discrete, nonhierarchical
Psychosocial theory	individuality	Individuality
Epistemological concepts	Rationalism	Empiricism
Belief systems	Monotheism	Naturalism
Ethical concepts	Deontological obligation	Consequentialism
Political theory	Classical conservative liberalism	Modern liberalism
Economic theory	Welfare state	Market exchange
Administrative theory	Orthodox administration	New Public Service

created by each element's meaning, we see a recognizable pattern of debate between perspectives, such as the debate between the classical conservative liberalism (republicanism) of Hierarchical Governance and the modern liberalism of Atomistic Governance that together form the "whole" of liberalism.

As shown in Table 9.2, when considering the dynamic ideal-types, Holographic and Fragmented Governance, we see the less common terrain. Here, the extreme ontological positions of both the One and Many—an ontology of abundance versus an ontology of lack—are placed in opposition, accentuating the differences between the elements in the static ideal-types.

When considering the vertical axis, we find the ideal-types can be paired under *collectivist* and *individualist* categories. Collectivist ontologies, Hierarchical and Holographic Governance, are shown in Table 9.3. In this pairing, it is their shared understanding of existence as One that forms commonalities across them. Communal worldviews consider how problems are shared and solved by the group as directed by the source of being, however it is conceived (Benson and Williams 1982).

Table 9.2 Dynamic state governance ideal-types: Holographic and Fragmented

	Holographic Governance	*Fragmented Governance*
Ontological assumptions	Dynamic state, transcendent source, singular expression	Dynamic state, immanent source, plural expression
Language characteristics	Gerundial, holistic	Gerundial, discrete
Psychosocial theory	Particular individuality	Singular Individuality
Epistemological concepts	Idealism	Epistemological anarchism
Belief systems	Pantheism	Anti-essentialism
Ethical concepts	Moral imperative	Moral skepticism/relativism
Political theory	Socialism	Individualist anarchism
Economic theory	Collectively planned economy	Self-sufficiency and barter
Administrative theory	New Public Administration	New Public Management

130 *Dystopian utopias*

Table 9.3 Collectivist governance ideal-types: Hierarchical and Holographic

	Hierarchical Governance
Ontological assumptions	Static state, transcendent source, singular expression
Language characteristics	Discrete, hierarchical
Psychosocial theory	individuality
Epistemological concepts	Rationalism
Belief systems	Monotheism
Ethical concepts	Deontological obligation
Political theory	Classical conservative liberalism
Economic theory	Welfare state
Administrative theory	Orthodox administration
	Holographic Governance
Ontological assumptions	Dynamic state, transcendent source, singular expression
Language characteristics	Gerundial, holistic
Psychosocial theory	Particular individuality
Epistemological concepts	Idealism
Belief systems	Pantheism
Ethical concepts	Moral imperative
Political theory	Socialism
Economic theory	Collectively planned economy
Administrative theory	New Public Administration

The individualist ontologies of Atomistic and Fragmented Governance are familiar contemporary Western perspectives. In this pairing, as shown in Table 9.4, it is their shared understanding of existence as Many that forms commonalities between them. As pluralism in various degrees tends to be the most accepted foundational assumption in modern and postmodern times, the elements are prevalent in current philosophical and theoretical discussion.

Ontological differences and similarities

This section begins the dialectical analysis by considering the basic differences and similarities of the four primary approaches found in each element of the Governance Typology. For the purpose of the following discussion, we provide a streamlined version of the familiar two-by-two matrix to emphasize and simplify the underlying ontological contrasts (see Table 9.5).

These differences between approaches engender mutual critiques and allow us to identify and explore the *dystopia* inherent in each ideal-type's utopia, which is discussed in Chapter 10. The collectivist ontologies yield critiques of the qualities shared among individualist ontologies, while the dynamic ontological positions fuel critiques of the qualities shared among static ontologies, and vice versa in both pairs. As also explained in Chapter 10, the paired sets of ontological positions, individualist–collectivist and static–dynamic, share characteristics. These similarities enable critiques to spark reform movements

Analysis of primary governance approaches 131

Table 9.4 Individualist governance ideal-types: Atomistic and Fragmented

	Atomistic Governance
Ontological assumptions	Static state, immanent source, plural expression
Language characteristics	Discrete, nonhierarchical
Psychosocial theory	Individuality
Epistemological concepts	Empiricism
Belief systems	Naturalism
Ethical concepts	Consequentialism
Political theory	Modern liberalism
Economic theory	Market exchange
Administrative theory	New Public Service
	Fragmented Governance
Ontological assumptions	Dynamic state, immanent source, plural expression
Language characteristics	Gerundial, discrete
Psychosocial theory	Singular Individuality
Epistemological concepts	Epistemological anarchism
Belief systems	Anti-essentialism
Ethical concepts	Moral skepticism/relativism
Political theory	Individualist anarchism
Economic theory	Self-sufficiency and barter
Administrative theory	New Public Management

between the approaches in practice. These movements further produce governance hybrids, which is explained in Chapter 11.

Both similarities and differences have a clear grounding in the respective ontological assumptions of each pairing. As shown in Table 9.6, the two *static state* approaches to governance (Hierarchical and Atomistic) share a notion of stasis and continuity of being and identity, along with foundational Truth. This stability carries through all other elements of the framework. However, in Hierarchical Governance, the assumption of collectivism (One) means that Truth, Right, and Good are determined by a higher power and accessed through reason; therefore, laws can be identified to guide political, economic, and administrative structures and procedures. Alternatively, in Atomistic Governance, the assumption of methodological individualism (Many) means that Truth is identified through observation and a firm belief based in science. Since Good is a matter of personal preference, ends can be negotiated and chosen to guide political, economic, and administrative structures and procedures for Right

Table 9.5 Streamlined ontological matrix

	Collectivist	*Individualist*
Static state	Hierarchical	Atomistic
Dynamic state	Holographic	Fragmented

132   *Dystopian utopias*

action. These differences are emphasized in collectivist individuality versus individualist Individuality.

The similarities and differences between the two *dynamic state* approaches to governance (Holographic and Fragmented) are depicted in Table 9.7. These approaches share a notion of dynamic being and identity that makes stability in all other elements of the framework impossible. However, in Holographic Governance, the assumption of collectivism (One) creates a sense of substantive abundance—whether it is divinely or humanly crafted. Thus, while there is ontological change, it is anchored in the understanding of a transcendent source that can provide a stable system of belief, which can guide Truth, Right, Good, and the organization of social institutions. Alternatively, in Fragmented Governance, the assumption of extreme individualism (Many) coupled with dynamism creates a sense of substantive lack and absolute flux, to the point where meaning and identity cannot be achieved for a duration long enough to support stability in any other element of the framework. Thus, truth is a matter of subjectivity, there can be no certainty of belief, both good and right are matters of shifting preferences, and there is no firm ground upon which to build legitimate social institutions.

The similarities and differences between the two *collectivist* approaches to governance (Hierarchical and Holographic) are outlined in Table 9.8. They share the notion of transcendent holism that rejects all notions of an ontological Many. An assumption of the One is relatively moderate in Hierarchical Governance and accentuated in Holographic Governance, but the common theme of unity and an affirmation of positive liberty runs throughout the other elements of the framework. However, in Hierarchical Governance the assumption of a static transcendent source leads to a hierarchical ordering throughout the social system. Foundational Truth determined by a static One means that social institutions must be guided by a predetermined understanding of what is Right and Good. Hierarchical social ordering asserts that those at the top of the structure are best able to determine how to utilize the power of the state to implement right action, thereby necessitating an elite ruling class who moderate and regulate market exchange to achieve the most equitable distribution of goods. Alternatively, in Holographic Governance the rejection of hierarchical ordering and insistence on equal potential to intuit a changing notion of Truth, Right, and Good prevent a top-down approach to guiding social institutions. While the interchangeability of members allows for any member to step into a political leadership role to guide a collectively planned economy, the emphasis on unity and equality requires that all members engage in and agree upon matters of governance.

The similarities and differences between the two *individualist* approaches to governance (Atomistic and Fragmented) are shown in Table 9.9. They share the notion of immanent pluralism that rejects all notions of a transcendent One. An assumption of the Many is relatively moderate in Atomistic Governance and accentuated in Fragmented Governance, but the common theme of pluralism and a rejection of external constraints reflects an ideal of negative liberty that runs throughout the other elements of the framework. However, in the Atomistic approach the assumption of stasis means that individuals have stable identities and predictable interests. These qualities allow for representation and pluralist competition through which individuals form stable social contracts based on a shared understanding of the Good as maximization of individual utility, guiding Right action. Alternatively, in the Fragmented approach the absence of substantive foundations and ongoing flux prevent stable identities and shared meaning among individuals. Thus, no social contract between individuals and no shared notions of truth, good, and right are possible.

The tables appended to this chapter after the Notes provide detailed analyses of how these differences and similarities logically play out in each element of the Governance Typology. These tables are meant as a reference for: (1) understanding how the differences between these sets of ideal-types fuel reforms sparked by critique, as discussed in Chapter 10; and (2) understanding how the similarities among these sets of ideal-types are the qualities that enable reifying hybrid positions to form between pairings, as discussed in Chapter 11.

Establishing a dynamic model

The dialectical differences are accentuated between the collectivist and individualist approaches as underlying ontological assumptions of the One and the Many move from static to dynamic states. As Davis (2003) notes, extreme collectivism "appears to exhibit an evolution that increasingly *emphasizes individuals as active beings able to act upon and change social frameworks*," while extreme individualism is "subject to collapse in the direction of collectivism" (108). Such escalation ultimately "must end in the breakdown of the system" (Bateson 1972, 68)—dialectical tension becomes a polarized chasm that would require an ideological leap to move from one to the other.

The extremity of the differences between the two dynamic positions push ontological assumptions so far apart that we must reconsider the two-by-two Streamlined Ontological Matrix depicted in Table 9.5. We reconfigure the matrix as an arc with the static state ontologies in the center (Hierarchical and Atomistic Governance) and the dynamic state ontologies on either end (Holographic and Fragmented Governance) (see Figure 9.1). Working from

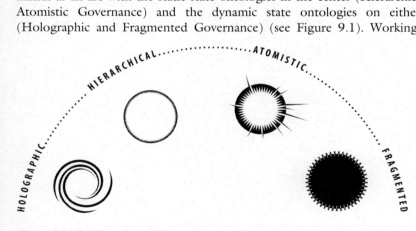

Figure 9.1 The Governance Arc.

134 *Dystopian utopias*

this Governance Arc, we can then analyze reform movements between the primary approaches to governance and the hybrids that emerge in the spaces between.

In governance theory we find *vertical* movements between Hierarchical and Holographic approaches as well as between Atomistic and Fragmented approaches. We also find *horizontal* movement between Hierarchical and Atomistic approaches. However, fluid horizontal movement between the Holographic and Fragmented approaches is not evident in governance theory.

Notes

1 Stout (2013) argues that it is more accurate to depict this as the Citizen/Maker dialectic, which is resolved in the synthesis of the mutually obligated Answerer given Niebuhr's (1963) own interpretation of his triadic model. However Harmon only employs two of three types.
2 It should be noted that in subsequent work, Harmon (2006) moves toward a synthesis position with his call to "dissolve dualisms" (28).

Table 9.6 Dialectical differences and similarities in static state ontologies

Framework element	Hierarchical Governance	Atomistic Governance	Both
Ontological assumptions	Hierarchical, transcendent cosmological order	Order established by Nature and laws of natural selection	Sufficient ontological stability to establish order
Language characteristics	Discrete, hierarchical	Discrete, nonhierarchical	Entities are stable and discrete and can be arranged
Psychosocial theory	Identity is established by the group; innate social contract	Identity is innate; fabricated social contract	Stable and reliable identities that persist through time and space
Epistemological concepts	Truth is known by a transcendent being and accessed through reason	Truth is determined by the laws of nature and verified through empirical observation	Stable, foundational knowledge can exist through time
Belief systems	Theistic terms used to describe a cosmological order	Nontheistic terms used to describe cosmological order	Belief systems can be universal and stable through time
Ethical concepts	Right is pre-determined and accessed through reason; Good follows Right	Individuals define Good; voluntary social contract defines Right; Right follows Good	Sources of ethical guidance can be externally imposed
Political theory	Representation established through elite leadership characteristics	Representation established through competitive pluralism	Sufficient stability exists to establish political institutions of representation
Economic theory	State control of exchange should guide positive liberty to ensure welfare	The state should ensure negative liberty as a basis for a natural market system	Outcomes of economic exchange are predictable
Administrative theory	Authority and discretion are constrained and directed by political oversight	Authority and discretion is moderated by political and citizen engagement	Administrators should have only moderate levels of authority and discretion

Table 9.7 Dialectical differences and similarities in dynamic state ontologies

Framework element	Holographic Governance	Fragmented Governance	Both
Ontological assumptions	Changing, transcendent, nonhierarchical whole	Immanent change based on cause and effect and social construction	Insufficient ontological stability to establish a permanent cosmological order
Language characteristics	Gerundial, holistic	Gerundial, discrete	Entities are dynamic
Psychosocial theory	Identity changes with the whole; innate social bond	Identity changes based on individual choice; no social bond	Identity changes in time and space
Epistemological concepts	Truth is accessed directly through introspection	Knowledge is empirically subjective but socially mediated via language	Knowledge is coherent rather than foundational; it is what makes sense in a given context
Belief systems	The sacred is manifest in all; all are valued equally	Beliefs are subjective, relative, and unfounded	Beliefs are formed internally
Ethical concepts	Right action determined through introspection; Good follows Right	Good is individually defined based on preference; Right is not considered or is equated to Good	Sources of ethical guidance are internal
Political theory	Egalitarianism within one-party rule is the only just approach to representation	Representation is impossible and therefore illegitimate	Representation is problematic due to suspicions of domination
Economic theory	Producers and consumers are unified in one self-organizing system	Any regulation of producers or consumers is coercion and illegitimate	Self-organizing economic activity is the only legitimate approach
Administrative theory	Solidarity ensures fair process and outcomes regardless of the administrative role	The absence of positional administrative authority empowers private actors	Administrators should have a high level of authority and discretion

Table 9.8 Dialectical differences and similarities in collectivist ontologies

Framework element	Hierarchical Governance	Holographic Governance	Both
Ontological assumptions	Hierarchical, transcendent cosmological order	Changing, transcendent, nonhierarchical whole	Existence is whole in expression and transcendent in source
Language characteristics	Discrete, hierarchical	Gerundial, holistic	Entities are unified
Psychosocial theory	Identity is established by the group; innate social contract	Identity changes with the whole; innate social bond	Embedded individuals; society is the unit of analysis
Epistemological concepts	Truth is known by a transcendent being and accessed through reason	Truth is accessed directly through introspection	Knowledge is obtained from a metaphysical source
Belief systems	Theistic terms used to describe a cosmological order	The sacred is manifest in all; all are equally valued	Beliefs grounded in a universal "higher power"
Ethical concepts	Right is pre-determined and accessed through reason; Good follows Right	Right action determined through introspection; Good follows Right	Both prioritize the collective Right
Political theory	Representation established through elite leadership characteristics	Egalitarianism within one-party rule is the only just approach to representation	The group has a right to sovereignty
Economic theory	State control of exchange should guide positive liberty to ensure welfare	Producers and consumers are unified in one self-organizing system	Control of exchange is necessary for the best results
Administrative theory	Authority and discretion are constrained and directed by political oversight	Solidarity ensures fair process and outcomes regardless of the administrative role	Administration exists to ensure the common good as determined by the group or its leaders

Table 9.9 Dialectical differences and similarities in individualist ontologies

Framework element	Individualist ontologies		
	Atomistic Governance	Fragmented Governance	Both
Ontological assumptions	Order established by Nature and laws of natural selection	Immanent change based on cause and effect and social construction	Existence is plural in expression and immanent in source
Language characteristics	Discrete, nonhierarchical	Gerundial, discrete	Entities are separate
Psychosocial theory	Identity is innate; fabricated social contract	Identity changes based on individual choice; no social bond	Independent individuals are the unit of analysis
Epistemological concepts	Truth is determined by the laws of nature and verified through empirical observation	Knowledge is empirically subjective but socially mediated via language	Knowledge is affected by external sources
Belief systems	Nontheistic terms used to describe cosmological order	Beliefs are subjective, relative, and unfounded	There is no transcendent "higher power"
Ethical concepts	Individuals define Good; voluntary social contract defines Right; Right follows Good	Good is individually defined based on preference; Right is not considered or is equated to Good	Both prioritize the individual Good
Political theory	Representation established through competitive pluralism	Representation is impossible and therefore illegitimate	The individual is the only legitimate sovereign
Economic theory	The state should ensure negative liberty as a basis for a natural market system	Any regulation of producers or consumers is coercion and illegitimate	Free market exchange among individuals or households and firms achieves the best results
Administrative theory	Authority and discretion is moderated by political and citizen engagement	The absence of administrative positional authority empowers private actors	Administration enables pluralist processes among individuals

10 The Arc of Reform

As shown in Part II, while never appearing in perfect form, the proponents of each particular approach to governance present their ideal as a utopian vision. Despite their similarities, from any one ontological perspective at least some characteristics of the others are deemed negative or even dystopian. Due to incommensurable and incompatible assumptions and characteristics, these perspectives confront one another in governance practice and compete for primacy. In this type of contestation advocates of each governance approach challenge and critique other approaches in hopes of either achieving dominance or persuading opponents to accept a compromise position.

Furthermore, because actuality rarely reflects ideals, the lived experiences or preferences of the individuals within each paradigm are generally at odds with practice, inevitably resulting in some degree of dissatisfaction. Indeed, true to ideal-types in general, the four primary approaches to governance are rarely present in pure form within any one philosopher's thinking, in any one political theory, or at any one place or time in history. However, patterns of emphasis are apparent in historical events and places. Similarly, ideological themes and mutual critiques are evident in social and political theory.

This chapter exposes the dystopia inherent in each ideal-type's utopia in order to explore why governance reform movements emerge. According to dialectics, each thesis/antithesis pair produces pathological dynamics "when one of the two opposing principles is neglected in favor of the other" (Harmon 1995, 7). These imbalances produce unsatisfactory experiences that ultimately lead to either submission or resistance by individuals. When the resulting existential angst generates refusal of the dominant ideal, reforms push toward a competing approach. Because there are simultaneous resistances pushing toward competing ideologies, this process often results in escalation between two opposing positions (Bateson 1935). These dynamics hinder the progress of both individuals and society.

To make clear how dystopian conditions emerge, we examine movements along the Governance Arc (refer back to Figure 9.1). We explore the dystopian characteristics of each of the primary approaches to governance by considering how the critiques of the static positions move us down the Arc toward the dynamic positions on either end. To explain these reform movements, we

140 *Dystopian utopias*

first augment the Governance Arc by inserting three reform categories placed in the direction they push ideology—Neoliberal, Neoconservative, and Communitarian—in the Arc of Reform (see Figure 10.1).

Liberalism's multiple personality disorder

We begin our analysis at the top of the Arc in the most familiar terrain—the ongoing tension between classical conservative (Hierarchical) and modern (Atomistic) liberalisms. Most contemporary Western theories of politics and administration are associated with liberalism in either its classical or its modern form. To best understand how the movement between these political ideologies is possible it is important to recognize not only what distinguishes classical conservative and modern liberalism, thereby fueling mutual critique, but also what *connects* them ontologically, as it is this overlap that allows reform movements as opposed to revolution. American liberalism, for instance, moves along an agonistic continuum between the two static state ontological positions that are most often associated with their political theory roots: Hobbesian (Hierarchical) and Lockean (Atomistic) perspectives on liberalism's social contract. Donati (2014) argues that these binary positions are complementary in that they "'dance together' so to speak" (16).

This choreography is conceived as a contest between control and freedom, between government and individual, between state and market, and among dominant and weak group identities. Constraining this contest is presented as "the best of all possible worlds.... The West believes it has harnessed the freedom/control antithesis as the engine of history" (Donati 2014, 18), and so the ontological underpinnings fueling this dynamic are frequently left unexamined. The control side of the dialectic is simply downplayed as a necessary evil. As Laclau (2005) notes, liberal democracy is often conceptualized as a political regime comprised of a particular set of universal institutional rules meant to

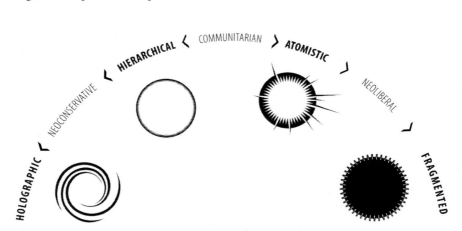

Figure 10.1 The Arc of Reform.

secure freedom and equality, yet which presuppose and potentially reinforce their opposites (a lack of freedom, unequal political power, discrimination, etc.).

As shown in Figure 10.2, the ontological continuum moves between the assumption of the One and the Many. Although these assumptions seem quite different in many respects, they are similar in that they both assume a static, unitary, unchanging, vision of human nature (Love 2012, Stout 2012b, White 1990). In the first instance, the individual is unified by a role within the group; in the latter the Individual is isolated but unitary in identity. As explained in Chapter 9, both sides of this dialectic are built upon the assumptions that (1) existence is static and therefore knowable, and (2) persons are discrete, unitary entities regardless of whether we prioritize the individual's group role or the Individual's unique identity. Psychosocially, both approaches assume that individuals are driven by self-interest to accept a social contract. Taken together, these assumptions frame the political ontology of liberalism.

However, liberalisms differ in how each responds to self-interest and these differences reflect ontological disagreements regarding the source of existence (transcendent versus immanent), the expression of existence (One versus Many), and the psychosocial condition of human beings (embedded versus independent). Beginning at the level of ontology, critique emerges from the dialectic between *singular expression* (One) and *plural expression* (Many) (Stout 2012a, Stout and Love 2013, 2015c). We draw considerably from the Progressive era pragmatist, Mary Follett, as her critique of both forms of liberalism is exceptional (see Stout and Love 2015b). Follett (1998) argues that although the aristocratic founders of the United States feared the tyranny of the masses in modern liberalism, they also feared the executive and legislative powers embodied in classical conservative liberalism. For this reason she insists that fear and suspicion of both the individual and society underlie "the foundation of our

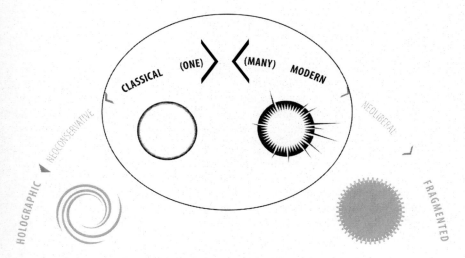

Figure 10.2 Ontological dialectic in liberalism.

142 *Dystopian utopias*

early [American] government" (165). We argue these same fears continue to fuel liberal reform arguments.

According to Marx and Engels (1998), modes of production have moved from feudalism to capitalism to socialism. According to Lacan (1977), societal discourses have moved from Master to University to Hysteric. Considering Hierarchical Governance to be most analogous to feudalism and the discourse of the Master, our analysis begins there.

The bondage of Hierarchical Governance

The centrifugal force of democratic reform movements depicted in the Arc of Reform (see Figure 10.1) often take the classical conservative ideal as the historical and theoretical starting point—the thesis position. Hierarchical Governance assumes that individuality is embedded in a social whole directed by a transcendent source. Therefore, classical conservative liberalism starts from a position of distrust of autonomy in which "the individual [is] feared and suspected" (Follett 1998, 164). Self-interest is understood to be a potential threat to the cosmological order and social good (Bercovitch 1978, Kaufmann 1998). Order must be asserted and deference to societal roles and authority is required. Hierarchical Governance imposes a political hierarchy that replicates the metaphysical hierarchy controlled by a superior guiding force—with the state standing in for the One (Hobbes 2000). In classical conservative liberalism, this hierarchy justifies political leadership in which decisions regarding the public good are made through a trustee model of representation.

From other perspectives, however, this social hierarchy is *not* cosmologically given, and therefore the existing political system is a form of representative elitism that "has produced 'privilege'" (Follett 1998, 132) through laws that perpetuate the subordination of certain groups. From the Hierarchical perspective, these systems of privilege are justified and reinforced by a "faith in the idea of a divinely created *hierarchy*—of the righteous domination of some parts over others" (Bennett 2010, 61). But from other perspectives the result is a problematic perpetuation of "otherwise inexplicable ideas that the rich deserve to get richer, that war is prolife, and that force can set us free" (61). According to Farmer (2005b), this hierarchical dominance is reified through the "cult of the leader" (141), a phenomenon that is "so ingrained psychologically and socially that most cannot imagine a society without hierarchy" (145)—we assume we *must* have superiors.

These hierarchical assumptions carry forward in psychosocial theory through an innate social order. This hierarchy is even woven into Western languages, which emphasize static, binary relationships between things that create a structure of dominance of one over the other, generating a "violent hierarchy" (Derrida 1981, 41). For example, fact is better than value, reason is better than emotion, mind is better than body, spirit is better than material, reality is better than perception, and so forth. Derrida (1976) deconstructs these supposedly natural hierarchies, revealing them to be socially determined values.

The Arc of Reform   143

Unfortunately, these values also play out in social identities. Foucault (1972) argues that one of the most oppressive aspects of (Western) language is its tendency toward categorization, which enables domination and exclusion. His ideas are explored in a variety of cultural studies that analyze the hierarchical nature of binaries (e.g., Barker 2000), such as male/female, straight/queer, Caucasian/people of color, colonizer/indigenous, Western/Eastern, and global North/South. From these perspectives, language fundamentally frames our subject positions as individuals and members of social groups—and this process is laced with power dynamics. In each set, the dominant identity forces individuals to align with its position in the dualism or become marginalized: "Those excluded claim rights that the community theoretically accepts as legitimate but denies them in practice" (Laclau 2005, 259). Therefore, Marcuse (1964, 1969) calls on minorities, outsiders, and public intellectuals to promote radical thinking, opposition, and refusal through identity politics. Keating (2013) takes this call a step further, arguing that even identity politics "reinforce the very systems against which we struggle" (3).

The same cultural dynamic plagues political representation. Catlaw (2007a) insists that the political project of representation rests on an inherent paradox in which the need to *fabricate* a hierarchical political regime demonstrates that the ontological assumptions underlying it are mistaken. This project of "fabricating a People"—or universal identity—and attempting to mitigate disorder and maintain social roles will necessarily lead to system failure "because the People as such *does not exist*" (114). These critiques undermine the democratic legitimacy of Hierarchical Governance—even when those at the top of the hierarchy are chosen by the citizens. Follett (1998) describes representative democracy as the "fiction of the 'consent of the governed'" (168), arguing "this is not enough, to elect officials and then to listen to their policy and consent.... There is no democracy without contribution" (Follett 2013b, 215). She argues that systems of representation are "hardly distinguishable from coercion" (200) and are at best a "first step" for "backward countries" where no form of consent currently exists (Follett 2003e, 211). Indeed, Follett (1998) asserts that the founders of the United States were at core elitist. Their objective was to limit the active participation of ordinary citizens and retain decision-making authority with elite leaders. Consent of the governed simply creates "a tendency towards aristocracy" (164). Even now, vestiges of authoritarian governance remain in democracies (Thorne and Kouzmin 2007).

Economic and administrative theory follow suit. As Kouzmin (1980) explains, "hierarchy provides the frame and the setting of analysis. Resulting theory ignores the fact that hierarchy masks crucial differentiation in power, rank and reward" (142). This phenomenon has been referred to as living "in the shadow of organization" (Denhardt 1981); the hierarchical ideals have spread to all domains of society, echoing Weber's concern about "the extension of formal rationality to all areas of life as a *form of domination*" (Hamilton 1991, 86). In what Catlaw (2007a) calls a "disciplinary society" (142), order and efficiency are exerted from the macrolevel through disciplinary processes at the

144 *Dystopian utopias*

microlevel in all organizations and groups. He argues that discipline is precisely the purpose that government is meant to achieve as it regulates and constrains all those who fall outside the hierarchical categories through administrative action.

Organizations and groups of all types mirror societal ordering; individuals increasingly truncate their own sense of identity and potential actions, becoming ever more defined by roles circumscribed by their place in the hierarchy. Catlaw (2007a) explains this constrains identity because such roles do not imagine whole beings; instead, individuals are "broken down into representational political categories and identities of discrete disciplinary enclosure (home, workplace, etc.)" (141). As Katz and Kahn (1978) note, when the system "neither requires nor wants the whole person" (46), individuals are merely functional parts. Over time, this "depersonalized actor" suffers a form of "psychosis" (Ramos 1981, 86) because "their basic humanity [is] denied" (Ritzer 2008, 27).

Even in the best-case scenarios, command and control hinders productive processes by resolving conflict through domination (Follett 2003b), destroying creative capacity as well (Evans 2000b). Input to decision making is limited to the facts and values held by those at the very top echelons of the hierarchy. The ultimate decision on what to do and how to do it lies with the executive at the helm; therefore, orders may not be appropriately responsive to the situation (Follett 2003b). Fulfillment of those orders is then demanded through hierarchical authority, rules, procedures, and laws; a fear of reprimand drives action. While this system may enjoy high levels of efficiency and compliance, at both an individual and societal level, control serves to inhibit development—which may be understood as progress in the material sense, or more broadly as the betterment of the ecological and psychological conditions of the world and its beings.

In sum, Hierarchical Governance binds people in social roles that do not fit identities and truncate self-expression. Hierarchy perpetuates domination in all spheres of society, limiting social action through command and control. In the dystopian extreme, we find that these hierarchical controls and role constraints produce the pathology of *bondage*. On this point, it matters little where one is in the hierarchy; although top positions have significantly more autonomy, one's societal role may have little fit to one's authentic sense of self, causing both "masters" and "slaves" to feel trapped (Denhardt 1981). Indeed, it has been argued that "even the ruling class does not *like* government, but needs the state for the purpose of exploiting, and thereby oppressing, the mass" (Goodwin 2007, 129). When control becomes too pervasive and untenable, individuals may reassert autonomy and self-interest in an attempt to renegotiate or resist the social contract through an Atomistic Governance approach.

The isolation of Atomistic Governance

When refusals of classical conservativism are driven by efforts to claim Individuality, as depicted in the Arc of Reform (see Figure 10.1), the centrifugal forces of democratic reform push liberalism toward its modern ideal. Atomistic

The Arc of Reform   145

Governance can be seen as a critical response to the bondage of Hierarchical Governance in which "no institution was trusted" (Follett 1998, 165). The independent individual was argued to be "peculiarly sacred" (Follett 1919, 579) and thus should be protected from threats from the political and economic hierarchy. According to Follett (1998), perpetuation of this underlying fear of social control "is in part a reaction to a misunderstood Hegelianism" (263–264), in which individual interest and state interest are thought to be fundamentally in conflict and mutually exclusive.

Atomistic Governance assumes that all individuals are unitary entities motivated by self-interest. Weber (1946) describes such pluralism as an irreconcilable host of "possible attitudes toward life" (152) and likens it to polytheism, whereby "many old gods ascend from their graves; they are disenchanted and hence take the form of impersonal forces. They strive to gain power over our lives and again they resume their eternal struggle with one another" (149). The discrete, noun-based structure of Western languages reiterates this separation and competition (Bohm 1980). Thus, rational Individuals must voluntarily enter into a social contract to form the state to protect their freedoms to the greatest degree possible (Locke 1980). Modern liberalism seeks to maximize individual freedom, with social order emerging only as "a result of the free interplay of its members' interests" (Ramos 1981, 31). This requires that all social contracts be voluntarily fabricated to be legitimate. Individuals may choose to band together—forming agreements and shared interests—but the individual is not beholden to such groups and may enter or leave them at will. The ontological disenchantment of modernity produced atomism and political pluralism (Howe 2006). In short, Atomistic Governance is guided by a vision of freedom in which government interference is minimized and the individual is protected from the encroachment of others (Fineman 2004).

Walzer (1984) suggests that liberal individualism resulted historically from breaking apart the once unified society through a separation of the spheres of social action—public, economic, and civic. This separation was created and supported "through the collaborating powers of capitalism, science, and the state" (Wolin 1981, 26). Translating into our terminology, the positivist ontology undergirding modern liberalism and the free-market economy also created a separation of individual and social action. Critics argue "the goal that liberalism sets for the art of separation—every person within his or her own circle—is literally unattainable" (Walzer 1984, 324); we are mutually interdependent in social groups. Follett (2013b) argues that the supposed mutual exclusivity of individual versus group is "a myth of the pluralists" (220), invented to support their opposition to representative elitism and their promotion of populist pluralism. Follett (1919) questions the assertion that there is a pre-social, independent "individual who stands outside and looks at his groups" (579), and instead insists "the fallacy of pluralism is not its pluralism, but that it is based on a non-existent individual" (579). Similarly, Bakunin (1972a) argues that this concept of Individuality rests on problematic "metaphysics [which] overlook the fact that man is a social animal," and therefore mistakenly views society as a "wholly

146   *Dystopian utopias*

artificial conglomerate of individuals, who suddenly organise themselves on the basis of some secret or sacred compact out of their free will" (57). In other words, while it is reasonable to remove the individual from a hierarchical cosmological order, it is impossible to separate human beings from their physical and social context.

Grounded in these erroneous philosophical assumptions, the pluralist state is a laissez-faire state—one in which the government minimizes centralized control, leaving decisions and actions up to pluralist competition to the greatest degree possible. Given this ongoing contest, ballot box democracy is presented as the ideal method for decision making in the polis; individuals and interest groups engage in a winner-takes-all political competition. Follett (1998) likens this process of competition and aggregation to "the helter-skelter strivings of an endless number of social atoms" and insists such competition "can never give us a fair and ordered world" (154). She argues that majority rule faces a conundrum because "democracy is not a sum in addition. Democracy is not brute numbers" (5). She points to the problems of aggregate public will, demanding to know, "Who are the people? Every individual? The majority? A theoretical average? A compromise group?" (220).

In best-case scenarios the majority may enact a compromise solution in an attempt "if not to gain power, at least to produce an equilibrium" (Follett 2013b, 182). However, in compromise all parties lose something, with some groups consistently losing more than others. Balance in such a system cannot be maintained, either because interests change or because the original desires, unfulfilled in compromise, re-emerge. Instead of achieving balance, the minority must continually reassert itself through ongoing competition with the majority. Indeed, pluralism leads to intensified efforts on the part of individuals and groups to achieve dominance. Individuals set themselves against one another in order to win through persuasion, which typically reflects de facto domination, even in compromise (Follett 2003a). Those who are in a position of privilege within the system are able to maintain their control because choices within pluralism are framed by the elite (Follett 2013b). The competition is rigged because "mere consent, bare consent, gives us only the benefit of the ideas of those who put forward the propositions for consent" (Follett 2003e, 210). Thus, atomistic competition fails to eliminate social hierarchy as promised, resulting instead in a form of oligarchy by monied interests (Gilens and Page 2014).

In the worst-case scenarios "it is the desire of the dominant classes which by the sorcery of consent becomes 'the will of the people'" (Follett 2013b, 209). Pluralism hinders productive public processes by utilizing an oppositional politics (Keating 2013) that resolves conflict through bargaining and competitive negotiation toward a compromise rather than creative and cooperative integration (Follett 2003a). Input to decision making is limited to the facts and values linked to self-interest (Follett 2013b) and "premised on a series of winners and losers, [in which] we struggle fiercely to come out—as one of the winners" (Keating 2013, 8). If the decision does not reflect one's preferences, self-interest drives a refusal to comply and attempts to find loopholes for desired behavior.

The Arc of Reform   147

This lack of compliance will limit the successful implementation of public decisions. While this system may enjoy high levels of effectiveness with those in agreement with the decision, self-interested behavior will tend to subvert the overall public benefit as it can leave many minorities indifferent or defiant (Follett 2003a). Because all parties lose something, agreements are short-lived and the competition continues to re-emerge.

Unfortunately, these failures of pluralism repeat throughout the political economy. Atomistic Governance expects individuals to maintain a high degree of self-sufficiency by pursuing individual interests that are equated with "economic advantage" (Follett 2013b, 35) in a monetized system of scarce resources. In this system, "each one of us is an individual who wins human dignity by earning property through hard work in competition with others" (Hummel 2008, 56) in a zero-sum game—what one party wins, another party loses. Polyani (1944) argues that individuals see each other as threats to their own self-interest and understand differences in status as reflecting differences in merit, rather than opportunity or privilege. Pluralism merely gives "lip service to these ideals in a society in which policy and law protect and perpetuate existing and historic inequality" (Fineman 2004, 3).

Marx and Engels (1998) describe aspects of the human condition that have been destroyed by capitalism's system of competitive market exchange.[1] At core, personal worth is reduced to mere production and exchange value. "The bourgeoisie has torn away from the family its sentimental veil, and has reduced the family relation to a mere money relation" (chapter 1). Family ties are broken and both spouses and children become instruments of material accumulation. All social relations are disrupted and labor loses its quality of self-expression and authentic purpose. Building on these concerns, conservatives fear that as the economy shifts from feudalism to capitalism, replacing land with capital as the principle source of wealth creates a new hierarchy of power that destroys the bastions of social strength: bonds with family, neighborhood, church, and community. Under such conditions, the social contract commodifies relationship by turning it into transaction rather than an authentic sharing of experience (McSwite 1997, 2006), making people function like a crowd rather than a group (Follett 1998, Stivers 2008). Social isolation transforms social *action*—a concept differentiated by having subjective meaning assigned to it by the actor (Weber 1994c)—into habitual or reactive *behavior* that has no shared subjective meaning (Weber 1994e).

As Davis (2003) notes, when relationships are reduced to market transactions, Individuals are assumed to be substantively unchanged by their interactions. Follett (2013c) similarly asserts that this myth of independence "does a great deal of harm" because "we cannot have any sound relations with each other as long as we take [individuals] out of the setting which gave them their meaning and value" (24). The myth of independence distorts how people "conceive themselves in relation to other humans, to human structures and institutions, and to the nonhuman or natural environment" (Gauthier 1977, 131), in a manner that undermines both the individual and society. Indeed, modern

148 *Dystopian utopias*

liberal capitalism causes many to experience a sense of loss of community and a growing sense of isolation in the expectation of self-sufficiency (Macpherson 1962, Phillips 2002). This creates a social pathology in which all others are to be feared as a threat, making trust in others risky or even foolhardy.

Consent through voting along with equality of opportunity in market exchange is "our Great Illusion" (Follett 1998, 220) in this political economy. Even in ideal circumstances, it "reflects only a majority's imposition of its will upon minorities" (Thayer 1980, 126). Furthermore, pluralist competition and the expectation of independent self-sufficiency weakens social ties among political minorities, minimizing their political and economic power. Paradoxically, the shift from Hierarchical control to Atomistic pluralism enables *better* control of individuals and social groups because, as observed by Foucault (1977, 1991), governmentality is transferred from the state to the individual through voluntary self-control. Individuals monitor and adjust their own behavior in order to win their place among the privileged elite.

In sum, pluralist democracy and market exchange do not provide a mechanism to escape the domination feared in Hierarchical Governance—they only provide a veneer of liberty through competition that perpetuates inequalities. Within this system one can never hope to achieve freedom from domination unless one's interests happen to align with the majority on an ongoing basis. As a result, this system fails to eliminate the bondage of hierarchies, which pluralism allegedly abhors. Instead, we argue that the pluralist democracy, capitalist market economy, and the associated laissez-faire state of Atomistic Governance produce the pathology of *isolation*. This existential condition allows for a new form of domination under the auspices of negative liberty. While those who share the interests and characteristics of the "winners" of pluralist competition may feel they are a part of a social contract, the "losers" in pluralist politics and market exchange are excluded and set adrift. Adding the assumption of meritocracy, these separations legitimate discrimination against or domination of particular groups of individuals. Therefore, the demand for more universal identity and rights encourages a move toward Hierarchical Governance.

The dialectic between liberalisms

Considering the fundamental assumption of static, unitary i/Individuality joined through social contract—either natural or fabricated—means that while the two liberal positions "may at times be incompatible ... they are not incommensurable ... [They] offer alternatives utilizing a common currency" (Zanetti 2004, 136). The commonality of static actors joined through a social contract is what allows movement between the two positions, but their different understandings of ontological collectivism versus individualism leads to an underlying tension as individuals find themselves simultaneously bound and isolated.

The dialectical tension between ontological assumptions of One versus Many drives the critiques that the two forms of liberalism make of one another. The dialectic is clearly one between the order of the state (a Hierarchical, collectivist

The Arc of Reform 149

One) versus the liberty of the individual (an Atomistic, individualist Many). This is classically articulated in de Tocqueville's (2000) observation of the way in which Americans keep the tension between community and individualism in balance (Vetter 2008). Rohr (1989) similarly outlines a "structured ambiguity" in the US Constitutional heritage—one in which human needs for community and governance compete with a commitment to individual rights to equality, freedom, and property (291). This tension also reveals itself in competing public ethics and political ideologies, particularly in the tenuous balance between the liberal ideals of equality and liberty (Follett 1998, Potter 1976). On one hand, the notion of equality emphasizes treatment relative to others as part of the whole, pushing liberalism toward Hierarchical Governance. On the other hand, liberty tends to be framed in terms of freedom from interference (from the state or other individuals) to pursue one's own unique goals, pushing liberalism toward Atomistic Governance.

From these mutual critiques, we might say that we have not escaped the paradox of liberalism. Instead, political theory seems to run in circles trying to resolve the dialectic, or it attempts to "paper over" the divide (Fox and Miller 1995, 258). Rather than being a tradition firmly rooted in either Hierarchical Governance or Atomistic Governance, liberalism is engaged in a constant back-and-forth between the two static state ontological positions. As MacIntyre (1988) argues,

> So-called conservatism and so-called radicalism of these contemporary guises are in general mere stalking-horses for liberalism: the contemporary debates within modern political systems are almost exclusively between conservative liberals, liberal liberals, and radical liberals. There is little place in such political systems for the criticism of the system itself, that is, for putting liberalism in question.
>
> (392)

These opposing positions reflect the two dominant ideas about the relationship between the political subject and the polis in Western political ideology. From an ontological perspective, liberalism attempts to balance its collectivist and individualistic extremes in an odd form of multiple personality disorder. The theoretical choice is to "let the contradiction stand" (King and Zanetti 2005, 50), or seek some form of compromise that is likely to result in domination by "pro-state liberalism" (Ventriss 1989, 175). The value of the former approach is to ensure that the important conflicts and differences revealed by thesis and antithesis moments are not obscured (Padgett 2002). Therefore, the most common narrative found in discussions of a globally appropriate approach to governance—an effective common ground—is that the tenuous balance held in tension between the characteristics of Hierarchical Governance and Atomistic Governance is the best model we have. However, as Thayer (1981) might argue, we simply continue leaping back and forth between the frying pan of hierarchy and the fire of competition, not really improving our lot as human beings at all.

150 *Dystopian utopias*

An attempt to establish equilibrium is seen most vividly in the communitarian proposals, examined in detail below. However, analyzing the underlying ontological continuum demonstrates that the two liberal positions cannot produce a satisfactory compromise between centralized hierarchical authoritarianism and decentralized competitive chaos; instead, too much hierarchy for some demands more competition, and an excess of competition for others demands more hierarchy (Thayer 1981). Furthermore, the dialectic can never produce a universal subject. As Laclau (2005) argues, liberal populism is particularist, based on multiple group identities; and as Catlaw (2007a) argues, these and even more singular identities will always undermine attempts to fabricate a People.

Marcuse (1964) describes this pervasive condition of domination by liberalism's obscured tenets as "one-dimensional" and Ramos (1981) calls it "unidimensional." Because fear of self-interest drives liberal democracy toward social organization and because domination by elites or majorities is ultimately the result of both forms, liberal institutions of all types tend to organize social action to curb self-interested behavior and subdue conflict (Marcuse 1964, Ramos 1981, Thayer 1981). The structure and top-down bureaucratic control central to classical conservative liberalism reflects Hierarchical Governance's fear of the uninhibited individual (Follett 1998). And, while modern liberalism also fears selfishness, Atomistic Governance resolves the problem through democracy's voluntary social contract (Harmon 1981). Thus, we see that the shared assumption of "fear, not faith" (Follett 1998, 165) produces the assumed need for social control of the individual in both hierarchy and competition (Thayer 1981).

This ongoing tension creates generalized angst: "fear of others and fears of the government" (Catlaw 2007c). This means that the "the state as apparatus or state as nation is always a security state, always dependent on fear, on terror, to justify the protection that only it can provide" (Heckert 2011, 204). But like a self-fulfilling prophecy, the fears and mistrust then exacerbate the very self-interest meant to be controlled (Denhardt 1981, Harmon and Mayer 1986, Reich 1988, Ross 1996, Will 1983). These mutual fears generate governance approaches that produce either bondage or isolation. Paradoxically, at the level of lived experience, bondage isolates from authentic identity and isolation causes the minority to bind themselves to the majority. Thus, the imagined ideal of letting the contradiction stand between liberalisms fails to produce acceptable governance outcomes.

The calcification of the Reified Community

Communitarianism seeks to resolve the liberal dialectic by addressing the problems of self-interest on a smaller scale. Donati (2014) describes this as an anti-modern theory that refutes the differentiation between freedom and control. We suggest that communitarianism does so by pushing either side of the static ontological continuum (see Figure 10.3) toward the center rather than apart.

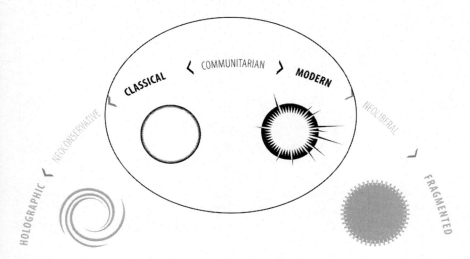

Figure 10.3 Communitarian liberalism.

Thus, there are two basic types of communitarian critique: (1) a call for a greater sense of community, pushing modern liberalism (Atomistic Governance) toward classical conservative liberalism (Hierarchical Governance), and (2) a call for more diversity within unity, pushing classical conservative liberalism (Hierarchical Governance) toward modern liberalism (Atomistic Governance). Thus, rather than being fundamentally different from the dialectic between liberalisms, communitarian reforms actually reiterate the same dynamics, but at a more nuanced level of debate.

While not as prevalent today, there is a historical precedent of political reforms that push classical conservative liberalism toward modern liberalism. For example, the American Revolution "set loose a libertarian spirit that terrified moderate and propertied democrats" (Bercovitch 1978, 134). In response, both the Federalist and Antifederalist movements sought to moderate the shift toward Atomistic Governance that had emerged; the former sought a return to Hierarchical terrain while the latter stopped short at a centrist position.

Federalists, concerned with what they regarded as extreme decentralization of power and the potential for popular insurrection, responded to modern liberal political rhetoric with classical conservative perspectives that called for centralization of power in the hands of the political elite. Writings warned of the "lusts and boundless appetites of men" (anonymous author quoted in Bercovitch 1978, 135), and promised disastrous consequences for the newly minted country if these self-interested impulses in the populace were left unchecked. These urges needed to submit to the guidance and control of more enlightened representatives. Thus, we see a countervailing push back toward Hierarchical Governance. As noted by Box (2004), such classical republicanism has evolved into the contemporary communitarian movement.

152 *Dystopian utopias*

Attempts to moderate this reform were made by the Antifederalists, who emphasized a moderate version of the individualism idealized in Atomistic Governance. Antifederalists sought to keep "government close to home so that homogeneous groupings of people in particular locales could more easily reach agreement, govern themselves without great strife, and live in harmony" (Cooper 2011, 9). From this position, particular groupings of citizens are not "national collectivities, but ... neighborhoods, associations, regions, networks, subcultures, age groups, ethnicities, and lifestyle sectors—in short, communities" (Rose 2000, 1398). McSwite (1997) argues that Antifederalists were motivated by a desire to "guard against the encroachment of social divisions based on class" (90), instead emphasizing active citizen involvement in communities as a form of reclaiming self-governance. Cooper (2011) suggests that "Antifederalists saw moral community as the solution" (9). Ostensibly, community members are more able to express their unique perspectives and have a meaningful impact on the voluntary social contract than in society writ large, thereby pushing Hierarchical Governance toward Atomistic Governance.

These early communitarians also anticipated the need for Hierarchical Governance characteristics that would become prominent in contemporary communitarianism; they placed an emphasis on morality and group cohesion where self-interest was situated within a general "moral sentiment" (Smith 2000a), in which natural rights produce an "obligation to mutual love amongst men" (Locke 1980, 8) alongside "self love ... ill nature, passion and revenge" (12). This "self-interest rightly understood" (de Tocqueville 2000, 525) is enabled by "positive liberty" and a desire "to participate in the process by which my life is controlled" (Berlin 2013, 178). For example, Montesquieu (1989) identifies "virtue" as the primary principle of democracies, in which individuals are guided by considerations of both private and public good, but are willing to suspend private gains at times for the benefit of the social group. Similarly, contemporary communitarian reforms (Etzioni 1996, 1998, Putnam 2000) and Third Way governance (Blair 1998, Giddens 1999) are much more prone to act as counterweights to Atomistic Governance, pushing back toward the classical conservative liberalism of Hierarchical Governance. These reforms lament the severed link between individual and community, charging that the modern liberal ethos is "oblivious to that essential human interdependency that underlies all political life" (Barber 1984, 25). It is this desire for belongingness that drives these reform efforts.

The commonality among communitarian reform efforts is that they each seek to push modern liberalism back toward its classical conservative roots, while maintaining some sphere of protection for negative liberty. As Clark (1998) suggests, communitarians seek to balance the liberal focus on rights, autonomy, and choice with the conservative emphasis on duty, participation, and commitment. Communitarians believe that greater democratic participation and commitment to community will ultimately revitalize civil society, expanding liberty by creating greater civility, trust, and a sense of shared purpose that will guide individuals in both the market and government. However, we argue that so long as reforms are offered along the same static ontological continuum, they

The Arc of Reform 153

will be unable to produce an acceptable universal identity. While not the bondage associated with Hierarchical Governance, the community identity demanded produces the pathology we call *calcification*. To maintain belonging within the community, identity must be inflexible and unchanging. Furthermore, communitarian liberalism fails to resolve the dialectic between order and liberty. The debate remains over who should control the coercive powers of hierarchy (state versus community) and how much competition is too extreme for social order—maintaining the existential tension in an unending back and forth, albeit traversing less ontological ground in these centrist positions.

Schismogenic escalation

The tension described above results in an ongoing process of mutual critique between competing liberalisms. While communitarianism seeks to anchor liberalism to an elusive stable center, other appeals to collectivism and individualism escalate, moving toward increasingly extreme manifestations. *Schismogenesis* is a term that describes a progressive distortion of opposing dualities (Bateson 1935). Due to the dynamics of ontological colonization discussed in Chapter 3, we see this dialectic between the One (Hierarchical/Holographic) and the Many (Atomistic/Fragmented) as a "symmetrical differentiation" (Bateson 1935, 68) of competing moves toward the extremes—starting with the static state ideals and then moving toward the dynamic state ideals.

As Proudhon (1979) argues, authority and liberty are "two complementary, opposed, and irreducible principles" such that neither can be fully realized but each must "make mutual borrowings" of the another leading to "incessant revolution" (31). The two sides of the dialectic engage in a reflexive hegemony, leading to "more and more extreme rivalry and ultimately to hostility and the breakdown of the system" (Bateson 1935, 68). Each pushes in opposing ideological directions toward ever stronger ideals, resulting in movement down either side of the Arc of Reform. New freedoms are met with new controls in what Donati (2014) describes as "the schizophrenia typical of daily life in our times" (22), where these systems of freedom and control become increasingly abstract and disconnected from one another both conceptually and in practice.

Referring again to the Arc of Reform (see Figure 10.1), neoconservative and neoliberal appeals to the One and the Many are mutually amplified (Love 2013). Each ideological side first draws upon the ideals of the static state ontological positions, as described in reference to the dialectic between liberalisms and the two communitarian reform movements. However, as the positions polarize, both sides of the debate begin to draw ideals from their radical counterparts of socialism and individualist anarchism in argumentation for nationalist solidarity versus increased autonomy from the state. The following sections will trace the trajectory of these countervailing reform movements as excesses of monism and pluralism.

154 *Dystopian utopias*

The absorption of Holographic Governance

Neoconservative reforms push Hierarchical Governance toward Holographic Governance based on a pronounced fear of unhampered self-interest (Curtis 2004, Brown 2006). The concern is that "the politics of liberty could degenerate into a libertinism" that will destroy the bonds of society (Weinstein 2004, 204). If public policy is driven only by rational self-interest, society will decline into a chaos of conflicting greed. Therefore, governments should focus on strengthening traditional values and institutions to balance out the effects of the market economy.

Neoconservative reforms begin with the rejection of individualist relativism within liberalism (Curtis 2004) and seek to "convert" classical conservative liberalism into a "new kind of conservative politics" (Kristol 2004b, 33). This emerges as an extension of the welfare state in which strong government is utilized to create a safety net for those who reflect specific cultural and moral ideals and are therefore deemed worthy (Brown 2006, Kristol 2004a, 2004b). These reforms amplify myths of unity and nation while calling for the positioning of a strong elite that can enforce social and moral norms, both domestically and abroad (Brown 2006, Curtis 2004, Kristol 2004b, Kristol and Kagan 2004). In these appeals to nationalism and unity, the Holographic Governance ideals of unity and the safety it affords are held up as desirable goals, while the Hierarchical Governance ideals of strong central authority and elite control are maintained.

Continuing the emphasis of the whole, the radical socialist critique is not satisfied with any stratification of society. In particular, socialist reforms or "old social movements" of the mid 1800s sought to eradicate the stratification of society through economic class (Day 2011). New social movements of the 1960s to 1980s sought to free all political and economic identities from state oppression. From these perspectives, the individual must be understood as socially embedded, but true unity and equality requires that individuals must also be freed from hierarchy. Thus, further critique of both classical conservative liberalism and neoconservativism pushes ideology toward the monist extreme of Holographic Governance—we really *can* be one egalitarian People. Thus, Holographic Governance seeks to establish a harmonious order that eliminates class conflict once and for all (Stavrakakis 2005).

However, in a system where all are envisioned as the same, inclusion within the whole becomes coercive as opposed to participative. As Mueller (2011) explains, Marxism held that one need only take over the institutions of the state to bring capitalism to heel—by empowering the workers to control the means of production. But this ignores the coercive powers of the state itself. Each person is forced into a "mechanical solidarity" that emphasizes similarities and discourages differentiation (Durkheim 1984). In Holographic Governance, individuality is frowned upon because the social ideal is one of total unification and homogeneity, marking a movement from a disciplinary society to a "society of control" in which discipline creeps across boundaries, such that "the confinement never ends" (Catlaw 2007a, 167). This is a perspective that emphasizes

The Arc of Reform 155

unity through "an appeal to consensus that is overwhelmingly tyrannical and totalitarian" (Eze 2008, 391), a form of "conceptual terrorism" (392), in that it suppresses individuation and gains unanimity through social coercion.

As Proudhon (1979) explains, this extreme vision of unity requires viewing "everything that may divide their will, break up their mass, create diversity, plurality, [and] divergence" as "affronts" to the unified People and therefore difference must be eradicated to the fullest extent possible. This is seen in contemporary social movements that seek to unify groups of individuals under the auspices of a common identity while denying difference; the result is likely to reinforce "authoritarian, racist, sexist, heteronormative policies in the new society that they create" (Adams 2011, 118).

These perspectives reflect a common critique of an ontology of abundance—the source of existence within is so substantively full that it crowds out individual identity. As Stuart Hall (1998) describes it, ontologically there is "total encapsulation" (447). Durkheim (1984) similarly explains, "When the collective consciousness completely envelops our own consciousness, coinciding with it at every point. At that moment our individuality is zero" (84). Paradoxically, under such conditions individuals have ceased to be *social* because there is no difference across which to relate to one another: "They are all imprisoned in the subjectivity of their singular experience, which does not cease to be singular if the same experience is multiplied innumerable times" (Arendt 1998, 58).

These encounters between the individual and the group or society can be expected to hinder productive public processes by resolving conflict through voluntary homogenization that Follett (1998) describes as the "imitation" (37) of "the crowd trying to preserve itself as it is" (Follett 2013b, 128). Input to decision making is limited to established societal norms. While this is an efficient decision-making approach, it suppresses authentic perspectives. Even if participation is invited, the expectation of homogeneity will prevent disagreement. This lack of authentic engagement limits the effectiveness of public decisions, as they will be the result of a "herd" mentality that congregates based on similarities or the purpose of "seeking the 'comfort' of fellowship" (Follett 1998, 89). While this approach may enjoy high levels of consistency, the lack of creative choice limits societal progress. When the group becomes homogeneous, there are no longer differences that enable individuals to learn from one another (Eze 2008).

Some critiques see the problem as being one of scale. Durkheim (1984) argues that group identity

> alters in nature as societies grow more immense. Because they are spread over a much vaster area, the common consciousness is itself forced to rise above all local diversities, to dominate more the space available, and consequently become more abstract.
>
> (230)

The alienating effects of this expansion are also depicted by Catlaw (2007a); as the identity of the People expands to include ever-increasing categories of

156   *Dystopian utopias*

diversity, eventually none experiences authentic identification with the People. However, while some agrarian communal societies (Baradat 2012) and tribal societies (Durkheim 1984) may exist successfully for a period of time, the short-lived experiments of communities such as New Harmony in the United States reveal that these issues occur on a small scale as well. Regardless of the size of the whole, individuals will eventually seek to escape assimilation through their assertion of authentic identity. As Durkheim (1984) warns, "individuality cannot arise until the community fills us less completely" (84).

In sum, the Holographic Governance perspective assumes and demands homogeneity in a way that denies authentic uniqueness and puts the individual at the effect of the whole. The differentiated role classifications in Hierarchical Governance are rejected, but the negative impact of socially imposed roles is accentuated by collapsing all roles into one universal identity. Relationally, centralized state power "percolate[s] into the associations themselves, modifying their structure and their whole inner life" (Buber 1971, 131). As a result, the collectivist pathology of bondage found in Hierarchical Governance expands into *absorption* in Holographic Governance. As Davis (2003) explains, the "pure embedding" of the individual is an "unsustainable conception" (108)—regardless of the scale of this absorptive identification with the group, individuals will attempt to assert their individuality and self-generated connections with others.

The alienation of Fragmented Governance

In the other ontological direction, neoliberal reforms push Atomistic Governance toward Fragmented Governance based on a pronounced fear of authoritarian control and a rejection of centralized authority created by majority rules. Neoliberalism asserts that attempts to balance individual and group in both forms of liberalism can only lead to a "Frankenstein that will destroy the very freedom we establish it to protect" (Friedman 2002, 2). Indeed, those who try suffer from what Hayek (1973) calls the *synoptic delusion*—the "assumption that we know everything needed for full explanation or control" (12). For neoliberals like Hayek, this assumption of omniscience plagues any attempts to control or regulate political and economic behavior. These critiques are echoed in Ayn Rand's objectivism, which is presented as the "opposite" of both conservativism (Peikoff 1991) and socialism (Rand 1964). Objectivism accentuates the negative liberty of Atomistic Governance through a complete separation of government and market (Rand 1964), while falling just shy of individualist anarchism (Peikoff 1991).

Insisting on "the significance of our institutional ignorance in the economic sphere" (Hayek 1973, 13), neoliberals demand a radical decentralization of both economic and political authority (Friedman 2002, Hayek 2001). This demand is justified because the only way to coordinate the economic transactions of millions of people is either radical centralization or radical decentralization: only the latter is acceptable (Friedman 2002). To achieve these ends, neoliberals push the moderate laissez-faire economics of Atomistic Governance even further, promoting the eradication of all regulation in the free market. This extreme market-based polity draws upon the Fragmented Governance ideals of self-sufficiency and free choice, while maintaining the stability promised by Atomistic Governance in limiting economic regulation to what is required for a functional market (e.g., stable currency, contract laws, etc.).

However, postmodern and libertarian critiques of modern liberalism are aimed at neoliberalism as well—particularly the accusation that political pluralism and the market merely obfuscate, rather than eliminate, social control. This "McDonaldization" of contemporary society (Ritzer 2008) systematically hollows out the state (Milward and Provan 2000), as the market is deregulated and privatization increasingly replaces state functions (Osborne and Gaebler 1992). As political theorist Wendy Brown (2006) notes, neoliberalism redefines political subjects as both "entrepreneurs and consumers whose moral autonomy is measured by their capacity for 'self-care'—their ability to provide for their own needs and service their own ambitions" (694). However, rather than fulfilling the promise of self-sufficiency, individuals find themselves subject to the whims of the market. Individuals are simply encouraged to enjoy varied, fleeting, and even contradictory pursuits no matter what the cost; this injunction is even presented as a citizen's duty (Dean 2006).

In response, postmodern critiques of neoliberalism push ideology even further down the Arc of Reform into the pluralist extreme of Fragmented Governance, "a worldview in which individualism is taken to extremes" (Zanetti and Adams 2000, 536), eventually devolving into a complete lack of commonality.[2] In an effort to escape systems of control found in any liberal ideology, postmodern and radical individualist critiques are centrally preoccupied with the deconstruction of grand narratives and social identities through resistance and refusal. This leads to a proliferation of counter-hegemonic social movements—a "constellation of opposition" (Adams 2011). While the libertarian and anarchist social movements succeed in deconstructing the hegemony of the state and capitalism, they often result in particularist counter-hegemonies. These power-seeking groups stand alone in attempts to secure their own identities, making them vulnerable to cooptation. Thus, all such social movements must be rejected, leading ultimately to libertarian anarchism, which promises the ideals of full self-sufficiency and complete liberation from the coercion of hegemonic social forces through the dissolution of society itself.

At this extreme, the ideal of Fragmented Governance comes into play. This nihilistic strand of postmodern thought (Bogason 2001) has been described as the "dark side of postmodernism" (Boje 2006, 483). This perspective depicts a world in which society is deconstructed and there is a "total acceptance of the ephemerality, fragmentation, discontinuity" (Harvey 1990, 44). As Rosenau (1992) explains, "The skeptical post-modernist (or merely skeptics), offering a pessimistic, negative, gloomy assessment, argue that the postmodern age is one of fragmentation, disintegration, malaise, meaninglessness, a vagueness or even absence of moral parameters and societal chaos" (15). The ontology of lack associated with this perspective insists that there "is no universal principle"

158 *Dystopian utopias*

(Tønder and Thomassen 2005b, 6), and that any such claims are necessarily social constructions (Antliff 2011).

Individuals "hold mostly incommensurable concepts and notions, as universal truths retreat into the background" (Ruccio and Amariglio 2003, 15). This disruption of meaning leads to "preoccupation with the fragmentation and instability of language" (Harvey 1990, 53) engendering "a sense of loss and meaninglessness" (White 1999, 157). Such conditions of "extreme" critique and disruption of meaning (Best and Kellner 1991) inevitably lead to an "epistemological crisis" (Adams 1992, Haque 1996). The loss of shared meaning "prevent[s] us even picturing coherently, let alone devising strategies to produce, some radically different future" (Harvey 1990, 53–54).

In this epistemological context human beings become a "mass of individual atoms thrown into the absurdity of Brownian motion" (Lyotard quoted in Hummel 2008, 51). In the process of resisting social construction, each individual "submits to a multitude of incompatible juxtaposed logics, all in perpetual movement without possibility of permanent resolution or reconciliation" (Rosenau 1992, 55). There is no possibility of a "stable identity" (Tønder and Thomassen 2005b, 6). This perspective "exaggerates [the] atomistic self" (Zanetti and Adams 2000, 544), leading to "the fragmentation of subjects (within as well as among themselves)" (Ruccio and Amariglio 2003, 15) to the point of "self-disintegration" (Boje 2006, 484). The Singular Individual is left with an empty charge to "be yourself" (Bogason 2001, 168) without a *self* to be.

Because meanings cannot be sustained long enough to form community (Anderson 2006), the postmodern condition serves as "a kind of reverse social contract: it dissolves the bonds that tie us together into free communities and democratic republics" (Barber 2007, 143). Furthermore, attempts to act collectively are met with active resistance or revolt because from the perspective of individualist anarchy any form of organized governance—state or market—is associated with the manipulative power of metanarratives (Lyotard 1984). Therefore, in terms of practicality, this perspective is "a negative radical attitude, unable to propose forms of popular democracy in place of the illusionary forms it criticizes" (Simons 2005, 155). As Chomsky (1970) notes, anarchism's continuous dismantling of forms of authority and oppression leave little room for rebuilding. Such perspectives destroy any capacity for society to be managed relationally (Donati 2014) because

> when lack is fundamentalised in ways that ultimately diminish or deny the corporeal abundance of others and world, it tends to misconstrue negativity and the protean character of otherness, and replicate the least-desirable aspects of modern subjectivity, ethics and politics.
>
> (Coles 2005, 68)

In addition to fragmenting reality, meaning, identity, and community, an important ethical problem with dismantling societal systems is that only those who are economically privileged are able to exit the system. This option is out

The Arc of Reform 159

of reach for those who are most hurt by the system. Therefore, individualist anarchism is an inherently elitist perspective (Franks 2011).[3] This reality, paired with an ideological assumption of equivalence across individuals, inadvertently reinserts liberal assumptions about power and creates a vanguard elite.

In sum, this "too fragmentary an existence" (Follett 1998, 314) of Fragmented Governance expands the isolation of Atomistic Governance into a "pure autonomy" (Hall 1998, 447) that is experienced as *alienation*, both from the self and others. Indeed, this deconstruction of all foundations leaves little to work with. We have no reality, no identity, no meaning, no community, no political or economic system, and no organizing strategy. It is like a nihilistic wormhole from which there is no way out. Such an existential state is likely to produce severe angst and a desire to produce some sort of stable reality, meaning, identity, and social connection. As Braidotti (2013) notes, "Jacques Lacan's notion of the symbolic is as out-dated as a Polaroid shot of a world that has since moved on" (188).

Notes

1 We note that the contexts described in the *Manifesto of the Communist Party* reflect characteristics of both Hierarchical and Atomistic Governance, even presaging the emergence of Fragmented Governance. While they thoroughly describe the developmental path from one from of governance to the next, all such reforms perpetuate elite (Bourgeoisie) rule over commoners (Proletariat).
2 Some assert that "modernism and postmodernism … are simply two versions of the same thing" (Harmon and McSwite 2011, 239). In our model, this equates to anything along the Atomistic–Neoliberal–Fragmented continuum of the Arc.
3 For example, the families living in hundreds of landless worker settlements and camps across Brazil cannot simply reject state power because they must rely on the public goods the state provides (Tarlau 2014).

11 The Arc of Reification

The analysis in Chapter 10 demonstrates that the ideals held up by both Hierarchical and Atomistic approaches to governance produce pathologies of bondage and isolation, and that each perspective attempts to remedy the pathology of its counterpart. A fear of systemic crisis leads to the tenuous decision to let the contradictions stand between liberalisms, or to anchor the dualism to more centrist positions that produce the pathology of calicification. Yet attempts to find a kind of Golden Mean repeatedly fail. In contemporary times, more common is the dialectical escalation of mutual critiques and calls for reform that push ideologies toward polarized dynamic ideals. In these extreme Holographic and Fragmented positions, the pathologies of absorption and alienation are quite likely to lead to existential crisis. As found in other schismogenic systems, these existential crises bring the tension between collectivist and individualist positions to a breaking point. As a result, there is a widespread and "deep existential resentment of late modernism" (Connolly 2011, 8).

Because there is insufficient ontological similarity to enable fluid movement from one extreme end of the Governance Arc to the other, the only options provided by Holographic and Fragmented are either an existential leap of revolution or retrenchment back toward more static ontological terrain to form hybrid positions aligned with liberal reform movements. This chapter explores these responses to existential crisis, noting that a leap from one extreme to the other simply lands the individual in the opposite pathology—from absorption to alienation or from alienation to absorption. To explain the dynamic of retrenchment from these positions, we replace the neoconservative, neoliberal, and communitarian reform movements with their respective hybrid approaches to governance in the Arc of Reification (see Figure 11.1)—the Reified State, the Reified Market, and the Reified Community.

Existential crisis

The Arc of Reform is driven by the unresolved tensions between the desire of individuals to be autonomous and the fear of what unleashed individualism may bring. This creates a situation in which the collective and the individual are placed at odds with one another, with classical conservative liberalism creating a

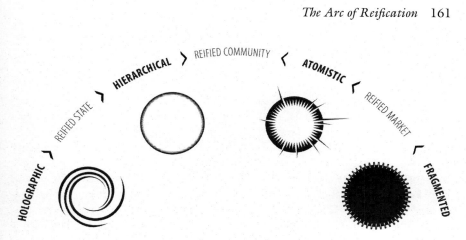

Figure 11.1 The Arc of Reification.

condition of bondage and modern liberalism creating an experience of isolation. As was explored in the last chapter, these psychosocial pathologies are amplified through reform efforts that engage in reflexive hegemony, resulting in schismogenic escalation (Bateson 1935). This process and the pathologies it engenders eventually lead to an existential crisis; one simply cannot be at once part of the group and independent from it. These existential crises make individuals vulnerable to the strategic use of fear in politics, exacerbating angst even further. Here, we will explore the continuing schismogenic escalation and the implications of these untenable extremes.

The dialectic between extremes: paradox of the i/Individual

In the explanation of the Arc of Reform, we saw the schismogenic process clearly in the movement between the individualist and collective positions wherein "the more individual rights expand, the more the individual becomes subject to centralised control and regulation" (Turner 1988, 60). As decentralization fans the flames of neoconservative reforms for greater controls over self-interest, the movement back toward centralized control ends up "producing the very conditions that justify its [neoliberalism's] continued existence" (Catlaw 2007a, 184). This leads Catlaw to wryly observe, "neoliberalism succeeds in the face of its failure" (184). Adding the neo-extensions to the dialectic between liberalisms "is like throwing gasoline on a fire: the exacerbation of hostility toward *government* that thereby precipitates a *simultaneous reduction and expansion*" of state authority (184). The symmetrical differentiation in play continues to push the process of critique and reform all the way down the Governance Arc into the most extreme positions.

At the psychosocial level of analysis, the dialectic between liberalisms and their neo-extensions generate contradictions in *lived experience*. This paradox of the **i**/Individual (Love 2008, 2010a, 2010b, 2012, 2013)[1] is created when

162   *Dystopian utopias*

human beings simultaneously attempt to exist as both embedded within groups and socially independent beings—the two sides of the ontological divide between collectivism and individualism. When individualism/Particular individualism is emphasized, individual identity is crowded out by group identity, resulting in the pathology of bondage (Hierarchical) and eventually absorption (Holographic). When Individualism/Singular Individualism is emphasized, the individual is separated from others, resulting in the pathology of isolation (Atomistic) and eventually alienation (Fragmented). The communitarian solution also fails to resolve the paradox fully because even at the community level of analysis, agreements about identity (as well as all other issues of social life) are based on static ontological ground that sustains the paradox between group and individual identity. While communities provide a sense of belongingness, the group identity calcifies the individual's ability to evolve and sustains fear of exclusion. These fears keep governmentality intact through voluntary self-control to retain group membership (Foucault 1977, 1991). Furthermore, securing a smaller-scale particularity perpetuates community regimes that exclude and remain in pluralist competition with one another (Rose 2007). Therefore, none of the primary approaches to governance or the proposed reform movements can overcome the paradox because they perpetuate the One/Many dialectic—indeed, movement along the Arc of Reform relies on this dialectic.

Some critiques are lodged against multiple ideal-types simultaneously. For example, the problem of representation presents itself in all but one ideal-type—Fragmented Governance. We suggest that the Fragmented Governance perspective challenges the very possibility of representation—all the way down to an ontology of lack. In short, the void cannot be represented by *any* substantive meaning—innate or man-made. However, the ontological assumptions in each of the other three ideal-types enable representation: someone can be authorized to represent the One (Hierarchical); someone can be authorized through majority rules to represent the preferences of the Many (Atomistic); or anyone has the potential to represent the common good (Holographic).

Aligning with the Fragmented ontology of lack, Catlaw's (2007a) criticism of what he calls "the ontology of representation" (127) provides an important articulation of how political representation of any type causes an increasingly dissociative experience and alienation from self.[2] He argues that the shared liberal understanding of the People as a popular (i.e., mass aggregate) sovereign assumes a stable ontological status of sameness and interchangeability—that someone can represent everyone within the People as constituted and modeled within a given governance regime. However, because no individual actually replicates the model of the People, representation is a fiction that perpetuates a "double exclusionary movement" (66), in which individuals first feel excluded because their situational experience is not mirrored back to them by the model, and are doubly excluded because this failure is understood as a fault of the copy (the individual) rather than the model (the People).

Representational governance provides a method of creating a popular sovereign that then *represents* the community or whole (the People)—and the

The Arc of Reification 163

individuals within that community. However, those who are represented necessarily experience a sense of exclusion because *no one* is actually coterminous with that universal identity. The response is a corresponding and increasing emphasis on the Many (Love 2013), in which focus is placed on differences—uniqueness—rather than similarities (Michaels 2007, Niedzviecki 2006). As explained in the Arc of Reform, this provides the basis for a schismogenic escalation that deepens rather than alleviates the pathologies of Atomistic and Hierarchical Governance. The creation of the People envisioned in modern liberalism pulls Atomistic individuals together through social contract, creating roles or categorizations (e.g., citizen, non-citizen) that are given ontological status in Hierarchical Governance. Thus, the pathology of isolation is addressed as individuals (the Many) are fit into abstract subcategories of the People (functionaries under the One), but this ultimately results in the pathology of bondage due to "underlying ontological commitment to the One" (Catlaw 2007a, 186).

As Singular Individuals insist on liberation from bondage or absorption through autonomy, the state tightens its hold over the individual, which in turn yields stronger assertions of Individuality—hence schismogenic escalation. This dynamic reinforces reciprocal calls for social order (One) and suspicion of conformity (Many), in which the One becomes ever more concentrated and the Many become increasingly fragmented. These accelerations are the result of the underlying dialectical paradox between liberalisms and their neo-extensions, driven by a perfect storm of unfulfilled ideals, fear, and existential angst.

The utopias professed by these perspectives, particularly in the extreme positions, are difficult to achieve and to maintain from an existential perspective. On the one hand, in Holographic Governance the individual is simply an undifferentiated part of the whole, resulting in the pathology of absorption into a universal identity. This pathology fuels the paradox of the i/Individual because the expectation of unity is in conflict with the actual difference manifested in the world and felt within oneself. As yearnings to express an *authentic* self are quashed by the societal expectation of sameness within the whole and connections to others through an absorptive cosmological order prevents *authentic* relations, the paradox escalates to existential crisis. On the other hand, within Fragmented Governance there is no stable or common ground for developing a coherent identity or social context. The result is a nihilistic pathology of alienation from both self and others. Therefore, the problem associated with representation is not actually resolved. Here, existential crisis ensues as yearnings to find and express *authentic* connection are quashed by fragmenting social attachments and the inability to stabilize identity prevents expression of an *authentic* self.

The result for the individual is an ontological and existential crisis wherein the "fabric of the world is coming undone" (Catlaw 2007a, 2). We see this as an unraveling of the *static* world as increasing tensions lead to ever more pronounced iterations along the One–Many continuum, pushing ideology down the Governance Arc (refer back to Figure 9.1) toward the *dynamic* state ontologies. Through escalating neoconservative and neoliberal critique, the qualities of

164 *Dystopian utopias*

each become ever more extreme. Unfortunately, the paradox of the i/Individual escalates between the Particular individual and the Singular Individual. An absorptive socialism (Holographic) is pitted against an alienating individualist anarchism (Fragmented). The result of both contexts is the dissolution of an authentic experience of both self and social connection. If the fear generated through such estrangement is not addressed, existential crisis seems likely.

Untenable extremes: revolution or retreat?

Once one is at either end of the Governance Arc, fluid horizontal movement toward a centrist hybrid is difficult because the philosophical breach between Holographic and Fragmented Governance is much larger than that between Hierarchical and Atomistic Governance—hence the Arc metaphor. The core of each thing or being is either completely filled with whatever stands in for the One (the Holographic ontology of abundance) or void of all substantive content (the Fragmented ontology of lack). Yet both extremes produce a sense of alienation from authentic expressions of self and social connection.

The question of an authentic self can be understood as "a result of the ego perceiving itself as separate from others in the world" (Bourne 2008, 136), where "self-identity consists of the development of a consistent feeling of biographical continuity where the individual is able to sustain a narrative about the self and answer questions about doing, acting, and being" (Kinnvall 2004, 746). Similarly, an authentic relation must be self-organizing as opposed to imposed by external sources (Follett 1919). Thus, at the psychosocial level of analysis, the resulting state of angst leads to existential crisis. Because fluid movement between the dynamic positions is not possible, the response is either a revolutionary leap from one dynamic position to the other, or a retrenchment toward the static ontological positions.

In Holographic Governance, the desire is to make real one's difference and to choose one's roles and relations. Such an existential crisis may lead to revolutionary impulses to reject any and all imposed relations and identities in order to grasp the complete freedom promised by the Fragmented ideal. An example of this can be seen in the call to revolution articulated in Theodore Kaczynski's (1995) manifesto, *The Industrial Society and its Future*. Best known as the Unabomber, Kaczynski explicitly rejects reform movements, calling instead for a revolution that "offers to solve all problems at one stroke and create a whole new world" (34). Kaczynski denounces what he calls "oversocialized leftists" (aligned most explicitly with socialism), and the collectivist Holographic ideal that "seeks to bind together the entire world (both nature and the human race) into a unified whole" (48). He calls for a movement to dismantle industrial–technological society and the system that bends human nature to its needs, and advocates replacing it with a decidedly Fragmented ideal that calls for a return to "wild nature" (42), insisting that "it is not necessary ... to set up some chimerical utopia or any new kind of social order. Nature takes care of itself" (42). In this return to "spontaneous creation" in nature, Kaczynski envisions the

The Arc of Reification 165

Fragmented Governance ideal of greater power and freedom within individuals and survivalist groups and the utter destruction of all social organizations that might control or absorb the individual.

A less extreme revolutionary example is the extent to which some Amish youth go during the period of *Rumspringa*, known as the "running around" years, during which teenagers are freed from the constraints of the community. The experimentation of most youth may be limited to playing card games or attending an amusement park, after which they choose to be baptized and stay within the community (Stevick 2007). However, as is depicted in the documentary *Devil's Playground* (Walker 2002), there are some youth who go through a process of existential crisis in which "the teens have cast aside their plain inhibitions for unbridled hedonism" (Stevick 2007, 152), some choosing to permanently leave the community in search of autonomy and the fulfillment of self-interest.

On the other side of the divide, in Fragmented Governance the desire is to make real one's connection with others and to feel a secure sense of identity. Existential crisis in Fragmented Governance may lead to revolutionary impulses that seek the anchor of community identity promised by the Holographic ideal. From a Buddhist perspective, the failure of Fragmented Governance to provide the autonomous identity it promises is seen in

> our frantic search and grasping for "things" ... a way of masking, suppressing, or diverting the painful awareness of that lack—and a desperate attempt to fill the void with an acquirable "identity," a self which one owns—one's own self.
>
> (Lusthaus 2002, 2)

This dynamic can be seen in the *Communist Manifesto* offered by Marx and Engels. In their mental experiment exploring the ultimate ends of capitalism, they describe government in the service of capitalism and a resulting social condition of isolation and alienation—what we associate with the movement from Atomistic to Fragmented Governance. Foreseeing the nihilistic trap it would ultimately produce, they urge modern liberal society to instead make the leap to socialism in order to reclaim a social life experience for all.

A similar impulse can be seen in the lure of cult societies (Durkin 2011). Individuals who experience existential anxiety based on social isolation become particularly vulnerable to "the vestiges of religion and of the family" (Debord 1994, 38), seeking "*one* stable identity that answers to the need for securitized subjectivity" (Kinnvall 2004, 758). Niedzviecki (2006) calls this form of ontological crisis "neo-traditionalism" (155) and offers up the example of John Walker Lindh, the American Taliban, as an illustration. He argues that Lindh's "explanation for leaving the United States and adopting a fundamentalist religion is heartbreaking, a damning condemnation of pseudo-individualist society: He felt alone" (151). In contrast to alienation within the postmodern context, Lindh sought absorption in a community identity.

166 *Dystopian utopias*

Interestingly, individuals in both Holographic and Fragmented scenarios experience a loss of either authentic identity or connection that generates a sense of existential angst rather than agonistic discomfort. In extreme experiences of existential crisis, individuals take a revolutionary leap, seeking the sense of authenticity that the alternative position offers. Unfortunately, a leap from one dynamic position to the other may merely swap the potential pathology of alienation for absorption and vice versa. Furthermore, because these revolutionary leaps move from one dynamic extreme to the other they may also perpetuate the uncertainty and fear that many feel when confronted with ontological dynamism.

This leap across the divide from one end of the Governance Arc to the other can be considered an ontological revolution, as such a movement indicates an extreme reality shift. Following the logic outlined herein, such a move results in profound restructuring in both philosophical foundations and practice. However, both dynamism and change, particularly in the West, are associated with a lack of control, entropy, and chaos. A common feeling is that "any form of present stasis is preferable to the known future of deterioration" (Wheatley 2006, 77). Indeed, our Western languages themselves shield us from such instability through their structure. Language that subordinates gerunds tends toward reification (Bohm 2004). Individuals who yearn for an authentic sense of self (Holographic) or interpersonal connection (Fragmented) can be led to believe that only stasis—either within the group or within the individual—can provide the desired sense of security.

We argue that the existential angst produced by the two dynamic approaches to governance (Holographic and Fragmented) fuel fears that are more likely to drive ideological reification than revolution, countervailing the Arc of Reform. A lack of individual agency and control in either position enflames a desire for stability, making people suggestible to fear-based rhetoric. Efforts by elites to maintain control lead to the politics of fear, which drive an ideological retrenchment along the Arc of Reification (see Figure 11.1). Those in power play upon existential fears and yearnings, each attempting to inject stability through the fabrication of strong economic, political, and social institutions that are naturalized "as something other than human product" (Berger and Luckmann 1966, 61). Instead, they are presented as Truth.

Specifically, neoconservative reforms pull Holographic Governance back toward Hierarchical Governance, creating a Reified State that obscures domination within supposed unity, while neoliberal reforms pull Fragmented Governance back toward Atomistic Governance, creating a Reified Market that obscures static power relations. Communitarian reforms offer perfect blends of diversity within unity to balance the freedom and control found in Atomistic and Hierarchical Governance, creating a Reified Community. In all instances, these movements are framed as attempts to "keep everything under control" (Bourne 2008, 136). Thus, reification is understood here as an attempt to resolve the dialectic between *static state* and *dynamic state* ontologies or to stop dialectical movement between the collectivist and individualist ontologies. Existential angst in these dynamic positions provides the fuel for a powerful mechanism to drive

The Arc of Reification   167

retrenchment through reification: fear. The elite use the politics of fear in the process of reification.

As explained in the Arc of Reform, neoconservatives play on the fear of conflict inherent in individualist approaches (Atomistic and Fragmented Governance) and rhetorically profess the ideals of order and unity. Neoliberals play on the fear of control inherent in collectivist approaches (Hierarchical and Holographic Governance) and rhetorically profess ideals of liberty and autonomy. Communitarians play on the fear of exclusion, claiming that diversity within unity will establish a stable sense of belonging. But because proponents of these reforms also want to maintain power and control, rather than giving it over to unpredictable collectivity (socialism) or unpredictable flux (individualist anarchism), operationally they move back toward their respective static ontological positions: Hierarchical and Atomistic Governance, or a hybrid of the two.

Some critical theorists feel that forthright attempts to maintain dialectical tensions between positions is a preferable approach because any claim to synthesis is suspected of being a dominating or obfuscating compromise (Adorno 1973). The argument is that such hybrids hide underlying philosophical commitments for manipulative purposes. We agree: proponents may claim the dynamic ideal as their purpose, while actually securing their own power positions. One who has traditionally been empowered wishes "to induce others to hold on to the *status quo* because he feels comfortable and smug under conditions as they are" (Mannheim 1936, 78).

Recognizing the power dynamics that are hidden under rhetorical assurances of stable ideals, Witt and deHaven-Smith (2008) describe the "holographic state" as one in which strategic shifting between neoliberal and neoconservative rhetoric allows for the increasing concentration of power in the hands of political elites who act above the law while disempowering average citizens (Brown 2006, Thorne and Kouzmin 2004, 2006, Witt and Kouzmin 2010).[3] Connolly (2013) refers to this dynamic relationship as "the evangelical–neoliberal resonance machine" (67). This machine was built by a collusion among the social sciences and political leaders that disempowered the ability of citizens to question what they make transparent (deHaven-Smith 2013, Thorne and Kouzmin 2012, Witt and deHaven-Smith 2008). The result is an accelerating exertion of elite control over government, market, and community.

Specifically, neoconservative rhetoric plays on the anxiety produced by isolation and holds up the ideal of unity while calling for the stabilization of centralized authority in the state, only to obscure control by governing elites. Likewise, neoliberal rhetoric plays on the fear of absorption and holds up the ideal of autonomy while calling for the support of the market, only to obscure the concentration of capitalist power. Indeed, "the sophistication of the rhetorical weaving of visibility/invisibility has become so artful that one can no longer even call out conspiracy without being labelled paranoid or insane" (Stout 2016, 91). The manipulative flux of visibility and invisibility (Thorne and Kouzmin 2012) within the Arc of Reification is not limited to the state and the market, however. While Thorne and Kouzmin draw upon communitarian

168   *Dystopian utopias*

critiques to bring democratic values back into focus, we see efforts to resolve the One/Many dialectic within liberalism by stabilizing the social contract in civil society as fruitless. Therefore we discuss all three products of reification—state, market, and community—in turn.

The Reified State

The ideal of Holographic Governance is socialism in which a shared group identity enables egalitarian participation by all; however, the pathology of absorption coupled with the instability of a dynamic group identity drives fears that provide fertile ground for reforms offering a stable, egalitarian group identity. Moving away from Holographic and toward Hierarchical Governance, these reform movements pull back from the socialist ideal toward more ontologically stable ground, including vanguard socialism, fascism, and neoconservativism. The result is the hybrid formation we classify as the Reified State.

Initial retrenchment from the Holographic ideal is illustrated in the state socialist political movements that sought to transfer sovereignty from the vanguard party of the proletariat to centralized party leaders. These reformers insisted that, "The party is obliged to maintain its dictatorship, regardless of the temporary vacillations even in the working class. This awareness is the indispensable unifying element" (Trotsky as quoted in Deutscher 2003, 424). This is perhaps best seen in the October Revolution, during which Lenin "seized at once upon all the possible differentiations, social, national, professional, that might bring some structure into the population, and he seemed convinced that in such stratification lay the salvation of the revolution" (Arendt 1968, 318). In essence, Lenin was making appeals to Hierarchical structure, while holding firm to Holographic ideals. This retrenchment was further articulated by Joseph Stalin (1953), who warned that a truly classless society would eliminate the possibility of a dictatorship of the proletariat but would also lead to the elimination of the Party. One might interpret this as a warning against the chaos of a changing proletariat identity. The Party can ensure the codification of a stable national identity better than the proletariat.

Such arguments by Lenin, Trotsky, and Stalin demonstrate the tendency for those with authority (often through both economic and cultural capital) to monopolize leadership positions and capitalize on the "belief that utopian ideals are mere fantasies" (Hoffman and Graham 2009, 227). These reforms also leverage the tensions created by schismogenic escalation by reinforcing fears of "anarchist subjectivity" and a leaderless state while offering themselves as the necessary answer (Antliff 2011, 165). As argued in the *Manifesto of the Communist Party*, such a hybrid position gives the "Socialistic bourgeois ... the existing state of society, minus its revolutionary and disintegrating elements" (Marx and Engels 1998, chapter 3).

A similar emphasis of Holographic unity with strong Hierarchical leadership is seen in fascist reform movements. Fascist reforms tend to arise initially as a rejection of socialism, yet proceed to promote socialist ideals in their rhetoric of

The Arc of Reification   169

nation and unity and a fierce rejection of both liberalism and capitalism: "Fascists see the state itself as central to human identity and vital to the idea of community" (Hoffman and Graham 2009, 307). Griffin (2013) refers to this as a form of "populist ultra-nationalism" (37) that rejects both liberalism and socialism, appealing instead to the concept of "palingenesis" or the rebirth of the nation. It is perhaps best illustrated by the rise of the Italian Fascist Party. Early advocates of fascism, such as Papini, argued that "a small elite of leaders, commanding the collective energy of the masses, could move Italy to higher stages of civilized life" (Gregor 1979, 200), instilling the "aristocratic virtues of authority and heroism" (Griffin 2013, 57). Mussolini's turn to fascism, for instance, was a direct rejection of his earlier association with the socialist party, and the Italians drawn to his cause rejected both the ruling political liberals and socialist ideals, seeing fascism as "a way of reasserting control over the workers and peasants" (DeGrand 2000, 20).

Contemporary neoconservative reforms continue this pattern of retrenchment set forth in vanguard socialism and fascism by promising stability through group solidarity, nationalism, patriotism, and moral authority. Chomsky (2002) notes that these characteristics are found in both the Leninist socialist concept of the vanguard and the classical conservative liberal precursors to neoconservatism. Neoconservative rhetoric embraces a strong, centralized state that enforces stable national identity, thus reducing the risk and soothing the anxiety of being absorbed by a changing collective in which the dominant ideals no longer reflect one's morals. Drawing further force from the schismogenic divide, neoconservative rhetoric simultaneously fuels fear of fragmentation, diversity, and self-interest (Kristol 2004b). These fears are placated by the promise of reinforcing a state-instituted morality that is predetermined and fixed (Brown 2006, Kristol 2004b).

Drawing on the escalating fear of others and latent class conflict, the neoconservative critique leads to an "increasingly fearful and intolerant political culture" and an "authoritative mindset" (Manwell 2010, 869). Neoconservatives promise security through mechanisms that "selectively favor government intrusion, censorship, and regulation for the under-races and underclasses," both domestically and globally (Brown 2006, 700). Such interventions may take the form of morally guided domestic policy (Kristol 2004a) or hawkish foreign policy (Kristol and Kagan 2004). Both conserve the dominant regime values while eradicating changing minority views and minoritarian Particular identities. As King and Zanetti (2005) suggest, such political rhetoric can promote the reinstitutionalization of power hierarchies based on "the importance of asserting our 'good' over 'evil'" (523).

The emphasis on a battle of good versus evil is reflected in appeals to religious morality, supported by a static transcendent source such as the Christian God or the Muslim Allah. In the American context, this allows neoconservatives to "shore-up flagging confidence in their familiar ethical faiths with ever-increasing doses of authority" (Howe 2006, 423) that can be used to orchestrate the enforcement of social and moral norms (Curtis 2004, Kristol 2004b).

170 *Dystopian utopias*

In tying this sense of religious morality to the notion of a unified public, neo-conservatives are able to hide the Hierarchical aspects of their position using the rhetorical ploys of the Holographic emphasis on unity and equality. However, rather than being crafted and instituted by the group as a whole, it is determined by political leaders and enforced by the state.

In such reforms, enforcement occurs through "an increase in state surveillance" (Manwell 2010, 869). For example, taken to extreme, NPA reforms argue for a Platonic guardian class composed of public administrators rather than elected representatives. Furthermore, methods of citizen engagement are seen only as "important *supplements* to representational democracy" (Nabatchi 2010, S310, emphasis added). Administrators are charged with ensuring democratic regime values (see for example, Denhardt and Denhardt 2007, Frederickson 1997, Rohr 1990, Terry 1995, Wamsley 1990), and becoming gatekeepers and enforcers of the state. Such a caricature reveals the approach to be "at best paternalistic and at worst a totalitarian dictatorship" (Fox and Cochran 1990, 93) of autonomous and controlling "mandarins" capable of a bureaucratic *coup d'état* (Riggs 1998). Indeed, this approach could be likened to Leninist vanguard reforms (Lukács 1998) or Chinese Maoism seeking to substitute the state for religion (Cobb Jr. 2012).

In his critique of the ontology of representation, Catlaw (2007a) argues that we have moved from a "society of discipline" to a "society of control" (184), in which individuals are defined by their roles within an organic Unity and controlled through an imposition of discipline by political elites and their functionaries. Historically this dynamic occurred only within specific organizations or groups; however, there has been a creeping of disciplinarity from confined spaces into all aspects of lived experience from which there is no private retreat. Similarly, Heckert (2011) explains, "The state may be considered that name which we give to the oppressive effects produced through decentralized relations of domination, surveillance, representation and control" (199).

The emphasis of egalitarian unity and shared identity in these varied reform hybrids provides rhetorical cover for what is actually elite control. Neoconservatives play on the fear of conflict inherent in individualist approaches (Atomistic and Fragmented Governance) and rhetorically profess ideals of order and unity. From an ontological perspective, where an ontology of abundance becomes stable, a nondemocratic socialism or authoritarianism may form (Marchart 2005)—as it has in many communist states. As in Hegel's idealized Unity, the state is reified and citizens are forced through coercion to become mere manifestations of the state, pursuing the state's own ends (Willoughby 1930). In other words, while the Holographic rhetoric of unity and solidarity is used to engender support for such reforms, the hidden Hierarchical assumption is that the state will be led by elite party leaders. Follett similarly insists, "socialists wish to give us ... state control and they mean by that state coercion—we find again and again in their pamphlets the words force, coerce" (Follett 2013d, 89). In sum, fixed ontologies of abundance discourage citizens from "contestation in thought, ethics and politics, and so on" (Coles 2005, 68).

The Reified Market

The ideal of Fragmented Governance is individualist anarchism in which Singular Individuals are self-sufficient, entering only into fleeting voluntary exchanges with others to meet their individual needs; however, the pathology of alienation coupled with fears of dynamic instability sets the stage for reforms that promise to preserve the goal of autonomy, while providing not only market stability but also existential stability. These reforms pull back from the full Fragmented ideal of individualist anarchism toward more ontologically stable ground—first in the form of libertarianism and objectivism, followed second by neoliberalism, stopping short of full retrenchment into Atomistic Governance. The result is the hybrid formation we classify as the Reified Market.

The Fragmented ideal strives to free the individual from manipulation by social construction. In this effort, classical anarchists such as Max Stirner reject any metaphysics that claim an absolute Truth, insisting instead that science, as well as religion, is a social construction (Antliff 2011). However, rather than being relationally generative, the individualist ontology of lack in Fragmented Governance actually makes people more weak and vulnerable to social construction. As Adams (2011) argues, the fragmentation of universality does not disintegrate or eliminate hegemony to produce Singular Individuality. Instead, its divisions make particularities vulnerable to cooptation. Objectivists are critical of individualist anarchists who attempt to "fill the void of the egos they do not possess, by the means of the only form of 'self-assertiveness' they recognize: defiance for the sake of defiance"—accusing them instead of "counterfeit individualism" (137). This realization that full autonomy cannot be achieved due to continued social construction provides the impetus for a movement away from post-structuralist individualist anarchism toward a position that protects liberty.

Proponents of libertarianism purport to maintain the autonomy of Fragmented Governance, while advocating minimal government that provides the social stability necessary for a reliable free-market economic system. This perspective is often aligned with the work of economist Ludwig von Mises (1998) who insists on a completely deregulated market where government's function is to protect private property and market transactions.

Recognizing that the ontological, psychosocial, and epistemological assumptions associated with Fragmented Governance are a danger to market pursuits, objectivist Ayn Rand (1964) explicitly rejects "the concept of a fluid, plastic, indeterminate, Heraclitean universe" (34). From the Fragmented Governance perspective, the "real" is understood as the *hyperreal* (Baudrillard 1994), a fabricated and ever-changing and contested spectacle (Debord 1994). Therefore, Branden (1964) chides subjectivists for "their rebellion against 'the tyranny of reality'" (137) and in response pulls back toward the stability of the Atomistic perspective by emphasizing the priority of rationality, reason, and autonomy. While these perspectives agree upon the *separation* of government and market, they do not wish to *eliminate* government; it is necessary to secure the market through stable philosophical assumptions.

172 *Dystopian utopias*

The libertarian insistence on a laissez-faire capitalism based on a complete separation of state and market sets the stage for the next phase of retrenchment: neoliberalism. Like objectivism, neoliberal rhetoric promises to empower individuals with autonomy and choice in the marketplace by disempowering government. However, whereas Rand advocates complete separation of government and market, neoliberals argue instead for government support of unregulated markets (Friedman 2002). In this configuration, government subsidies and bailouts are acceptable. Further, neoliberalism encourages the construction of a unified identity through consumption. As such, neoliberalism "wraps itself in the mantle of 'liberty' and 'democracy' " (Brown 2006, 701), but only promises the ability to assert one's individuality through the marketplace (Barber 2007, Niedzviecki 2006). Both objectivists and neoliberals emphasize the centrality of the capitalist market with no to limited regulation as the central sociopolitical institution for protecting the ideal of autonomy—thereby producing what we call the Reified Market.

The utopian ideal of Fragmented Governance appeals to autonomy from social construction. In contrast, the Reified Market promises to empower individuals to construct their own identity within a stabilized market. In response to the desire to fabricate (or perhaps find) Individuality through consumption, producers proliferate ever-increasing niche markets. This relationship between fracturing identities and niche marketing is mutually reinforcing as "manufacturers, advertisers, marketers, and political operatives became invested in segmenting the whole, thereby encouraging social and cultural divisions for their own profit" (Cohen 2003, 408). With the splintering of mass markets into ever narrower niche markets, individuals are thought to gain "more opportunity to express their separate identities through their choices as consumers" (309). Faced with these choices, individuals attempt to create a pastiche of identities and may come "to occupy so many different positions and hold ... a bewildering variety of perspectives" (Ruccio and Amariglio 2003, 15).

Marcuse (1964) insists that while proponents of this Reified Market—whether laissez-faire or limited regulation—may claim the free market protects autonomy and negative liberty, it is actually authoritarian in that the economic elite dictate our choices to buy happiness. Careful manipulation of social narratives through the use of marketing allows those with power (i.e., capital) to shape the desires and therefore the very identities of individuals subject to those narratives (Debord 1994). Therefore, in contrast to rhetoric of choice and consumer autonomy, producers are actually in control of identity (Thorne 2010).

Due to their inability to access an authentic identity, consumers are left "vulnerable, unprotected, and susceptible to outside manipulation" (Barber 2007, 32); they are "malleable and weak" (McSwite 1996, 200) in the face of vast market choices that replace true needs with manufactured needs (Marcuse 1964). Desires are fleeting and are constantly refreshed and redefined by producers, leading to continual consumption (Harvey 1990, Jameson 1991), or hyper-consumption (Frey 2004). Thus, the "counterfeit individualism" of

The Arc of Reification 173

Fragmented Governance critiqued by Rand (1964) is actually a matter of individuals being manipulated to consume market identities.

This preoccupation with identity construction obfuscates the underlying power dynamics inherent in late capitalism. Indeed, Debord (1994) likens the neoliberal marketplace to "spectacle" because it is intended to distract and mislead the consumer in order to obscure power imbalances. The market-oriented policies and rhetoric of objectivism and neoliberalism work to make concentrated power within the globalizing market invisible while creating a visible, though false, sense of individual empowerment (Thorne and Kouzmin, 2004, 2006). Neoliberal reforms thereby produce a Reified Market that promises individual empowerment through consumption while obfuscating elite market control and domination of consumers (Barber 2007).

This reification of the market has profound implications for the social bond and the project of democracy. Objectivist and neoliberal retrenchment efforts promise a social contract through voluntary exchange in the free market (Friedman 2002, Peikoff 1991, Rand 1964). However, under such conditions the public realm is transformed into a sphere for desire manipulation (Lyotard 1984) with little to no substantive democratic dialogue (Fox and Miller 1995). Although populists purport to uphold the Fragmented Governance ideal of "social and cultural change while analysing the effectiveness of domination" (Simons 2005, 159), attempts to resist domination remain anemic in the face of the "colonization of the life-world" (Habermas 1989, 54) by market principles.

In this consumerist post-democracy, political antagonism is redirected into the marketplace where existential lack is transformed into a never-ending series of desires that are alleviated but the consumer is never satisfied (Stavrakakis 2005). This market hegemony in the public sphere has been described as "Leviathan in sheep's clothing: its function is not to encourage and perpetuate freedom (let alone freedom of a political variety) but rather to repress it" (Jameson 1991, 273). Economic power rather than political sovereignty controls the market-based social contract and representation is subsumed by market forces and niche identity politics. Because neoliberalism obfuscates these power dynamics in the free-market political economy, this "false economic philosophy" leads to "non-conservation of our national resources, exploitation of labor, and political corruption. We see the direct outcome in our slums, our unregulated industries, our 'industrial unrest,' etc." (Follett 1998, 170–171).

In sum, the existential angst of Fragmented Governance leads people to accept a dystopian hybrid in which the market becomes the dominant force in society. Neoliberals play on the fear of control inherent in collectivist approaches (Hierarchical and Holographic Governance) and rhetorically profess ideals of liberty and autonomy. But neoliberalism is "a project that empties the world of meaning, that cheapens and deracinates life and openly exploits desire" (Brown 2006, 692). Many government activities are divested or contracted out to the marketplace in response to consumption demands. In so doing, government plays a proactive role in extending the grip of the market to issues previously considered public (Miller and Fox 2007), replacing the public realm with a

174 *Dystopian utopias*

Reified Market. As summarized in Chapter 2, this globally "untamed capitalism" is leading to ecological disaster (Bogason 2001, 167).

The Reified Community

As we saw in Chapter 10, in an effort to prevent schismogenic escalation, communitarian reformers moderate both the ideal of liberty and the ideal of social order. Deeply troubled by the failure of the Reified Market to adequately address the existential crisis resulting from Fragmented Governance, and yet demanding more unity than what is offered in Atomistic Governance, they pull back toward Hierarchical Governance. However, equally troubled by the existential crisis of Holographic Governance and the nationalistic solutions offered by the Reified State, because Hierarchical Governance fails to accommodate diversity, communitarians retrench only so far as the center of the Governance Arc.

In the process of reification, communitarianism promises a *fixed* balance of hierarchy and competition through diversity within unity (Stout and Love 2014a). Reformists such as Jürgen Habermas (1975), Michael Walzer (1984), and Alberto Guerreiro Ramos (1981) suggest that the solution is to reinstate social boundaries in order to reclaim the polity from both the chaos of the market and the hierarchical control of the state. Reforms would delimit the market (while leaving it unchanged) and thereby reclaim spaces for political and community life. The argument is that the value of equality among diversity would once again check the value of liberty, thereby creating unity. Reforms are presented as means to fight the collapse of state, market, and civil society under the domain of market values, by reasserting a firm separation among them and placing civil society in a privileged position over the other two. Civil society could then revitalize the public sphere by restructuring interactions according to communicative ethics and action in substantive relationship.

While all communitarian reforms call for unity and virtuous citizenship, they shift the locus of action from the state to mediating civic institutions of various types. As noted by Dewey, traditional communitarians value established social roles, rules, and norms (Kahne 1996). The logic of this move is that through communities, individuals can be governed by social norms and dynamics as opposed to law and governance. This moves much of what once was the domain of government into the sphere of civil society and nonprofit organizations.

However, in this utopian vision, the polity becomes governed "through the micromanagement of the self-steering practices of its citizens" (Rose 2000, 1408). While the formal instruments of state and elected leaders recede, the informal leaders in civil society continue to mirror many of the same regime values. Furthermore, through what has been labeled the nonprofit industrial complex, the third sector has merely become "a set of symbiotic relationships that link political and financial technologies of state and owning class control with surveillance over public political ideology, including and especially emergent progressive and leftist social movements" (Smith 2007, 8). In this way, the Reified Community obfuscates elite control. For this reason, Berlin (2013) asserts that positive liberty, despite the rhetoric of self-mastery, lays the foundation for an authoritarian regime in which individuals are enslaved yet "declare themselves free" (211).

As Rose (2000) explains, civil society becomes a tool of establishing and enforcing regime values. Communitarians play on the fear of exclusion, claiming diversity within unity will establish a stable sense of belonging. In the communitarian ideal, *community* becomes the stand-in for the One in order to accommodate locally determined differences among the Many. As a result, community becomes an instrument of social control because it takes on and administers the public ethic; civil society reproduces the institutions of power in the state (Mueller 2011). We refer to this as the Reified Community.

We use this label because all of the arguments for balancing the individual and society are grounded in the static state ontological continuum and therefore do not address the static/dynamic state dialectic. This leaves both collectivist and individualist anarchists wanting because all static positions are suspect as mechanisms of domination. Furthermore, Berlin (2013) argues that in such conditions of social control, it is inevitable that individuals will attempt to reassert their individual will. The Reified Community does not resolve the dialectical tension between the individual and society; instead it merely provides a platform from which the schismogenic cycle of reform to begin anew. Thus, like the unending swing of a metronome pendulum, all approaches on the Governance Arc find themselves caught in the dialectic between collectivism and individualism.

Notes

1 Herein we extend Love's (2010a) individuals within social groups (Hierarchical) and independent Individuals (Atomistic) with the Particular individual and the Singular Individual to accommodate the Holographic and Fragmented extremes.
2 We must point out that our critique of Singular Individuality contradicts Catlaw (2007a) who argues for its benefits.
3 We note the difference in our use of the holographic metaphor—this alternative perspective refers to the notion that it is an illusion pretending actuality.

Part IV

Affirmation of a radically democratic approach to governance

The goal of Part IV is to affirm a radically democratic approach to governance—the perspective we hold and claim in the Preface. Chapter 12 first explores the need for a radically democratic approach to governance based on both experiential and theoretical reasons. In short, the failure of all other governance approaches to achieve social, economic, and environmental sustainability demonstrates their lack of viability for universal acceptance in the contemporary global context. In response to these failures, we analyze how the dialectical paradoxes they generate can be resolved through synthesis. After an explanation of dialectical synthesis, we consider how it would play out in each element of the Governance Typology. Taken together, these syntheses generate what we call Integrative Governance, an approach that is grounded in what we call "relational process ontology" (Stout and Love 2015c). This ontological terrain does not fall anywhere along the Governance Arc critiqued in Part III.

Chapter 13 argues that Integrative Governance provides a robust framework for radical democracy and that it has the potential to produce more fruitful outcomes due to its flexibility and openness. Explaining and then applying the method of integration, we consider the manner in which Integrative Governance pursues the desires held by the positions on the Governance Arc, as well as how it addresses their fears and resolves their pathologies. We then explore the pathways for discourse that could support the integration of each position on the Governance Arc into Integrative Governance. We argue that by accommodating the driving concerns in each, Integrative Governance represents a synthesis of all.

We close by describing the next steps in this project of affirmation. To flesh out Integrative Governance theoretically, we need to explore the diverse literatures that promulgate its characteristics. From there, to complete the ideal-type method, we must use the full Governance Typology to evaluate experience. While assessments along the lines of what has been presented in Part III abound, we lack understanding of the nascent practices of Integrative Governance. Future empirical research can expand our understanding and help us in drawing conclusions about the usefulness of this approach. We will focus on various social and economic movements to identify groups practicing radical democracy prefiguratively. From these studies, the theory and practice of Integrative Governance will be fine-tuned.

12 Why Integrative Governance?

Considering what we have presented in the first three parts of this book, there are sufficient empirical and theoretical reasons to consider a different approach to governance. Furthermore, we argue that experiential evidence is causally linked to ontological rationales through prefiguration. In concurrence and as if prophesying the contemporary global context summarized herein, Follett (1998) argues in her 1918 book *The New State*, that "chaos, disorder, destruction, come everywhere from refusing the syntheses of life" (93). In contemporary terminology, the crises of social, economic, and environmental sustainability stem from our dialectical ontological assumptions and the practices they prefigure.

However, these issues of sustainability are interwoven with governance crises that conventional approaches appear unable to resolve. Many agree modernity has generated such dramatic challenges that "it has become impossible to ignore the consequences of this progress" (Stengers 2011, 12). We are globally interconnected through mass communication, travel, immigration, economic interdependence, and global environmental impacts (Wang 2012). Together—across nations and forms of government—we seem to be careening toward disaster. We need a new approach to political economy based on generative principles that replace fear with trust, the assumption of scarcity with the possibility of abundance, self-interest with mutual interest, and dialectical competition/hierarchy with collaboration (Stout 2010a). As Mesle (2008) puts it, if we do not begin to understand ourselves in relational process, "we imperil the web in which we live" (9). We will reconsider the experiential and ontological aspects of this claim before beginning the project of constructing Integrative Governance.

Experiential rationales

Due to contemporary governance crises—the questions of sovereignty, governance, and participation—the context of governance is no longer exclusively the government agency or even the nation, but rather an intersectoral, international process. Governance is increasingly conducted through a global political economy that is most aptly described as capitalist markets operating with state-actor support—a plutocracy rather than a democracy. Given our history to date,

180 *A radically democratic approach*

it is fair to say that *every* governance approach attempting world order thus far has failed to attain global acceptance. Assuming that arguments regarding the prefigurative nature of ontology are correct, then both the barriers to acceptance and the tools to overcome them can be traced to these foundational assumptions.

It is reasonable to argue that the vast majority of Western/Global North governance theory is grounded in Hierarchical/Atomistic assumptions, but leaning toward static, individualist, positivist, humanist, teleological, liberal, and capitalist foundations. We also find evidence of Holographic/Fragmented alternatives and responses to that hegemony—although most often these ideologies are met with retrenchment into Reified State/Market hybrids. The economic and social stratification of Hierarchical Governance is maintained while many rules of engagement have changed to Atomistic Governance, with strong moves into the Reified Market of neoliberalism and late capitalism. There are ongoing attempts to balance this extreme with the hybrid position of the Reified State of neoconservativism, and at times with the Reified Community of communitarianism.

However, none of these approaches to governance fits all cultural perspectives and preferences (Brinkerhoff and Goldsmith 2005) and as a result many voices are silenced and experiences are disregarded through ontological colonization. In short, we find our beliefs and practices lacking legitimate answers to the new questions that we face in the postmodern condition (MacIntyre 1988). We are confronted with an unresolvable pluralism in which incompatible and incommensurate ideologies coexist in a state of unending conflict. As Follett (1998) argues, "we have not yet learned how to live together" (3)—at least not in a true democratic fashion. Proponents of radical democracy argue that "neither hierarchy nor markets are appropriate forms of governance" (Marsh 1998, 8), and demand that we return sovereignty to the people impacted by collective decisions and actions and allow them to engage directly in the governance process. As sociologist Patricia Hill Collins (2012) cogently argues,

> Democracy is not a thing that can be achieved but, rather, a relational process honed in the crucible of lived experience across differences in power.... These characteristics of the construct of community not only describe the dynamics of actual power relations; they can also serve as a template for aspirational political projects.
>
> (448)

Absent such participatory practice, political unrest is escalating globally. To effectively bring people into the governance process, a new ontological grounding is necessary.

Addressing the movement toward radical democracy, Connolly (2011) argues that we cannot simply forego the state as an institution. Instead, we can marry state politics with a new micropolitics to achieve not only social, but economic and environmental sustainability. To achieve such ends, the new state

Why Integrative Governance? 181

"must permit greater social differentiation while assuring greater integration" by "offering more coordination and political direction towards the common good" (Donati 2014, 79). We do not find these "plastic state" (Follett 1998, 314) characteristics in the largely fear-driven governance approaches described thus far. But it is also not easy to reinvent these governance practices due to the fears they generate. As Catlaw (2007c) observes, "Thinking political life beyond fear is a huge challenge—perhaps *the* challenge for us." As demonstrated in Chapter 11, the politics of fear is at play in all points on the Governance Arc—as demonstrated through the processes of schismogenic escalation as well as strategic retrenchment. Our fears of other positions on the Governance Arc drive attempts at ontological colonization. As environmentalist Paul Hawken (2007) notes, we try to "prevent diversity" through hegemony "rather than nurturing natural evolution and the flourishing of ideas" (16).

We argue that due to ontological impositions, many people find themselves experiencing discomfort at a very deep level—an existential crisis created by holding a worldview that is mismatched to societal expectations. These types of experiences are reported globally, regardless of the particular governance regime at hand. Ontological angst reveals itself wherever collectivist worldviews have overtaken individualist worldviews, and vice versa. It also emerges wherever those holding a relational process perspective are constrained by dominant worldviews of either a collectivist or individualist orientation. This has led to processes of counter-hegemony in which there is a proliferation of political perspectives, a "*minoritization of the world*" (Connolly 2011, 59) that pushes back against ideological hegemony. However, such counter-hegemonic moves do not succeed in claiming the seat of power—nor can they independently transform that system of power.

As a result, many scholars and activists hope that meaningful responses to shared economic and environmental crises will foster a "reactive form of pan-human planetary bond," which will encourage us to restructure society (with consideration of other species as well) (Braidotti 2013, 111) and become planetary citizens (Keating 2013). This requires reconsidering our situation as a complex and changing *predicament* in which we are fully implicated, rather than an objective *condition* subject to divine salvation or remediation via better scientific and technological knowledge (Connolly 2011). We must understand how dominant worldviews drive the social, economic, and environmental crises experienced globally.

If such calls were easily disregarded or refuted in times past, perhaps it is only now, in the face of extreme life-threatening crises, that we can recognize their significance and value. None of the ideological positions along the Governance Arc is sufficient to resolve these crises: "neither neoliberal theory, nor socialist productivism, nor deep ecology, nor social democracy in its classic form" (Connolly 2013, 37). As the collective statement from the New System Project puts it,

> When the old ways no longer produce the outcomes we are looking for, something deeper is occurring. We have fundamental problems because of

182 *A radically democratic approach*

fundamental flaws in our economic and political system. The crisis now unfolding in so many ways across our country [world] amounts to a systemic crisis.

(Democracy Collaborative 2015)

A successful and sustainable response to the crises we face requires fundamental changes to the manner in which we shape individual and collective action together—we must move beyond attempting to hold the tensions in balance and instead seek a synthesis.

While the contemporary circumstances are certainly dire, they are by no means immutable. When individuals and groups feel dominated or alienated, there are several common responses—join the competition for incremental reforms, acquiesce voluntarily, succumb to domination, or refuse and resist through a variety of methods. While militancy may indeed be needed to move forward, a fruitful response to the contemporary condition "seems insufficiently articulated in radical theory today" (Connolly 2013, 31). But there is another possibility in which action seeks systemic transformation—not through domination or compromise, but rather through intentional social process—what Follett (2013b) calls "the method of integration" (178).

We agree that transformation of these existing systems requires a dialogue among physical science, social science, philosophy, and theology (Connolly 2011); "systemic problems require systemic solutions" (Democracy Collaborative 2015). Additionally, this dialogue must be fully inclusive and integrative, moving beyond traditional approaches to these spheres of knowledge production by embracing experiential knowledge. In sum, theories and practices based on discrete individual subjects and objects clearly divide public and private organizations, and separate political, economic, and civil spheres; these independent sectors no longer work. Our current dominant political and social theories are ill-equipped to function within a world that is woven together through intersecting networks, a world in which who we are, what we do, and what we will become are inescapably bound together in perpetual motion (Suchocki 1985); *this is a world of co-creation.* We are socially, economically, and environmentally interdependent and our governance theories have yet to catch up. We must grapple with "the fundamental challenge" of working out "what is involved in construing the world as a world of processes rather than things and then reformulate both the natural and the human sciences on this foundation" (Gare 2000, 5). To do so, we must turn to the ontological rationales for a different grounding for governance in the contemporary global context.

Ontological rationales

Catlaw (2007a) suggests we seek a "politics of the subject" in which we "theorize a government that does not exist to represent and replicate the division between those who rule and those who are ruled" (189). To prefigure this radical democracy, he calls for a political ontology that does not force unique

Why Integrative Governance? 183

individuals into the oppressive and exclusionary model-copy condition of representation. However, his proposition does not provide much in the way of explanation, so we must go further. Indeed, reflecting on the Arab Spring and similar social movements, Tugal (2014) argues, "If we do not develop solid alternatives (and organizations and institutions that will implement them), the downfall of the system will not mean the making of a better world" (3). Like a hologram, regime values are reflected in the smallest acts of administrative behavior; to transform that regime, we must all become part of the solution (Thorne and Kouzmin 2012). This will require altering the very managerial logic that infuses everything we do.

The challenge is to make effective criticism through resistance and refusal while also taking purposeful action toward effective systemic social change. This has been described as an affirmative, as opposed to a skeptical, postmodern philosophy (Rosenau 1992). Queer anarchist Jamie Heckert (2012) suggests that we must ask, "What ways of living and relating can we practice that are even more effective at meeting the needs of everyone for life, love, and freedom?" (71). While we must continue critique, refusal, and resistance of unsustainable philosophies and practices, we must also affirm alternatives that will not be colonizing through domination or shallow compromise, but are rather malleable and integrative: "The way to create a new world is to take steps *to* create it, to live the life we want to live" (Ackelsberg 2012, 3).

It may be that the movements described in the Arcs of Reform and Reification believe they are in this pursuit. But as shown in Table 12.1, from the perspective of one or more of the others, each primary approach to governance and its associated hybrid yields a dystopian social condition that binds us or absorbs us (Hierarchical, Reified State, and Holographic), isolates us or alienates us (Atomistic, Reified Market, and Fragmented), or calcifies us (Reified Community). Regardless of where one is along the ontological continuum of the Governance Arc, the individual ends up with some sense of alienation from either authentic self or relation.

We argue these pathological conditions are the result of the dialectical imbalances in collectivist and individualist ontological assumptions. All positions on the Governance Arc perpetuate the One/Many dialectic. When group role is emphasized, the individual is alienated from self as group identity crowds out individual identity in the pathologies of bondage (Hierarchical) and eventually absorption (Holographic). Similarly, when the individual is emphasized, the person is separated from others as a result of the pathologies of isolation (Atomistic) and eventually alienation (Fragmented). Communitarian attempts

Table 12.1 Dystopian pathologies

	Collectivist/Reified State	*Reified Community*	*Individualist/Reified Market*
Static state	Bondage	Calcification	Isolation
Dynamic state	Absorption		Alienation

184 *A radically democratic approach*

to resolve this dialectic between the group and the individual are based on static ontological ground, and any stable balance comes at the cost of rigidity, which calcifies group identity. Taken together, we argue that all positions on the Governance Arc remain in dialectical tension and imbalance, in terms of both the collectivist and individualist divide and the static and dynamic divide—all of which produce pathologies. Considering the movements down and up the Arcs of Reform and Reification, we can see that the pathologies spur perpetual movement among the ideological positions without ever resolving the community–individual dialectic. We cannot remain trapped in ontological tension that leads to doubt, suspicion, and fear. We must figure out how we can effectively and democratically constitute community (Braidotti 2013).

From our critique, we conclude that all approaches on the Governance Arc fail to offer a sustainable and satisfactory response to the contemporary global context. However, taken together, each has valuable insight to provide. As cogently argued by Coles (2005),

> *Both* lack and abundance provide rich insight into contemporary problems and alternative possibilities. Yet this richness hinges significantly on articulating their *intertwinement* in ways that better illuminate each concept: checking the dangers of their reification and sharpening their ethical and political suggestiveness.
>
> (68)

We add resolution of the paradox of stasis (being) versus process (becoming) to this challenge.

In crafting an alternative, we must also avoid the pitfalls of what White (2000) calls strong ontological positions. Both the Holographic and Fragmented ontologies are strong in that they are not open to contestation—the Holographic ontology of abundance denies the Many, while the Fragmented ontology of lack denies the One. These issues remain true in their respective hybrids of the Reified State and the Reified Market. Even the relatively moderate Hierarchical, Atomistic, and Reified Community positions are still strong because they are static in their understanding of existence, leaving no possibility for malleability. Thus, as it stands, should any of the approaches on the Governance Arc be employed in the global context, we can anticipate ontological colonization and resulting resistance and refusal.

We believe that in a dynamic, globalizing, pluralistic context that has become deeply fragmented and competitive, and in which claims to truth and legitimacy are regularly contested, we must disregard ontologies that claim either a bounded Whole or a static Is. This eliminates all but one ideal-type: Fragmented Governance. However, a fiercely held ontology of lack disables any sort of stable identity or social bond beyond recognition of our common plight in the face of ontological blindness and psychosocial domination. In other words, all positions on the Governance Arc are *strong* in ways that undermine collective action through radical democracy.

Why Integrative Governance? 185

In a global context, the challenge is to provide critique paired with pragmatic affirmation that is not dominating in its prescriptions, but rather tentative and inclusive—in other words, a weak ontology (White 2000) or an unstable ontology (Marchart 2005). We must find a universalism that will not produce particular substantive content that can become hegemonic or totalizing (Prozorov 2014a). Instead, we must seek to affirm an ontology grounded in "fluid, transcultural universals" (Keating 2013, 117).

It is this need for the in-between that drives some scholars to search for an integrative position drawing from apparently opposing theories of abundance and lack (see for example, Patton and Protevi 2003, Tønder and Thomassen 2005b). As Laclau (2005) argues, we must reconsider these concepts as "two necessary moments of a unique ontological condition" (256):

> Each illuminates something vital about the human condition and modes of power that damage this vitality. Yet in isolation, they greatly misconstrue our condition and the ethical and political contours of radical democracy. Hence, when lack is fundamentalised in ways that ultimately diminish or deny the corporeal abundance of others and world, it tends to misconstrue negativity and the protean character of otherness, and replicate the least-desirable aspects of modern subjectivity, ethics and politics. Similar dangers appear among those who would theorise abundance "beyond negativity" in ways that tend to diminish the ongoing need to attend to the tragic elements of political life, the importance of contestation in thought, ethics and politics, and so on.
>
> (Coles 2005, 68)

To avoid both monist and pluralist extremes and reifying hybrids, we propose that it is possible to resolve these dialectical tensions through synthesis.

Following Follett's lead, rather than attempting to hold approaches to governance in an ostensibly creative tension with one another, we suggest that synthesis may offer a better approach. Joining others, we argue that synthesis is the only way to resolve paradoxes in ontological arguments over transcendence versus immanence (Wang 2012), abundance versus lack (Tønder and Thomassen 2005b), and One versus Many—or in more psychosocial terms, identity versus difference (Tønder and Thomassen 2005a). However, dialectical synthesis is not a revolution that leaps from one known position to another. It is an open-ended transformation that pursues the imaginable through co-creation of an entirely new alternative. This requires a willingness to jump off the Governance Arc into the abyss of the unknown.

Thus, we must take a leap of faith (not fear) and move toward a wholly different approach—a radical democracy, which we call Integrative Governance. The "relational process ontology" (Stout and Love 2015c) grounding this approach does not fall anywhere along the Governance Arc. Instead, we will demonstrate that Integrative Governance generates new ontological territory through the *dialectical synthesis* of concepts found on the Governance Arc. We

186 *A radically democratic approach*

will also show that as a synthesis, Integrative Governance provides transformational pathways from each position on the Governance Arc to its ontological terrain. Due to its relational character, Integrative Governance prevents the hegemony of either collectivism or individualism and its grounding in process prevents reification.

Employing dialectical synthesis

To avoid the traps of liberalism, monist and pluralist extremes, and the reification of hybrids, we must identify a wholly different position which "dissolves" the dualisms (Harmon 2006) that create the Governance Arc. If we imagine folding the Governance Arc down on itself, or folding the four corners of the two-by-two Governance Typology matrix inward like an origami fortune teller, we might be able to identify the characteristics of a *synthesis* of each dialectic in operation. Donati (2014) notes that etymologically, the term synthesis implies composition. It is formed by *syn* (with, together) and *thesis* (action of placing something). Thus, to synthesize means to actively put together—in this case overlaying ontological assumptions in dialectical opposition to create a new assumption.

As discussed in Chapter 9, an awareness of conceptual differences and the whole they create can produce a synthesis that transcends both elements of the originating unity, thus establishing a new thesis. In this way, dialectic is useful in catalyzing both enlightenment *and* emancipatory change (Carr 2000a). One need only think of the Socratic method of questioning a proposition as well as its opposite to arrive at a new conclusion, or the notion of a "third way" out of ethical dilemmas (Kidder 1995), to grasp the meaning of dialectical synthesis and its value in transcending binary oppositional thinking. Wang (2012) suggests that synthesis is similar to the Chinese notion of *harmonism*, which seeks to escape "essentialist universalism and isolating particularism [that] both rely on dualistic or either/or thinking" (7).

As Follett (1998, 2013b) explains Hegelian synthesis and her own concept of integration, synthesis/integration represents an authentically *third position* that resolves the problems created by both domination (what we call ontological colonization) and compromise (what we call ontological hybridization) between two concepts in dialectical tension. This is valuable because as social theorist Gloria Anzaldúa (2015) notes, "I need a different mode of telling stories, one that can simultaneously hold the different models of what I think reality is. I need a new way of organizing reality" (43). Relating integrative process to formative dialectical assumptions, Follett (2013b) explains,

> The full acceptance of life as process gets us further and further away from the old controversies. The thought I have been trying to indicate is neither conventional idealism nor realism. It is neither mechanism nor vitalism: we see mechanism as true within its own barriers; we see the *élan vitale* (still a thing-in-itself) as a somewhat crude foreshadowing of a profound truth.

Why Integrative Governance? 187

It is now possible to rid ourselves of the limitations of these more partial points of view; we have now given to us new modes of thinking, new ways of acting.

(91)

This argument is not far from Hegel's synthesis of being and nothing as *becoming*, the synthesis of essence and appearance as *actuality*, and the synthesis of the universal and particular as the *singular*. However, rather than imagining synthesis as a static Unity or an end to history—a predetermined point of ultimate development—we follow Bookchin's (1994) open-ended dialectical naturalism, which "advances the vision of an ever-increasing wholeness, fullness and richness of differentiation and subjectivity" (20). This view matches the contemporary understanding of assemblage (Deleuze and Guattari 1983, 1987).

As shown in Figure 12.1, as the dialectical cycle of thesis–antithesis–synthesis repeats, developmental progression is anticipated:

> The struggle between the thesis and the anti-thesis goes on until some solution develops which will, in a certain sense, go beyond both thesis and antithesis by recognizing the relative value of both, *i.e.*, by trying to preserve the merits and to avoid the limitations of both.... Once attained, the synthesis may in turn become the first step of a new dialectic triad.
>
> (Popper 1940, 404)

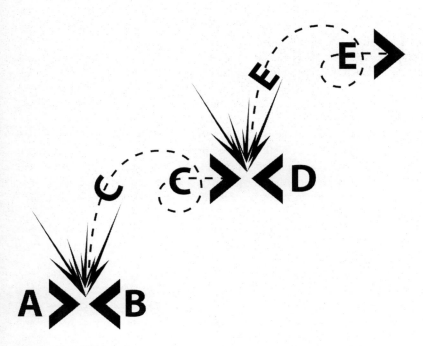

Figure 12.1 Dialectical progression.

188 *A radically democratic approach*

Indeed, many feel that progressive development is the true purpose of dialectic: "It implies interaction leading to an improved synthesis" (Stever 1988, 82). This is how Hegel imagined dialectic playing out historically: "It is a process that develops from lower to higher, from simpler to more complex, from abstract to concrete. In other words, it is an organic process of unfolding and progressing" (Wang 2012, 23).

We agree that there is developmental value to synthesis and seek to identify and explain the various syntheses needed to resolve dialectical tensions on the Governance Arc. A fifth ideal-type, Integrative Governance, can be developed through (1) dialectical analysis of opposing pairs of concepts within the four primary governance approaches, and (2) identification of the synthesis concepts in a diverse array of philosophical, spiritual, scientific, and theoretical sources, albeit those which have been marginalized by dominant perspectives (see Stout and Love 2017). To accomplish the first task here, we apply the same theoretical framework used to explain the primary approaches to governance, providing a conceptual map for comparison across competing prescriptions.

Seeking synthesis

A framework for Integrative Governance can be crafted by examining the possibility of dialectical synthesis in each element of the Governance Typology. Each synthesis must include important characteristics of the thesis and antithesis while presenting a wholly unique position of its own, as explained in the sections that follow. It is important to note, however, that because of process assumptions, none of the resulting concepts holds to "any absolute truth, or … definite goals"; each synthesis is "always straining after higher forms of expression" with "no definite terminus nor … fixed goal" (Rocker 2004, 15).

Like many "post" theoretical positions (i.e., post-humanism, post-colonialism, and post-communism) that resolve dialectic through synthesis (Braidotti 2013), the relational process ontology assumptions of Integrative Governance resolve the collectivist/individualist (One/Many) dialectic through a relational perspective that accommodates both without privileging either the group or the individual. Its process assumptions also resolve the static/dynamic dialectic through an ongoing dynamic state punctuated by moments of stability. In so doing, this integrative position introduces ontological dynamism to many communitarian assumptions in order to prevent the reification of community (Stout and Love 2014a). We argue that these relational process syntheses may provide conceptual grounding for more effective social action—*without becoming a reified, static unity.*

We agree that this alternative "relationship approach" as described by Harmon and McSwite (2011) "*does not fall anywhere along the continuum from principle on the one hand to discourse on the other*" (226)—what we refer to as the Governance Arc. We assume that "principle" connotes the rationalism and idealism of Hierarchical and Holographic Governance and their hybrids, while "discourse" connotes the empiricism and constructivism of Atomistic and

Fragmented Governance and their hybrids. However, we argue that the "relationship-based" approach, as described by Harmon and McSwite (2011), is grounded in an "ontology of relational consciousness" (McSwite 2011, 38) that is *static*.[1] As such, it goes no further than the Reified Community. We must add the dynamism of process to relation—relational *process* ontology—in order to avoid reification. Therefore, as shown in Figure 12.2, Integrative Governance creates ontological terrain in the space encompassed by the Governance Arc, but not on the Arc itself.

To develop this new governance approach, we must first determine the concepts that resolve dialectical tensions in every element of the Governance Typology. We will begin with the deconstruction of those concepts herein and carefully explicate the meaning of synthesis based on relational process at each conceptual level.

Ontological assumptions and associated language

From First Peoples to the newest scientific discoveries, the call is ringing out to adopt an understanding of existence that ensures social, economic, and environmental sustainability. At the ontological level, the dialectic of *static* versus *dynamic state of being* must be resolved. The notion of process accommodates both stable and changing characteristics because the process of becoming is punctuated with moments of full expression. The dialectic of *transcendent* versus *immanent source of being* is resolved by accommodating a nontheistic potentiality similar to transcendence because it accepts the nonmaterial as "real," but imagines an embodied creation similar to immanence. Within all that exists, there is the capacity to create from nontemporal, nonmaterial potentiality. This radical form of immanence includes the material and nonmaterial within an open-ended whole. Thus, it can be understood as a "space *in between* immanence and transcendence" (Tønder 2005, 204).

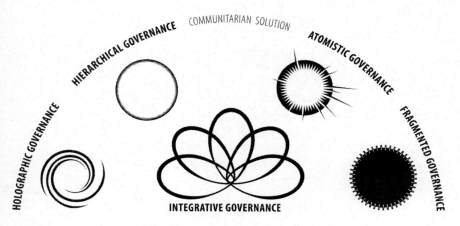

Figure 12.2 The ontological terrain of Integrative Governance.

190 *A radically democratic approach*

Finally, the dialectic of *unified* versus *plural expression of being* is resolved through relational expression in which unique entities co-create themselves and co-compose an open-ended whole from a combination of potentiality, prior states, and environmental influences (Whitehead 1979). Each and every instance of becoming is happening in a relational context of assemblage that interconnects everything from quantum particles to the universe as a whole (Bohm 1980). There is no "beyond" that transcends the universe.

Thus, in relational process ontology, becoming is a seamless emergent process of creative, relational assemblage from embodied potentiality to actuality. Cultural theorist Stuart Hall (1998) describes this as an ontological point between the dialectic of "pure 'autonomy or total encapsulation'" (447). It is this relational, generative quality that uniquely synthesizes ontologies of abundance and lack by assuming a foundational void—but one that is filled with the creative potential of each entity. From this perspective, difference is "the constant play between presence and absence which simply renders impossible the attainment of either full presence (totality) or full absence (radical lack)" (Marchart 2005, 26). It is this dynamic quality that avoids the reification of stability found in the hybrid attempts at ontological compromise.

As explained in Chapter 3, ontological assumptions are encoded within language that serves to reinforce those assumptions through the shaping of consciousness, identity, belief, and knowledge (Gadamer 2004, Heidegger 1996, Lakoff 2003, Saussure 1960). Western languages are imbued with atomism and rank ordering in their use of binaries in meaning making (Derrida 1976). Discrete binaries not only reflect a static, isolated ontology, they establish the opportunity for one of the halves to be dominant. Even Alfred North Whitehead (1979), the founder of process philosophy, could not escape this problem in his use of terminology such as hierarchy, dominance, and importance when referring to the manner in which inanimate and animate entities experience and assemble. Perpetuating categorical differentiation based on complexity or sentience enables destruction of the physical planet in the same way that hierarchical differentiation between races of humans or humans and animals enables their use as commodities.

To express the relational process understanding of "'a world in motion'" where "everything is moving, even if some things are (temporarily) at rest" (Holm *et al.* 2003, 32), the dialectics in language itself must be resolved. *Noun-based* and *verb-based* as well as *holistic* and *binary* languages must be synthesized through concepts that are gerundial (dynamic), non-discrete (holistic or relational), and nonbinary (nonhierarchical) in character. Gerundial language takes the verb rather than the noun as primary, reflecting dynamism and synthesizing the subject–object relationship into a relational subject–subject shared experience. Verb-based languages are "full of potentiality, that which can be" (Maryboy 2004, 12). Furthermore, these languages are nonhierarchical; therefore, they are non-colonizing in nature.

Psychosocial theory

The ongoing proliferation of social crises around the world indicates that our very survival demands a transformation of psychosocial theory in order to discover "new ways of perceiving each other" (Carlsson and Ramphal 1995, 46). In response, critical social theorists are "analyzing current events and development in a way that is congruent with the pluralist, contingent rhythms of materialization" (Coole and Frost 2010, 25)—what we describe as relational process ontology. Human existence cannot be fully explained physically, nor can it be limited simply to phenomenological subjectivity. Human potential is located in an "intercorporeal depth" that is an "*intertwining* between self and world" (Coles 2005, 76–78). Thus, the processes of becoming can create new forms of both individuality and collective life (Patton 2005). Identity formation is a complex process of relational becoming in which unique individuals are permeable and interconnected within themselves, with others, and with their environments in a "nested relatedness" (Bird-David 1999, S78). Process synthesizes the dialectic of *unitary* and *decentered identity* while relation synthesizes the dialectic of *embedded* and *independent social condition*. Because the individual is both socially embedded and co-creative of that society, the social bond is innate and socially constructed, demanding neither complete unity nor pure autonomy. This psychosocial state enables both an authentic sense of self and community, resolving many of the existential crises found in the positions on the Governance Arc.

Epistemological concepts

To resolve social, economic, and environmental crises, how knowledge is constructed must change. Epistemologies have been a principal focus in governance scholarship because, as leading social theorists Michel Foucault and Bent Flyvbjerg argue, "power defines what constitutes knowledge and rationality; indeed, power ultimately defines 'what counts as reality'" (Brooks 2002, 91). Distinctive patterns of political decision making are based on "embedded assumptions and social constructions of reality" (Schneider and Ingram 1997, x). Thus, some argue that global citizens must "see with new eyes and understand with new minds before they can truly turn to new ways of living" (Carlsson and Ramphal 1995, 47).

The bifurcation of mind and matter, philosophy and science, enables the splitting of the *why* of phenomena from the *how*. We must use methods that enable us to consider both simultaneously (Stengers 2011). This suggests that traditional approaches to knowing and understanding are not working; rationalism, empiricism, idealism, and constructivism are not producing the knowledge needed to live sustainably. An integrative approach resolves the dialectic between *internal* and *external justification* by using multiple sources of information that are accessed in a variety of ways. It synthesizes the dialectic of knowledge *structuration* between *foundations* and *coherence* by enabling both in a

192 *A radically democratic approach*

participatory process. Such a pragmatist approach eliminates the "epistemological gap" (Ferré 1998) between the internal (mind) and the external (empirical world) because thought (hypothesis and analysis) and action (experience and observation) are intertwined in an ongoing process of co-creating knowledge. This synthesis empowers all forms of knowing and all participants in knowledge production, making truth flexible and non-dominating.

Belief systems

Competing belief systems are often the identified source of global and civil conflict. If ontology is the understanding of existence, belief systems are the translators of those understandings into action. In other words, *what are the implications of seeing the universe, the world, and the people in it in a particular way?* Connolly (2011) notes that faith disciplines perception by establishing anticipation. If one is raised to believe in a world that operates in a particular way, one anticipates and measures one's experience against that assumption, always seeking to restore experience to one's expectation when it is not met. Therefore, how one responds to the increasingly problematic human predicament has much to do with one's belief system.

An integrative approach would synthesize the dialectic of *unitary transcendent* and *plural immanent sources of existence* through a type of materiality imbued with a metaphysical quality within a relational whole. The dialectic of *static* and *dynamic states of existence* would be synthesized through the ongoing process of becoming punctuated with moments of completion. For the purposes of illustration, in understanding the source of existence as a transcendent One, static state monotheism asserts a divine being that is separate from and hierarchically above the physical universe, establishing a fundamental dualism. As a dynamic alternative, pantheism asserts a transcendent divinity that expresses itself through the parts of the whole, thus denying autonomy within differentiated parts through non-duality. A synthesis would need to accommodate the nonmaterial aspect of existence as well as some understanding of wholeness. In understanding the source of existence as an immanent Many, static state naturalism denies any form of noumena and asserts a material world made up of many individual phenomena. Its belief systems include both atheistic science and secular humanism. The dynamic alternative, anti-essentialism, simply refutes all belief systems as grand narratives that a radical plural must refuse. Thus, a synthesis would have to accommodate material phenomena as a core feature of existence, as well as plurality and difference. A belief system grounded in these assumptions would provide sufficient common ground for mutually respectful dialogue among faiths.

Ethical concepts

As the philosophical assumptions come together, they prefigure particular attitudes and norms of behavior in practice. Therefore, faulty ethics are often

Why Integrative Governance? 193

assumed to be the culprit in social, economic, environmental, and governance crises. An integrative approach to ethics would synthesize the dialectic in *sources of ethical guidance* between *internal motivation* and *external criteria* through a collaborative determining process. Both what motivates each participant and the criteria upon which they agree are considered in developing an ethic. The synthesis lies between norms and facts (Habermas 1998). The dialectic that demands prioritizing *Right* or *Good* as a *normative structure* is resolved through intersubjective agreement.

This participatory, relational approach resolves the dialectic between *man-the-citizen* and *man-the-maker* in *man-the-answerer*, who is mutually obligated with others (Niebuhr 1963). There is no transcendent source providing the substantive content of an ethic; there are no predetermined moral mandates. Instead, we generate together our shared moral guidance. This suggests a universal ethic that is relationally respectful, mutually caring, and mutually answerable, while its dynamic relativity is constrained by nesting, interconnected groups. These characteristics support what we currently pursue through international law: a public morality that is at once local and global, democratic in process, and voluntary in adoption.

Political theory

Similar to ethics, political ideologies and governance practices are often blamed for crises of sustainability. Contemporary crises of both governance and sustainability demand "a redefinition of people's relationship with their society" (Lemus and Barkin 2013, 6). Based on this relationship, the primary dialectic in political theory is in regard to the *structure of authority* through *hierarchy* or *competition*, and the *relative strength of that authority* as *moderate* or *strong*. An integrative approach would need to structure authority in a manner that synthesizes hierarchy and competition. This would demand new organization forms and institutional rules of engagement: a different mode of human coexistence (Buber 1971). A type of confederation that enables deeply nesting and broadly inclusive interlocking networks, from the neighborhood to the global level of analysis, would achieve such a synthesis (Follett 1998).

To resolve the problem of the relative strength of authority, we must dismantle dominating power relations and prevent their recurrence in politics. To do so, radical democracy often demands a return of authority to the individual. However, this would not eliminate the system of power in play. Instead, Follett (1998) calls for a "coöperative sovereignty" (316) that reformulates power-over as power-with (Follett 2003d). Rather than eliminating authority assigned to particular roles, participatory practice *transforms* authority by shifting it from individuals or institutions to the process itself. Government becomes a convener—an institution that provides "the space and the process for working out understanding across lines of difference" (McSwite 2002, 113). Participation resolves the paradox of freedom and control between the individual and the group because restraint is not domination when it is authentically self-generated

194 *A radically democratic approach*

and self-imposed as an active member of the whole. Interlocking networks build the whole in an inclusive and dynamic manner. We believe this approach to radical democracy will be most fruitful.

Economic theory

In response to the various crises of sustainability, there is a growing movement to find the "next system" (Alperovitz *et al.* 2015)—one that supports an Earth community as opposed to an empire (Korten 2006). This movement emphasizes the centrality of economics in social life. Radical democracy asserts that "democratic control of the economy is both desirable and possible" (Simons 2005, 151). For a radically democratic approach to resource use, production, distribution, and consumption, "We need another economic logic" (Donati 2014, 50). A relational process approach would synthesize the dialectic of *external* and *internal regulation* of the market through the practices of participatory democracy. A global economy of this nature would look more like an interlocking network.

Similar to authority in political theory, the *intensity of that regulation* (*weak* or *strong*) would be transformed through self-governance. Such an economy understands economic actors as interdependent rather than competitively independent or dependent on the state, reflecting an "intersubjectivist economics" in which "agents and structures influence one another" (Davis 2003, 125). These agents pursue a combination of self-development and expression, mutual interest, and cooperation in production and consumption. These complex motivations would enable multiple bottom lines to guide action on the part of both firms and households, production and consumption. Considering the implications for people, place, and profits would result in greater sustainability across social, economic, and environmental domains.

Administrative theory

In order to resolve the crises of governance that have fostered or allowed social, economic, and environmental crises to emerge, both political and economic life must be administered in a different manner. An integrative approach to administration would transform authority, leadership, management, and procedures. The primary dialectic in administrative theory is *organizing* via *hierarchy* versus *competition*, with the *relative strength of administrative authority* (*weak* or *strong*) within governance being secondary. As noted in political theory, an integrative approach would resolve the dialectic between *hierarchy* and *competition* through confederation. But rather than empowering administrators to manage interlocking networks, they would instead adopt a facilitative coordinating role without command authority. Once again, this transforms authority by placing it in the process, while enabling the facilitation of that process.

Coordination is an ongoing process through which the perspectives, expertise, and functions of all parties are interwoven. In a radically democratic approach, procedures become emergent and open-ended processes. Coordination requires identifying shared concerns, analyzing possible responses, coming to decisions about what to do, acting collectively, and then considering how things went. Facilitative leaders can help groups coordinate action in each phase, while consensus-oriented decision making enables collective choice. These participatory practices foster a sense of collective responsibility and experientially founded commitment to shared implementation. We believe this approach will foster more sustainable outcomes.

Note

1 We make this observation based on their employment of Heidegger's *being-with*, which does not assume process ontology (Shaviro 2009).

13 Pursuing Integrative Governance

Based on the syntheses proposed in Chapter 12, we agree with others who argue, "The abundant version of radical democratic theory offers the better hope of fulfilling democratic ideals on condition that it is articulated with a theory of hegemony to give it a political strategy" (Simons 2005, 151). In other words, we must affirm an approach grounded in relational process ontology while maintaining critique—both of other governance approaches *and* the one we pursue. Furthermore, while radical democracy requires a revolution in ontological perspective and engagement for many, we don't believe it demands a structural revolution. As Stavrakakis (2005) argues, "most forms of democracy—liberal democracy included—still contain a kernel of that potential—often repressed and marginalised and certainly in need of radical revitalisation and re-activation" (192). We can nurture this revitalization through a shift that allows for authentic participation and interrelation through what Keating (2013) refers to as post-oppositional politics within existing institutions.

In this sense, Integrative Governance is a prefigurative approach. Its purpose is to facilitate a radically democratic, ongoing process of *integrating* that interconnects all levels of experience (material, intrapersonal, and interpersonal) within all social groups (family and friendships, community, politics, work, and economic exchange) at all levels of analysis (neighborhood, city, region, nation, the world). In other words, it is *radical democracy as a way of life.*

Integrative Governance is grounded in relational process ontology, which makes a commitment to a notion of life as an ongoing process of becoming among interdependent beings, things, and places—each of which is a unique expression of existence. We are a dynamic, mutually influencing multitude of unique but interrelating parts. Our co-creative potential is infinite and bounded only by our interdependent choices. Such an ontology provides a logically coherent basis for political, economic, and administrative practices that consider the entire situation, allowing for mutual influence and change in an ongoing integrative group process: one that accommodates both disrupting and unifying, disintegration and integration, change and stability. It is, by definition and practice, a radical approach that transforms democracy.

To address misunderstandings in responses to our preliminary work, we feel it is important to make clear that due to its radical grounding and relational

Pursuing Integrative Governance 197

process assumptions, integration is definitively *non-Hegelian*; we seek a unifying process, not static unity. To defend this claim, we turn to Follett's (1998) explanation of the differentiating features:

> I have said that the political pluralists are fighting a misunderstood Hegelianism. Do they adopt the crudely popular conception of the Hegelian state as something 'above and beyond' men, as a separate entity virtually independent of men? Such a conception is fundamentally wrong and wholly against the spirit of Hegel. As James found collective experience not independent of distributive experience, as he reconciled the two through the 'compounding consciousness,' so Hegel's related parts received their meaning only in the conception of total relativity. The soul of Hegelianism is total relativity, but this is the essence of the compounding of consciousness. As for James the related parts and their relations appear simultaneously and with equal reality, so in Hegel's total relativity.
>
> (266)

From a relational process understanding, "true Hegelianism finds its actualized form in federalism" (Follett 1998, 267)—Follett's way of describing *organic wholes a-making in evolving situations*. Because each person is a co-creator in this process, this type of open-ended whole is democratically acceptable. In interlocking networks of radically democratic communities, "our loyalty is neither to imaginary wholes nor to chosen wholes, but is an integral part of that activity which is at the same time creating me" (Follett 1919, 579).

Any synthesis position must successfully integrate the driving concerns within the thesis and antithesis. Follett (2013b) calls this process *integration*, explaining that it is an intentional process of creating "*functional unity*" (256) among individuals actively engaging in collective action in any sector of society. As she understands it, "the method of integration" (178) is composed of a number of processual elements that are iterative rather than linear in nature. These elements include a disposition, a style of relating, a mode of association, and an approach to action.

Integrating begins with an attitude—a *disposition* that she describes as "*the will to will the common will*" (Follett 1998, 49). This relational disposition generates a cooperative *style of relating* and enables participatory interactions— or "*modes of association*" (147)—in which we feel an obligation to engage in public life and to consider others in all we do. Thus, the second characteristic of integrating is genuine participation: "You have to have participation before you can get co-operation" (Follett 2003c, 171).

In this participatory cooperation, the group co-produces knowledge, shared desire, purpose, choice of method, and so forth—in short, all activities common to the group decision-making process. In these activities, integrating seeks "the interpenetration of the ideas of the parties concerned" (Follett 2003e, 212). This requires a dialogic "interpermeation" (Follett 1998, 209) that includes "a cooperative gathering of facts" (Follett 2013b, 17), and "genuine discussion"

198 *A radically democratic approach*

that "is truth-seeking" (Follett 1998, 210) in the situation. Its synergistic effect produces more creative and effective methods because nothing is lost through domination or compromise: "By integrating these interests you get the increment of the unifying" (Follett 2013b, 45–46).

It "often takes ingenuity, a 'creative intelligence,' to find the integration" (163). But from the perspective of *constructive conflict* (Follett 2003a), differing interests are more easily integrated through the techniques of disintegration and revaluation. Disintegration is necessary in order to move from fully formulated *a priori* positions to the nuanced driving desires underneath. *Interests* are typically composed of a desire, an idea about how to get the desire met, and a passion to make it happen. To enable integration, desire must be split from method, which may be achieved either through change in the desire or change in the preferred method of fulfillment. Once divided, "revaluation is the flower of comparison" (38) that precipitates an organic change of opinion through dialogue and value comparison.

However, Follett (2013b) also notes that such revaluation occurs in response to changes in the situation, changes in oneself, and new sources of knowledge. Regardless of the relational source, "through an interpenetrating of understanding, the quality of one's own thinking is changed" (163). "The course of action decided upon is what we all together want, and I see that it is better than what I had wanted alone. It is what *I* now want" (Follett 1998, 25). Today, we would call this a consensus building process (Susskind *et al.* 1999) or a conflict resolution process (Forester 2009) that addresses both normative and causal beliefs (Sabatier 1988).

Because of this integration of desires and/or preferred methods, commitment to what is co-created is ensured not through consent or the binding authority of law or contract, "but in the fact that it has been produced by the community" (Follett 1998, 130); loyalty is *experientially* founded. Similarly, a sense of mutual responsibility is engendered by this shared ownership: "collective responsibility is not a matter of adding but of interweaving" (Follett 2013a, 75).

Following the method of integration, Integrative Governance must answer the desire for *order* sought by Hierarchical Governance, the *liberty* sought by Atomistic Governance, the *unity* sought by Holographic Governance, the *autonomy* sought by Fragmented Governance, and the sense of *belonging* sought by the communitarian hybrid. If these fundamental characteristics are not accommodated in the governance approach, integration will not be successful.

As suggested in Figure 13.1, Integrative Governance accomplishes integration because it is placed at the pivot of the metronome's pendulum in the Governance Arc. In dialogue with Hierarchical and Atomistic Governance, it accommodates both *order* and *liberty* through moments of harmony and stability amidst ongoing contestation and change. In dialogue with Holographic and Fragmented Governance, it enables us to achieve both *unity* and *autonomy* through respect for difference within a social condition of interdependence. Taken together, these characteristics enable the sense of *belonging* sought in the

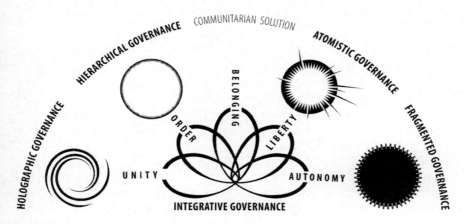

Figure 13.1 Pathways for discourse.

Reified Community, but one that resists reification through openness and ongoing process.

Delving below these desires, Integrative Governance also addresses the fears held at the various positions on the Governance Arc. The shared fear of *conflict* held by Hierarchical and Holographic Governance is mitigated by transforming the understanding of conflict as constructive conflict, a creative opportunity that enables the progress of both the individual and society. The shared fear of *control* held by Atomistic and Fragmented Governance is abated through self-organizing participation. Because agreements are co-created and experientially founded, mutual consent is not dominating. The fear of *exclusion* felt in the Reified Community is relieved through open-ended inclusion in ongoing integration—the substantively undefined and changing *we*.

In accommodating these desires and relieving these fears, Integrative Governance heals the pathologies generated by the positions on the Governance Arc. The experience of *bondage* or *absorption* created by Hierarchical and Holographic Governance is averted by self-organizing confederation. Because all are involved in composing the assemblage, its identity is not externally imposed but rather co-created—the People is "a-making" (Follett 2013b, 102). The experience of *isolation* or *alienation* felt in Atomistic and Fragmented Governance is prevented through relationality. Interconnectedness enables a sense of belonging that is not dominating. The pathology of *calcification* generated by the Reified Community is precluded through process punctuated with moments of stability—becoming a group-self is emergent and evolutionary.

Considering these analyses, Integrative Governance meets the tenets of radical democracy because it assumes the possibility of an accessible authentic self and an ontological relation that encourages social connection while being sufficiently dynamic and open-ended as to be non-colonizing and non-fundamentalist in terms of substantive meanings. In other words, its relational

200 *A radically democratic approach*

process ontology is sufficiently *weak* (see White 2000) for radical democracy. Its embrace of both disintegration and integration, like a synthesis of lack and abundance, is "unsurpassed in its potential fecundity" (Norval 2005, 99).[1]

Therefore, while we wish to establish *pathways for discourse* that proponents of the other approaches to governance may travel—a conceptual starting point for the integrative process—we unabashedly affirm Integrative Governance. We believe it provides a more fruitful grounding for global governance and our ability to co-create a more sustainable, flourishing future. It can help in the project of transforming governance in all areas of life because progress of the individual and society is understood in both substantive and process terms.

Substantively, enabling a greater emphasis of social bottom lines while considering more traditional economic and environmental outcomes contributes to sustainability. In terms of process, Integrative Governance provides an open approach to dialogue that can support ever-widening circles of agreement. This approach does not seek to persuade those holding a different perspective to simply give it up, as this would merely replace one form of ontological colonization with another. Instead, the method of integration invites the "*emergence of another, even if it, too, is punctuated by ambivalence and hesitation*" (Connolly 2005, 242). In this invitation, Integrative Governance follows what Nietzsche calls a "spiritualization of enmity," by which he means that those of different creeds "come to terms with each other by weaving reciprocal forbearance, hesitation and presumptive generosity into their relations" (245).

Next steps

As a research agenda, exploring the relationship between the individual and society is a project that is not likely to end soon. Indeed, it is a question that Integrative Governance would say should never be "answered" due to the problem of reification. We undertook an exploration of the theoretical barriers to global governance because existing approaches have not managed to negotiate the dialectic between collectivism and individualism at state levels of action, let alone globally. We are experiencing a global crisis of sustainability that can be seen in social, economic, and environmental predicaments, as well as a loss of legitimacy in governments of all forms. To sustain our collective life, we must sort out how we live together on this planet. This requires *some* type of approach to global governance. We feel Integrative Governance holds the most promise.

However, to support our affirmation of Integrative Governance, we must continue to develop it theoretically. A full explication of each conceptual element in the Governance Typology will require more in-depth analysis than can be presented herein. To flesh out a robust explication, we will delve more deeply into sources describing concepts aligned with relational process ontology. Specifically, we will more fully explore the theories and practices of perspectives and cultures beyond mainstream societies—the minoritarian understandings that can be found around the world.

Pursuing Integrative Governance 201

From there, empirical research will be used in an iterative fashion to fine-tune both theory and practice. As noted in Chapter 4, typologies are used in empirical study to analyze a particular situation and identify what is similar to and different from the various ideal-types in order to make recommendations. We will use the Governance Typology in case assessment, the formation of recommendations, and implementation of change efforts—the results of which will feed back into theoretical development and refinement.

We will focus our empirical research on groups already expressing characteristics of Integrative Governance. Increasingly, people the world over are demanding more direct participation in the processes of governance—a key characteristic of radical democracy. Giving us a clue for where to begin, Follett (2013b) looked to the social movements of her time for nascent examples:

> The community centre movements, the workmen's education movement, the cooperative movement, to mention only two or three.... The central aim of these, the most democratic movements we have, is to train ourselves, to learn how to use the work of experts, to find our will, to educate our will, to integrate our wills.
>
> (5)

Of particular interest to us today are the indications we see of Integrative Governance in various social and economic movements: large-scale cooperatives (Mondragon, Evergreen), indigenous land rights (the Zapatista Army of National Liberation, Australian Aboriginal Sovereignty), food sovereignty (the Coalition of Immokalee Workers, La Via Campesina), community building (Blacks in Green), social and racial justice (Showing Up for Racial Justice, Black Lives Matter, embodied solidarity), political accountability (the Arab Spring), and economic accountability (Occupy, Next System Project).

We believe these types of collective action have much to teach us about Integrative Governance. While post-anarchist and radical democratic theory look to these sources for a prefigurative *politics*, we look toward a prefigurative *administration* as well. Specifically, we seek to assess the degree to which participants and groups in these movements exhibit characteristics in the Governance Typology: *to what degree do their practices reflect Integrative Governance from administration to ontology? If we delve all the way in to philosophical assumptions, do we find consistency? Why, or why not? Does our premise that inconsistent ontological assumptions will eventually pull practice out of alignment hold?* The potential answers to these research questions spur us onward in our pursuit of Integrative Governance.

Note

1 This is Norval's assessment of Laclau's unique approach to ontological abundance working in concert with psychosocial lack in hegemony and counter-hegemony.

References

Abigail, Ruth Anna, and Dudley D. Cahn. 2011. *Managing Conflict through Communication*. 4th edition. Boston, MA: Allyn & Bacon.

Ackelsberg, Martha. 2012. "Preface." In *Queering Anarchism: Addressing and Undressing Power and Desire*, edited by C. B. Daring, J. Rogue, Deric Shannon and Abbey Volcano, 1–4. Oakland: AK Press.

Adams, Guy B. 1992. "Enthralled with Modernity: The Historical Context of Knowledge and Theory Development in Public Administration." *Public Administration Review* no. 52:211–218.

Adams, Guy B., Priscilla V. Bowerman, Kenneth M. Dolbeare, and Camilla M. Stivers. 1990. "Joining Purpose to Practice: A Democratic Identity for the Public Service." In *Images and Identities in Public Administration*, edited by Henry D. Kass and Bayard L. Catron, 219–240. Newbury Park, CA: Sage Publications.

Adams, Jason. 2011. "The Constellation of Opposition." In *Post-Anarchism: A Reader*, edited by Duane Rousselle and Süreyyya Evren, 117–138. London: Pluto Press.

Adams, Robert Merrihew. 1975. "Where do our Ideas Come From? Descartes vs. Locke." In *Innate Ideas*, edited by Stephen P. Stich, 71–88. Los Angeles: University of California Press.

Adler, Margot. 1986. *Drawing Down the Moon*. Boston: Beacon Press.

Adorno, Theodor W. 1973. *Negative Dialectics*. New York: Seabury Press.

Allan, George. 1993. "Process Ideology and the Common Good." *Journal of Speculative Philosophy* no. 7 (4):266–285.

Alperovitz, Gar, James Gustave Speth, and Joe Guinan. 2015. "The Next System Project: New Political-Economic Possibilities for the 21st Century." In *NSP Report*. Washington, DC: New Systems Project.

Amoah, Lloyd G. Adu. 2010. "Public Policy Formation in Africa: Toward a Grounded Ontology." *Administrative Theory & Praxis* no. 32 (4):606–610.

Amoah, Lloyd G. Adu. 2012. "Reflections on Philosophical Clarity and the Process-orientation Turn." *Administrative Theory & Praxis* no. 34 (3):385–406.

Anderson, Benedict. 2006. *Imagined Communities: Reflections on the Origin and Spread of Nationalism*. Revised edition. New York: Verso.

Antliff, Allan. 2011. "Anarchy, Power, and Post-Structuralism." In *Post-Anarchism: A Reader*, edited by Duane Rousselle and Süreyyya Evren, 160–167. London: Pluto Press.

Anzaldúa, Gloria. 2015. *Light in the Dark: Luz En Lo Oscuro*. Durham, NC: Duke University Press.

Appleby, Paul H. 1945. *Big Democracy*. New York: Knopf.

Appleby, Paul H. 1952. *Morality and Administration in Democratic Government*. Baton Rouge: Louisiana State University Press.

Archie, Lee C. 2010. *Ethics: Ethical Relativism*. Lander University.

Arendt, Hannah. 1968. *The Origins of Totalitarianism*. New York: Harcourt.

Arendt, Hannah. 1998. *The Human Condition*. Chicago: University of Chicago Press. Original edition, 1958.

Aristotle. 1908. *The Organon*. London: George Bell and Sons.

Aristotle. 2000. *Nichomachean Ethics*. Translated by T. H. Irwin. Indianapolis: Hackett Publishing.

Armstrong, Karen. 2005. *A Short History of Myth*. New York: Cannongate.

Arnstein, Sherry. 1969. "A Ladder of Citizen Participation." *Journal of the American Institute of Planners* no. 35 (3):216–224.

Augustine, Saint. 1961. *Confessions*. Translated by R. S. Pine-Coffin. Baltimore: Penguin Books.

Ayer, A. J. 1952. *Language, Truth and Logic*. New York: Dover Publications.

Ayer, A. J., Ed. 1959. *Logical Positivism*. New York: The Free Press.

Bachrach, Peter. 1967. *The Theory of Democratic Elitism: A Critique*. Boston: Little, Brown.

Bagavad Gita, The. 2007. *The Bagavad Gita*. Translated by Eknath Easwaran. Canada: Nilgiri Press.

Bailey, Mary Timney. 1992. "Do Physicists Use Case Studies? Thoughts on Public Administration Research." *Public Administration Review* no. 52 (1):47–55.

Bakunin, Mikhail. 1972a. "Politics and the State." In *Bakunin's Writings*, edited by Guy A. Aldred, 42–64. New York: Kraus Reprint Corporation. Original edition, 1871.

Bakunin, Mikhail. 1972b. "The Red Association." In *Bakunin's Writings*, edited by Guy A. Aldred, 21–25. New York: Kraus Reprint Corporation. Original edition, 1870.

Bakunin, Mikhail. 1972c. "Solidarity in Unity." In *Bakunin's Writings*, edited by Guy A. Aldred, 18–21. New York: Kraus Reprint Corporation. Original edition, 1871.

Baradat, Leon P. 2012. *Political Ideologies: Their Origins and Impact*. 11th edition. New York: Longman.

Barber, Benjamin R. 1984. *Strong Democracy: Participatory Politics for a New Age*. Berkeley, CA: University of California Press.

Barber, Benjamin R. 2007. *Consumed: How Markets Corrupt Children, Infantilize Adults, and Swallow Citizens Whole*. New York: W.W. Norton and Company.

Barker, Chris. 2000. *Cultural Studies: Theory and Practice*. Thousand Oaks, CA: Sage Publications.

Barnard, Chester I. 1968. *The Functions of the Executive*. 30th Anniversary edition. Cambridge, MA: Harvard University Press. Original edition, 1938.

Barnosky, Anthony D., Nicholas Matzke, Susumu Tomiya, Guinevere O. U. Wogan, Brian Swartz, Tiago B. Quental, Charles Marshall, Jenny L. McGuire, Emily L. Lindsey, Kaitlin C. Maguire, Ben Mersey, and Elizabeth A. Ferrer. 2011. "Has the Earth's Sixth Mass Extinction Already Arrived?" *Nature* no. 471.

Barry, Brian. 2005. *Why Social Justice Matters*. Cambridge, MA: Polity Press.

Bartels, Koen P. R. 2013. "Public Encounters: The History and Future of Face-to-face Contact between Public Professionals and Citizens." *Public Administration* no. 91 (2):469–483.

Bartels, Koen P. R. 2014. "Communicative Capacity: The Added Value of Public Encounters for Participatory Democracy." *American Review of Public Administration* no. 44 (6):656–674.

204 *References*

Barzelay, Michael. 1993. "The Single Case Study as Intellectually Ambitious Inquiry." *Journal of Public Administration Research and Theory* no. 3:305–318.

Bateson, Gregory. 1972. *Steps to an Ecology of Mind*. Chicago: University of Chicago Press.

Baudrillard, Jean. 1994. *Simulacra and Simulation*. Ann Arbor: University of Michigan Press.

Bauman, Zygmunt. 2001. "Individually Together." In *Individualization: Institutionalized Individualism and its Social and Political Consequences*, edited by Ulrich Beck and Elisabeth Beck-Gernsheim, xiv. Thousand Oaks: Sage Publications.

Beck, Ulrich, and Elisabeth Beck-Gernsheim. 2001. Authors' preface: "Institutionalized individualism." In *Individualization: Institutionalized Individualism and its Social and Political Consequences*, edited by Ulrich Beck and Elisabeth Beck-Gernsheim, xx–xxv. Thousand Oaks: Sage Publications.

Beck, Ulrich, and Elisabeth Beck-Gernsheim. 2001. *Individualization: Institutionalized Individualism and its Social and Political Consequences*. Vol. 13. Thousand Oaks: Sage Publications.

Beeman, Chris, and Sean Blenkinsop. 2008. "Might Diversity Also Be Ontological? Considering Heidegger, Spinoza and Indigeneity in Educative Practice." *Encounters on Education* no. 9 (Fall):95–107.

Bell, Michael. 2006. "Toward an Ecology of Spirit." In *Business Within Limits: Deep Ecology and Buddhist Economics*, edited by Zsolnai Laszlo and Knut Johannessen Ims, 269–318. Bern, Switzerland: Peter Lang AG.

Bellone, Carl J., and George Frederick Goerl. 1993. "In Defense of Civic-regarding Entrepreneurship or Helping Wolves to Promote Good Citizenship." *Public Administration Review* no. 53 (4):396–398.

Bennett, Jane. 2001. *The Enchantment of Modern Life: Attachments, Crossings, and Ethics*. Princeton, NJ: Princeton University Press.

Bennett, Jane. 2010. "A Vitalist Stopover on the Way to a New Materialism." In *New Materialisms: Ontology, Agency, and Politics*, edited by Diana Coole and Samantha Frost, 47–69. Durham, NC: Duke University Press.

Benson, Peter L., and Dorothy L. Williams. 1982. *Religion on Capitol Hill: Myths and Realities*. New York: Harper & Row.

Bentham, Jeremy. 1988. *An Introduction to The Principles of Morals and Legislation*. Buffalo, NY: Prometheus Press. Original edition, 1789.

Bercovitch, Sacvan. 1978. "The Typology of America's Mission." *American Quarterly* no. 30 (2):135–155.

Berger, Peter L., and Thomas Luckmann. 1966. *The Social Construction of Reality: A Treatise in the Sociology of Knowledge*. Garden City, NY: Anchor Books.

Berkely, George. 1712. "Passive obedience: or, the Christian doctrine of not resisting the supreme power, proved and vindicated…. In a discourse deliver'd at the College-chapel." Available at http://ota.ox.ac.uk/id/4115 via http://writersinspire.org/content/passive-obedience-or-christian-doctrine-not-resisting-supreme-power-proved-vindicated (accessed August 1, 2016).

Berlin, Isaiah. 2013. "Two Concepts of Liberty." In *Liberty*, edited by Henry Hardy, 166–217. Oxford: Oxford University Press. Original edition, 1969.

Bernstein, Richard J. 1991. *The New Constellation: The Ethical–Political Horizons of Modernity/Postmodernity*. Cambridge, MA: MIT Press.

Bertalan, Hilton. 2011. "When Theories Meet: Emma Goldman and 'Post-Anarchism'." In *Post-Anarchism: A Reader*, edited by Duane Rousselle and Süreyyya Evren, 208–230. London: Pluto Press.

References 205

Best, Steven, and Douglas Kellner. 1991. *Postmodern Theory: Critical Interrogations, Critical Perspectives*. New York: Guilford Press.

Bevir, Mark. 2012. *Governance: A Short Introduction*. Oxford: Oxford University Press.

Bingham, Lisa Blomgren, Tina Nabatchi, and Rosemary O'Leary. 2005. "The New Governance: Practices and Processes for Stakeholder and Citizen Participation in the Work of Government." *Public Administration Review* no. 65 (5):547–558.

Bird-David, Nurit. 1999. "'Animism' Revisited: Personhood, Environment, and Relational Epistemology." *Current Anthropology* no. 40 (S1):S67–S91.

Blair, Tony. 1998. *The Third Way: New Politics for a New Century*. London: Fabian Society.

Blake, William. 2008. "Auguries of Innocence." In *The Complete Poetry & Prose of William Blake*, edited by David V. Erdman, 490–493. Los Angeles: University of California Press. Original edition, 1863.

Blasi, Joseph. 2009. *The Communal Experience of the Kibbutz*. New Brunswick: Transaction Publishers.

Bogason, Peter. 2001. "Postmodernism and American Public Administration in the 1990s." *Administration & Society* no. 33 (2):165–193.

Bohm, David. 1980. *Wholeness and the Implicate Order*. London: Routledge & Kegan Paul.

Bohm, David. 1985. *Unfolding Meaning*. London: Routledge.

Bohm, David. 2004. *On Dialogue*. New York: Routledge.

Boje, David M. 2006. "What Happened on the Way to Postmodern? Part II." *Administrative Theory & Praxis* no. 28 (4):479–494.

Bookchin, Murray. 1994. *The Philosophy of Social Ecology: Essays on Dialectical Naturalism*. 2nd edition. Montreal: Black Rose Books.

Bookchin, Murray. 2002. "Theses on Libertarian Municipalism." In *The Anarchist Papers*, edited by Dimitrios Roussopoulos, 9–22. New York: Black Rose Books.

Borsodi, Ralph. 1927. *The Distribution Age: A Study of the Economy of Modern Distribution*. New York: D. Appleton and Co.

Borsodi, Ralph. 1929. *This Ugly Civilization*. New York: Simon and Schuster.

Borsodi, Ralph. 1933. *Flight from the City*. New York: Harper and Brothers.

Bourne, Edmund J. 2008. *Global Shift: How a New Worldview is Transforming Humanity*. Oakland, CA: New Harbinger Publications.

Bowman, James S. 1978. "Managerial Theory and Practice: The Transfer of Knowledge in Public Administration." *Public Administration Review* no. 38 (6):563–570.

Box, Richard C. 1992. "An Examination of the Debate over Research in Public Administration." *Public Administration Review* no. 52:62–69.

Box, Richard C. 1998. *Citizen Governance: Leading American Communities into the 21st Century*. Thousand Oaks, CA: Sage Publications.

Box, Richard C. 1999. "Running Government like a Business: Implications for Public Administration Theory and Practice." *American Review of Public Administration* no. 29 (1):19–43.

Box, Richard C., Ed. 2004. *Public Administration and Society: Critical Issues in American Governance*. Armonk, NY: M.E. Sharpe.

Box, Richard C. 2008. *Making a Difference: Progressive Values in Public Administration*. Armonk, NY: M.E. Sharpe.

Boyte, Harry C. 2005. "Reframing Democracy: Governance, Civic Agency, and Politics." *Public Administration Review* no. 65 (5):536–546.

206 References

Bozeman, Barry, and Stuart Bretschneider. 1994. "The 'Publicness Puzzle' in Organization Theory: A Test of Alternative Explanations of Differences Between Public and Private Organizations." *Journal of Public Administration Research and Theory* no. 4 (April):197–223.

Brady, F. Neil. 2003. "'Publics' Administration and the Ethics of Particularity." *Public Administration Review* no. 63 (5):525–534.

Braidotti, Rosi. 2006. *Transpositions: On Nomadic Ethics.* Cambridge, MA: Polity Press.

Braidotti, Rosi. 2010. "The Politics Of 'Life Itself' and New Ways of Dying." In *New Materialisms: Ontology, Agency, and Politics*, edited by Diana Coole and Samantha Frost, 201–218. Durham, NC: Duke University Press.

Braidotti, Rosi. 2013. *The Posthuman.* Cambridge, MA: Polity Press.

Branden, Nathaniel. 1964. "Counterfeit Individualism." In *The Virtue of Selfishness: A New Concept of Egoism*, by Ayn Rand, 135–138. New York: New American Library.

Brigg, Morgan. 2007. "Biopolitics Meets Terrapolitics: Political Ontologies and Governance in Settler-colonial Australia." *Australian Journal of Political Science* no. 42 (3):403–417.

Brinkerhoff, Derick W., and Arthur A. Goldsmith. 2005. "Institutional Dualism and International Development: A Revisionist Interpretation of Good Governance." *Administration & Society* no. 37 (2):199–224.

Brodd, Jefferey. 2003. *World Religions.* Winona, MN: Saint Mary's Press.

Brooks, Michael P. 2002. *Planning Theory for Practitioners.* Chicago: American Planning Association.

Brown, Wendy. 2006. "American Nightmare: Neoliberalism, Neoconservatism, and De-democratization." *Political Theory* no. 34 (6):690–714.

Buber, Martin. 1971. *Paths in Utopia.* Translated by R. F. C. Hull. Boston: Beacon Press. Original edition, 1949.

Buchanan, James M. 1966. "An Individualistic Theory of Political Process." In *Varieties of Political Theory*, edited by David Easton, 25–37. Englewood Cliffs, NJ: Prentice-Hall.

Butler, Ann Caldwell. 1980. "Josiah Warren and the Sovereignty of the Individual." *Journal of Libertarian Studies* no. IV (4):433–448.

Caiden, Gerald E. 1984. "In Search of an Apolitical Science of American Public Administration." In *Politics and Administration: Woodrow Wilson and American Public Administration*, edited by Jack Rabin and James S. Bowman, 51–76. New York: Dekker.

Caldwell, Lynton K. 1988. *The Administrative Theories of Hamilton & Jefferson: Their Contribution to Thought on Public Administration.* 2nd edition. New York: Holmes & Meier Publishers. Original edition, 1944.

Capra, Fritjof. 1983. *The Turning Point: Science, Society, and the Rising Culture.* New York: Bantam Books.

Capra, Fritjof. 1999. *The Tao of Physics: An Exploration of the Parallels between Modern Physics and Eastern Mysticism.* Boston: Shambhala Publications.

Carino, Ledvina V. 2001. "Private Action for public good? The public role of Voluntary Sector Organizations." *Public Organization Review: A Global Journal* no. 1:55–74.

Carley, Michael, and H. Smith. 2001. "Civil Society and New Social Movements." In *Urban Development and Civil Society: The Role of Communities in Sustainable Cities*, edited by Michael Carley, Paul Jenkins and Harry Smith, 192–203. London: Earthscan.

Carlson, Allan. 2004. *The New Agrarian Mind: The Movement Toward Decentrist Thought in Twentieth-Century America.* New Brunswick: Transaction Publishers.

References 207

Carlsson, Ingvar, and Shridath Ramphal. 1995. *Our Global Neighborhood: The Report of the Commission on Global Governance*. Oxford: The Commission on Global Governance.

Carnap, Rudolf. 1959. "The Old and New Logic." In *Logical Positivism*, edited by A. J. Ayer, 133–146. New York: The Free Press. Original edition, 1930.

Carr, Adrian. 2000a. "Critical Theory and the Management of Change in Organizations." *Journal of Organizational Change Management* no. 13 (3):208–220.

Carr, Adrian. 2000b. "Critical Theory and the Psychodynamics of Change: A Note about Organizations as Therapeutic Settings." *Journal of Organizational Change Management* no. 13 (3):289–299.

Carr, Adrian, and Lisa A. Zanetti. 1999. "Metatheorizing the Dialectic of Self and Other." *American Behavioral Scientist* no. 43 (2):324–345.

Castells, Manuel. 2015. *Networks of Outrage and Hope: Social Movements in the Internet Age*. 2nd edition. Boston: Polity.

Catlaw, Thomas J. 2005. "Constitution as Executive Order: The Administrative State and the Political Ontology of We the People." *Administration & Society* no. 37 (4):445–482.

Catlaw, Thomas J. 2006. "Authority, Representation, and the Contradictions of Post-traditional Governing." *American Review of Public Administration* no. 36 (3):261–287.

Catlaw, Thomas J. 2007a. *Fabricating the People: Politics & Administration in the Biopolitical State*. Tuscaloosa, AL: University of Alabama Press.

Catlaw, Thomas J. 2007b. "From Representations to Compositions: Governance beyond the Three-sector Society." *Administrative Theory & Praxis* no. 29 (2):225–259.

Catlaw, Thomas J. 2007c. In discussion with the author, January–February, Tempe, AZ.

Catlaw, Thomas J. 2008. "Frederick Thayer and the Structural Transformation of the Public Sphere." *Administration & Society* no. 40 (4):358–383.

Catlaw, Thomas J., and Gregory M. Jordan. 2009. "Public Administration and 'the Lives of Others': Toward an Ethics of Collaboration." *Administration & Society* no. 41:290–312.

Catlaw, Thomas J., and Margaret Stout. 2007. "Postmodernism and Public Policy." In *Encyclopedia of Public Administration & Public Policy*, edited by Jack Rabin, 1524–1529. New York: Taylor & Francis.

Catron, Bayard L., and Barry R. Hammond. 1990. "Reflections on Practical Wisdom—Enacting Images and Developing Identity." In *Images and Identities in Public Administration*, edited by Henry D. Kass and Bayard L. Catron, 241–252. Newbury Park, CA: Sage Publications.

Caulkins, D. Douglas. 1999. "Is Mary Douglas' Grid/Group Analysis Useful for Cross-cultural Research?" *Cross-Cultural Research* no. 33 (1):108–128.

Center for Responsive Politics. 2016. *Agribusiness: Sector Profile, 2015*. Available from www.opensecrets.org/lobby/indus.php?id=a&year=2015 (accessed July 1, 2016).

Chomsky, Noam. 1965. *Aspects of the Theory of Syntax*. Cambridge, MA: MIT Press.

Chomsky, Noam. 1970. *Anarchism: From Theory to Practice*, Translated by Mary Klopper, edited by Daniel Guerin and Noam Chomsky. New York: Monthly Review Press.

Chomsky, Noam. 2002. *Media Control: The Spectacular Achievements of Propaganda*. 2nd edition. New York: Seven Stories Press.

Christ, Carol P. 2003. *She Who Changes: Reimagining the Divine in the World*. New York: Palgrave Macmillan.

Clark, Barry. 1998. *Political Economy: A Comparative Approach*. 2nd edition. Westport, CT: Praeger Publishers.

208 References

Cobb, Jim. 2014. *Prepper's Long-Term Survival Guide: Food, Shelter, Security, Off-Grid Power and More Life-Saving Strategies for Self-Sufficient Living.* Berkeley: Ulysses Press.

Cobb Jr., John B. 2002. *Postmodernism and Public Policy.* Albany: SUNY Press.

Cobb Jr., John B. 2012. "Foreword." In *Process and Pluralism: Chinese Thought on the Harmony of Diversity,* edited by Zhihe Wang, v–vii. Frankfurt: Ontos Verlag.

Cohen, Lizabeth. 2003. *A Consumers' Republic: The Politics of Mass Consumption in Postwar America.* New York: Knopf: Distributed by Random House.

Coles, Romand. 2005. "The Wild Patience of Radical Democracy: Beyond Žižek's Lack." In *Radical Democracy: Politics between Abundance and Lack,* edited by Lars Tønder and Lasse Thomassen, 68–85. New York: Manchester University Press.

Collingwood, V. 2003. "Assistance with Fewer Strings Attached." *Ethics and International Affairs* no. 17 (1):55–68.

Collins, Patricia Hill. 2012. "Social Inequality, Power, and Politics: Intersectionality and American Pragmatism in Dialogue." *Journal of Speculative Philosophy* no. 26 (2):442–457.

Commanger, Henry Steele. 1950. *The American Mind: An Interpretation of American Thought and Character Since the 1880s.* New Haven, CT: Yale University Press.

Comte, August. 1883. *The Catechism of Positive Religion.* Translated by Richard Congreve. London: Ballantyne Press.

Comte, August. 2009. *A General View of Positivism.* Translated by J. H. Bridges. Cambridge, UK: Cambridge University Press. Original edition, 1865.

Connolly, William E. 2005. "Immanence, Abundance, Democracy." In *Radical Democracy: Politics between Abundance and Lack,* edited by Lars Tønder and Lasse Thomassen, 239–255. New York: Manchester University Press.

Connolly, William E. 2011. *A World of Becoming.* Durham, NC: Duke University Press.

Connolly, William E. 2013. *The Fragility of Things: Self-Organizing Processes, Neoliberal Fantasies, and Democratic Activism.* Durham, NC: Duke University Press.

Coole, Diana, and Samantha Frost. 2010. "Introducing the New Materialisms." In *New Materialisms: Ontology, Agency, and Politics,* edited by Diana Coole and Samantha Frost, 1–43. Durham, NC: Duke University Press.

Cooley, Charles Horton. 1922. *Human Nature and the Social Order.* Revised edition. New York: Charles Scribner's Sons. Original edition, 1902.

Cooper, Terry L. 1984. "Citizenship and Professionalism in Public Administration." *Public Administration Review* no. 44:143–149.

Cooper, Terry L. 1991. *An Ethic of Citizenship for Public Administration.* Englewood Cliffs, NJ: Prentice Hall.

Cooper, Terry L. 2011. "Building Ethical Community." *American Review of Public Administration* no. 41 (1):3–22.

Cox, Robert W. 1995. "Critical Political Economy." In *International Political Economy: Understanding Global Disorder,* edited by Bjorn Hetne, 30–52. Halifax, Nova Scotia: Fernwood Publishing.

Critchley, Simon. 2005. "True Democracy: Marx, Political Subjectivity and Anarchic Meta-Politics." In *Radical Democracy: Politics between Abundance and Lack,* edited by Lars Tønder and Lasse Thomassen, 219–235. New York: Manchester University Press.

Crosby, Barbara C. 2010. "Leading in the Shared-power World of 2020." *Public Administration Review* no. 70 (S1):S69–S77.

Crowley, Terry. 1997. *An Introduction to Linguistics.* 3rd edition. Oxford: Oxford University Press.

Curtis, Adam. 2004. *The Power of Nightmares: The Rise of the Politics of Fear.* London: BBC.

References 209

Dahl, Robert A. 1998. *On Democracy*. New Haven, CT: Yale University Press.

Dalai Lama, and Thubten Chodron. 2014. *Buddhism: One Teacher, Many Traditions*. Somerville, MA: Wisdom Publications.

Darwall, Stephen 1998. *Philosophical Ethics*. Boulder, CO: Westview Press.

Davies, Tony. 1997. *Humanism (The New Critical Idiom)*. edited by John Drakakis. London: Routledge.

Davis, John B. 2003. *The Theory of the Individual in Economics: Identity and Value, Advances in Social Economics*. New York: Routledge.

Day, Richard J. F. 2011. "Hegemony, Affinity and the Newest Social Movements: At the End of the 00s." In *Post-Anarchism: A Reader*, edited by Duane Rousselle and Süreyyya Evren, 95–116. London: Pluto Press.

De Tocqueville, Alexis. 2000. *Democracy in America*. Chicago: University of Chicago Press.

Dean, Jodi. 2006. *Žižek's Politics*. New York: Routledge.

Debord, Guy. 1994. *The Society of the Spectacle*. New York: Zone Books.

Degrand, Alexander. 2000. *Italian Fascism: Its Origins & Development*. 3rd edition. Lincoln, NE: University of Nebraska Press.

deHaven-Smith, Lance. 2013. *Conspiracy Theory in America*. Austin, TX: University of Texas Press.

Deleuze, Gilles, and Félix Guattari. 1983. *Anti-Oedipus: Capitalism and Schizophrenia*. Minneapolis: University of Minnesota Press.

Deleuze, Gilles, and Félix Guattari. 1987. *A Thousand Plateaus: Capitalism and Schizophrenia*. Translated by Brian Massumi. New York: Continuum.

Democracy Collaborative. *It's Time to Think Boldly about Building a New American System*. Democracy Collaborative 2015 [cited May 30, 2016]. Available from http://democracycollaborative.org/content/its-time-think-boldly-about-building-new-american-system (accessed July 1, 2016).

Denhardt, Janet Vinzant, and Austin Lane Crothers. 1998. *Street-Level Leadership: Discretion and Legitimacy in Front-Line Public Service*. Washington, DC: Georgetown University Press.

Denhardt, Janet Vinzant, and Robert B. Denhardt. 2007. *The New Public Service: Serving, Not Steering*. Expanded edition. New York: M. E. Sharp.

Denhardt, Kathryn G. 1989. "The Management of Ideals: A Political Perspective on Ethics." *Public Administraiton Review* no. 49 (2):187–193.

Denhardt, Robert B. 1981. *In the Shadow of Organization*. Lawrence: Regents Press of Kansas.

Denhardt, Robert B. 2000. *Theories of Public Organization*. 3rd edition. New York: Harcourt Brace.

Denhardt, Robert B., and Barry R. Hammond. 1992. *Public Administration in Action: Readings, Profiles, and Cases*. Pacific Grove, CA: Brooks/Cole Publishing.

Derbyshire, Philip. 2007. "Lacan and Ethics: The Ends of Analysis and the Production of the Subject." In *Origins and Ends of the Mind: Philosophical Essays on Psychoanalysis*, edited by Christian Kerslake and Ray Brassier, 87–100. Leuven, Belgium: Leuven University Press.

Derrida, Jacques. 1976. *Of Grammatology*. Baltimore: Johns Hopkins University Press.

Derrida, Jacques. 1981. *Positions*. Translated by Alan Bass. Chicago: University of Chicago Press.

Descartes, René. 1980. *Discourse on Method, and Meditations on First Philosophy*. Translated by Donald Cress. Indianapolis: Hackett Publishing.

210 References

Deutsch, Eliot. 1969. *Advaita Vedānta*. Honolulu: East–West Center Press.

Deutscher, Isaac. 2003. *The Prophet Armed: Trosky 1879–1921*. New York: Verso. Original edition, 1954.

Dewey, John. 1993. "The Democratic State." In *The Political Writings*, edited by Debra Morris and Ian Shapiro, 173–183. Indianapolis: Hackett Publishing Company. Original edition, 1927.

Dilthey, Wilhelm. 1988. *Introduction to the Human Sciences: An Attempt to Lay a Foundation for the Study of Society and History*. Detroit: Wayne State University Press. Original edition, 1883.

Dimock, Marshall E. 1936. "The Criteria and Objectives of Public Administration." In *The Frontiers of Public Administration*, edited by John M. Gaus, Leonard D. White and Marshall E. Dimock, 116–133. Chicago: University of Chicago Press.

Dolbeare, Kenneth M., and Janette Kay Hubbell. 1996. *USA 2012: After the Middle-Class Revolution*. Chatham, NJ: Chatham House Publishers.

Donati, Pierpaolo. 2014. *Transcending Modernity: The Quest for a Relational Society*. Bologna: University of Bologna, Cesis-Department of Sociology and Business Law.

Doty, D. Harold, and William H. Glick. 1994. "Typologies as a Unique Form of Theory Building: Toward Improved Understanding and Modeling." *Academy of Management Review* no. 19 (2):230–251.

Douglas, Mary. 1996. *Natural Symbols: Explorations in Cosmology*. New York: Routledge. Original edition, 1970.

Drayton, William. 2002. "The Citizen Sector: Becoming as Competitive and Entrepreneurial as Business." *California Management Review* no. 44 (3):120.

Dryzek, John S. 1990. *Discursive Democracy: Politics, Policy, and Political Science*. New York: Cambridge University Press.

Dryzek, John S. 1996. *Democracy in Capitalist Times: Ideals, Limits, and Struggles*. New York: Oxford University Press.

Durkheim, Emile. 1984. *The Division of Labor in Society*. New York: Free Press. Original edition, 1933.

Durkin, Sean. 2011. *Martha Marcy May Marlene*. Film. United States: Fox.

Dworkin, Ronald. 1986. *Law's Empire*. Cambridge, MA: Harvard University Press.

Dye, Thomas R. 2002. *Understanding Public Policy*. 10th edition. Upper Saddle River, NJ: Prentice Hall.

Dziadkowiec, Jakub 2011. "The Layered Structure of the World in N. Hartmann's Ontology and a Processual View." In *The Philosophy of Nicolai Hartmann*, edited by Roberto Poli, Carlo Scognamiglio and Frederic Tremblay, 95–123. Berlin: Walter de Gruyter.

Easton, David. 1966. "Alternative Strategies in Theoretical Research." In *Varieties of Political Theory*, edited by David Easton, 1–13. Englewood Cliffs, NJ: Prentice Hall.

Easwaran, Eknath. 2007. "Introduction." In *The Bagavad Gita*. Canada: Nilgiri Press.

Edwards, Jason. 2010. "The Materialism of Historical Materialism." In *New Materialisms: Ontology, Agency, and Politics*, edited by Diana Coole and Samantha Frost, 281–298. Durham, NC: Duke University Press.

Eisenhardt, Kathleen M. 1995. "Building Theories from Case Study Research." In *Longitudinal Field Research Methods*, edited by Goerge P. Huber and andrew H. Van De Ven, 65–90. Thousand Oaks, CA: Sage Publications.

Elias, Maria Veronica. 2010. "Governance from the Ground Up: Rediscovering Mary Parker Follett." *Public Administration and Management* no. 15 (1):9–45.

Ellsworth, William L. 2013. "Injection-induced Earthquakes." *Science* no. 341 (6142) (July 12). DOI: 10.1126/science.1225942.

References 211

Emery, Carla. 2012. *The Encyclopedia of Country Living*. 40th Anniversary edition. Seattle: Sasquatch Books.

Emmert, Mark A., and Michael M. Crow. 1988. "Public, Private and Hybrid Organizations: An Empirical Examination of the role of Publicness." *Administration and Society* no. 20 (2):216–244.

Engels, Friedrich. 2000. "Anti-Dühring." In *What is Justice? Classic and Contemporary Readings*, edited by Robert C. Solomon and Mark C. Murphy, 174–175. New York Oxford University Press.

Epstein, Wendy Netter. 2013. "Contract Theory and the Failure of Public–private Contracting." *Cordozo Law Review* no. 34:2211–2259.

Erikson, Erik O., and Jarle Weigard. 2003. *Understanding Habermas: Communicative Action and Deliberative Democracy*. New York: Continuum.

Etzioni, Amitai. 1996. *The New Golden Rule: Community and Morality in a Democratic Society*. New York: Basic Books.

Etzioni, Amitai. 1998. *The Essential Communitarian Reader*. Lanham, MD: Rowman & Littlefield Publishers.

Evans, Karen G. 2000a. "Imagining Anticipatory Government." In *New Sciences for Public Administration and Policy: Connections and Reflections*, edited by Goktug Morcol and Linda F. Dennard, 195–220. Burke, VA: Chatelaine Press.

Evans, Karen G. 2000b. "Reclaiming John Dewey: democracy, inquiry, pragmatism, and public management." *Administration & Society* no. 32 (3):308–328.

Evans, Karen G., and Gary L. Wamsley. 1999. "Where's the Institution? Neoinstitutionalism and Public Management." In *Public Management Reform and Innovation: Research, Theory, and Application*, edited by George H. Frederickson and Jocelyn M. Johnston, 117–144. Tuscaloosa, AL: University of Alabama Press.

Evren, Süreyyya. 2011. "Introduction: How New Anarchism Changed the World (of Opposition) After Seattle and Gave Birth to Post-Anarchism." In *Post-Anarchism: A Reader*, edited by Duane Rousselle and Süreyyya Evren, 1–19. London: Pluto Press.

Eze, Michael Onyebuchi. 2008. "What is African communitarianism? Against consensus as a regulative ideal." *South African Journal of Philosophy* no. 27 (4):386–399.

Faber, Roland, Henry Krips, and Daniel Pettus. 2010. *Event and Decision: Ontology and Politics in Badiou, Deleuze, and Whitehead*. Newcastle: Cambridge Scholars.

Fagence, M. 1977. *Citizen Participation in Planning*. New York: Pergamon Press.

Farmer, David John. 1995. *The Language of Public Administration: Bureaucracy, Modernity, and Postmodernity*. Tuscaloosa, AL: University of Alabama Press.

Farmer, David John. 1997. "Derrida, Deconstruction, and Public Administration." *American Behavioral Scientist* no. 41 (1):12–27.

Farmer, David John. 1999. "Public Administration Discourse: A Matter of Style?" *Administration & Society* no. 31 (3):299–320.

Farmer, David John. 2002a. "The Discourses of Anti-Administration." In *Rethinking Administrative Theory: The Challenge of the New Century*, edited by Jong S. Jun, 271–287. Westport, CT: Praeger.

Farmer, David John. 2002b. "Introduction." *Administration & Society* no. 34:87–90.

Farmer, David John. 2005a. "Quintet: Introduction to Post-traditional Theory." *International Journal of Public Administration* no. 28 (11–12):903–908.

Farmer, David John. 2005b. *To Kill the King: Post-Traditional Governance and Bureaucracy*. Armonk, NY: M.E. Sharpe.

Farmer, David John. 2006. "Imagine! Preface to the Post-traditional." *Administrative Theory & Praxis* no. 28 (2):169–175.

212 References

Farmer, David John. 2010. *Public Administration in Perspective: Theory and Practice through Multiple Lenses.* Armonk, NY: M.E. Sharpe.

Fernández De Rota, Antón. 2011. "Acracy_Reloaded@Post1968/1989: Reflections on Postmodern Revolutions." In *Post-Anarchism: A Reader,* edited by Duane Rousselle and Süreyyya Evren, 139–148. London: Pluto Press.

Ferré, Frederick. 1998. *Knowing and Value: Toward a Constructive Postmodern Epistemology.* Albany, NY: SUNY Press.

Feyerabend, Paul. 1993. *Against Method.* London: Verso.

Fineman, Martha. 2004. *The Autonomy Myth: A Theory of Dependency.* New York: New Press.

Finer, Herman. 1941. "Administrative Responsibility in Democratic Government." *Public Administration Review* no. 1 (4):335–350.

Fink, Bruce. 1995. *The Lacanian Subject: Between Language and Jouissance.* Princeton: Princeton University Press.

Fink, Bruce. 1998. "The Master Signifier and the Four Discourses." In *Key Concepts of Lacanian Psychoanalysis,* edited by Dany Nobus, 29–47. New York: Other Press.

Fischer, Claude S. 2008. "Paradoxes of American individualism." *Sociological Forum* no. 23 (2):363–372.

Fischer, Frank. 1995. *Evaluating Public Policy.* Chicago: Nelson-Hall Publishers.

Fischer, Mark. 1992. "The Sacred and the Secular: An Examination of the 'Wall of Separation' and its Impact on the Religious World View." *University of Pittsburgh Law Review* no. 54 (Fall):325.

Fish, Stanley. 1999. *The Trouble with Principle.* Cambridge, MA: Harvard University Press.

Flyvbjerg, Bent. 2001. *Making Social Science Matter: Why Social Inquiry Fails and How it Can Succeed Again.* Translated by Steven Sampson. Cambridge, UK: Cambridge University Press.

Foley, Jonathan A., Ruth Defries, Gregory P. Asner, Carol Barford, Gordon Bonan, Stephen R. Carpenter, F. Stuart Chapin, Michael T. Coe, Gretchen C. Daily, Holly K. Gibbs, Joseph H. Helkowski, Tracey Holloway, Erica A. Howard, Christopher J. Kucharik, Chad Monfreda, Jonathan A. Patz, I. Colin Prentice, Navin Ramankutty, and Peter K. Snyder. 2005. "Global Consequences of Land Use." *Science* no. 309 (22 June):570–574.

Follett, Mary Parker. 1918. *The New State: Group Organization the Solution of Popular Government.* New York: Longmans, Green and Co.

Follett, Mary Parker. 1919. "Community is a Process." *Philosophical Review* no. 28 (6):576–588.

Follett, Mary Parker. 1924. *Creative Experience.* New York: Longmans, Green and Co.

Follett, Mary Parker. 1998. *The New State: Group Organization the Solution of Popular Government.* University Park, PA: Pennsylvania State University Press. Original edition, 1918.

Follett, Mary Parker. 2003a. "Constructive Conflict." In *Dynamic Administration: The Collected Papers of Mary Parker Follett,* edited by Henry C. Metcalf and Lyndall Urwick, 30–49. New York: Routledge. Original edition, 1942.

Follett, Mary Parker. 2003b. "The Giving of Orders." In *Dynamic Administration: The Collected Papers of Mary Parker Follett,* edited by Henry C. Metcalf and Lyndall Urwick, 50–70. New York: Routledge. Original edition, 1942.

Follett, Mary Parker. 2003c. "The Influence of Employee Representation in a Remoulding of the Accepted Type of Business Manager." In *Dynamic Administration: The*

References   213

Collected Papers of Mary Parker Follett, edited by Henry C. Metcalf and Lyndall Urwick, 167–182. New York: Routledge. Original edition, 1942.

Follett, Mary Parker. 2003d. "Power." In *Dynamic Administration: The Collected Papers of Mary Parker Follett*, edited by Henry C. Metcalf and Lyndall Urwick, 95–116. New York: Routledge. Original edition, 1942.

Follett, Mary Parker. 2003e. "The Psychology of Consent and Participation." In *Dynamic Administration: The Collected Papers of Mary Parker Follett*, edited by Henry C. Metcalf and Lyndall Urwick, 210–229. New York: Routledge. Original edition, 1942.

Follett, Mary Parker. 2013a. "Co-ordination." In *Freedom and Co-Ordination: Lectures in Business Organization by Mary Parker Follett*, edited by Lyndall Urwick, 61–76. Abingdon: Routledge. Original edition, 1949.

Follett, Mary Parker. 2013b. *Creative Experience*. Peabody, MA: Martino Fine Books. Original edition, 1924.

Follett, Mary Parker. 2013c. "The Giving of Orders." In *Freedom and Co-Ordination: Lectures in Business Organization by Mary Parker Follett*, edited by Lyndall Urwick, 16–33. Abingdon: Routledge. Original edition, 1949.

Follett, Mary Parker. 2013d. "The Process of Control." In *Freedom and Co-Ordination: Lectures in Business Organization by Mary Parker Follett*, edited by Lyndall Urwick, 77–89. Abingdon: Routledge. Original edition, 1949.

Forester, John. 2009. *Dealing With Differences: Dramas of Mediating Public Disputes*. Oxford: Oxford University Press.

Foucault, Michel. 1972. *The Archaeology of Knowledge & the Discourse on Language*. Translated by A. M. Sheridan Smith. New York: Pantheon Books.

Foucault, Michel. 1977. *Discipline and Punish*. New York: Vintage Books.

Foucault, Michel. 1980. *Power/Knowledge: Selected Interviews and Other Writings, 1972–1977*. Translated by Colin Gordon, John Mepham, Kate Soper and Leo Marshall. New York: Pantheon Books.

Foucault, Michel. 1991. "Governmentality." In *The Foucault Effect: Studies in Governmentality*, edited by Graham Burchell, Colin Gordon and Peter Miller, 87–104. Chicago: University of Chicago Press.

Fox, Charles J. 1996. "Reinventing Government as Postmodern Symbolic Politics." *Public Administration Review* no. 56 (3):256–262.

Fox, Charles J., and Clarke E. Cochran. 1990. "Discretionary Public Administration: Toward a Platonic Guardian Class?" In *Images and Identities in Public Administration*, edited by Henry D. Kass and Bayard L. Catron, 87–112. Newbury Park, CA: Sage Publications.

Fox, Charles J., and Hugh T. Miller. 1995. *Postmodern Public Administration: Toward Discourse*. Thousand Oaks, CA: Sage Publications.

Frakes, Jonathan. 1996. Star Trek: First Contact. USA: Paramount Pictures.

Franks, Benjamin. 2011. "Post-Anarchism: A Partial Account." In *Post-Anarchism: A Reader*, edited by Duane Rousselle and Süreyyya Evren, 168–180. New York: Pluto Press.

Fraser, Nancy, and Linda Nicholson. 1988. "Social Criticism Without Philosophy: An Encounter between Feminism and Postmodernism." *Theory, Culture & Society* no. 5:373–394.

Frederickson, H. George. 1971. "Toward a New Public Administration." In *Toward a New Public Administration: The Minnowbrook Perspective*, edited by Frank Marini, 309–331. Scranton, OH: Chandler.

214 *References*

Frederickson, H. George. 1996. "Comparing the Reinventing Government Movement to The New Public Administration." *Public Administration Review* no. 56 (3):263–270.

Frederickson, H. George. 1997. *The Spirit of Public Administration*. San Francisco: Jossey-Bass.

Fremond, Olivier, and Mierta Capaul. 2002. "The State of Corporate Governance: Experience from County Assessments." Policy Research Working Paper. Washington, DC: The World Bank.

Freudenburg, William R., and Robert Gramling. 2011. *Blowout in the Gulf: The BP Oil Spill Disaster and the Future of Energy in America*. Cambridge, MA: MIT Press.

Frey, Théo. 2004. "Perspectives for a Generation." In *Guy Dubord and the Situationist International: Texts and Documents*, edited by Tom McDonough, 167–171. Cambridge, MA: MIT Press.

Friedman, Milton. 2002. *Capitalism and Freedom*. 40th Anniversary edition. Chicago: University of Chicago Press. Original edition, 1962.

Friedrich, Carl J. 1940. "Public Policy and the Nature of Administrative Responsibility." In *Public Policy: A Yearbook of the Graduate School of Public Administration, Harvard University*, edited by Carl J. Friedrich and Edward S. Mason, 3–24. Cambridge, MA: Harvard University Press.

Gadamer, Hans-Georg. 2004. *Truth and Method*. Translated by Joel Weinsheimer and Donald G. Marshall. 2nd edition. New York: Continuum.

Gare, Arran. 2000. "Human Ecology, Process Philosophy, and the Global Ecological Crisis." *Concrescence: The Australian Journal of Process Thought* no. 1:1–11.

Garvey, Gerald. 1997. *Public Administration: The Profession and the Practice, a Case Study Approach*. Belmont, CA: Wadsworth/Thomson Learning.

Gauthier, David. 1977. "The Social Contract as Ideology." *Philosophy & Public Affairs* no. 6 (2):130–164.

Gehring, Abigail. 2011. *The Homesteading Handbook: A Back to Basics Guide to Growing Your Own Food, Canning, Keeping Chickens, Generating Your Own Energy, Crafting, Herbal Medicine, and More*. New York: Skyhorse Publishing.

George, Henry. 1929. *Progress and Poverty, the Remedy: An Inquiry into the Causes of Industrial Depressions and the Increase of Want with Increase of Wealth, the Modern Library*. New York: Random House. Original edition, 1879.

Giddens, Anthony. 1984. *The Constitution of Society: Outline of the Theory of Structuration*. Berkeley: University of California Press.

Giddens, Anthony. 1999. *The Third Way: The Renewal of Social Democracy*. Malden, MA: Polity Press.

Gilens, Martin, and Benjamin I. Page. 2014. "Testing Theories of American Politics: Elites, Interest Groups, and Average Citizens." *Perspectives on Politics* no. 12 (3):564–581.

Godwin, William. 1842. *Enquiry Concerning Political Justice and its Influence on Morals and Happiness*. Vol. 1. London: J. Watson.

Golembiewski, Robert T., Jerry G. Stevenson, and Michael White. 1997. *Cases in Public Management*. 5th edition. Itasca, IL: F.E. Peacock Publishers.

Goodnow, Frank J. 2003. *Politics and Administration: A Study in Government*. New Brunswick, NJ: Transaction Publishers. Original edition, 1900.

Goodwin, Barbara. 2007. *Using Political Ideas*. 5th edition. West Sussex: John Wiley & Sons.

Gore, Al, and Bill Clinton. 1993. *From Red Tape to Results: Creating a Government That Works Better and Costs Less*. Washington, DC: US Government Printing Office.

References 215

Gottlieb, Robert, and Anupama Joshi. 2010. *Food Justice*. Cambridge, MA: MIT Press.

Gould, Rebecca Kneale. 2005. *At Home in Nature: Modern Homesteading and Spiritual Practice in America*. Berkely: University of California Press.

Graham, Daniel W. 2002. "Heraclitus and Parmenides." In *Presocratic Philosophy: Essays in Honour of Alexander Mourelatos* edited by Alexander P. D. Mourelatos, Victor Miles Caston, and Daniel W. Graham, 27–44. Farnham, UK: Ashgate.

Graham, Daniel W. 2008. "Heraclitus." In *The Stanford Encyclopedia of Philosophy* edited by Edward N. Zalta. Stanford, CA: Stanford University Press.

Gregor, A. James. 1979. *Young Mussolini and the Intellectual Origins of Fascism*. Los Angeles: University of California Press.

Griffin, David Ray. 2007. *Whitehead's Radically Different Postmodern Philosophy: An Argument for its Contemporary Relevance*. Albany, NY: State University of New York Press.

Griffin, Roger. 2013. *The Nature of Fascism*. New York: Routledge.

Grodzins, Morton. 1966. *The American System: A New View of Government in the United States*. Chicago: Rand McNally.

Gulick, Luther. 1937a. "Notes on the Theory of Organization." In *Papers on the Science of Administration*, edited by Luther Gulick and Lyndall Urwick, 3–13. New York: Institute of Public Administration.

Gulick, Luther. 1937b. "Science, Values and Public Administration." In *Papers on the Science of Administration*, edited by Luther Gulick and Lyndall Urwick, 191–195. New York: Institute of Public Administration.

Gyekye, Kwame. 1995. *African Philosophical Thought: The Akan Conceptual Scheme*. Revised edition. Philadelphia: Temple University Press.

Habermas, Jürgen. 1975. *Legitimation Crisis*. Boston: Beacon Press.

Habermas, Jürgen. 1989. *The Structural Transformation of the Public Sphere: An Inquiry into a Category of Bourgeois Society*. Cambridge, MA: MIT Press.

Habermas, Jürgen. 1998. *Between Facts and Norms*. Cambridge, MA: MIT Press.

Habermas, Jürgen, and Maeve Cooke, eds. 1998. *On the Pragmatics of Communication: Studies in Contemporary German Social Thought*. Cambridge, MA: MIT Press.

Halden, Rolf U., and Kellog J. Schwab. 2008. "Environmental Impact of Industrial Farm Animal Production." Pew Commission on Industrial Farm Animal Production.

Hales, Steven D., and Timothy A. Johnson. 2003. "Endurantism, Perdurantism and Special Relativity." *The Philosophical Quarterly* no. 53 (213):524–539.

Hall, Douglas John. 1990. *The Steward: A Biblical Symbol Come of Age*. New York: Friendship Press.

Hall, Stuart. 1998. "Notes on Deconstructing the 'Popular'." In *Cultural Theory and Popular Culture: A Reader*, edited by John Storey, 442–453. Essex: Pearson Education.

Hamilton, Peter. 1991. *Max Weber: Critical Assessment 2*. Vol. 3. London; New York: Routledge.

Haque, M. Shamsul. 1996. "The Intellectual Crisis in Public Administration in the Current Epoch of Privatization." *Administration & Society* no. 27 (4):510–536.

Harmon, Michael M. 1981. *Action Theory for Public Administration*. New York: Longman.

Harmon, Michael M. 1990. "The Responsible Actor as 'Tortured Soul': The Case of Horatio Hornblower." In *Images and Identities in Public Administration*, edited by Henry D. Kass and Bayard L. Catron, 151–180. Newbury Park, CA: Sage Publications.

Harmon, Michael M. 1995. *Responsibility as Paradox: A Critique of Rational Discourse on Government*. Thousand Oaks, CA: Sage Publications.

216 References

Harmon, Michael M. 2006. *Public Administration's Final Exam: A Pragmatist Restructuring of the Profession and the Discipline.* Tuscaloosa, AL: University of Alabama Press.

Harmon, Michael M., and Richard T. Mayer. 1986. *Organization Theory for Public Administration.* Burke, VA: Chatelaine Press.

Harmon, Michael M., and O. C. McSwite. 2011. *Whenever Two or More are Gathered: Relationship as the Heart of Ethical Discourse.* Tuscaloosa, AL: The University of Alabama Press.

Harper, Phillip Brian. 1994. *Framing the Margins: The Social Logic of Postmodern Culture.* New York: Oxford University Press.

Hart, David K. 1974. "Social Equity, Justice, and the Equitable Administrator." *Public Administration Review* no. 34 (January–February):3–10.

Hart, David K. 1984. "The Virtuous Citizen, the Honorable Bureaucrat, and Public Administration." *Public Administration Review* no. 44:111–120.

Hart, David K. 1989. "A Partnership in Virtue among All Citizens: The Public Service and Civic Humanism." *Public Administration Review* no. 49 (2):101–105.

Harvey, David. 1990. *The Condition of Postmodernity: An Enquiry into the Origins of Cultural Change.* Cambridge, MA: Blackwell.

Hawken, Paul. 2007. *Blessed Unrest: How the Largest Social Movement in History is Restoring Grace, Justice, and Beauty to the World.* New York: Penguin Books.

Hayek, Friedrich. 1973. *Law, Legislation, and Liberty: Rules and Order.* Vol. 1. Chicago: University of Chicago Press.

Hayek, Friedrich. 1978. *The Constitution of Liberty.* Chicago: University of Chicago Press.

Hayek, Friedrich. 2001. *The Road to Serfdom.* New York: Routledge. Original edition, 1944.

Häyry, Matti. 2012. "*Passive Obedience* and Berkely's moral philsophy." *Berkely Studies* no. 23:3–14.

Heckert, Jamie. 2011. "Sexuality as State Form." In *Post-Anarchism: A Reader*, edited by Duane Rousselle and Süreyyya Evren, 195–207. New York: Pluto Press.

Heckert, Jamie. 2012. "Anarchy Without Oppression." In *Queering Anarchism: Addressing and Undressing Power and Desire*, edited by C. B. Daring, J. Rogue, Deric Shannon and Abbey Volcano, 63–75. Oakland: AK Press.

Hegel, Georg W. F. 1977. *Phenomenology of Spirit.* Translated by Arnold V. Miller. Oxford: Clarendon Press. Original edition, 1807.

Hegel, Georg W. F. 1991. *Elements of the Philosophy of Right.* Cambridge, UK: Cambridge University Press.

Hegel, Georg W. F. 2000. "The Philosophy of Right." In *What is Justice? Classic and Contemporary Readings*, edited by Robert C. Solomon and Mark C. Murphy, 155–166. New York: Oxford University Press. Original edition, 1821.

Hegel, Georg Wilhelm Friedrich. 2010. *The Science of Logic.* Translated by George Di Giovanni. New York: Cambridge University Press.

Heidegger, Martin. 1992. *Parmenides.* Translated by Andre Schuwer and Richard Rojcewicz. Bloomington, IN: Indiana University Press.

Heidegger, Martin. 1996. *Being and Time.* Translated by J. Stambaugh. Albany, NY: State University of New York Press.

Heidegger, Martin. 1998. *Pathmarks.* Cambridge, UK: Cambridge University Press.

Helms, Douglas. 1992. Readings in the History of the Soil Conservation Service. In *NHQ Readings in the History of the Soil Conservation Service.* USDA Economics and Social Sciences Division.

References 217

Hempel, Carl G. 1959. "The Empiricist Criterion of Meaning." In *Logical Positivism*, edited by A. J. Ayer, 108–132. New York: The Free Press.

Hendriks, Frank. 2010. *Vital Democracy: A Theory of Democracy in Action*. New York: Oxford University Press.

Henton, Douglas, John Melville, and Kimberly Walesh. 1997. *Grassroots Leaders for a New Economy: How Civic Entrepreneurs are Building Prosperous Communities*. San Francisco: Jossey-Bass.

Hobbes, Thomas. 2000. "Leviathan." In *What is Justice? Classic and Contemporary Readings*, edited by Robert C. Solomon and Mark C. Murphy, 63–74. New York: Oxford University Press. Original edition, 1651.

Hodgson, Godfrey. 2009. *The Myth of American Exceptionalism*. New Haven: Yale University Press.

Hoffman, John, and Paul Graham. 2009. *Introduction to Political Theory*. 2nd edition. Essex: Pearson Education.

Holm, Wayne, Irene Silentman, and Laura Wallace. 2003. "Situational Navajo: A School-based, Verb-centered Way of Teaching Navajo." In *Nurturing Native Languages*, edited by Jon Reyhner, Octaviana V. Trujillo, Roberto Luis Carrasco and Louise Lockard, 25–52. Flagstaff, AZ: Northern Arizona University.

Hood, Christopher. 1991. "A Public Management for All Seasons?" *Public Administration* no. 69 (1):3–19.

Hood, Christopher. 1996. "Exploring Variations in Public Management Reform of the 1980s." In *Civil Service Systems in Comparative Perspective*, edited by H. A. Bekke, James L. Perry and T. A. Toonen, 268–287. Bloomington, IN: Indiana University Press.

Houston, David J., and Sybil M. Delevan. 1990. "Public Administration Research: An Assessment of Journal Publications." *Public Administration Review* no. 50:674–681.

Howe, Louis E. 2006. "Enchantment, Weak Ontologies, and Administrative Ethics." *Administration & Society* no. 38 (4):422–446.

Howe, Louis E. 2010. "Temporality and Reconciliation." *Administrative Theory & Praxis* no. 32 (4):611–619.

Huddleston, Mark W. 1981. "Comparative Perspectives on Public Administration Ethics: Some Implications for American Public Administration" *Public Personnel Management* no. 10 (1):67–76.

Hume, David. 1988. *Dialogues Concerning Natural Religion: The Posthumous Essays of the Immortality of the Soul and of Suicide*. 2nd edition. Indianapolis: Hacket Publishing Company.

Hummel, Ralph P. 1990. "Circle Managers and Pyramid Managers: Icons for the Post-Modern Public Administrator." In *Images and Identities in Public Administration*, edited by Henry D. Kass and Bayard L. Catron, 202–218. Newbury Park, CA: Sage Publications.

Hummel, Ralph P. 1991. "Stories Managers Tell: Why They Are as Valid as Science." *Public Administration Review* no. 51 (1):31–41.

Hummel, Ralph P. 1998. "Practice Illuminating Theory." *Administrative Theory & Praxis* no. 20 (2):150–158.

Hummel, Ralph P. 2002. "Critique of 'Public Space'." *Administration & Society* no. 34:102–107.

Hummel, Ralph P. 2008. *The Bureaucratic Experience: The Post-Modern Challenge*. 5th edition. Armonk, NY: M.E. Sharpe.

Husserl, Edmund. 1982. *General Introduction to a Pure Phenomenology*. Translated by F. Kerston. Boston: Kluwer. Original edition, 1931.

218 References

Institute for Humanist Studies. 2016. "What is Humanism?" available at http://humanist studies.org/about-us/ (accessed August 1, 2016).

International Panel on Climate Change (IPCC). 2014. *Climate Change 2014: Impacts, Adaptation, and Vulnerability [Summary for Policymakers]*, edited by C. B. Field, V. R. Barros, D. J. Dokken, K. J. Mach, M. D. Mastrandrea, T. E. Belir, M. Chatterjee, K. L. Ebi, Y. O. Estrada, R. C. Genova, E. S. Kissel, A. N. Levy, S. MacCracken, P. R. Mastrandrea and L. L. White. Cambridge, UK: Cambridge University Press.

James, William. 1907. *Pragmatism: A New Name for Some Old Ways of Thinking*. Cambridge, MA: Harvard University.

James, William. 1996. *A Pluralistic Universe*. Lincoln, NE: University of Nebraska Press.

James, William. 1997. *The Varieties of Religious Experience: A Study in Human Nature*. New York: Simon & Schuster. Original edition, 1902.

Jameson, Fredric. 1991. *Postmodernism, or, the Cultural Logic of Late Capitalism, Post-Contemporary Interventions*. Durham: Duke University Press.

Jenkins-Smith, Hank C. 1990. *Democratic Politics and Policy Analysis*. New York: Harcourt Brace.

Jensen, Jason L., and Robert Rodgers. 2001. "Cumulating the Intellectual Gold of Case Study Research." *Public Administration Review* no. 61 (2):235–246.

Jisheng, Yang. 2008. *The Great Chinese Famine 1958–1962*. Translated by Stacy Mosher and Guo Jian. New York: Farrar, Straus and Giroux.

Johnson, Galen A. 1990. "Introduction." In *Ontology and Alterity in Merleau-Ponty*, edited by Galen A. Johnson and Michael B. Smith, xvii–xxx. Evanston, IL: Northwestern University Press.

Jung, Carl Gustav. 1969. *The Archetypes and the Collective Unconscious*. Princeton, NJ: Princeton University Press.

Kaczynski, Theodore. 1995. *Industrial Society and its Future*. Camberley, UK: Green Anarchist.

Kagan, Shelly 1998. *Normative Ethics*. Boulder, CO: Westview Press.

Kahne, Joseph. 1996. *Reframing Educational Policy: Democracy, Community, and the Individual, Advances in Contemporary Educational Thought Series*. New York: Teachers College Press.

Kakabadse, Andrew, Alexander Kouzmin, Nada K. Kakabadse, and Nikolai Mouraviev. 2013. "Auditing Moral Hazards for the Post-Global Financial Crisis (GFC) Leadership." In *State Crimes Against Democracy: Political Forensics in Public Affairs*, edited by Alexander Kouzmin, Matthew T. Witt and andrew Kakabadse, 79–106. New York: Palgrave Macmillan.

Kamensky, John M. 1996. "Role of the 'Reinventing Government' movement in federal management reform." *Public Administration Review* no. 56 (3):247–255.

Kane, Douglas D., Joseph D. Conroy, R. Peter Richards, David B. Baker, and David A. Culver. 2014. "Re-eutrophication of Lake Erie: Correlations between Tributary Nutrient Loads and Phytoplankton Biomass." *Journal of Great Lakes Research*. DOI: 10.1016/J.Jglr.2014.04.004.

Kant, Immanuel. 1998. *Critique of Pure Reason*. Cambridge, UK: Cambridge University Press.

Kanter, Rosabeth Moss. 1972. *Commitment and Community: Communes and Utopias in Sociological Perspective*. Cambridge, MA: Harvard University Press.

Kaplan, Rachel, and Ruby Blume. 2011. *Urban Homesteading: Heirloom Skills for Sustainable Living*. New York: Skyhorse Publishing.

References 219

Kapleau, Philip. 2000. *The Three Pillars of Zen: Teaching, Practice, and Enlightenment.* New York: Anchor Books.

Kass, Henry D. 1990. "Stewardship as a Fundamental Element in Images of Public Administration." In *Images and Identities in Public Administration,* edited by Henry D. Kass and Bayard L. Catron, 113–131. Newbury Park, CA: Sage Publications.

Kassotis, Christopher D., Donald E. Tillitt, J. Wade Davis, Annette M. Hormann, and Susan C. Nagel. 2014. "Estrogen and Androgen Receptor Activities of Hydraulic Fracturing Chemicals and Surface and Ground Water in a Drilling-dense Region." *Endocrinology* no. 155 (3):897–907.

Kathlene, L., and J. A. Martin. 1991. "Enhancing Citizen Participation: Panel Designs, Perspectives, and Policy Formation." *Journal of Policy Analysis and Management* no. 10 (1):46–63.

Katz, Daniel, and Robert Louis Kahn. 1978. *The Social Psychology of Organizations.* 2nd edition. New York: Wiley.

Kaufmann, Michael. 1998. *Institutional Individualism: Conversion, Exile, and Nostalgia in Puritan New England.* Hanover, NH: Wesleyan University Press.

Keating, AnaLouise. 2013. *Transformation Now! Toward a Post-Oppositional Politics of Change.* Chicago: University of Illinois Press.

Keller, Catherine. 2003. *Face of the Deep: A Theology of Becoming.* New York: Routledge.

Kelly, Rita Mae. 1998. "An Inclusive Democratic Polity, Representative Bureaucracies, and the New Public Management." *Public Administration Review* no. 58 (3):201–208.

Kensen, Sandra. 2008. "Reflections on Theory in Action: Invitation to Participate." *Administrative Theory & Praxis* no. 30 (3):376.

Keohane, R. O., and J. S. Nye. 2000. "Globalization: What's New? What's Not? (and So What?)." *Foreign Policy* no. 118 (Spring):104–119.

Kettl, Donald F. 1993. *Sharing Power: Public Governance and Private Markets.* Washington, DC: Brookings Institution.

Kettl, Donald F. 2000a. "Public Administration at the Millennium: The State of the Field." *Journal of Public Administration Research and Theory* no. 10 (1):7–34.

Kettl, Donald F. 2000b. "The Transformation of Governance: Globalization, Devolution, and the Role of Government." *Public Administration Review* no. 60 (6):488–497.

Kidder, Rushworth M. 1995. *How Good People Make Tough Choices: Resolving the Dilemmas of Ethical Living.* New York: Fireside.

Kinchloe, J. L. 2006. "Critical Ontology and Indigenous Ways of Being: Forging a Postcolonial Curriculum." In *Curriculum as Cultural Practice: Postcolonial Imaginations,* edited by Yatta Kanu, 181–202. Toronto: University of Toronto Press.

King, Cheryl Simrell, and Sandra Kensen. 2002. "Associational Public Space: Politics Administration, and Storytelling." *Administration & Society* no. 34:108–113.

King, Cheryl Simrell, Patricia M. Patterson, and Frank E. Scott. 2000. "Still Enthralled with ernmodernity? Toward Postrationalist Discourse Theories." *American Review of Public Administration* no. 30 (3):221–224.

King, Cheryl Simrell, Camilla Stivers, and Collaborators, eds. 1998. *Government is Us: Public Administration in an Anti-Government Era.* Thousand Oaks, CA: Sage Publications.

King, Cheryl Simrell, and Lisa A. Zanetti. 2005. *Transformational Public Service: Portraits of Theory in Practice.* Armonk, NY: M.E. Sharpe.

Kingdon, John W. 2003. *Agendas, Alternatives, and Public Policies.* 2nd edition. New York: Addison-Wesley Longman.

220 References

Kingsley, J. Donald. 1944. *Representative Bureaucracy: An Interpretation of the British Civil Service*. Yellow Springs, OH: Antioch Press.

Kingsolver, Barbara. 2007. *Animal, Vegetable, Miracle: A Year of Food Life*. New York: Harper Perennial.

Kinnvall, Catarina. 2004. "Globalization and Religious Nationalism: Self, Identity, and the Search for Ontological Security." *Political Psychology* no. 25 (5):741–767.

Kirlin, John J. 1996. "The Big Questions of Public Administration in a Democracy." *Public Administration Review* no. 56 (5):416–423.

Klein, Naomi. 2014. *This Changes Everything: Capitalism vs the Climate*. New York: Simon & Schuster.

Klingner, Donald E. 2004. "Globalization, Governance, and the Future of Public Administration: Can We Make Sense out of the Fog of Rhetoric Surrounding the Terminology?" *Public Administration Review* no. 64 (6):737–743.

Kobrak, Peter. 1996. "The Social Responsibilities of a Public Entrepreneur." *Administration & Society* no. 28 (2):205–237.

Kooiman, Jan. 2001. *Interactive Governance*. London: Routledge.

Kooiman, Jan. 2003. *Governing as Governance*. Thousand Oaks, CA: Sage Publications.

Korea Saumaul Undong Center. April 15, 2015. *SMU in Korea* 2014. Available from www.saemaul.or.kr/eng/whatSMU/koreaSMU (accessed August 1, 2016).

Korten, David C. 2006. *The Great Turning: From Empire to Earth Community*. Bloomfield, CT: Kumarian Press.

Kouzmin, Alexander. 1980. "Control and Organization: Towards a Reflexive Analysis." In *Work and Inequality: Ideology and Control in the Capitalist Labour Process*, edited by Paul Boreham and Geoff Dow, 130–162. South Melbourne: The Macmillan Company of Australia.

Kreft, Sönke, David Eckstein, Lukas Dorsch, and Livia Fischer. 2015. "Global Climate Risk Index 2016: Who Suffers Most from Extreme Weather Events?" In *Weather-Related Loss Events in 2014 and 1995 to 2014*, edited by Joanne Chapman-Rose, Gerold Krier and Daniela Baum. Berlin: Germanwatch.

Krislov, Samuel. 1974. *Representative Bureaucracy*. Englewood Cliffs, NJ: Prentice Hall.

Kristol, Irving. 2004a. "A Conservative Welfare State." In *The Neocon Reader*, edited by Irwin Stelzer, 143–146. New York: Grove Press.

Kristol, Irving. 2004b. "The Neoconservative Persuasion." In *The Neocon Reader*, edited by Irwin Stelzer, 31–38. New York: Grove Press.

Kristol, William, and Robert Kagan. 2004. "National Interest and Global Responsibility." In *The Neocon Reader*, edited by Irwin Stelzer, 57–77. New York: Grove Press.

Kropotkin, Peter. 1992. *Words of a Rebel*. Translated by George Woodcock. New York: Black Rose Books.

Lacan, Jacques. 1977. *Écrits*. Translated by Allan Sheridan. London: Routledge.

Laclau, Ernesto. 1990. *New Reflections on the Revolution of Our Time, Phronesis*. London: Verso.

Laclau, Ernesto. 2005. "The Future of Radical Democracy." In *Radical Democracy: Politics between Abundance and Lack*, edited by Lars Tønder and Lasse Thomassen, 256–262. New York: Manchester University Press.

Laclau, Ernesto, and Chantal Mouffe. 1985. *Hegemony and Socialist Strategy: Towards a Radical Democratic Politics*. 2nd edition. London: Verso Books.

Lakoff, George. 1987. *Women, Fire, and Dangerous Things: What Categories Reveal about the Mind*. Chicago: University of Chicago Press.

References 221

Lakoff, George. 2003. "Embodied Mind, and How to Live with One." In *The Nature and Limits of Human Understanding*, edited by Anthony Sanford, 47–48. Dorsett, England: T&T Clark International.

Lang, Tim, and Michael Heasman. 2015. *Food Wars: The Global Battle for Mouths, Minds and Markets*. 2nd edition. New York: Routledge.

Lazarsfeld, Paul F., and Allen H. Barton. 1951. "Qualitative Measurement in the Social Sciences: Classification, Typologies, and Indices." In *The Policy Sciences: Recent Developments in Scope and Method*, edited by Daniel Lerner and Harold D. Lasswell, 155–192. Stanford, CA: Stanford University Press.

Leach, Edmund. 1974. *Levi-Strauss*. Glasgow: Collins.

Leibniz, Gottfried Wilhelm. 1991. *Discourse on Metaphysics and Other Essays*. Translated by Daniel Garber and Roger Ariew. Indianapolis, IN: Hacket Publishing Company.

Lemus, Blanca, and David Barkin. 2013. *Rethinking the Social and Solidarity Economy in Light of Community Practice*. Geneva: United Nations Research Institute for Social Development.

Lenin, Vladimir I. 2002a. "Marxism and Insurrection." In *Revolution at the Gates: A Selection of Writings from February to October 1917*, edited by Slavoj Žižek, 117–123. New York: Verso.

Lenin, Vladimir I. 2002b. "The Tasks of the Proletariat in the Present Revolution ('April Theses')." In *Revolution at the Gates: A Selection of Writings from February to October 1917*, edited by Slavoj Žižek, 56–61. New York: Verso.

Lennon, Thomas M., and Dea Shannon. 2012. *Continental Rationalism*. In *The Stanford Encyclopedia of Philosophy*, edited by Edward N. Zalta. Stanford, CA: Stanford University Press.

Lerner, Allan W., and John Wanat. 1998. *Public Administration: Scenarios in Management*. Upper Saddle River, NJ: Prentice Hall.

Leviatan, Uriel. 2013. "Kibbutzim as Real-life Utopia: Survival Depends on Adherence to Utopian Values." *Psychology and Developing Societies* no. 25 (2):249–281.

Lewis, Eugene. 1980. *Public Entrepreneurship: Toward a Theory of Bureaucratic Political Power*. Bloomington, IN: Indiana University Press.

Lietaer, Bernard. 2013. *The Future of Money: Creating New Wealth, Work and a Wiser World*. New Ed: Cornerstone Digital.

Lippmann, Walter. 2004. *Public Opinion*. Mineola, NY: Dover Publications. Original edition, 1922.

Lipsky, Michael. 1983. *Street-Level Bureaucracy: Dilemmas of the Individual in Public Service*. New York: Russell Sage Foundation.

Locke, John. 1980. *Second Treatise of Government*, edited by C. B. Macpherson. Indianapolis: Hackett Publishing Company. Original edition, 1690.

Long, Norton E. 1954. "Public policy and administration: the goals of rationality and responsibility." *Public Administration Review* no. 14 (1):22–31.

Love, Jeannine M. 2008. "The Rugged Individualist Club." *Administrative Theory & Praxis* no. 30 (4):424–449.

Love, Jeannine M. 2010a. *The Rugged Individualist Club: The Paradox of the I/individual in American Governance*. Dissertation, Public Policy and Public Administration, George Washington University, Washington, DC.

Love, Jeannine M. 2010b. "The Webs We Weave: (Re)Envisioning the *I*ndividual as Situated in Emergent Social Fabrics." Presentation at the Annual Conference of the American Society for Public Administration, San Jose, CA.

222 References

Love, Jeannine M. 2011. "Finding the (inter)Connections: Re-Examining Contemporary Theories of Public Administration." Presentation at the Annual Conference of the American Society for Public Administration, Baltimore, MD.

Love, Jeannine M. 2012. "From Atomistic to Interwoven: Utilizing a Typology of I/individualisms to Envision a Process Approach to Governance." *Administrative Theory & Praxis* no. 34 (3):362–384.

Love, Jeannine M. 2013. "A Society of Control: The Paradox of the People and the Individual." *Public Administration Quarterly* no. 37 (4): 576–593.

Lovejoy, Arthur O. 1964. *The Great Chain of Being: A Study of the History of an Idea.* Cambridge, MA: Harvard University Press. Original edition, 1936.

Lukács, Georg. 1998. *Lenin: A Study in the Unity of His Thought, Verso Classics.* New York: Verso.

Lusthaus, Dan. 2002. *Buddhist Phenomenolgy: A Philosophical Investigation of Yogācāra Buddhism and the Ch'eng Wei-Shih Lun.* London: Routledge Curzon.

Lutrin, Carl E., and Allen K. Settle. 1992. *American Public Administration: Concepts and Cases.* 4th edition. New York: West Publishing Company.

Lynn, Lawrence E., Jr. 1996. *Public Management as Art, Science, and Profession.* Chatham, NJ: Chatham House.

Lynn, Lawrence E., Jr. 2006. *Public Management: Old and New.* New York: Routledge.

Lyons, Nona Plessner. 1983. "Two Perspectives: On Self, Relationships, and Morality." *Harvard Educational Review* no. 53 (2):125–145.

Lyotard, Jean-François. 1984. *The Postmodern Condition: A Report on Knowledge.* Translated by G. Bennington and Brian Massumi. Vol. 10, *Theory and History of Literature.* Minneapolis: University of Minnesota Press.

MacIntyre, Alisdair. 1988. *Whose Justice? Which Rationality?* Notre Dame, IN: University of Notre Dame Press.

Mackie, J. L. 1990. *Ethics: Inventing Right and Wrong.* New York: Penguin Books.

Macpherson, C. B. 1962. *The Political Theory of Possessive Individualism: Hobbes to Locke.* Oxford: Oxford University Press.

MacRae, Duncan Jr., and James A. Wilde. 1979. *Policy Analysis for Public Decisions.* Belmont, CA: Wadsworth.

Malebranche, Nicolas. 1980. *The Search After Truth.* New York: Press Syndicate of the University of Cambridge. Original edition, 1674.

Mallin, Michael A., and Lawrence B. Cahoon. 2003. "Industrial Animal Production: A Major Source of Nutrient and Microbial Pollution." *Population and Environment* no. 24 (5):369.

Mander, William. 2013. "Pantheism." In *The Stanford Encyclopedia of Philosophy,* edited by Edward N. Zalta. Stanford, CA: Stanford University.

Mannheim, Karl. 1936. *Ideology and Utopia: An Introduction to the Sociology of Knowledge, International Library of Psychology, Philosophy and Scientific Method.* New York: Harcourt, Brace and Company.

Manwell, Laurie A. 2010. "In Denial of Democracy: Social Psychological Implications for Public Discourse on State Crimes against Democracy post-9/11." *American Behavioral Scientist* no. 53 (6):848–884.

Marchart, Oliver. 2005. "The Absence at the Heart of Presence: Radical Democracy and the 'Ontology of Lack'." In *Radical Democracy: Politics between Abundance and Lack,* edited by Lars Tønder and Lasse Thomassen, 17–31. New York: Manchester University Press.

References 223

Marcuse, Herbert. 1964. *One-Dimensional Man: Studies in the Ideology of Advanced Industrial Society*. Boston: Beacon Press.

Marcuse, Herbert. 1969. *An Essay on Liberation*. Boston: Beacon Press.

Margulis, Lynn, Celeste A. Asikainen, and Wolfgang E. Krumbein, eds. 2011. *Chimeras and Consciousness: Evolution of the Sensory Self*. Cambridge, MA: The MIT Press.

Mao Tse-Tung. 1965a. "Our Economic Policy." In *Selected Works of Mao Tse-Tung*. Vol. 1, 141–146. New York: Pergamon Press. Original edition, 1934.

Mao Tse-Tung. 1965b. "Report on an Investigation of the Peasant Movement in Hunan." In *Selected Works of Mao Tse-Tung*. Vol. 1, 23–59. New York: Pergamon Press. Original edition, 1927.

Marsh, David. 1998. "The Development of the Policy Network Approach." In *Comparing Policy Networks*, edited by David Marsh, 3–17. Philadelphia: Open University Press.

Marshall, T. H. 1950. *Citizenship and Social Class: and Other Essays*. Cambridge, UK: Cambridge University Press.

Marx, Karl. 2008. *Critique of the Gotha Program*. Rockville, MD: Wildside Press. Original edition, 1875.

Marx, Karl, and Friedrich Engels. 1998. *The Communist Manifesto: A Modern Edition*. New York: Verso. Original edition, 1848.

Maryboy, Nancy C. 2004. "Balancing the Flux: A Native Woman's Views of the Language of Spirituality." *Revision* no. 26 (3):11–12.

Maturana, Humberto R., and Francisco Varela. 1987. *Tree of Knowledge*. Boston: Shambhala Publications.

Maynard-Moody, Steven, and Michael Musheno. 2003. *Cops, Teachers, Counselors: Stories from the Front Lines of Public Service*. Ann Arbor, MI: University of Michigan Press.

McCutcheon, Russell T. 2005. "Introduction." In *The Insider/Outsider Problem in the Study of Religion: A Reader*, edited by Russell T. McCutcheon, 15–22. London: Continuum.

McKay, Iain. 2011. "Introduction: General Idea of the Revolution in the 21st Century." In *Property is Theft!: A Pierre-Joseph Proudhon Anthology*, edited by Iain Mckay, 1–54. Oakland: AK Press. Original edition, 1840.

McKay, Iain. 2008. *Anarchist FAQ*. Stirling: AK Press.

McSwite, O. C. 1996. "Postmodernism, Public Administration, and the Public Interest." In *Refounding Democratic Public Administration: Modern Paradoxes, Postmodern Challenges*, edited by Gary L. Wamsley and James F. Wolf, 198–224. Thousand Oaks: Sage Publications.

McSwite, O. C. 1997. *Legitimacy in Public Administration: A Discourse Analysis*. Thousand Oaks, CA: Sage Publications.

McSwite, O. C. 2000. "On the Discourse Movement—A Self Interview." *Administrative Theory & Praxis* no. 22 (1):49–65.

McSwite, O. C. 2001a. "The Psychoanalytic Rationale for Anti-administration." *Administrative Theory & Praxis* no. 23 (4):493–506.

McSwite, O. C. 2001b. "Reflections on the role of Embodiment in Discourse." *Administrative Theory & Praxis* no. 23 (2):243–250.

McSwite, O. C. 2002. *Invitation to Public Administration*. New York: M.E. Sharpe.

McSwite, O. C. 2003. "Now More than Ever—Refusal as Redemption." *Administrative Theory & Praxis* no. 25 (2):183–204.

McSwite, O. C. 2004. "Creating Reality through Administrative Practice: A Psychoanalytic Reading of Camilla Stivers' Bureau Men, Settlement Women." *Administration & Society* no. 36 (4):406–426.

224 *References*

McSwite, O. C. 2005. "Taking Public Administration Seriously: Beyond Humanism and Bureaucrat Bashing." *Administration & Society* no. 37:116–125.

McSwite, O. C. 2006. "Public Administration as the Carrier of the New Social Bond." *Administrative Theory & Praxis* no. 28 (2):176–189.

McSwite, O. C. 2011. "Human Relationship: The Heart of Ethical Discourse." In *Whenever Two or More Are Gathered: Relationship as the Heart of Ethical Discourse*, edited by Michael M. Harmon and O. C. McSwite, 14–38. Tuscaloosa, AL: The University of Alabama Press.

Mesle, C. Robert. 2008. *Process-Relational Philosophy: An Introduction to Alfred North Whitehead*. West Conshohocken, PA: Templeton Foundation Press.

Meyer, C. Kenneth, and Charles H. Brown. 1989. *Practicing Public Management: A Casebook*. 2nd edition. New York: St. Martin's Press.

Michaels, Walter Benn. 2007. *The Trouble With Diversity: How We Learned to Love Identity and Ignore Inequality*. New York: Holt Paperbacks.

Mies, Maria, and Vandana Shiva. 2014. *Ecofeminism*. New York: Zed Books. Original edition, 1993.

Mill, John Stuart. 1909. *Principles of Political Economy: With Some of Their Application to Social Philosophy*. New York: Longmans, Green, and Co.

Mill, John Stuart. 1999. *On Liberty*. 14th edition. Orchard Park, NY: Broadview Press. Original edition, 1859.

Mill, John Stuart. 2000. "Utilitarianism." In *What is Justice? Classic and Contemporary Readings*, edited by Robert C. Solomon and Mark C. Murphy, 166–174. New York: Oxford University Press. Original edition, 1861.

Miller, Hugh T. 2000. "Rational Discourse, Memetics, and the autonomous Liberal–Humanist Subject." *Administrative Theory & Praxis* no. 22 (1):89–104.

Miller, Hugh T. 2004. "The Ideographic Individual." *Administrative Theory & Praxis* no. 26 (4):469–488.

Miller, Hugh T., and Mohamad Alkadry, eds. 1998. *These Things Happen: Stories from the Public Sector*. Burke, VA: Chatelaine Press.

Miller, Hugh T., and Charles J. Fox. 2007. *Postmodern Public Administration*. Revised edition. Armonk, NY: M.E. Sharpe.

Milward, H. Brinton, and Keith G. Provan. 2000. "Governing the hollow state." *Journal of Public Administration Research and Theory* no. 10 (2):359–380.

Mingus, Matthew S. 2000. "Relational Holism and the Possibility of Quantum Administration: Farfetched Ideas or an Ascendant Worldview?" In *New Sciences for Public Administration and Policy: Connections and Reflections*, edited by Goktug Morcol and Linda F. Dennard, 243–263. Burke, VA: Chatelaine Press.

Mitchell Jr., Richard G. 2002. *Armaggedon: Survivalism and Chaos in Modern Times*. Chicago: University of Chicago Press.

Mitchell, Juliet. 1974. *Psychoanalysis and Feminism: A Radical Reassessment of Freudian Psychoanalysis*. London: Allen Lane.

Montesquieu, Charles De Secondat Baron De. 1989. *The Spirit of the Laws*. Translated by Anne M. Cohler, Basia Carolyn Miller and Harold Samuel Stone. Cambridge, UK: Cambridge University Press.

Morris, Brian. 1993. *Bakunin: The Philosophy of Freedom*. Montreal: Black Rose Books Ltd.

Morse, Ricardo S. 2006. "Prophet of Participation: Mary Parker Follett and Public Participation in public Administration." *Administrative Theory & Praxis* no. 28 (1):1–32.

Morstein Marx, Fritz. 1946. "The Lawyer's Role in Public Administration." *Yale Law Journal* no. 55 (3):498–526.

References   225

Mosher, Frederick. 1968. *Democracy and the Public Service.* New York: Oxford University Press.

Mouffe, Chantal. 2000. *The Democratic Paradox.* New York: Verso.

Mouffe, Chantal. 2005. "For an Agonistic Public Sphere." In *Radical Democracy: Politics between Abundance and Lack,* edited by Lars Tønder and Lasse Thomassen, 123–132. New York: Manchester University Press.

Mueller, Tadzio. 2011. "Empowering Anarchy: Power, Hegemony and Anarchist Strategy." In *Post-Anarchism: A Reader,* edited by Duane Rousselle and Süreyyya Evren, 75–94. New York: Pluto Press.

Murdoch, Iris. 1992. *Metaphysics as a Guide to Morals.* New York: Penguin Books.

Murray, Nancy. 2000. "In Search of Truth: Eastern Metaphysics, Quantum Science and Public Administration Philosophy." In *New Sciences for Public Administration and Policy: Connections and Reflections,* edited by Goktug Morcol and Linda F. Dennard, 221–242. Burke, VA: Chatelaine Press.

Nabatchi, Tina. 2010. "The (re)Discovery of the Public in Public Administration." *Public Administration Review* no. 70 (Supplement):S309–311.

National Performance Review. 2004. "From Red Tape to Results: Creating a Government That Works Better and Costs Less." In *Classics of Public Administration,* edited by Jay M. Shafritz, Albert C. Hyde and Sandra J. Parkes, 556–563. Belmont, CA: Wadsworth. Original edition, 1993.

Neufeldt, Victoria, Ed. 1996. *Webster's New World College Dictionary.* 3rd edition. New York: Macmillan.

New Internationalist. 2004. "Resistance is fertile!" Issue 365. Available at https://newint. org/features/2004/03/01/action/ (accessed August 1, 2016).

Newman, Lex. 2013. "Descartes' Rationalist Epistemology." In *A Companion to Rationalism,* edited by Alan Nelson, 179–205. Malden, MA: Blackwell Publishing Ltd.

Newman, Saul. 2005. *Power and Politics in Poststructuralist Thought: New Theories of the Political.* New York: Routledge.

Nichol, Lee. 2004. "Foreword." In *On Dialogue,* by David Bohm, xv–xx. New York: Routledge.

Niebuhr, H. Richard. 1963. *The Responsible Self: An Essay in Christian Moral Philosophy.* New York: Harper & Row.

Niedzviecki, Hal. 2006. *Hello, I'm Special: How Individuality Became the New Conformity.* San Francisco: City Lights Books.

North, Douglass Cecil. 1990. *Institutions, Institutional Change, and Economic Performance, the Political Economy of Institutions and Decisions.* Cambridge, UK: Cambridge University Press.

Norval, Aletta J. 2005. "Theorising Hegemony: Between Deconstruction and Psychoanalysis." In *Radical Democracy: Politics between Abundance and Lack,* edited by Lars Tønder and Lasse Thomassen, 86–102. New York: Manchester University Press.

Nozick, Robert. 2000. "Anarchy, State, and Utopia." In *What is Justice? Classic and Contemporary Readings,* edited by Robert C. Solomon and Mark C. Murphy, 106–112; 301–308. New York: Oxford University Press. Original edition, 1974.

NRCS. *About.* Natural Resource Conservation Service 2016 [Cited 5–18–2016]. Available from www.nrcs.usda.gov/wps/portal/nrcs/main/national/about/history/ (accessed July 1, 2016).

Osborn, Stephen G., Avner Vengosh, Nathaniel R. Warner, and Robert B. Jackson. 2011. "Methane Contamination of Drinking Water Accompanying Gas-well Drilling and

226 *References*

Hydraulic Fracturing." *Proceedings of the National Academy of Sciences* no. 108:8172–8176.

Osborne, David, and Ted Gaebler. 1992. *Reinventing Government: How the Entrepreneurial Spirit is Transforming the Public Sector.* Reading, MA: Addison-Wesley.

Ostrom, Vincent. 1976. "Language, Theory, and Empirical Research in Policy Analysis." In *Problems of Theory in Policy Analysis,* edited by Phillip M. Gregg, 9–18. Lexington, MA: Lexington Books.

Ostrom, Vincent. 1989. *The Intellectual Crisis in American Public Administration.* 2nd edition. Tuscaloosa, AL: University of Alabama Press. Original edition, 1973.

Ostrom, Vincent. 1997. *The Meaning of Democracy and the Vulnerability of Democracy: A Response to Tocqueville's Challenge.* Ann Arbor, MI: The University of Michigan Press.

Oved, Yaacov. 1988. *Two Hundred Years of American Communes.* New Brunswick: Transaction Publishers.

Overeem, Patrick. 2005. "The Value of the Dichotomy: Politics, Administration, and the Political Neutrality of Administrators." *Administrative Theory & Praxis* no. 27 (2):311–329.

Padgett, Alan G. 2002. "Dialectical Realism in Theology and Science." *Perspectives on Science and Christian Faith* no. 54 (3):184–192.

Palmer, John. 2008. "Parmenides." In *The Stanford Encyclopedia of Philosophy* edited by Edward N. Zalta. Stanford, CA: Stanford University Press.

Pandit, Bansi. 2005. *Explore Hinduism.* Loughborough: Explore Books.

Paris, David C., and James F. Reynolds. 1983. *The Logic of Policy Inquiry.* New York: Longman.

Pariser, Eli. 2011. *The Filter Bubble: What the Internet is Hiding from You.* New York: Penguin Press.

Parry, Glenn R. 2004. "Seed Thoughts on Dialogue." *Revision* no. 26 (3):5–10.

Patton, Paul. 2005. "Deleuze and Democratic Politics." In *Radical Democracy: Politics between Abundance and Lack,* edited by Lars Tønder and Lasse Thomassen, 50–67. New York: Manchester University Press.

Patton, Paul, and John Protevi, eds. 2003. *Between Deleuze and Derrida.* London: Continuum.

Peikoff, Leonard. 1991. *Objectivism: The Philosophy of Ayn Rand.* New York: Meridian.

Perkins, John. 2004. *Confessions of an Economic Hit Man.* New York: Plume.

Pesch, Udo. 2008. "The Publicness of Public Administration." *Administration & Society* no. 40:170–193.

Peters, B. Guy. 1992. *The Future of Governing.* Lawrence, KS: University Press of Kansas.

Phillips, Kevin. 2002. *Wealth and Democracy: A Political History of the American Rich.* New York: Broadway Books.

Plato. 1961. *Meno.* New York: Cambridge University Press.

Plato. 1993. *Phaedo.* Cambridge, UK: Cambridge University Press.

Plato. 2004. *The Republic.* Translated by C. D. C. Reeve. Indianapolis: Hacket Publishing.

Polyani, Karl. 1944. *The Great Transformation: The Political and Economic Origins of Our Time.* Boston: Beacon Press.

Popper, Karl R. 1940. "What is Dialectic?" *Mind* no. 49 (196):403–426.

Potter, David Morris. 1976. *Freedom and its Limitations in American Life.* Stanford: Stanford University Press.

Proudhon, Pierre-Joseph. 1979. *The Principle of Federation and the Need to Reconstitute the Party of Revolution.* Translated by Richard Vernon. Toronto: University of Toronto Press. Original edition, 1863.

References 227

Proudhon, Pierre-Joseph. 2007. *What is Property? Or, an Inquiry into the Principle of Right and of Government.* New York: Cosimo. Original edition, 1840.

Prozorov, Sergei. 2014a. *Ontology and World Politics: Void Universalism I.* New York: Routledge.

Prozorov, Sergei. 2014b. *Theory of the political subject: Void Universalism II.* New York: Routledge.

Pugh, Darryl L. 1991. "The Origins of Ethical Frameworks in Public Administration." In *Ethical Frontiers in Public Management: Seeking New Strategies for Resolving Ethical Dilemmas,* edited by James S. Bowman, 9–33. San Francisco: Jossey-Bass.

Pulitano, Elvira. 2003. *Toward a Native American Critical Theory.* Lincoln, NE: University of Nebraska Press.

Putnam, Robert D. 2000. *Bowling Alone: America's Declining Social Capital.* New York: Simon and Schuster.

Raadschelders, Jos C. N. 1999. "A Coherent Framework for the Study of Public Administration." *Journal of Public Administration Research and Theory* no. 9 (2):281–303.

Raadschelders, Jos C. N. 2000. "Understanding Government in Society: We See the Trees, But Could We See the Forest?" *Administrative Theory & Praxis* no. 22 (2):192–225.

Ramos, Alberto Guerreiro. 1981. *The New Science of Organizations: A Reconceptualization of the Wealth of Nations.* Toronto: University of Toronto Press.

Rand, Ayn. 1964. *The Virtue of Selfishness: A New Concept of Egoism.* New York: New American Library.

Rand, Ayn. 1966. *Capitalism: The Unknown Ideal.* New York: Signet.

Rand, Ayn. 1982. *Philosophy: Who Needs It.* Indianapolis: The Bobbs-Merrill Company.

Randolph, John. 2012. "Creating the Climate Change Resilient Community." In *Collaborative Resilience: Moving through Crisis to Opportunity,* edited by Bruce Evan Goldstein, 127–148. Cambridge, MA: MIT Press.

Rawls, John. 2000. "A Theory of Justice." In *What is Justice? Classic and Contemporary Readings,* edited by Robert C. Solomon, Mark C. Murphy, 100–105; 286–287. New York: Oxford University Press. Original edition, 1971.

Redford, Emmette S. 1969. *Democracy in the Administrative State.* New York: Oxford University Press.

Reich, Robert B., Ed. 1988. *The Power of Public Ideas.* Cambridge, MA: Ballinger Publishing Company.

Reich, Robert B. 1990. *Public Management in a Democratic Society.* Englewood Cliffs, NJ: Prentice Hall.

Rein, Martin, and Donald Schön. 1993. "Reframing Policy Discourse." In *The Argumentative Turn in Policy Analysis and Planning,* edited by Frank Fischer and John Forester, 145–166. Durham, NC: University of North Carolina Press.

Ricardo, David. 1911. *The Principles of Political Economy and Taxation.* London: Dent.

Riggs, Fred W. 1998. "Public Administration in America: Why Our Uniqueness Is Exceptional and Important." *Public Administration Review* no. 58 (1):22–31.

Risse, Thomas. 2004. "Global Governance and Communicative Action." *Government and Opposition* no. 39 (2):288–313.

Ritzer, George. 2008. *The McDonaldization of Society.* 5th edition. Los Angles, CA: Pine Forge Press.

Roberts, Nancy. 2004. "Public Deliberation in an Age of Direct Citizen Participation." *American Review of Public Administration* no. 34 (4):315–353.

228   *References*

Rocker, Rudolf. 2004. *Anarcho-Syndicalism: Theory and Practice, Working Class Series.* Oakland: AK Press. Original edition, 1938.

Rohlf, Michael. 2010. "Immanuel Kant." In *The Stanford Encyclopedia of Philosophy,* edited by Edward N. Zalta. Stanford: Stanford University Press.

Rohr, John A. 1986. *To Run a Constitution: The Legitimacy of the Administrative State.* Lawrence, KS: University Press of Kansas.

Rohr, John A. 1989. *Ethics for Bureaucrats: An Essay on Law and Values.* 2nd edition. New York: Marcel Dekker.

Rohr, John A. 1990. "The Constitutional Case for Public Administration." In *Refounding Public Administration,* edited by Gary L. Wamsley, Robert N. Bacher, Charles T. Goodsell, Philip S. Kronenberg, John A. Rohr, Camilla Stivers, Orion F. White and James F. Wolf, 52–95. Newbury Park, CA: Sage Publications.

Rose, Nikolas. 2000. "Community, Citizenship, and the Third Way." *The American Behavioral Scientist* no. 43 (9):1395–1411.

Rose, Nikolas. 2007. *The Politics of Life Itself: Biomedicine, Power and Subjectivity in the Twenty-First Century.* Princeton, NJ: Princeton University Press.

Rosenau, Pauline Marie. 1992. *Postmodernism and the Social Sciences: Insights, Inroads, and Intrusions.* Princeton, NJ: Princeton University Press.

Rosenbloom, David H. 1983. "Public Administration Theory and the Separation of Powers." *Public Administration Review* no. 43 (3):219–227.

Rosenbloom, David H. 2009. *Public Administration: Understanding Management, Politics, and Law in the Public Sector.* 7th edition. New York: McGraw-Hill.

Ross, Rupert. 1996. *Return to Teaching: Exploring Aboriginal Justice.* Toronto: Penguin Books.

Rossiter, Clinton, Ed. 1999. *The Federalist Papers.* New York: Mentor.

Rousselle, Duane, and Süreyyya Evren, eds. 2011. *Post-Anarchism: A Reader.* London: Pluto Press.

Roy, Mathieu, and Harold Crooks. 2011. *Surviving Progress.* Canada: Big Picture Media Corporation.

Ruccio, David F., and Jack Amariglio. 2003. *Postmodern Moments in Modern Economics.* Princeton, NJ: Princeton University Press.

Runes, Dagobert D. 1962. *Dictionary of Philosophy: Ancient/Midieval/Modern.* Paterson, NJ: Little, Adams and Company.

Rutgers, Mark R. 2001. "Splitting the Universe: On the Relevance of Dichotomies for the Study of Public Administration." *Administration & Society* no. 33 (1):3–20.

Sabatier, Paul A. 1988. "An Advocacy Coalition Framework of Policy Change and the Role of Policy-oriented Learning Therein." *Policy Sciences* no. 21 (2/3):129–168.

Salamon, Lester M. 2005. "Training Professional Citizens: Getting beyond the Right Answer to the Wrong Question in Public Administration." *Journal of Public Affairs Education* no. 11 (1):7–20.

Sarup, Madan. 1989. *An Introductory Guide to Post-Structuralism and Postmodernism.* Athens, GA: University of Georgia Press.

Satariano, Nickie Bazell, and Amanda Wong. 2012. "Creating an Online Strategy to Enhance Effective Community Building and Organizing." In *Community Organizing and Community Building for Health and Welfare,* 3rd edition., edited by Meredith Minkler, 269–287. New Brunswick, NJ: Rutgers University Press.

Saussure, Ferdinand de. 1960. *Course in General Linguistics.* London: Peter Owen. Original edition, 1916.

References 229

Savas, E. S. 1982. *Privatizing the Public Sector: How to Shrink Government.* Chatham, NJ: Chatham House.

Savas, E. S. 2000. *Privatization and Public-Private Partnerships.* New York: Chatham House.

Schaff, Adam. 1970. *Marxism and the Human Individual.* Translated by O. Wojtasiewicz. New York: McGraw-Hill.

Schlager, Edella. 1999. "A Comparison of Frameworks, Theories, and Models of Policy Processes." In *Theories of the Policy Process: Theoretical Lenses on Public Policy,* edited by Paul A. Sabatier, 233–260. Boulder, CO: Westview Press.

Schmidt, Mary R. 1993. "Grout: Alternative Forms of Knowledge and Why They Are Ignored." *Public Administration Review* no. 53 (6):525–530.

Schmitt, Carl. 1985. *Political Theology: Four Chapters on the Concept of Sovereignty.* Translated by George Schwab. Cambridge, MA: MIT Press.

Schneider, Anne Larason, and Helen Ingram. 1997. *Policy Design for Democracy.* Lawrence, KS: University Press of Kansas.

Schneider, Louis. 1971. "Dialectic in sociology." *American Sociological Review* no. 36 (4):667–678.

Schultz, David. 2004. "Professional Ethics in a Postmodern Society." *Public Integrity* no. 6 (4):279–297.

Schutz, Alfred. 1967. *The Phenomenology of the Social World.* Translated by George Walsch and Frederick Lehnert. Evanston, IL: Northwestern University Press. Original edition, 1932.

Selznick, Philip. 1949. *TVA and the Grass Roots.* Berkeley: University of California Press.

Seymour, John. 2009. *The Self-Sufficient Life and How to Live It: The Complete Back-To-Basics Guide.* London: DK Publishing.

Sharma, Chandradhar. 1996. *The Advaita Tradition in Indian Philosophy: A Study of Advaita in Buddhism, Vedānta and Kāshmīra Shaivism.* Delhi: Shri Jainedra Press.

Shaviro, Steven. 2009. *Without Criteria: Kant, Whitehead, Deleuze, and Aesthetics.* Cambridge, MA: Massachusetts Institute of Technology Press.

Shields, Christopher. 2013. "Aristotle." In *The Stanford Encyclopedia of Philosophy,* edited by Edward N. Zalta. Stanford, CA: Stanford University.

Shun'ei, Tagawa. 2009. *Living Yogācār: An Introduction to Consciousness-Only Buddhism.* Translated by Charles Muller. Somerville, MA: Wisdom Publications.

Siddheswarananda, Swami. 1998. *Hindu Thought and Carmelite Mysticism.* Dehli, Inda: Motilal Banarsidass Press.

Sidgewick, Henry. 1884. *The Methods of Ethics.* London: Macmillan.

Sidhu, Kuldip S., Methichit Chayosumrit, and Khun H. Lie. 2012. "Stem Cells, Definition, Classification and Sources." In *Frontiers in Pluripotent Stem Cells Research and Therapeutic Potentials: Bench-To-Bedside,* edited by Kuldip S. Sidhu, 3–15. United Arab Emirates: Bentham Science Publishers.

Simon, Herbert A. 1946. "The Proverbs of Administration." *Public Administration Review* no. 6 (1):53–67.

Simon, Herbert A. 1947. "A comment on the 'Science' of Public Administration." *Public Administration Review* no. 7 (Summer):200–203.

Simon, Herbert A. 1976. *Administrative Behavior: A Study of Decision-Making Processes in Administrative Organization.* 3rd edition. New York: Macmillan. Original edition, 1945.

Simon, Herbert A., Donald W. Smithburg, and Victor A. Thompson. 1974. *Public Administration.* New York: Alfred A. Knopf. Original edition, 1950.

230 References

Simons, Jon. 2005. "The Radical Democratic Possibilities of Popular Culture." In *Radical Democracy: Politics between Abundance and Lack*, edited by Lars Tønder and Lasse Thomassen, 149–166. New York: Manchester University Press.

Smadja, Claude. 2000. "Time to Learn from Seattle." *Newsweek*, January 17, 64.

Smith, Adam. 2000a. "A Theory of the Moral Sentiments." In *What is Justice? Classic and Contemporary Readings*, edited by Robert C. Solomon and Mark C. Murphy, 144–147. New York: Oxford University Press. Original edition, 1759.

Smith, Adam. 2000b. "The Wealth of Nations." In *What is Justice? Classic and Contemporary Readings*, edited by Robert C. Solomon and Mark C. Murphy, 148–151. New York: Oxford University Press. Original edition, 1776.

Smith, Andrea. 2007. "Introduction: The Revolution Will Not Be Funded." In *The Revolution Will Not Be Funded: Beyond the Non-Profit Industrial Complex*, edited by Incite! Women of Color Against Violence, 1–18. Cambridge, MA: South End Press.

Smith, Linda Tuhiwai. 1999. *Decolonizing Methodologies: Research and Indigenous Peoples*. New York: University of Otago Press.

Solomon, Robert C., and Mark C. Murphy, eds. 2000. *What is Justice? Classic and Contemporary Readings*. New York: Oxford University Press.

Somasundaran, Ponisseril, Partha Patra, Raymond S. Farinato, and Kyriakos Papadopoulos. 2014. *Oil Spill Remediation: Colloid Chemistry-Based Principles and Solutions*. New York: John Wiley & Sons.

Sørensen, Eva, and Jacob Torfing. 2005. "The Democratic Anchorage of Governance Networks." *Scandinavian Political Studies* no. 28 (3):195–218.

Sorokin, Pitirim. 1957. *Social and Cultural Dynamics: A Study of Change in Major Systems of Art, Truth, Ethics, Law and Social Relationships*. Revised edition. Boston: Porter Sargent. Original edition, 1937.

Speth, James Gustave. 2008. *The Bridge at the Edge of the World: Capitalism, the Environment, and Crossing from Crisis to Sustainability*. New Haven, CT: Yale University Press.

Spicer, Michael W. 2004. "Public Administration, The History of Ideas, and the Reinventing Government Movement." *Public Administration Review* no. 64 (3):353–362.

Spicer, Michael W. 2010. *In Defense of Politcs in Public Administration: A Value Pluralist Perspective*. Tuscaloosa, AL: University of Alabama Press.

Stalin, Joseph. 1953. *Foundations of Leninism*. Moscow: Foreign Languages Publishing House.

Starratt, Robert J. 1996. *Transforming Educational Administration: Meaning, Community, and Excellence*. New York: McGraw-Hill.

Starratt, Robert J. 2003. *Centering Educational Administration: Cultivating Meaning, Community, Responsibility*. Mahwah, NJ: L. Erlbaum Associates.

Stavrakakis, Yannis. 2005. "Negativity and Democratic Politics: Radical Democracy Beyond Reoccupation and Conformism." In *Radical Democracy: Politics between Abundance and Lack*, edited by Lars Tønder and Lasse Thomassen, 185–202. New York: Manchester University Press.

Steinfeld, Henning, Pierre Gerber, Tom Wassenaar, Vincent Castel, Mauricio Rosales, and Cees De Haan. 2006. *Livestock's Long Shadow*. Rome: Food and Agriculture Organization of the United Nations.

Stengers, Isabelle. 2011. *Thinking With Whitehead: A Free and Wild Creation of Concepts*. Translated by Michael Chase. Cambridge, MA: Harvard University Press.

Stever, James A. 1988. *The End of Public Administration: Problems of the Profession in the Post-Progressive Era*. Dobbs Ferry, NY: Transnational Publishers.

References 231

Stevick, Richard A. 2007. *Growing Up Amish: The Teenage Years.* Baltimore: John Hopkins University Press.

Stewart-Harawira, Makere. 2005. *The New Imperial Order: Indigenous Responses to Globalization.* London: Zed Books.

Stiglitz, Joseph E. 2007. *Making Globalization Work.* New York: W.W. Norton & Co.

Stillman, Richard J., II. 2005. *Public Administration: Concepts and Cases.* New York: Houghton Mifflin Company.

Stillman, Richard Joseph, II. 1996. *The American Bureaucracy: The Core of Modern Government.* 2nd edition. Chicago: Nelson-Hall.

Stirner, Max. 1995. *The Ego and its Own (Cambridge Texts in the History of Political Thought).* Oxford: Cambridge University Press.

Stivers, Camilla. 2000. *Bureau Men, Settlement Women: Constructing Public Administration in the Progressive Era.* Lawrence, KS: University Press of Kansas.

Stivers, Camilla. 2002a. "Comments." *Administration & Society* no. 34:116–118.

Stivers, Camilla. 2002b. "Toward Administrative Public Space: Hannah Arendt Meets the Municipal Housekeepers." *Administration & Society* no. 34:98–102.

Stivers, Camilla. 2008. *Governance in Dark Times: Practical Philosophy for Public Service.* Washington, DC: Georgetown University Press.

Stout, Margaret. 2006. "A Samurai's Lineage: Theoretical Traditions in Public Administration." *Administrative Theory & Praxis* no. 28 (4):618–630.

Stout, Margaret. 2007. *Bureaucrats, Entrepreneurs, and Stewards: Seeking Legitimacy in Contemporary Governance.* Dissertation, School of Public Affairs, Arizona State University, Phoenix.

Stout, Margaret. 2009a. "Toward a Dialectical Synthesis of Competing Ontologies: A Basic Sketch." Presentation at the Annual Conference of the Public Administration Theory Network, Frankfort, KY.

Stout, Margaret. 2009b. "You Say You Want a Revolution?" *International Journal of Organization Theory and Behavior* no. 12 (2):291–309.

Stout, Margaret. 2010a. "Back to the Future: Toward a Political Economy of Love and Abundance." *Administration & Society* no. 42 (1):3–37.

Stout, Margaret. 2010b. "Climbing the Ladder of Participation: Establishing Local Policies for Participatory Practice." *Public Administration and Management* no. 15 (1):46–97.

Stout, Margaret. 2010c. "Co-creation and the Social Bond: A Collaborative Process of Becoming." Presentation at the Annual Conference of the American Society for Public Administration, San Jose, CA.

Stout, Margaret. 2010d. "Reclaiming the (Lost) Art of Ideal-typing in Public Administration." *Administrative Theory & Praxis* no. 32 (4):491–519.

Stout, Margaret. 2010e. "Refusing Ontological Colonization." *Administrative Theory & Praxis* no. 32 (4):600–605.

Stout, Margaret. 2011. "Relational Ontology: Toward a Public Philosophy and Ethic for an Interconnected World." Presentation at the Annual Conference of the American Society for Public Administration, Baltimore, MD.

Stout, Margaret. 2012a. "Competing Ontologies: A Primer for Public Administration." *Public Administration Review* no. 72 (3):388–398.

Stout, Margaret. 2012b. "Toward a Relational Language of Process." *Administrative Theory & Praxis* no. 34 (3):407–432.

Stout, Margaret. 2013. *Logics of Legitimacy: Three Traditions of Public Administration Praxis.* Boca Raton, FL: CRC Press.

232 *References*

Stout, Margaret. 2014. "The Many Faces of Unity." *Public Administration Quarterly* no. 38 (2): 273–281.

Stout, Margaret. 2016. "Remembering Kym Thorne (and Alexander Kouzmin): Reform, Revolution, or Mission Impossible?" *Administrative Theory & Praxis* no. 38 (2):90–92.

Stout, Margaret, and Jeannine M. Love. 2012. "Relational Process Ontology: A Grounding for Global Governance." Presentation at the Annual Conference of the Public Administration Theory Network, South Padre Island, TX.

Stout, Margaret, and Jeannine M. Love. 2013. "Ethical Choice Making." *Public Administration Quarterly* no. 37 (2):278–294.

Stout, Margaret, and Jeannine M. Love. 2014a. "Fraternity, Solidarity, and Unity: Concepts Grounded in Competing Ontologies." *Administrative Theory & Praxis* no. 36 (3):421–429.

Stout, Margaret, and Jeannine M. Love. 2014b. "The Unfortunate Misinterpretation of Miss Follett." *Public Voices* no. 13 (2):11–32.

Stout, Margaret, and Jeannine M. Love. 2015a. "Integrative Governance: A Method for Fruitful Public Encounters." *American Review of Public Administration*. DOI: 10.1177/0275074015576953.

Stout, Margaret, and Jeannine M. Love. 2015b. *Integrative Process: Follettian Thinking from Ontology to Administration*. Anoka, MN: Process Century Press.

Stout, Margaret, and Jeannine M. Love. 2015c. "Relational Process Ontology: A Grounding for Global Governance." *Administration & Society* no. 47 (4):447–481.

Stout, Margaret, and Jeannine M. Love. 2016. Follett, Mary Parker. In *Encyclopedia of Public Administration and Public Policy*, edited by Melvin J. Dubnick and Domonic A. Bearfield, 1503–1510. New York: Taylor & Francis Group.

Stout, Margaret, and Jeannine M. Love. 2017. *Integrative Governance: Generating Sustainable Responses to Global Crises*. London: Routledge.

Stout, Margaret, and Joao Salm. 2011. "What Restorative Justice Might Learn from Administrative Theory." *Contemporary Justice Review* no. 14 (2):203–225.

Stout, Margaret, and Carrie Staton. 2011. "The Ontology of Process Philosophy in Follett's Administrative Theory." *Administrative Theory & Praxis* no. 33 (2):268–292.

Stringham, Edward. 2005. *Anarchy, State, and Public Choice*. Cheltenham, UK: Edward Elgar.

Stringham, Edward. 2007. *Anarchy and the Law: The Political Economy of Choice*. Piscataway, NJ: Transaction Publishing.

Suchocki, Marjorie. 1985. "Weaving the World." *Process Studies* no. 14 (2):76–86.

Susskind, Lawrence, Sarah McKearnan, and Jennifer Thomas-Larme, eds. 1999. *The Consensus Building Handbook*. Thousand Oaks, CA: Sage.

Susskind, Leonard. 1995. "The World as a Hologram." *Journal of Mathematical Physics* no. 36 (11):6377–6396.

Suzuki, Daisetsu Teitaro. 1968. *On Indian Mahayana Buddhism*. New York: Harper & Row.

Tarlau, Rebecca. 2014. "Thirty Years of Landless Workers Demanding State Power." *Berkeley Journal of Sociology* no. 58:4.

Taylor, Charles. 1989. *Sources of the Self: The Making of the Modern Identity*. Cambridge, MA: Harvard University Press.

Taylor, Frederick Winslow. 1911. *The Principles of Scientific Management*. New York: Harper & Brothers.

Terry, Larry D. 1995. *Leadership of Public Bureaucracies: The Administrator as Conservator*. Thousand Oaks, CA: Sage Publications.

References   233

Thayer, Frederick C. 1980. "Organization Theory as Epistemology: Transcending Hierarchy and Objectivity." In *Organization Theory and the New Public Administration*, edited by Carl J. Bellone, 113–139. Boston: Allyn and Bacon.

Thayer, Frederick C. 1981. *An End to Hierarchy and Competition: Administration in the Post-Affluent World*. 2nd edition. New York: New Viewpoints.

Thomassen, Lasse. 2005. "In/Exclusions: Towards a Radical Democratic Approach to Exclusion." In *Radical Democracy: Politics between Abundance and Lack*, edited by Lars Tønder and Lasse Thomassen, 103–119. New York: Manchester University Press.

Thompson, Victor Alexander. 1975. *Without Sympathy or Enthusiasm: The Problem of Administrative Compassion*. University: University of Alabama Press.

Thoreau, Henry David. 2004. "Civil Disobedience." In *Walden and Other Writings*, edited by Joseph Wood Krutch, 89–110. New York: Bantam Dell.

Thorne, Kym. 2010. "Narcissistic and Dangerous 'Alphas': 'Sovereign Individuals' and the Problem of Cultivating the 'Civic' in Cyberspace." *International Journal of Critical Accounting* no. 2 (1):96–109.

Thorne, Kym, and Alexander Kouzmin. 2004. "Borders in an (In)visible World: Revisiting Communities, Recognizing Gulags." *Administrative Theory & Praxis* no. 26 (3):408–429.

Thorne, Kym, and Alexander Kouzmin. 2006. "Learning to Play the 'Pea and Thimble' Charade—The Invisible and Very Visible Hands in the Neo-Liberal Project: Towards a Manifesto for Reflexive Consciousness in Public Administration." *Administrative Theory & Praxis* no. 28 (2):262–274.

Thorne, Kym, and Alexander Kouzmin. 2007. "The Imperative of Reason and Rationality: A Politically—and Historically—Aware Netizen's Rejoinder." *Administrative Theory & Praxis* no. 29 (1):41–56.

Thorne, Kym, and Alexander Kouzmin. 2012. "Reform, Revolution, or Mission Impossible?" *Administrative Theory & Praxis* no. 34 (1):16–39.

Tilman, David, Kenneth G. Cassman, Pamela A. Matson, Rosamond Naylor, and Stephen Polasky. 2002. "Agricultural Sustainability and Intensive Production Practices." *Nature* no. 418 (8 August):671–677.

Tønder, Lars. 2005. "Inessential Commonality: Immanence, Transcendence, Abundance." In *Radical Democracy: Politics between Abundance and Lack*, edited by Lars Tønder and Lasse Thomassen, 203–218. New York: Manchester University Press.

Tønder, Lars, and Lasse Thomassen. 2005a. "Introduction." In *Radical Democracy: Politics between Abundance and Lack*, edited by Lars Tønder and Lasse Thomassen, 1–13. New York: Manchester University Press.

Tønder, Lars, and Lasse Thomassen, eds. 2005b. *Radical Democracy: Politics between Abundance and Lack*. New York: Manchester University Press.

Tugal, Cihan. 2014. "End of the Leaderless Revolution." *Berkeley Journal of Sociology* no. 58:3.

Turner, Bryan S. 1988. "Individualism, Capitalism and the Dominant Culture: A Note on the Debate." *Journal of Sociology* no. 24 (1):47–64.

Underhill, Evelyn. 1920. *The Essentials of Mysticism: and Other Essays*. London: J. M. Dent & Sons Ltd.

Urwick, L. (Lyndall). 1937. "The Function of Administration: With Special Reference to the Work of Henri Fayol." In *Papers on the Science of Administration*, edited by Luther Gulick and L. Urwick, 115–130. New York: Institute of Public Administration, Columbia University.

234 *References*

Ventriss, Curtis. 1989. "Toward a Public Philosophy of Public Administration: A Civic Perspective of the Public." *Public Administration Review* no. 49 (2):173–179.

Ventriss, Curtis. 1991. "Reconstructing Government Ethics: A Public Philosophy of Civic Value." In *Ethical Frontiers in Public Management: Seeking New Strategies for Resolving Ethical Dilemmas*, edited by James S. Bowman, 114–134. San Francisco: Jossey-Bass.

Verney, Marilyn Notah. 2004. "On Authenticity." In *American Indian Thought*, edited by Anne Waters, 133–139. Malden, MA: Blackwell Publishing.

Vetter, Lisa Pace. 2008. "Harriet Martineau on the Theory and Practice of Democracy in America." *Political Theory* no. 36 (3):424–455.

Vigoda, Eran. 2002. "From Responsiveness to Collaboration: Governance, Citizens, and the Next Generation of Public Administration." *Public Administration Review* no. 62 (5):527–540.

Von Mises, Ludwig. 1998. *Human Action*. Auburn, AL: Ludwig Von Mises Institute.

Vowell, Sarah. 2008. *The Wordy Shipmates*. New York: Riverhead Books.

Waddock, Sandra A., and James E. Post. 1991. "Social Entrepreneurs and Catalytic Change." *Public Administration Review* no. 51 (5):393–401.

Waldo, Dwight. 1984. *The Administrative State: A Study of the Political Theory of American Public Administration*. 2nd edition. New York: Holmes & Meier Publishers. Original edition, 1948.

Waldo, Dwight. 1988. "The End of Public Administration?" *Public Administration Review* no. 48 (5):929–932.

Walker, Lucy. 2002. *The Devil's Playground*. USA: Winstar Cinema.

Walzer, Michael. 1984. "Liberalism and the Art of Separation." *Political Theory* no. 12 (3):315–330.

Wamsley, Gary L. 1990. "The Agency Perspective: Public Administrators and Agential Leaders." In *Refounding Public Administration*, edited by Gary L. Wamsley, Robert N. Bacher, Charles T. Goodsell, Philip S. Kronenberg, John A. Rohr, Camilla Stivers, Orion F. White and James F. Wolf, 114–162. Newbury Park, CA: Sage Publications.

Wamsley, Gary L. 1996. "A Public Philosophy and Ontological Disclosure as the Basis for Normatively Grounded Theorizing in Public Administration." In *Refounding Democratic Public Administration: Modern Paradoxes and Postmodern Challenges*, edited by Gary L. Wamsley and James F. Wolf, 351–401. Thousand Oaks, CA: Sage.

Wamsley, Gary L., and James F. Wolf, eds. 1996. *Refounding Democratic Public Administration: Modern Paradoxes and Postmodern Challenges*. Thousand Oaks, CA: Sage.

Wamsley, Gary L., Robert N. Bacher, Charles T. Goodsell, Philip S. Kronenberg, John A. Rohr, Camilla Stivers, Orion F. White, and James F. Wolf, eds. 1990. *Refounding Public Administration*. Newbury Park, CA: Sage Publications.

Wang, Zhihe. 2012. *Process and Pluralism: Chinese Thought on the Harmony of Diversity*. edited by Nicholas Rescher, Johanna Seibt and Michel Weber. Vol. 23, *Process Thought*. Frankfurt: Ontos Verlag.

Watanabe, Tsuneo. 2009. "Eastern Epistemology and the Psychology of the Subjective Self." In *Varieties of Theoretical Psychology: International Theoretical and Practical Concerns*, edited by Thomas Teo, Paul Stenner, Alexandra Rutherford and Eri Park, 92–102. Concord, Ontario: Captus University Publications.

Waters, Anne, Ed. 2004a. *American Indian Thought*. Malden, MA: Blackwell Publishing.

Waters, Anne. 2004b. "Language Matters: Nondiscrete Nonbinary Dualism." In *American Indian Thought*, edited by Anne Waters, 97–115. Malden, MA: Blackwell Publishing.

References 235

Weber, Max. 1946. "Science as a Vocation." In *From Max Weber: Essays in Sociology*, edited by H. H. Gerth and C. Wright Mills, 129–156. New York: Oxford University Press.

Weber, Max. 1949a. "The Meaning of 'Ethical Neutrality' in Sociology and Economics." In *The Methodology of the Social Sciences*, edited by Edward Shils and Henry A. Finch, 1–47. New York: The Free Press.

Weber, Max. 1949b. *The Methodology of the Social Sciences*. New York: The Free Press.

Weber, Max. 1949c. "Objectivity in Social Science and Social Policy." In *The Methodology of the Social Sciences*, edited by Edward Shils and Henry A. Finch, 49–112. New York: The Free Press.

Weber, Max. 1968. *Economy and Society: An Outline of Interpretive Sociology*. New York: Bedminster Press. Original edition, 1922.

Weber, Max. 1993. *The Protestant Ethic and the Spirit of Capitalism*. London: Routledge. Original edition, 1930.

Weber, Max. 1994a. "Ideal-type Constructs." In *Sociological Writings: Max Weber*, edited by Wolf Heydebrand, 262–276. New York: Continuum Publishing Company.

Weber, Max. 1994b. "Legitimacy and the Types of Authority." In *Sociological Writings: Max Weber*, edited by Wolf Heydebrand, 28–32. New York: Continuum Publishing Company.

Weber, Max. 1994c. "The Methodological Foundations of Sociology." In *Sociological Writings: Max Weber*, edited by Wolf Heydebrand, 228–248. New York: Continuum Publishing Company.

Weber, Max. 1994d. "Rationality and Formalism in Law." In *Sociological Writings: Max Weber*, edited by Wolf Heydebrand, 204–205. New York: Continuum Publishing Company.

Weber, Max. 1994e. "The Types of Social Action." In *Sociological Writings: Max Weber*, edited by Wolf Heydebrand, 3–6. New York: Continuum Publishing Company.

Weimer, David L., and Aidan R. Vining. 1999. *Policy Analysis: Concepts and Practice*. 3rd edition. Upper Saddle River, NJ: Prentice Hall.

Weinstein, Kenneth R. 2004. "Philosophic Roots, the Role of Leo Strauss, and the War in Iraq." In *The Neocon Reader*, edited by Irwin M. Stelzer, 203–212. New York: Grove Press.

Wettenhall, Roger. 2001. "Public or private? Public Corporations, Companies and the Decline of the Middle Ground." *Public Organization Review: A Global Journal* no. 1:17–40.

Wheatley, Margaret J. 2006. *Leadership and the New Science: Discovering Order in a Chaotic World*. 3rd edition. San Francisco: Berrett-Kohler Publishers Inc.

White, Jay D. 1986. "On the Growth of Knowledge in Public Administration." *Public Administration Review* no. 46 (1):15–24.

White, Jay D. 1999. *Taking Language Seriously: The Narrative Foundations of Public Administration Research*. Washington, DC: Georgetown University Press.

White, Orion F. 1971. "Social Change and Administrative Adaptation." In *Toward a New Public Administration: The Minnowbrook Perspective*, edited by Frank Marini, 59–83. Scranton, OH: Chandler.

White, Orion F. 1990. "Reframing the Authority/Participation Debate." In *Refounding Public Administration*, edited by Gary L. Wamsley, Robert N. Bacher, Charles T. Goodsell, Philip S. Kronenberg, John A. Rohr, Camilla Stivers, Orion F. White and James F. Wolf, 182–245. Newbury Park, CA: Sage Publications.

236 References

White, Orion F., and Cynthia McSwain. 1990. "The Phoenix Project: Raising a New Image of Public Administration from the Ashes of the Past." In *Images and Identities in Public Administration*, edited by Henry D. Kass and Bayard L. Catron, 23–60. Newbury Park, CA: Sage Publications.

White, Orion F., and Cynthia J. McSwain. 1993. "The Semiotic Way of Knowing and Public Administration." *Administrative Theory & Praxis* no. 15 (1):18–35.

White, Stephen K. 2000. *Sustaining Affirmation: The Strengths of Weak Ontology in Political Theory*. Princeton, NJ: Princeton University Press.

Whitehead, Alfred North. 1966. *Modes of Thought*. New York: The Free Press. Original edition, 1938.

Whitehead, Alfred North. 1979. *Process and Reality: An Essay in Cosmology*, Edited by David Ray Griffin and Donald W. Sherburne. Corrected edition. New York: Simon and Shuster. Original edition, 1929.

Whyte, William Foote. 1956. *The Organization Man*. College Park, PA: University of Pennsylvania Press.

Widder, Nathan. 2005. "Two Routes from Hegel." In *Radical Democracy: Politics between Abundance and Lack*, edited by Lars Tønder and Lasse Thomassen, 32–49. New York: Manchester University Press.

Wildavsky, Aaron. 1979. *Speaking Truth to Power: The Art and Craft of Policy Analysis*. Boston: Little, Brown.

Wilde, Parke. 2013. *Food Policy in the United States: An Introduction*. New York: Routledge.

Will, George F. 1983. *Statecraft as Soulcraft: What Government Does*. New York: Simon and Schuster.

Williams, Raymond. 1983. *Keywords: A Vocabulary of Culture and Society*. Revised edition. New York: Oxford University Press.

Willoughby, Westel W. 1930. *The Ethical Basis of Political Authority*. New York: The Macmillan Company.

Witt, Matthew T. 2010. "Pretending Not to See or Hear, Refusing to Signify: The Farce and Tragedy of Geocentric Public Affairs Scholarship." *American Behavioral Scientist* no. 53 (6):921–939.

Witt, Matthew T., and Lance deHaven-Smith. 2008. "Conjuring the Holographic State: Scripting Security Doctrine for a (New) World of Disorder." *Administration & Society* no. 40 (Journal Article):547–485.

Witt, Matthew T., and Alexander Kouzmin. 2010. "Sense Making under 'Holographic' Conditions: Framing SCAD Research." *American Behavioral Scientist* no. 53 (6):783–794.

Wolf, James F., and Robert N. Bacher. 1990. "The Public Administrator and Public Service Occupations." In *Refounding Public Administration*, edited by Gary L. Wamsley, Robert N. Bacher, Charles T. Goodsell, Philip S. Kronenberg, John A. Rohr, Camilla Stivers, Orion F. White and James F. Wolf, 163–181. Newbury Park, CA: Sage Publications.

Wolin, Sheldon. 1981. "The New Public Philosophy." *Democracy: A Journal of Political Renewal and Radical Change* no. 1 (4):23–36.

Wong, John, Ed. 1979a. *Group Farming in Asia: Experiences and Potentials*. Singapore: Singapore University Press.

Wong, John. 1979b. "The Group Farming System in China: Ideology Versus Pragmatism." In *Group Farming in Asia: Experiences and Potentials*, edited by John Wong, 89–106. Singapore: Singapore University Press.

References 237

Yoder, Diane, E., and Terry L. Cooper. 2005. "Public-Service Ethics in a Transnational World." In *Ethics in Public Management*, edited by H. George Frederickson and Richard K. Ghere, 297–327. Armonk, NY: M.E. Sharpe.

Yogananda, Paramahansa. 1993. *Autobiography of a Yogi*. 12th edition. Los Angeles: Self-Realization Fellowship. Original edition, 1946.

Zanetti, Lisa A. 2004. "Repositioning the Ethical Imperative: Critical Theory, *Recht*, and Tempered Radicals in Public Service." *American Review of Public Administration* no. 34 (2):134–150.

Zanetti, Lisa A., and Guy B. Adams. 2000. "In Service of the Leviathan: Democracy, Ethics and the Potential for Administrative Evil in the New Public Management." *Administrative Theory & Praxis* no. 22 (3):534–554.

Zhang, Chun. 2015, "China's New Blueprint for an 'Ecological Civilization'." *The Diplomat* September 30.

Zhong, Yang. 2003. *Local Government and Politics in China: Challenges from Below*. New York: Routledge.

Žižek, Slavoj. 1997. "The Big Other Doesn't Exist." *European Journal of Psychology* no. 5. Available at www.lacan.com/zizekother.htm (accessed July 1, 2016).

Žižek, Slavoj. 2000. "Holding the Place." In *Contingency, Hegemony, Universality: Contemporary Dialogues on the Left*, edited by Ernesto Laclau Slavoj and Judith Butler, 308–326. London: Verso.

Žižek, Slavoj. 2006. *Jacques Lacan's Four Discourses* Available from www.lacan.com/zizfour.htm (accessed July 1, 2016).

Žižek, Slavoj. 2007. *How to Read Lacan*. New York: W.W. Norton and Company.

Žižek, Slavoj. 2009. *The Ticklish Subject: The Absent Centre of Political Ontology*. London: Verso.

Index

Page numbers in *italics* denote tables, those in **bold** denote figures.

Absolute 89–96, 99, 106n4
agonism/agonistic 22, 80, 81, 140, 166
agricultural policy/practices 15–16, 54, 69–70, 85–6, 105–6, 121–2
alterity 29, 30, 35
anarchism/anarchist: collectivist/social 93, 98–100; individualist/libertarian *49, 107*, 108, 112, 116–18, 119, 153, 156, 157–9, 171–2, 175; post/queer 36, 117, 175, 183, 201
Anzaldúa, Gloria 186
Aquinas, Thomas 78, 87n2
Aristotle 23, 42–3, 60, 73, 76, 78
Arnstein, Sherry *see* Ladder of Citizen Participation 20
authentic: connection 147, 163–4, 166, 183, 191, 199; self/identity 10, 46, 108, 111–12, 144, 147, 150, 156, 163–4, 166, 172, 183, 191, 199

Bartels, Koen 54
becoming 23–5, 33, 46, 89, **89**, 91, 109–10, **110**, 184, 189–90, 191, 196; *see also* dynamic ontology
being 23–5, 46, 56, **56**, 58, 72–3, **72**, 74, 184; *see also* static ontology
binary 24, 45, *45*, 73, 110, 140, 142, 186, 190; *see also* dualism/dualistic
Bohm, David 9–10, 15, 73, 108
Borg Collective (*Star Trek*) 93, 112
Brahman *see* Absolute
Braidotti, Rosi 10–11, 159

capitalism/capitalist 11–14, 66, 69, 82–3, 98, 100, 118–19, 147–8, 165, 167, 172–4, 179–80
Catlaw, Thomas 18, 32, 32, 46, 65, 116,

143–4, 150, 154–6, 162, 170, 175n2, 182–3
citizen/citizenship 3, 7n1, 11, 17–18, 20–1, 29–30, 50, 57, 60, 62–3, 65, 68, 79, 81, 83–5, 99–100, 102–4, 121, 123n2, 143, 152, 157, 167, 170, 174; global/planetary 181, 191
climate change 14–15
colonization 11, 22, 33–6, 153, 173, 180–1, 184, 186, 200; *see also* domination; hegemony
communism/communist 20, 31, 98, 100, 102, 105, 159n1, 165, 168, 170; *see also* anarchism, collectivist; Marx, Karl; Marxism; socialism
communitarianism/communitarian 3, 140, 150–3, **151**, 160, 162, 166–7, 174–5, 183–4, 188, 198
competition 13–14, 17, 24, *49*, 50, 70n6, 72, 74, 77, 79–84, 85, 114, 121, 137, 145, 146–8, 149–50, 153, 162, 174, 179, 193, 194
Comte, Auguste 77, 78
Connolly, William 12–13, 14, 16, 30, 167, 180, 181, 192
consequentialism *49, 71*, 78; *see also* utilitarianism
constructive conflict 198, 199
consumerism 120, 173
cooptation 21, 157, 171
cosmopolitanism 20
counter-hegemonic/counter-hegemony 22, 117–18, 125, 157, 181, 201n1

dialectic/dialectical 5, 17, 23–5, *42*, 140–1, *141*, 148–50, 167, 175, 179, 182–3; in analysis 5, 38, 42–3, 127–8,

130, *135*, *136*, *137*, *138*; in escalation 8, 139, 153, 160–2; in synthesis 6, 177, 185–8, *187*
dialogue 9–10, 173, 182, 198, 200
Delueze, Gilles 3, 109, 113, 117, 187
Derrida, Jacques 110, 142
Descartes, René/Cartesian 46, 60–1, 64, 76; *see also* rationalism
domination 17, 19, 24–5, 30, 33–5, 56, 98, 108, 116–17, 119, 142–4, 148–50, 166, 170, 173, 175, 182–4, 186, 193, 198; *see also* colonization; hegemony
Donati, Pierpaolo 9, 17, 140, 150, 153, 186
Douglas, Mary 47, 59, 74, 94, 113
dualism/dualistic 24–5, 35, 93, 143, 160, 186, 192; *see also* binary

elitism/elite 18–19, 36, 61, 65, 67, 69, 133, 142–3, 145–6, 148, 150, 151, 154, 159, 159n1, 166–7, 169–70, 172–5
Engels, Friedrich *see* Marx, Karl
existence 6, 22, 23–5, 28, 35, 36, 42, 44–5, 51, 56, 70n5, 72–3, 89–90, 108–9, 141, 155, 184, 189, 196; *see also* being; becoming
expressivism 96

fear, politics of 141–2, 161, 166–7, 168–9
Finer, Herman 67
Follett, Mary 4, 6, 18, 20–1, 34, 75, 141, 143, 144, 145–8, 155, 170, 179–80, 182, 186–7, 193, 197–9
Friedrich, Carl 65, 104

George, Henry 13–14, 26, 82
global financial crisis/GFC 12–14, 17
globalization/global context 9, 11, 12–13, 19, 33, 35, 37, 86, 173, 177, 179, 182, 184–5; *see also* governance, global
godhead 90–1; *see also* Absolute
Good, the 29, 36, 49, *49*, 56, 62, 64–5, 66, 70n6, 77–9, 80, 115, 128, 131, 132–3, 193
governance 3, 38; global 3, 5, 20–1, 200 (*see also* globalization)

hegemony/hegemonic 5, 6, 19, 22, 34–5, 36, 37, 114, 180, 181, 185, 201n1; reflexive 153, 161; *see also* colonization; domination
Habermas, Jürgen 77, 78, 174
Heckert, Jamie 183
Hegel, Georg Wilhelm Friedrich 6, 43, 90, 92, 97–8, 145, 170, 186–8, 197

Heidegger, Martin 32–3, 109–10, 195n1
Heraclitus 23–4, 25, 45
Hobbes, Thomas/Hobbesian 60, 63–4, 74, 79, 82, 140
holism/holistic 45, *45*, 57, 90–2, 105, 133, 190; *see also* non-dualism/non-dualistic
homesteading/survivalism 119, 122, 123n1, 165
Husserl, Edmund 114

ideal-type method 4, 6, 25–6, 40–3, *42*; and generic elements 40, 41, 44, 51, *51*; and genetic meanings 40, 42, *51*
idealism 94, 95, 97, 106n3, 188
identity 3, 6, 10, 11–12, 26, 27, 46–7, *46*, 58–9, 72, 74, 92–4, 97, 111–13, 117, 121, 131, 132
immanence/immanent 23, 24, 25, *25*, *45*, *45*, 72, *72*, 89, 90, 109, *110*, 132, 141, 185, 189; *see also* material; natural; physical
integration, method of 177, 182, 186, 197–9; *see also* Follett, Mary
intergovernmental 3, 18
international 3, 13, 19–20, 179
intersectoral 3, 18, 19, 20, 179

Jung, Carl 93, 94

Keating, AnaLouise 10, 143, 146, 185, 196

Lacan, Jacques 27, 32–3, 43, 46, 108–9, 110–11, 113, 117, 142, 159; *see also* Žižek, Slavoj
Ladder of Citizen Participation 20–1
Leibniz, Gottfried Wilhelm 73, 90
liberalism 3, 35, 140–2, **141**, 144, 148–50, 160–1; classical conservative 17, *49*, 49, 56, 64–5, 66, 70n3, 70n4, 142, 150; modern 17, 29, 49, *49*, 79–81, 82, 145, 150; *see also* communitarianism
libertarianism/libertarian 151, 157, 171–2; *see also* anarchism, individualist; objectivism
Locke, John/Lockean 74–6, 79, 82, 83, 140

Many, the 23, 24, *25*, 33, 36, 45, 48, *48*, 72, *72*, 108–9, **110**, 128–9, 131–3, 141, 148–9, 153, 162–3, 168, 175, 183–5, 188, 192; *see also* dialectic; One, the

240 *Index*

material (ontologically)/materialism/
materialist 23, 60, 66, 72, 73, 76, 77,
94, 189, 196; enchanted 32; new 9, 36,
191–2; *see also* immanent; natural;
physical
Marx, Karl 8, 43, 97–8, 100, 102, 142,
147, 165; *see also* anarchism, collectivist;
communism/communist; Marxism;
socialism
Marxism/post-Marxism 112, 154; *see also*
anarchism, collectivist; communism;
socialism
maya 91, 93, 102
metaphysical 4, 23, 24, 28, 34, 48, *48*, 51,
61, 73, 77, 93, 99, 109, 142, 192; *see
also* nonmaterial; transcendent
monism/monist 23, 24, 56, 153, 154,
185, 186
monotheism/monotheistic *48*, 55, 61,
70n5, 192
Morstein Marx, Fritz 30–1

natural (ontologically)/naturalism 48, *48*,
72–4, 77, 192; dialectical 187; *see also*
immanent; material; physical
Negri, Antonio 116
neoliberal/neoliberalism 11, 13–14, 17,
18, 20, 120, 140, **140**, 153, 156–7,
159n2, 160, 161, 163–4, 166–7, 171,
172–3, 180, 181
New Public Administration/NPA *50*, 83,
89, 102–4, 128, 170
New Public Management/NPM 18, *50*,
83, 108, 120–1, 128
New Public Service *50*, 72, 83–4, 128
Next System Project, the 14, 201
Niebuhr, H. Richard 48, 62–3, 77–8,
87n1, 138n1, 193
non-dualism/non-dualistic; *see also*
holism/holistic
non-governmental organizations (NGOs)
18–19, 119; *see also* nonprofit; voluntary
associations
nonmaterial 25, 56, 189, 192; *see also*
metaphysical; transcendent
nonprofit 18–19, 174

objectivism 77, 156, 171–3; *see also*
libertarianism
One, the 23, 24, *25*, 33, 36, 45, 48, *48*,
56, **57**, 57, 58–9, 61, 62, 89–90, **89**,
96, 128–9, 133, 137, 141, 142, 148–9,
153, 162–3, 164, 168, 175, 183, 185,
188, 192; *see also* dialectic; Many, the

ontic 22, 109, 111
ontology: of abundance 24, 32–3, 90, 92,
129, 133, 155, 158, 164, 170, 184,
184, 190, 200, 201n1; of lack 24, 32–3,
108–9, 111–12, 129, 133, 157–8, 162,
164, 171, 184–5, 190, 200, 201n1;
relational process 6, 177, 185, 188–90,
191, 196; strong 36, 184; weak 36, 37,
185, 199–200; *see also* worldview
Orthodox Administration *50*, 56, 66–8,
83, 102, 128

pantheism *48*, 96, 192
Parmenides 23–5, 45, 56, 73
participation/participatory 3, 13, 17,
20–1, 32–3, 64, 79, 81, 83–4, 101,
143, 152, 154–5, 168, 179–80, 192–5,
196–7, 199, 201
particularity 46, 92, 162; *see also* One, the
pathology/pathologies 125, 126, 139,
160–3, 166, 168, 171, 177, 183–4,
199; in Atomistic Governance 144–8; in
communitarianism/Reified Community
150–3; in Fragmented Governance
156–9; in Hierarchical Governance
142–4; in Holographic Governance
154–6
People, the 3, 17–18, 29, 46, 57, 64–5,
67, 68, 98, 104, 143, 150, 154–6,
162–3, 199; *see also* representation;
sovereignty
physical (ontologically) 4, 14, 24, 33, 48,
51, 71, 73, 182, 191; *see also*
immanent/immanence; material;
natural
Plato/Platonic 23, 42, 56, 59, 60, 62,
87n1, 94–5, 102, 103, 170
pluralism/pluralistic 17, 29, 35, 36, 49,
65, 72, 79–81, 82, 83–4, 86, 114, 121,
132–3, 145–8, 157, 162, 180, 184, 197
politics/administration dichotomy 67
postmodernism/postmodern 9, 31, 33,
83, 108–9, 112, 114, 115, 116–17,
120–1, 157–8, 159n2, 165, 180, 183
post-structuralism/post-structuralist 24–5,
108, 110–11, 171
potentiality 25, 90, 109, 189–90
Proudhon, Pierre-Joseph 98, 125, 153,
155
Prozorov, Sergei 6, 28, 30, 185
public/publicness 18–19, 20, 34, 182,
197
public administration theory 6, 27, 29–33,
37, 39, 44, 47, 50, *50*, 52n1, 53–4

Index 241

radical democracy 3, 7n1, 8, 33, 125, 143, 177, 180–1, 182–3, 185, 193–4, 196, 199–200, 201
radicalism *see* anarchism; socialism
Ramos, Alberto Guerreiro 32, 112, 150, 174
rationalism 60, 76, 94, 188, 191
Rawls, John/Rawlsian 63, 66, 79, 102
reify/reification 57, 137; avoiding 187–90, 199; process of 164–7
Reinventing Government 18, 120, 123n2
representation (political) 18, 21, 32, 33–4, 46, 49, 56, 65, 72, 81, 84, 107, 116–17, 133, 142, 143, 162–3, 170, 173; *see also* People, the; sovereignty
Right *49*, 49, 56, 62, 65–6, 69, 77–8, 89, 97, 115, 131–3, 193

semiotics 110
singularity 46, 109, 113; *see also* Many, the
Smith, Adam 66, 76, 79, 82
social bond 29, 46, 58–60, 74–6, 92–4, 105, 111–13, 173, 184, 191
social movements 10, 14, 117, 154–5, 157, 174, 183, 201
socialism/socialist 14, 17, *49*, 89, 97–102, 142, 153–4, 164, 167–70; *see also* anarchism, collectivist; communism/ communist; Marx, Karl; Marxism
sovereign/sovereignty 63; *see also* People, the; representation
Stirner, Max 112
stratalism 4
sustainability 1, 3, 8–18, 22, 177, 179–80, 189, 193–4, 200

Thayer, Frederick 13, 14, 24, 29, 49, 50, 70n6, 149, 150
transcendent/transcendence 23, 24, 25, *25*, 42, *42*, 45, *45*, 48, 55–6, **57**, 70n5, 76, 88, 89–90, **89**, 92, 95, 96, 106n3, 132, 141, 142, 169, 185, 189, 192, 193; *see also* metaphysical; nonmaterial
Transcendentalism/Transcendentalist 90, 96–7
transdisciplinary 6, 39

unity 23, 24, 43, 73, 89, 90–2, 92–4, 96, 100, 133, 163, 170, 187, 188, 191, 197
utilitarianism 62, 67, 78–80; *see also* consequentialism

void 23, 25, 108, 117, 162, 164, 165, 171, 190; *see also* ontology of lack
voluntary associations 19

Waldo, Dwight 31, 33, 67, 70n7
Wamsley, Gary 28, 30
Wang, Zhihe 43, 186
Weber, Max 23, 40, 61, 69, 70n1, 77, 79, 127, 143, 145, 147
welfare state 56, 66, 69, 154
White, Stephen 30, 36, 184–5; *see also* ontology, strong; ontology, weak
Whitehead, Alfred North 41, 190
worldview 1, 4, 6, 8, 10, 19, 22, 34–5, 44, 48, 54, 72, 78, 89, 92, 108, 121, 129, 157, 181; *see also* ontology

Žižek, Slavoj 8, 108, 113, 117; *see also* Lacan, Jacques